T0350777

Leveraged
Buyouts

Leveraged Buyouts

*A Practical Guide to Investment
Banking and Private Equity*

PAUL PIGNATARO

WILEY

Cover Design: Wiley

Cover Image: numbers © iStockphoto.com / wragg; gold lights © iStockphoto.com / vizualbyte

Library of Congress Cataloging-in-Publication Data:

Pignataro, Paul.
    Leveraged buyouts : a practical guide to investment banking and private equity / Paul Pignataro.
        pages cm. — (Wiley finance series)
    Includes index.
    ISBN 978-1-118-67454-3 (cloth)—ISBN 978-1-118-67458-1 (ePDF)—ISBN 978-1-118-67445-1 (ePub)   1. Leveraged buyouts. 2. Consolidation and merger of corporations. 3. Investment banking. 4. Private equity. I. Title.
    HD2746.5.P54 2013
    658.1'62—dc23

                                                                    2013023885

This book is dedicated to every investor in the pursuit of enhancing wealth. Those who have gained, and those who have lost—this continuous struggle has confounded the minds of many. This book should be one small tool to help further said endeavor; and if successful, the seed planted will contribute to a future of more informed investors and smarter markets.

Contents

Preface

In the 1970s and 1980s, the corporate takeover market began to surge. As a means to continue to enhance corporate wealth and leadership, growth through mergers or acquisitions flooded the corporate environment. Although such mergers and acquisitions had existed for decades, the mid-1970s led the multibillion-dollar hostile takeover race. This was followed by a surge in the 1980s of the leveraged buyout, a derivative of the takeover, culminating with the most noted leveraged buyout of its time, the $25 billion buyout of RJR Nabisco by Kohlberg Kravis Roberts in 1989.

A leveraged buyout, most broadly, is the acquisition of a company using a significant amount of debt to meet the acquisition cost. Arguably, the increase in leveraged buyouts in the 1980s was partly due to greater access to the high-yield debt markets (so-called junk bonds), pioneered by Michael Milken. Access to such aggressive types of lending allowed buyers to borrow more money to fund such large acquisitions. The more debt borrowed, the less equity needed out-of-pocket, leading to potentially higher returns. This concept of higher returns for less equity sparked interest among many funds and even individual investors, and extended worldwide. From buyouts of small $10 million businesses to the recent $25 billion potential buyout of Dell, small investors, funds, and enthusiasts alike have been fascinated by the mechanics, aggressiveness, and high-return potential of leveraged buyouts.

This book seeks to give any investor the fundamental tools to help analyze a leveraged buyout and determine if the potential returns are worth the investment. These fundamental tools are used by investment banks and private equity funds worldwide. We will evaluate the potential leveraged buyout of the H.J. Heinz Company, determining its current financial standing, projecting its future performance, and estimating the potential return on investment using the exact same methods used by the bulge bracket investment banks and top private equity firms. We will have you step into the role of an analyst on Wall Street to give you a firsthand perspective and understanding of how the modeling process works, and to give you the tools to create your own analyses. Whether you are an investor looking to make your own acquisitions or a fund, these analyses are invaluable in the process. This book is ideal for both those wanting to create their own analyses and those wanting to enter the investment banking or private equity field. This is also a guide designed for investment banking or private equity professionals themselves if they need a thorough review or simply a leveraged buyout modeling refresher.

THE HEINZ CASE STUDY

PITTSBURGH & OMAHA, Neb. & NEW YORK--(BUSINESS WIRE)—H.J. Heinz Company (NYSE: HNZ) ("Heinz") today announced that it has entered into a definitive merger agreement to be acquired by an investment consortium comprised of Berkshire Hathaway and 3G Capital.

Under the terms of the agreement, which has been unanimously approved by Heinz's Board of Directors, Heinz shareholders will receive $72.50 in cash for each share of common stock they own, in a transaction valued at $28 billion, including the assumption of Heinz's outstanding debt. The per share price represents a 20% premium to Heinz's closing share price of $60.48 on February 13, 2013, a 19% premium to Heinz's all-time high share price, a 23% premium to the 90-day average Heinz share price and a 30% premium to the one-year average share price.

(Heinz Press Release, February 14, 2013)

In this press release dated February 14, 2013, Heinz announces the possibility of being acquired by both Berkshire Hathaway and 3G Capital. We will analyze this potential buyout of Heinz throughout this book. Heinz manufactures thousands of food products on six continents, and markets these products in more than 200 countries worldwide. The company claims to have the number-one or number-two brand in 50 countries. Each year Heinz produces 650 million bottles of ketchup and approximately two single-serve packets of ketchup for every man, woman, and child on the planet. The company employs 32,000 people worldwide.

What is the viability of such a buyout? How are Berkshire Hathaway and 3G Capital finding value in such an investment? What are their potential returns? There is a technical analysis used by Wall Street analysts to help answer such questions. We will walk you through the complete buyout analysis as a Wall Street analyst would conduct that analysis.

It is important to note that the modeling methodology presented in this book is just one view. The analysis of Heinz and the results of that analysis do not directly reflect my belief, but rather, a possible conclusion for instructional purposes only based on limiting the most extreme of variables. There are other possibilities and paths that I have chosen not to include in this book. Many ideas presented here are debatable, and I welcome the debate. The point is to understand the methods and, further, the concepts behind the methods to equip you properly with the tools to drive your own analyses.

HOW THIS BOOK IS STRUCTURED

This book is divided into three parts:

1. Leveraged Buyout Overview
2. Leveraged Buyout Full-Scale Model
3. Advanced Leveraged Buyout Techniques

In Part One, we explain the concepts and mechanics of a leveraged buyout. Before building a complete model, it is important to step through, from a high level, the purposes of a leveraged buyout and the theory of how a leveraged buyout works. A high-level analysis helps us to understand the importance of key variables and is crucial to understanding how various assumption drivers affect potential returns.

In Part Two, we build a complete leveraged buyout model of Heinz. We analyze the company's historical performance and step through techniques to make accurate projections of the business's future performance. The goal of this part is not only to understand how to build a model of Heinz, but to extract the modeling techniques used by analysts and to apply those techniques to any investment.

Part Three also adds more modeling complexity, ideal for those who already have basic experience modeling leveraged buyouts. Adjusting scenarios, advanced securities such as paid-in-kind (PIK) securities and preferred dividends, and the capitalization and amortization of debt fees add more complexity and will further your understanding of using leveraged buyouts in practice.

The book is designed to have you build your own leveraged buyout model on Heinz step-by-step. The model template can be found on the companion website associated with this book and is titled "NYSF_ Leveraged_Buyout_Model_Template.xls" To access the site, see the About the Companion Website section at the back of this book.

Leveraged Buyout Overview

A leveraged buyout (LBO) is a fundamental, yet complex acquisition commonly used in the investment banking and private equity industries. We will take a look at the basic concepts, benefits, and drawbacks of a leveraged buyout. We will understand how to effectively analyze an LBO. We will further analyze the fundamental impact of such a transaction and calculate the expected return to an investor. Last, we will spend time interpreting the variables and financing structures to understand how to maximize investor rate of return (IRR).

The three goals of this part are:

1. Understanding leveraged buyouts (leveraged buyout theory).
   - Concepts.
   - Purposes and uses.
2. Valuation overview (What is value?)
   - Book value, market value, equity value, and enterprise value.
   - Understanding multiples.
   - Three core methods of valuation:
       i. Comparable company analysis.
       ii. Precedent transactions analysis.
       iii. Discounted cash flow analysis.
3. Ability to understand a simple IRR analysis (leveraged buyout analysis).
   a. Purchase price.
   b. Sources and uses.
   c. Calculating investor rate of return (IRR).

CHAPTER 1

Leveraged Buyout Theory

A leveraged buyout is an acquisition of a company using a significant amount of debt to meet the cost of the acquisition. This allows for the acquisition of a business with less equity (out-of-pocket) capital. Think of a mortgage on a house. If you take out a mortgage to fund the purchase of a house, you can buy a larger house with less out-of-pocket cash (your down payment). Over time, your income will be used to make the required principal (and interest) mortgage payments; as you pay down those principal payments, and as the debt balance reduces, your equity in the house increases. Effectively, the debt is being converted to equity. And maybe you can sell the house for a profit and receive a return. This concept, on the surface, is similar to a leverage buyout. Although we use a significant amount of borrowed money to buy a business in an LBO, the cash flows produced by the business will hopefully, over time, pay down the debt. Debt will convert to equity, and we can hope to sell the business for a profit.

There are three core components that contribute to the success of a leveraged buyout:

1. Cash availability, interest, and debt pay-down.
2. Operation improvements.
3. Multiple expansion.

CASH AVAILABILITY, INTEREST, AND DEBT PAY-DOWN

This is the concept illustrated in the chapter's first paragraph. The cash being produced by the business will be used to pay down debt and interest. It is the reduction of debt that will be converted into the equity value of the business.

It is for this reason that a company with high and consistent cash flows makes for a good leveraged buyout investment.

OPERATION IMPROVEMENTS

Once we own the business, we plan on making some sort of improvements to increase the operating performance of that business. Increasing the operating performance of the business will ultimately increase cash flows, which will pay down debt faster. But, more important, operating improvements will increase the overall value of the business, which means we can then (we hope) sell it at a higher price. Taking the previous mortgage example, we had hoped to make a profit by selling the house after several years. If we make some renovations and improvements to the house, we can hope to sell it for a higher price. For this reason, investors and funds would look for businesses they can improve as good leveraged buyout investments. Often the particular investor or fund team has particular expertise in the industry. Maybe they have connections to larger sources of revenue or larger access to distribution channels based on their experience where they feel they can grow the business faster. Or, maybe the investor or fund team sees major problems with management they know they can fix. Any of these operation improvements could increase the overall value of the business.

MULTIPLE EXPANSION

Multiple expansion is the expectation that the market value of the business will increase. This would result in an increase in the expected multiple one can sell the business for. We will later see, in a business entity, we will most likely base a purchase and sale off of multiples. We will also conservatively assume the exit multiple used to sell the business will be equal to the purchase multiple (the multiple calculated based on the purchase price of the business). This would certainly enhance the business returns.

WHAT MAKES GOOD LEVERAGED BUYOUT?

In summary, a good leveraged buyout has strong and consistent cash flows that can be expected to pay down a portion of the debt raised and related interest. Further, the investor or fund sees ways to improve the operating performance of the business. It is hoped that the combination of debt converting into equity and the increase in operating performance would significantly increase the value of the business. This results in an increase in returns to the investor or fund. The next pages of this book step through such an analysis in its entirety and are intended to give you the core understanding of how such an analysis can provide not only benefits to a company, but high returns to an investor. This will also indicate pitfalls many investors face and reasons why many LBOs may not work out as planned.

EXIT OPPORTUNITIES

The financial returns from a leveraged buyout are not truly realized until the business is exited, or sold. There are several common ways to exit a business leveraged buyout:

1. Strategic sale: The business can be sold to a strategic buyer, a corporation that may find strategic benefits to owning the business.
2. Financial sponsor: Although not too common, the business can be sold to another Private Equity firm, maybe one with a different focus that can help take the business to the next level.
3. Initial public offering (IPO): If the company is at the right stage, and if the markets are right, the company can be sold to the public markets—an IPO
4. Dividend recapitalization: Although not necessarily a sale, a dividend recapitalization is a way for a fund to receive liquidity from their business investments. Think of it like refinancing a mortgage or taking out a second mortgage on your home in order to receive cash. The business will raise debt and distribute the cash raised from the debt to business owners or fund management.

IS HEINZ A LEVERAGED BUYOUT?

There is a debate on whether the Heinz situation is technically a leveraged buyout. I believe we can all agree this is in fact a buyout; Heinz is being acquired by 3G Capital and Berkshire Hathaway. But is the buyout leveraged? Those believing that the Heinz deal is not a leveraged buyout argue that the debt raised to meet the acquisition cost is not significant enough to constitute a leveraged buyout. I agree that what justifies the amount of debt raised to be *significant* is not formally defined in the leveraged buyout world. However, we will see in Chapter 4 that the amount of debt raised is approximately 40 percent to 45 percent of total funds used to acquire Heinz; I believe this is a significant amount of debt. The second important thing to consider is *how* the debt is being raised. In a leveraged buyout, typically the debt raised is backed by the assets of the company being purchased. As this will most likely be the case for Heinz, I would certainly consider this a leveraged buyout.

Others also argue this is not technically a leveraged buyout based on intent. In other words, the Heinz buyers are stating that their intent is not to exit the investment after a fixed time horizon, as is often the case for large buyout funds. Although this may be true, I am not sure "intent" is an appropriate determinant of what constitutes a leveraged buyout. It is still a buyout; it is still leveraged. Whether you believe the transaction is a leveraged buyout still stands as a relatively subjective debate. For purposes of instruction, we will model the case as if it were a full-fledged leveraged buyout. What's interesting is that the modeling does not change either way.

CHAPTER 2

What Is Value?

Before getting into the leveraged buyout analysis, a valuation overview is in order. The most important question before even getting into the mechanics is "What is value?" To help answer this question, we note there are two major categories of value:

1. *Book value.* Book value is the value of an asset or entire business entity as determined by its books, or the financials.
2. *Market value.* Market value is the value of an asset or entire business entity as determined by the market.

BOOK VALUE

The book value can be determined by the balance sheet. The total book value of a company's property, for example, can be found under the net property, plant, and equipment (PP&E) in the assets section of the balance sheet. The book value of the shareholders' interest in the company (not including the noncontrolling interest holders) can be found under shareholders' equity.

MARKET VALUE

The market value of a company can be defined by its market capitalization, or shares outstanding times share price.

Both the book value and market value represent the equity value of a business. The equity value of a business is the value of the business attributable to just equity holders—that is, the value of the business excluding debt lenders, noncontrolling interest holders, and other obligations.

Shareholders' equity, for example, is the value of the company's assets less the value of the company's liabilities. So this shareholders' equity value (making sure noncontrolling interest is not included in shareholders' equity) is the value of the business excluding lenders and other obligations—an equity value. The market value, or market capitalization, is based on the stock price, which is inherently an equity value since equity investors value a company's stock after payments to debt lenders and other obligations.

ENTERPRISE VALUE

Enterprise value (also known as firm value) is defined as the value of the entire business, including debt lenders and other obligations. We will see why the importance of enterprise value is that it approaches an approximate value of the operating assets of an entity. To be more specific, "debt lenders and other obligations" can include short-term debts, long-term debts, current portion of long-term debts, capital lease obligations, preferred securities, noncontrolling interests, and other nonoperating liabilities (e.g., unallocated pension funds). So, for complete reference, enterprise value can be calculated as:

Enterprise value =
  Equity value
+ Short-term debts
+ Long-term debts
+ Current portion of long-term debts
+ Capital lease obligations
+ Preferred securities
+ Noncontrolling interests
+ Other nonoperating liabilities (e.g., unallocated pension funds)
– Cash and cash equivalents

We will explain why subtracting cash and cash equivalents is significant. So, to arrive at enterprise value on a book value basis, we take the shareholders' equity (book value) and add back any potential debts and obligations less cash and cash equivalents. Similarly, if we add to market capitalization (market value) any potential debts and obligations less cash and cash equivalents, we approach the enterprise value of a company on a market value basis.

Here is a quick recap:

Valuation Category	Book Value	Market Value
Equity Value	Shareholders' Equity	Market Capitalization
Enterprise Value	Shareholders' Equity plus potential debts and obligations less cash and cash equivalents	Market Capitalization plus potential debts and obligations less cash and cash equivalents

Note: "Potential debts and obligations" can include short-term debts, long-term debts, current portion of long-term debts, capital lease obligations, preferred securities, non-controlling interests, and other nonoperating liabilities (e.g., unallocated pension funds).

Let's take the example of a company that has shareholders' equity of $10 million according to its balance sheet. Let's also say it has $5 million in total liabilities. We will assume no noncontrolling interest holders in these examples to better illustrate the main idea. As per the balance sheet formula (where Assets = Liabilities + Shareholders' Equity), the total value of the company's assets is $15 million. So $10 million is the book equity value of the company.

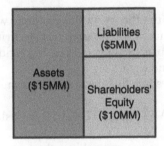

Book Value

Let's now say the company trades in the market at a premium to its book equity value; the market capitalization of the company is $12 million. The market capitalization of a company is an important value, because it is current; it is the value of a business as determined by the market (Share Price × Shares Outstanding). When we take the market capitalization and add the total liabilities of $5 million, we get a value that represents the value of the company's total assets as determined by the market.

However, in valuation we typically take market capitalization or book value and add back not the total liabilities, but just debts and obligations as noted earlier to get to enterprise value. The balance sheet formula can help us explain why:

$$\text{Shareholders' Equity} + \text{Liabilities} = \text{Assets}$$

Market Value

Using this equation, let's list out the actual balance sheet items:

Shareholders' Equity [or Market Capitalization] + Accounts Payable + Accrued Expenses + Short-Term Debt + Long-Term Debt = Cash + Accounts Receivable + Inventory + Property, Plant, and Equipment

To better illustrate the theory, in this example we assume the company has no noncontrolling interests, no preferred securities, and no other non-operating liabilities such as unallocated pension funds; it has just short-term debt, long-term debt, and cash.

We will abbreviate some line items so the formula is easier to read:

SE [or Mkt. Cap.] + AP + AE + STD + LTD = Cash + AR + Inv. + PP&E

Now we need to move everything that's not related to debt—the accounts payable (AP) and accrued expenses (AE)—to the other side of the equation. We can simply subtract AP and AE from both sides of the equation to get:

SE [or Mkt. Cap.] + STD + LTD = Cash + AR + Inv. + PP&E − (AP + AE)

And we can regroup the terms on the right to get:

SE [or Mkt. Cap.] + STD + LTD = Cash + PP&E + AR + Inv. − AP − AE

Notice that AR + Inv. − AP − AE, or current assets less current liabilities, is working capital, so:

SE [or Mkt. Cap.] + STD + LTD = Cash + PP&E + WC

Now remember that enterprise value is shareholders' equity (or market capitalization) plus debt less cash, so we need to subtract cash from both sides of the equation:

$$SE \text{ [or Mkt. Cap.]} + STD + LTD - Cash = PP\&E + WC$$

Short-term debt plus long-term debt less cash and cash equivalents is also known as net debt. So, this gives us:

$$SE \text{ [or Mkt. Cap.]} + Net Debt = PP\&E + WC$$

This is a very important formula. So, when adding net debt to shareholders' equity or market capitalization, we are backing into the value of the company's PP&E and working capital in the previous example, or more generally the core operating assets of the business. So, enterprise value is a way of determining the implied value of a company's core operating assets. Further, enterprise value based on market capitalization, or

$$\text{Enterprise Value} = \text{Market Capitalization} + \text{Net Debt}$$

is a way to approach the value of the operating assets as determined by the market.

Working Capital and PP&E ($13MM)	Net Debt ($3MM)		Implied Value of Operating Assets in the Market ($15MM)	Net Debt ($3MM)
	Shareholders' Equity ($10MM)			Market Cap ($12MM)
Book Value			**Market Value**	

Note that we had simplified the example for illustration. If the company had noncontrolling interests, preferred securities, or other nonoperating liabilities such as unallocated pension funds in addition to debts, the formula would read:

$$\text{Enterprise Value} = \text{Market Capitalization} + \text{Net Debt} + \text{Noncontrolling}$$
$$\text{Interests} + \text{Preferred Securities} + \text{Capital Lease Obligations} +$$
$$\text{Other Nonoperating Liabilities}$$

Quite often people wonder why cash needs to be removed from net debt in this equation. This is also a very common investment banking interview question. And, as illustrated here, cash is not considered an operating asset; it is not an asset that will be generating future income for the business (arguably). And so, true value of a company to an investor is the value of just those assets that will continue to produce profit and growth in the future. This is one of the reasons why, in a discounted cash flow (DCF) analysis, we are concerned only about the cash being produced from the operating assets of the business. It is also crucial to understand this core valuation concept, because the definition of an operating asset, or the interpretation of which portions of the company will provide future value, can differ from company to market to industry. Rather than depending on simple formulas, it is important to understand the reason behind them in this rapidly changing environment so you can be equipped with the proper tools to create your own formulas. For example, do Internet businesses rely on PP&E as the core operating assets? If not, would the current enterprise value formula have meaning? How about in emerging markets?

MULTIPLES

Multiples are metrics that compare the value of a business relative to its operations. A company could have a market capitalization value of $100 million, but what does that mean in relation to its operating performance? If that company is producing $10 million in net income, then its value is 10 times the net income it produces; "10x net income" is a market value multiple. These multiples are used to compare the performance of one company to another. So let's say I wanted to compare this business to another business that also has $100 million in market cap. How would I know which business is the better investment? The market capitalization value itself is arbitrary in this case unless it is compared to the actual performance of the business. So if the other company is producing $5 million in net income, its multiple is 20x; its market capitalization is 20 times the net income it produces. As an investor, I would prefer to invest in the lower multiple, as it is the cheaper investment; it is more net income for a lower market price. So, multiples help us compare relative values to a business's operations.

Other multiples exist, depending on what underlying operating metric one would like to use as the basis of comparison. Earnings before interest and taxes (EBIT); earnings before interest, taxes, depreciation, and amortization (EBITDA); and revenue can be used instead of net income. But how do we determine which are better metrics to compare? Let's take an example of two companies with similar operations. See Table 2.1.

TABLE 2.1 Business Comparison

Metric	Company A	Company B
Revenue	$10,000.0	$10,000.0
Cost of Goods Sold (COGS)	3,500.0	3,500.0
Operating Expenses	1,500.0	1,500.0
EBITDA	5,000.0	5,000.0
Depreciation	500.0	3,000.0
EBIT	4,500.0	2,000.0
Interest	0.0	2,000.0
EBT	4,500.0	0.0
Taxes (@ 35%)	1,575.0	0.0
Net Income	2,925.0	0.0

Let's say we want to consider investing in either Company A or Company B. Company A is a small distribution business, a package delivery business that has generated $10,000 in revenue in a given period. This is a start-up company run and operated by one person. It has a cost structure that has netted $5,000 in EBITDA. Company B is also a small delivery business operating in a different region. Company B is producing the same revenue and has the same operating cost structure, so it is also producing $5,000 in EBITDA. The current owner of Company A operates his business out of his home. He parks the delivery truck in his garage, so he has minimal depreciation costs and no interest expense. The owner of Company B, however, operates his business differently. He has built a warehouse for storage and to park the truck. This has increased the depreciation expense and has created additional interest expense, bringing net income to $0. If we were to compare the two businesses based on net income, Company A is clearly performing better than Company B. But, what if we are only concerned about the core operations? What if we are only concerned about the volume of packages being delivered, the number of customers, and the direct costs associated to the deliveries? What if we were looking to acquire Company A or B, for example? In that case, let's say we don't care about Company B's debt and its warehouse, as we would sell the warehouse and pay down the debt. Here, EBITDA would be a better underlying comparable measure. From an operations perspective, looking at EBITDA, both companies are performing well and we could have been misled in that case by looking only at net income.

So, although market capitalization/net income is a common multiple, there are other multiples using metrics such as EBIT or EBITDA. However, since EBIT and EBITDA are values before interest is taken into account, we cannot compare them to market capitalization. Remember that market capitalization, based on the share price, is the value of a business after lenders are paid; EBITDA (before interest) is the value before lenders have been paid. So, adding net debt (plus potentially other items as discussed previously in the enterprise value section) back to market capitalization gives us a numerator (enterprise value) that we can use with EBIT or EBITDA as a multiple:

$$\text{Enterprise Value} / \text{EBIT}$$

or:

$$\text{Enterprise Value} / \text{EBITDA}$$

So, in short, if a financial metric you want to use as the comparable metric is after debt or interest, it must be related to market capitalization—this is a market value multiple. If the financial metric is before debt or interest, it is related to enterprise value—an enterprise value multiple.

Market Value Multiples	Enterprise Value Multiples
Market Capitalization/Net Income	Enterprise Value/Sales
Price per Share/EPS	Enterprise Value/EBITDA
Market Capitalization/Book Value	Enterprise Value/EBIT

THREE CORE METHODS OF VALUATION

The value definitions and multiples from earlier in the chapter are applied in several ways to best approach how much an entity could be worth. There are three major methods utilized to approach this value:

1. Comparable company analysis.
2. Precedent transactions analysis.
3. Discounted cash flow analysis.

Each of these three methods is based on wide-ranging variables and could be considered quite subjective. Also, the methods approach value from very different perspectives. So we can have relatively strong support of value from a financial perspective if all three methods fall within similar valuation ranges.

Note that a leveraged buyout can also be considered a fourth method of valuation. The required exit in order to achieve a desired return on investment is the value of the business to the investor. This is a valuation method sometimes used by funds.

Comparable Company Analysis

The comparable company analysis compares one company with companies that are similar in size, product, and geography. The comparable company analysis utilizes multiples as a measure of comparison. If the peers' multiples are consistently higher than the multiples of the company we are valuing, it could mean that our company is undervalued. Conversely, if the peers' multiples are consistently lower than the multiples of the company we are valuing, it could mean that our company is overvalued. The comparable company analysis has one major advantage over the other valuation methods:

- *It is the most current of all three analyses.* It gives a market perspective. The comparable company analysis is based on the most recent stock prices and financials of the company.

  However, the comparable company analysis has the following drawbacks:

- *It may be difficult to find companies to compare.* If the company has a unique business model, is in a niche industry, or is not the size of a public company, it may be difficult to find the right peer group.
- *The markets as a whole may be undervalued or overvalued.* We could be in a market environment where the entire industry is overvalued or undervalued. If so, our analysis will be flawed.

Precedent Transactions Analysis

The precedent transactions analysis assesses relative value by looking at multiples of historical transactions. The perspective is that the value of the company we are valuing is relative to the price others have paid for similar companies. So, if we look for other companies similar to ours that have been acquired, we can compare their purchase multiples to assess the approximate value of our business.

Purchase Multiples

Purchase multiples are similar to market multiples (described previously), except the numerator in a purchase multiple is based on the price paid for an entity as opposed to the current market value.

Enterprise value/EBITDA, for example, is based on (market capitalization + net debt)/EBITDA in a market multiple. But in a purchase multiple, enterprise value/EBITDA is based on (purchase price + net debt)/EBITDA. Net debt is plus potentially noncontrolling interests, preferred securities, unallocated pension funds (and arguably other nonoperating liabilities), as discussed previously in the enterprise value section.

A precedent transactions analysis has this major advantage over the other valuation methods:

- *The purchase price includes a premium.* This could be advantageous if we were looking to acquire a company. It would help us determine how much of a premium we would need to consider to convince the owner or shareholders to hand over the company to us.

And there are several major drawbacks to the analysis:

- *Historical analysis.* Precedent transactions by definition are historical transactions. The analysis may be irrelevant if we are in a completely different economic environment.
- *Difficult-to-find relevant transactions.* Especially in an environment where there are not many acquisitions, it may not be possible to find acquisitions similar to the one we are analyzing.
- *Difficult-to-get data.* Even if we do find relevant transactions, it is not always easy to find the data to create the multiples.

TABLE 2.2 Multiples

	Market Value	Enterprise Value (EV)
Market Multiples	Market Cap/Net Income Price per Share/EPS (P/E)	EV/EBIT EV/EBITDA EV/Sales (where EV is Market Cap + Net Debt*)
Purchase Multiples	Purchase Price/Net Income	EV/EBIT EV/EBITDA EV/Sales (where EV is Purchase Price + Net Debt*)

*Plus potentially noncontrolling interests, preferred securities, and unallocated pension funds (and arguably other nonoperating liabilities), as discussed in the enterprise value section.

Discounted Cash Flow Analysis

The discounted cash flow (DCF) analysis is known as the most technical of the three major methods, as it is based on the company's cash flows. The discounted cash flow method takes the company's projected unlevered free cash flow (UFCF) and discounts it back to present value. We typically project the company's cash flows over a fixed time horizon (five to seven years, for example). We then create a terminal value, which is the value of the business from the last projected year into perpetuity. The enterprise value of the business is the sum of the present value of all the projected cash flows and the present value of the terminal value.

DCF Enterprise Value = Present Value (PV) of UFCF Year 1 + · · · + PV of UFCF Year n + PV of Terminal Value

The discounted cash flow analysis has this major advantage over the other valuation methods:

- *It is the most technical.* It is based on the company's cash flows from the model projections, as opposed to the comparable company analysis, which is mainly driven by market data.

The analysis also has several disadvantages:

- *Terminal value.* Although the first projected years are based on modeled cash flows, the terminal value accounts for a very significant portion of the overall valuation. That terminal value is based on a multiple or a perpetuity.
- *Model projections.* The model projections could be inaccurate; they could be overstated or understated, depending on what is driving the projections.
- *Discount rate.* The discount rate may be difficult to estimate.

Again, while all three major valuation methodologies have significant drawbacks, they do have strengths. It is important to play the strengths of each off of the others to come up with an approximate value of the entire business. If you are interested in seeing how that is technically done, I recommend reading my book *Financial Modeling and Valuation: A Practical Guide to Investment Banking and Private Equity* (John Wiley & Sons, 2013), which steps through a complete valuation analysis on Walmart.

CHAPTER 3

Leveraged Buyout Analysis

There are three major steps to conducting a leveraged buyout (LBO) analysis:

Step 1: Obtaining a purchase price.
Step 2: Estimating sources and uses of funds.
Step 3: Calculating investor rate of return (IRR).

PURCHASE PRICE

In order to conduct a leveraged buyout analysis, we first need to obtain a potential purchase price of the entity. Conducting a valuation analysis on the entity will help us arrive at an approximate current value of the entity. The book *Financial Modeling and Valuation* steps through how to model and value a company. Although a valuation analysis is helpful in providing an indication of what the appropriate value of the entity is today, one will most likely have to consider a control premium. A control premium is the percentage above current market value one would consider paying to convince the business owner or shareholders to hand over the business or shares. Let's take another look at the Heinz press release presented in the Preface.

> **Heinz Leveraged Buyout Press Release**
> *PITTSBURGH & OMAHA, Neb. & NEW YORK–(BUSINESS WIRE)—H.J. Heinz Company (NYSE: HNZ) ("Heinz") today announced that it has entered into a definitive merger agreement to be acquired by an investment consortium comprised of Berkshire Hathaway and 3G Capital.*
>   *Under the terms of the agreement, which has been unanimously approved by Heinz's Board of Directors, Heinz shareholders will*

receive $72.50 in cash for each share of common stock they own,
in a transaction valued at $28 billion, including the assumption of
Heinz's outstanding debt. The per share price represents a 20%
premium to Heinz's closing share price of $60.48 on February 13,
2013, a 19% premium to Heinz's all-time high share price, a 23%
premium to the 90-day average Heinz share price and a 30% pre-
mium to the one-year average share price."

(Heinz Press Release, February 14, 2013)

This states that the company will be purchased for $72.50 per share. Heinz, however, at the time this article was written, was trading at $60.48 per share. So the buyers are paying a price per share ($72.50) that is approximately 20 percent higher than the current trading price per share—a control premium.

Public versus Private Company Purchase

It is important to note that for a public company the purchase price is most likely based on a percentage above the current market trading value per share as exemplified in the preceding press release. However, private companies are popular leveraged buyout candidates as well. If we are evaluating a private company, we do not have a current market trading value from which to value the business. So, we need to use multiples to establish an estimated purchase price. Multiples of a private company can be based on public company comparables or historical transactions. In other words, to find an appropriate value of a private company, you can look for companies that are similar in product and size to that company: comparable companies. The multiples ranges of these comparable companies can determine the value of the private company. Also, looking at the price paid for historical transactions similar in product and size to the private company as a multiple can help establish an appropriate purchase price.

Types of Acquisitions

A business acquisition can be considered an asset acquisition or a stock acquisition. There are several differences between the two.

Asset acquisition

In an asset acquisition, the buyer purchases selected assets in the business and may take on the liabilities directly associated with the assets selected. Here, the net value of the assets purchased are "stepped-up," or written up,

SHIPCO EXAMPLE

Let's take an example of a local package delivery business—a private company that makes money delivering packages to consumers. Let's say in 2012 it has produced $20 million in revenue. After cost of goods sold (COGS) and operating expenses, the company produces $5 million in earnings before interest, taxes, depreciation, and amortization (EBITDA). This is a private business, so we can look to public comparable companies (if they exist) to assess a proper value. Or we can look at precedent transactions—other acquisitions of local delivery businesses. The goal of this book is to assess leveraged buyout (LBO) returns, not valuation, so let's assume the comparable company analysis results in a range of 4.0x to 6.0x EBITDA and we found a few historical transactions where buyers paid 4.5x to 5.5x EBITDA for a local delivery business. For this example we will base a purchase price on a 5.0x EBITDA multiple, as it is the midpoint of both the comparable company analysis and the precedent transaction analysis. That will result in a $25 million estimated purchase price (5 times $5 million EBITDA). Keep this example in mind, as we will use it to illustrate core LBO concepts in this chapter before we get to the actual Heinz case.

on the acquirer's tax balance sheet. In other words if a buyer pays a higher value for an asset than what is stated on the seller's balance sheet, and that purchase price represents the fair market value of the asset, then that incremental value paid can be amortized over 15 years (under U.S. tax law) for tax purposes. This amortization is tax deductible. The value of the asset can also be "stepped-down" or written down if the purchase price is less than what is stated on the seller's balance sheet.

Stock acquisition

In a stock acquisition, the buyer purchases the target's stock from the selling shareholders. This would result in an acquisition of the entire business entity—all of the assets and liabilities of the seller (some exceptions will be later noted). In a stock acquisition, if the purchase price paid is higher than the value of the entity as per its balance sheet, the difference needs to be further scrutinized. Unlike in an acquisition of assets, where the difference can be amortized and tax deductible, here the difference cannot all be attributed to an asset "stepped-up" and may be attributed to other items such as intangibles assets or Goodwill. While intangible assets can still be amortized, Goodwill cannot under us G.A.A.P rules. Because Goodwill cannot be amortized, it will not receive the same tax benefits as amortizable assets. We will detail this further in Chapter 8.

338(h)(10) Elections

To a buyer, an acquisition of assets is generally preferred for several reasons: First the buyer will not be subject to additional liabilities beyond those directly associated with the assets, and second the buyer can receive the tax benefits of an asset "step-up."

However, to a seller an acquisition of equity is generally preferred as the entire business, including most liabilities, are sold. This also avoids the double-taxation issue sellers face related to an asset purchase. See Table 3.1.

The 338(h)(10) election is a "best of both worlds" scenario allowing the buyer to record a stock purchase as an asset acquisition in that the buyer can still record the asset "step up." The section 338(h)(10) election historically has been available to buyers of subsidiaries only, but are now permitted in acquisitions of S corporations even though, by definition, S corporations do not fulfill the statute's requirement that the target be a subsidiary. Thus, an S corporation acquisition can be set up as a stock purchase, but it can be treated as an asset purchase followed by a liquidation of the S corporation for-tax purposes.

Since Heinz is a public company, the buyers will consider the acquisition a stock acquisition.

See Table 3.1 from the popular website Breaking Into Wall Street for a nice summary of all the major differences between an Asset Acquisition, a Stock Acquisition, and the 338(h)(10) Election.

SOURCES AND USES OF FUNDS

Once a purchase price has been established, we need to determine the amount of funds we actually need raised to complete the acquisition (uses), and we need to know how we will obtain those funds (sources).

Uses of Funds

The uses of funds represent how much funding we need to complete the acquisition. These uses generally fall into three major categories:

1. Purchase price.
2. Net debt.
3. Transaction fees.

TABLE 3.1 Types of Acquisitions

	Stock Purchase	Asset Purchase	338(h)(10) Election
Sellers	Shareholders	Corporate entity	Shareholders
Assets and Liabilities	Buyer gets everything	Buyer picks and chooses	Buyer gets everything
Valuation of Assets and Liabilities	Book values used, but modified for any step-ups or step-downs	Every single asset/liability must be valued separately	Book values used, but modified for any step-ups or step-downs
Seller Taxes	Single taxation—shareholders pay capital gains tax	Double taxation—taxes on purchase price minus fair market value as well as on shareholder proceeds	Double taxation—taxes on purchase price minus fair market value as well as on shareholder proceeds
Book Basis	Assets/liabilities stepped up or down for accounting purposes	Assets/liabilities stepped up or down for accounting purposes	Assets/liabilities stepped up or down for accounting purposes
Tax Basis	Buyer assumes seller's tax basis for assets/liabilities	Buyer receives tax step-up for assets/liabilities	Buyer receives tax step-up for assets/liabilities
Goodwill and Other Intangibles	Not amortized for tax purposes and not tax-deductible	Amortization is tax-deductible; amortized over 15 years for tax purposes	Amortization is tax-deductible; amortized over 15 years for tax purposes
Seller Net Operating Losses (NOLs)	Buyer can apply Section 382 after transaction to reduce taxes	Completely lost in transaction	Completely lost in transaction
Complexity	Inexpensive and quick to execute	Complex and time-consuming—need to value and transfer each asset	Inexpensive and quick to execute
Used For	Most public/large companies	Divestitures; distressed sales; some private companies	Private companies; compromise between buyer and seller
Preferred By	Sellers	Buyers	Both
Combined Balance Sheet	Add all seller's assets and liabilities (assume shareholders' equity is wiped out); adjust for write-ups, write-downs, and new items	Add only the seller's assets and liabilities that the buyer is acquiring; adjust for write-ups, write-downs, and new items created in acquisition	Add all seller's assets and liabilities (assume shareholders' equity is wiped out); adjust for write-ups, write-downs, and new items

(continued)

TABLE 3.1 (Continued)

	Stock Purchase	Asset Purchase	338(h)(10) Election
Goodwill Created	= Equity Purchase Price – Seller Book Value + Seller Existing Goodwill – PP&E Write-Up – Intangibles Write-Up – Seller Existing Deferred Tax Liability (DTL) + Write-Down of Seller Existing Deferred Tax Asset (DTA) + New DTL Created	= Equity Purchase Price – Seller Book Value + Seller Existing Goodwill – PP&E Write-Up – Intangibles Write-Up – Seller Existing DTL + Write-Down of Seller Existing DTA	= Equity Purchase Price – Seller Book Value + Seller Existing Goodwill – PP&E Write-Up – Intangibles Write-Up – Seller Existing DTL + Write-Down of Seller Existing DTA
Goodwill Treatment	Not amortized for accounting purposes; not amortized for tax purposes and not tax-deductible	Not amortized for accounting purposes; amortized over 15 years for taxes and tax-deductible	Not amortized for accounting purposes; amortized over 15 years for taxes and tax-deductible
Intangibles Treatment	Amortized for accounting purposes; not tax-deductible	Amortized for accounting purposes; tax-amortized over 15 years and tax-deductible	Amortized for accounting purposes; tax-amortized over 15 years and tax-deductible
Depreciation from PP&E Write-Up	Affects pretax income but not tax-deductible	Affects pretax income and tax-deductible	Affects pretax income and tax-deductible
New DTL Created	Total Asset Write-Up* Buyer Tax Rate	$0	$0
Annual NOL Usage Allowed	Seller's Equity Purchase Price* MAX(Previous 3 Month's Adjusted Long-Term Rates)	$0	$0
DTA Write-Down	=MAX(0, NOL Balance – Allowed Annual Usage* Years until Expiration)	Subtract entire NOL balance from DTA	Subtract entire NOL balance from DTA

Source: Breaking into Wall Street (BIWS): http://samples.breakingintowallstreet.com.s3.amazonaws.com/22-BIWS-Acquisition-Types.pdf.

Purchase Price

As discussed previously in the purchase price section of this chapter, the purchase price is based either on the current market trading value of the business or on some multiple.

Net Debt

Quite often, in addition to the purchase price, a buyer is responsible for raising additional funds to pay off the target company's outstanding debt obligations. This can also include other liabilities such as capital lease obligations. The need to pay down such obligations is dependent on several factors including whether the company is public or private.

Public Company If the company is public, which means the buyer is buying all existing shares from the shareholders, the buyer must assume responsibility for obligations on the target company's balance sheet. Certainly the shareholders cannot be responsible for the corporate debt. So the buyer has to determine whether it can or should assume the debt that will carry over after purchase, or if it must raise additional funds to pay down those obligations. The buyer must conduct some due diligence on the company's debts. Most likely, when lenders lend to companies, those debts come with covenants and bylaws that state if there are any major company events, such as a change in control (an acquisition), so those lenders would require to be paid back. If that is the case, then the buyer has no choice but to re-finance or raise additional funds to pay those obligations. If there are no such requirements, then the buyer must make the decision whether it would prefer to pay back the obligations or take them on and just keep them outstanding on the balance sheet. That decision will most likely be based on the interest rates or other terms of the outstanding loans. If the buyer can get a loan with a better rate, the buyer will most likely prefer to pay back the old debt and raise new debt.

Private Company If the company is private, the buyer has most likely negotiated a purchase price based on some multiple. Remember that there are market value multiples and enterprise value multiples (see Chapter 2). The multiple becomes an important factor here because this multiple determines whether the purchase price is effectively a market value or an enterprise value. In other words, if the purchase price was derived based on a market value multiple, then of course the purchase price is an effective market value, whereas if the purchase price was derived based on an enterprise value multiple, then the purchase price is an effective enterprise value. This is important to consider because if the purchase price negotiated is effectively an enterprise value, then that purchase price includes the value of debt. And that means we should not have to raise additional funds to pay down the target company's debt obligations. We are basically saying that the seller should be responsible for such obligations. Let's say, for example, that we negotiated to buy a company for 5x EBITDA. If the company's EBITDA is $100,000, then we will pay $500,000 for the company. However, since $500,000 is based on an enterprise value, which is the value of the business including obligations, then the $500,000 effectively includes the value of debt and obligations and the seller should assume responsibility for paying them down.

On the other hand, let's say we negotiated a purchase price based on a market value multiple of 10x net income. If the net income is $25,000, then the purchase price is $250,000. However, that purchase price is a market value (because it is based on net income—after debt and obligations), which means the value of debt is not included. Inherently, the buyer is now responsible for the obligations on the business. This should make sense because this is a lower purchase price than that obtained when we used the EBITDA multiple.

Let's say the total value of obligations is $250,000. If we have negotiated a purchase price based on EBITDA, then we pay $500,000 and are not responsible for the debt (the seller holds responsibility). However, if the negotiated purchase price is based on net income and the purchase price is $250,000, then we are responsible for raising additional funds to pay the obligations of $250,000, which totals $500,000.

	Public Company	**Private Company**
Valuation Methods Used	Percent premium above market price, multiples	Multiples
Net Debt Responsibility	Goes to the buyer; is either rolled over, refinanced, or paid down upon acquisition.	Can go to the buyer or seller; depends on valuation method, negotiations, and debt contracts

So, depending on how the buyer has arrived at a purchase price, net debt may or may not need to be included in uses of funds. Note that we mention net debt as opposed to total debt, as net debt is the total debt less cash and cash equivalents. In other words, we assume if there is any outstanding cash on the target company balance sheet at acquisition, it will be used to pay target obligations. Note that for a private company, it is likely that a seller will pocket all outstanding cash before sale. In that situation, the cash will be $0 on the balance sheet.

SHIPCO EXAMPLE (*Continued*)

In the ShipCo example, we used an EBITDA multiple to arrive at the purchase price. So the $25 million purchase price is effectively an enterprise value, and it includes the effects of debt. Therefore, if we actually purchase the business, the seller is responsible for taking the $25 million and paying down debt. We will receive a debt-free business.

Transaction Fees

Transaction fees are expenses related to the pursuit and close of the transaction. Lawyers and investment bankers need to get paid for their services in helping the deal come together, for example. The buyer needs to allocate additional funds to pay such fees. The fees can run from a small retainer to a percentage of the transaction size. The amount depends on negotiations and firmwide policy. Some of these fees can be capitalized. (See Table 3.2.) Examples of a few of the more common transaction fee categories follow.

Investment Banking Fees Investment banks will often be hired to help pursue the purchase or sale of a business on behalf of a client. The investment banking fees are often based on a percentage of the transaction value (1 percent to 3 percent, for example, or even less than 1 percent for some multibillion-dollar businesses). Investment banks also receive fees for conducting business valuations, seeking out other investing parties such as lenders, and conducting due diligence.

Legal Fees Attorneys are needed for contract negotiation, regulatory review and approval, legal due diligence, preparation of documents for approval, and closing documents. There will also be attorney fees for negotiating, reviewing, and preparing the documents necessary for funding the transaction, which can include private placement memoranda for debt and/ or equity. Investment banks also aid in authoring memoranda hand-in-hand with legal council.

Due Diligence Costs Due diligence refers to examining and auditing a potential acquisition target. This process includes reviewing all financial records, appraising assets, and valuing the entity and anything deemed material to the sale.

Environmental Assessment   If land or property is involved in the acquisition, an environmental assessment may be required to assess the positive or negative impacts the asset may have on the environment.

Human Resources   Quite often if the strategy of a leveraged buyout is to improve the operational performance of the business, there will be a need to search for better talent. New management such as a CEO with a proven track record may be key to achieving such desired operational results. A human resources search may then need to be conducted.

Debt Fees   Lenders often charge a fee, either a flat rate or a certain percentage of the debt lent out. This percentage can be less than 1 percent for standard term loans or 1 percent to 3 percent for more aggressive types of debt. It can also vary significantly based on the size of debt lent. Sometimes fees charged associated with term loans can be capitalized and amortized on the balance sheet. We discuss in detail the capitalization and amortization of debt fees in Chapter 16.

Equity Fees   The equity investor may also charge a fee upon transaction closing. Such fees are again dependent on the size of equity invested and are one of several ways a private equity fund can generate operating profit. Table 3.2 is an example of a transaction fee structure for a recent $30 million leveraged buyout transaction.

In the example, the equity investor is the private equity firm purchasing the business. He has charged a 2 percent fee on the $30 million purchase price. The senior lender has raised $7,500,000 and receives a 0.5 percent fee.

TABLE 3.2   Transaction Fee Table Example

Transaction Fees	Rate	Amount
Equity Investor	2.00%	$ 600,000
Senior Lender	0.50%	37,500
Mezzanine Lender	2.00%	120,000
Legal		150,000
Accounting		75,000
Environmental		10,000
Due Diligence		15,000
Human Resources		25,000
Miscellaneous		25,000
Total		$1,057,500

The mezzanine lender has raised $6,000,000 and receives a 2 percent fee. There are also several other fees that are flat fees. This is based on a real example, so it gives you an indication of fee amounts for a $30 million acquisition. In total, these fees amounted to 3.33 percent of the overall transaction size.

In summary, the purchase price, net debt, and transaction fees all represent the uses of cash. This is the amount of money a buyer needs to raise to meet the total cost of acquisition.

SHIPCO EXAMPLE (*Continued*)

Let's keep the ShipCo example simple and assume there are no transaction fees. Again, we want to use ShipCo to illustrate the LBO process, so we don't want to complicate the example with distracting details.

Sources of Funds

Now that we know how much we need to raise in total to fund the acquisition, we need to source such funds. Funds are sourced either by raising equity or debt or by using cash on hand. Table 3.3 gives an example of the types of sources one would see in a leveraged buyout. The percentage ranges in the left column represent on average the percentage of total sources raised by each security. The expected returns can vary depending on the market environment. Also note that the expected equity returns of >25% stated in Table 3.3 is the percentage many funds hope to achieve; different from what has actually been achieved on average given the recent market environment.

Debt

A company can raise various types of debts in order to obtain funding for an acquisition. Common debts raised exist in several categories.

Bank Debt Bank debt or a term loan is the most fundamental type of debt. It usually carries 5 percent to 12 percent interest and can be backed by the core assets of the business. Such debt is also typically amortized over the transaction horizon, five to seven years for example. Bank debts can come from commercial or investment banks, private funds, or investors. It is also possible, but more difficult, to receive multiple loans from different lenders. However, there is almost always a hierarchy where one

TABLE 3.3   Example of Leveraged Buyout Capital Structure

Bank Debt (30% to 50%)	■ Has initial rights on the assets ■ Lowest-risk security ■ Expected returns (interest): 5% to 12%
High Yield Debt (0% to 10%)	■ Junk bonds ■ Higher-risk security ■ High interest ■ Not used as often (mezzanine is more common today) ■ Expected returns: 12% to 15%
Mezzanine Lending (20% to 30%)	■ Combination of debt and equity; downside protection (debt) and upside potential (equity) ■ Also can be considered convertible debt or preferred equity ■ Helpful in increasing equity returns ■ Expected returns: 13% to 25%
Equity (20% to 30%)	■ Financial sponsors ■ No downside protection ■ Expected returns: >25%

is subordinate to another. Subordinated debt would be riskier and warrant a higher interest rate.

Note that the purpose of this book is not to educate on all the various debt instruments. The selection is vast and there are other great books out there that focus solely on debt instruments. This is meant to be a brief overview to better illustrate how various debts are applied to a leveraged buyout analysis.

A private entity can attempt to raise not only standard term debt, but more aggressive types of debt that would arguably not be doable if the company were public. A public company receiving a significant amount of high-interest debt might send shareholders running. This ability for a private company to access debts that a public market might not allow is key to a leveraged buyout.

High Yield Debt   High yield debt is a more aggressive type of debt borrowed at much higher interest rates to compensate for additional risk of defaulting on such debt. Interest in such debt can be upward of 15 percent, but it varies depending on the situation at hand. We mention in Table 3.3 that 0 percent to 10 percent of high yield debt typically is used in a leveraged buyout transaction because we've seen two schools of thought. Some funds we have spoken to used high yield debt previously but not anymore. Other funds are starting to access high yield debt markets again. If you are the buyer, it really depends on who is willing to lend and at what cost (interest rate).

Seller Notes Upon purchasing the business, a smart buyer would want to find ways to incentivize the prior owner of the business to help aid in the business transition. In a worst-case scenario, the seller could attempt to build a competing business directly after the sale. To try to prevent such scenarios from happening, and further to encourage the seller of the business to stick around and help transition the business to the new buyer, seller incentives such as a seller note or rollover equity is put in pace. A seller note is a loan from the seller to the buyer paid back in agreed-upon installments. For example, let's say that in the $25 million ShipCo purchase, we agreed on paying the seller $20 million up front and $5 million will be a seller note payable over five years. The seller is now incentivized to help out in the business until he has received his $5 million in full in five years. Such seller notes may or may not incur interest, depending on the agreement between the seller and the buyer. As a side note, sellers often sign noncompete agreements, which prevent the seller from starting a new business competitive to the one recently sold. Seller notes are a good way to help enforce such agreements.

Mezzanine

Mezzanine securities are hybrids between debt and equity. Convertible bonds or preferred securities are examples of mezzanine securities. The general concept of a mezzanine security is that it is initially considered debt that will convert to equity after a certain amount of time or after certain hurdles are met. We're being a bit vague here because virtually any combination of debt and equity can be created if there is an investor willing to invest in such a security and if there is a company willing to borrow such a security. As such, convertible markets departments exist in investment banks whose sole purpose is to create unique hybrid structures designed to match a buyer with a seller of a mezzanine security.

The benefit of mezzanine lending to an investor is there is some downside protection (as it is debt for the first specified number of years), but there is upside potential if the security converts into equity. Given the fact that there is an equity component to such securities, and knowing equity is more risky than debt, the effective combined return of a convertible security should be higher than that of debt. In Table 3.3 we suggested that anywhere from 20 percent to 30 percent of the total sources are typically made up of mezzanine securities. Again, this depends on the company and respective markets.

Chapter 15 in the book steps through more detail on preferred securities and specifically demonstrates how to model out preferred securities as they pertain to Heinz.

Just a note: Preferred securities can technically be considered equity, although they are also considered mezzanine as they often simulate debt in some form. See Chapter 15 for a more complete overview of preferred securities.

Equity

A public company can raise shares in the open market in order to obtain funding for an acquisition. A private entity can attempt to raise equity from funds or investors, or they can use their own funds. Typically, in a leveraged buyout 20 to 30 percent of equity is raised to meet the total amount needed. That number can change depending on the transaction situation and market environment.

Rollover Equity In private companies the seller of the business can also invest some funds back into the business and receive a small equity stake. This is helpful in incentivizing the seller to continue to consult with the business, especially as the seller may be tied to clients and important relationships necessary to sustain or further business growth.

Cash

If an entity has adequate cash on hand to meet the total funding needs, raising equity or debt may not be necessary.

● ● ●

The sources of funding are totaled and should match the uses of funding.

Sources of Funds = Uses of Funds

SHIPCO EXAMPLE (*Continued*)

Let's say in the ShipCo example we have been able to raise 35 percent in bank debt, 25 percent in high yield debt, and 40 percent in equity. So, 35 percent of the $25 million is $8.75 million, 25 percent of the $25 million is $6.25 million, and $10 million is the equity we will use to purchase the company. We also note that the company has $100 thousand in net debt on the business. Because the net debt is effectively included in the purchase price in this case, we separate out the portion of net debt from the purchase price. In other words, of the $25 million we agreed to pay the seller, $100 thousand will be used to pay down net debt. (See Table 3.4.) There are other ways to look at this, which we will reserve for the more advanced Heinz analysis.

TABLE 3.4 ShipCo Sources and Uses

Uses	Amount	Sources	Amount	%
Purchase Price (equity value)	$24,900.0	Bank Debt	$ 8,750.0	35%
Transaction Fees	0.0	High Yield Debt	6,250.0	25%
Net Debt	100.0	Equity	10,000.0	40%
Total	$25,000.0	Total	$25,000.0	100%

IRR ANALYSIS

Once we have our sources and uses of cash, we can now proceed to determine the annualized rate of return for our potential investment.

Initial Assumptions

First, we begin with the following assumptions:

Time Horizon

It is first important to consider a time horizon. How long do we expect to own and hold the business before selling it? This time horizon could be dependent on how long we deem it would take to make adequate improvements, or maybe it is based on the timing of investment funds required to be returned to investors. Often the horizon is five, seven, or ten years.

Exit Value Method

Once we know when we will sell the business, we need to determine the exit value—how much we can expect to sell the business for. Since the company is now private, we would most likely base the sale on a multiple at the time of sale, an exit multiple. Here, comparable companies or precedent transactions can help determine a fair exit multiple. But often, we can conservatively use the same multiple as we paid for the business. In other words, if we paid 10x EBITDA for the company, we would hope in five years to sell the business for at least 10x EBITDA. The idea is that we would have most likely improved business performance and increased EBITDA, so although the multiple remains unchanged, the sale value would have increased. Therefore, it is useful to consider in advance, for the analysis, what method we will use to arrive at the exit value; that is, will it be a multiple of EBIT, EBITDA, or some other method? It is most common to use EBIT or EBITDA, as they are unlevered metrics and better represent performance of the business operations (see Chapter 2 on valuation).

SHIPCO EXAMPLE (*Continued*)

For the ShipCo example, let's use five years as the time horizon. Since we paid 5x EBITDA for the business, let's assume conservatively we will sell the business for 5 times the year 5 EBITDA.

Steps to Investor Return

Once we have the core assumptions—the purchase price, the uses of funds, the sources of funds, time horizon, and exit value method—we can proceed with the analysis.

Step 1: Unlevered Free Cash Flow Projections

Once we have our core assumptions, we would most likely need five-year projections in order to interpret the exit multiple into an actual exit value. Further, once we have an exit value, we note that this exit value, if calculated based on an enterprise value multiple, will produce an enterprise exit value. If so, we need to convert enterprise value into equity value by removing net debt. It is equity value that reflects our actual return. In other words, when selling the business, we will most likely be responsible for paying down the business debts. Again, the company we are selling is private, and if the sale is based on an EBIT or EBITDA multiple, then the sale value is an enterprise value, and therefore includes the value of debt.

However, in order to predict the level of debt in year 5, for example, we need to understand not only the impact of interest incurred over the five years, but also the cash produced by the business over the five years. The cash produced can be used to pay down debts. Unlevered free cash flow projections contain both EBIT and EBITDA projections, which can be used for our exit value, and also contain cash projections, which can be used to project cash. So, for a simple IRR analysis it is first recommended to build simple unlevered free cash flow projections.

Unlevered Free Cash Flow   Unlevered free cash flow is cash that is available to all capital providers, including equity holders and lenders. In other words, it is a measure of cash flow before equity holders and lenders have been paid. Further, as valuation is a measure of a company's core operating assets of a business, unlevered free cash flow should represent the cash generated or lost based on the core operations of the business. To clarify, let's take a look at a complete cash flow statement. We will give a more thorough review of the components of a cash flow statement in Chapter 6, so if you find your understanding of cash flows is weak, we recommend you review this discussion again after reading Chapter 6. (See Table 3.5.)

To get to an unlevered cash flow amount, we want to remove all cash flows related to the capital structure. So we eliminate dividend payouts, noncontrolling interests, share issuances, share buybacks, debt raises, and debt pay-downs; the entire financing activities section is removed. Further, we want a measure of cash that approaches everyday activity, so nonrecurring and extraordinary items such as acquisitions and divestitures will be removed. In the investing activities section, we are left with capital expenditures. (See Table 3.6.)

Simplifying the leftover cash flows gives us:

Unlevered Free Cash Flow
Net income
+ Depreciation and amortization
+ Deferred taxes
+ Other noncash items
+ Working capital changes
− Capital expenditures

Finally, since we are trying to capture an unlevered measure of cash, we also need to adjust the net income for interest expense. So we need to add one more line item: after-tax net interest expense.

Unlevered Free Cash Flow
Net income
+ Depreciation and amortization
+ Deferred taxes
+ Other noncash items
+ Working capital changes
− Capital expenditures
+ A/T net interest expense
= Total unlevered free cash flow

TABLE 3.5 Consolidated Statements of Cash Flows

Consolidated Statements of Cash Flows (in US$ millions)

Period Ending January 31	Actuals			Estimates				
	2010A	2011A	2012A	2013E	2014E	2015E	2016E	2017E
Cash flows from operating activities								
Net income	$14,883.0	$16,993.0	$16,387.0	$17,192.1	$18,030.3	$18,665.9	$19,066.2	$19,215.5
Loss (income) from discontinued operations to net cash	79.0	(1,034.0)	67.0	0.0	0.0	0.0	0.0	0.0
Depreciation and amortization	7,157.0	7,641.0	8,130.0	8,591.7	9,188.6	9,809.4	10,448.9	11,101.1
Deferred income taxes	(504.0)	651.0	1,050.0	715.9	1,003.5	791.0	596.3	411.4
Other operating activities	318.0	1,087.0	398.0	318.0	318.0	318.0	318.0	318.0
Changes in operating working capital								
Changes in accounts receivable	(297.0)	(733.0)	(796.0)	146.5	(289.5)	(243.2)	(189.7)	(130.3)
Changes in inventory	2,213.0	(3,205.0)	(3,727.0)	(148.4)	(2,043.1)	(1,716.2)	(1,338.7)	(919.2)
Changes in prepaid expenses and other	0.0	0.0	0.0	(773.9)	(122.9)	(103.3)	(80.6)	(55.3)
Changes in accounts payable	1,052.0	2,676.0	2,687.0	701.2	1,865.5	1,567.0	1,222.2	839.3
Changes in accrued liabilities	1,348.0	(433.0)	59.0	1,425.7	979.0	822.3	641.4	440.5
Changes in accrued income taxes	0.0	0.0	0.0	(460.7)	34.3	26.0	16.4	6.1
Net changes in operating working capital	$ 4,316.0	$ (1,695.0)	$ (1,777.0)	$ 890.4	$ 423.1	$ 352.6	$ 271.2	$ 181.1
Total cash flows from operating activities	$26,249.0	$23,643.0	$24,255.0	$27,708.1	$28,963.6	$29,936.9	$30,700.5	$31,227.1
Cash flows from investing activities								
Payments for property and equipment (CAPEX)	(12,184.0)	(12,699.0)	(13,510.0)	(14,213.0)	(14,923.7)	(15,520.6)	(15,986.2)	(16,305.9)
CAPEX % of revenue	3.0%	3.0%	3.0%	3.0%	3.0%	3.0%	3.0%	3.0%

Proceeds from disposal of property and equipment	1,002.0	489.0	580.0	0.0	0.0	0.0	0.0	0.0
Investments and business acquisitions, net of cash acquired	0.0	(202.0)	(3,548.0)	0.0	0.0	0.0	0.0	0.0
Other investing activities	(438.0)	219.0	(131.0)	(438.0)	219.0	(131.0)	(438.0)	219.0
Total cash from investing activities	**$(11,620.0)**	**$(12,193.0)**	**$(16,609.0)**	**$(14,651.0)**	**$(14,704.7)**	**$(15,651.6)**	**$(16,424.2)**	**$(16,086.9)**
Cash flows from financing activities								
Short-term borrowings (repayments)	(1,033.0)	503.0	3,019.0	0.0	0.0	0.0	0.0	0.0
Long-term borrowings (repayments)	(487.0)	7,316.0	466.0	0.0	0.0	0.0	0.0	0.0
Long-term debt due within one year	0.0	0.0	0.0	0.0	0.0	0.0	0.0	0.0
Capital lease obligations due within one year	0.0	0.0	0.0	0.0	0.0	0.0	0.0	0.0
Dividends paid	(4,217.0)	(4,437.0)	(5,048.0)	(5,344.7)	(5,187.3)	(5,029.9)	(4,872.5)	(4,715.1)
Dividends paid ($/share)			1.59	1.59	1.59	1.59	1.59	1.59
Purchase of common stock (treasury stock)	(7,276.0)	(14,776.0)	(6,298.0)	(7,318.8)	(7,318.8)	(7,318.8)	(7,318.8)	(7,318.8)
Purchase of redeemable noncontrolling interest	(436.0)	0.0	0.0	0.0	0.0	0.0	0.0	0.0
Capital lease obligations	(346.0)	(363.0)	(355.0)	0.0	0.0	0.0	0.0	0.0
Other	(396.0)	(271.0)	(242.0)	0.0	0.0	0.0	0.0	0.0
Total cash from financing activities	**$(14,191.0)**	**$(12,028.0)**	**$(8,458.0)**	**$(12,663.5)**	**$(12,506.1)**	**$(12,348.7)**	**$(12,191.3)**	**$(12,033.9)**
Effect of exchange rate on cash	194.0	66.0	(33.0)	194.0	66.0	(33.0)	194.0	66.0
Total change in cash and cash equivalents	**$632.0**	**$(512.0)**	**$(845.0)**	**$587.6**	**$1,818.8**	**$1,903.6**	**$2,279.0**	**$3,172.3**
Supplemental Data:								
Cash flow before debt pay-down				587.6	1,818.8	1,903.6	2,279.0	3,172.3

TABLE 3.6 Consolidated Statements of Cash Flows—Unlevered and Free

Consolidated Statements of Cash Flows (in US$ millions)

Period Ending January 31	Actuals			Estimates				
	2010A	2011A	2012A	2013E	2014E	2015E	2016E	2017E
Cash flows from operating activities								
Net income	$14,883.0	$16,993.0	$16,387.0	$17,192.1	$18,030.3	$18,665.9	$19,066.2	$19,215.5
Loss (income) from discontinued operations to net cash	79.0	(1,034.0)	67.0	0.0	0.0	0.0	0.0	0.0
Depreciation and amortization	7,157.0	7,641.0	8,130.0	8,591.7	9,188.6	9,809.4	10,448.9	11,101.1
Deferred income taxes	(504.0)	651.0	1,050.0	715.9	1,003.5	791.0	596.3	411.4
Other operating activities	318.0	1,087.0	398.0	318.0	318.0	318.0	318.0	318.0
Changes in operating working capital								
Changes in accounts receivable	(297.0)	(733.0)	(796.0)	146.5	(289.5)	(243.2)	(189.7)	(130.3)
Changes in inventory	2,213.0	(3,205.0)	(3,727.0)	(148.4)	(2,043.1)	(1,716.2)	(1,338.7)	(919.2)
Changes in prepaid expenses and other	0.0	0.0	0.0	(773.9)	(122.9)	(103.3)	(80.6)	(55.3)
Changes in accounts payable	1,052.0	2,676.0	2,687.0	701.2	1,865.5	1,567.0	1,222.2	839.3
Changes in accrued liabilities	1,348.0	(433.0)	59.0	1,425.7	979.0	822.3	641.4	440.5
Changes in accrued income taxes	0.0	0.0	0.0	(460.7)	34.3	26.0	16.4	6.1
Net changes in operating working capital	$4,316.0	$(1,695.0)	$(1,777.0)	$890.4	$423.1	$352.6	$271.2	$181.1
Total cash flows from operating activities	$26,249.0	$23,643.0	$24,255.0	$27,708.1	$28,963.6	$29,936.9	$30,700.5	$31,227.1
Cash flows from investing activities								
Payments for property and equipment (CAPEX)	(12,184.0)	(12,699.0)	(13,510.0)	(14,213.0)	(14,923.7)	(15,520.6)	(15,986.2)	(16,305.9)
CAPEX % of revenue	3.0%	3.0%	3.0%	3.0%	3.0%	3.0%	3.0%	3.0%

Proceeds from disposal of property and equipment	1,002.0	489.0	580.0	0.0	0.0	0.0	0.0	0.0
Investments and business acquisitions, net of cash acquired	0.0	(202.0)	(3,548.0)	0.0	0.0	0.0	0.0	0.0
Other investing activities	(438.0)	219.0	(131.0)	(131.0)	219.0	(131.0)	(438.0)	219.0
Total cash from investing activities	$(11,620.0)	$(12,193.0)	$(16,609.0)	$(14,651.0)	$(14,704.7)	$(15,651.6)	$(16,424.2)	$(16,086.9)
Cash flows from financing activities								
Short-term borrowings (repayments)	(1,033.0)	503.0	3,019.0	0.0	0.0	0.0	0.0	0.0
Long-term borrowings (repayments)	(487.0)	7,316.0	466.0	0.0	0.0	0.0	0.0	0.0
Long-term debt due within one year	0.0	0.0	0.0	0.0	0.0	0.0	0.0	0.0
Capital lease obligations due within one year	0.0	0.0	0.0	0.0	0.0	0.0	0.0	0.0
Dividends paid	(4,217.0)	(4,437.0)	(5,048.0)	(5,344.7)	(5,187.3)	(5,029.9)	(4,872.5)	(4,715.1)
Dividends paid ($/share)	—	—	—	1.59	1.59	1.59	1.59	1.59
Purchase of common stock (treasury stock)	(7,276.0)	(6,298.0)	(6,298.0)	(7,318.8)	(7,318.8)	(7,318.8)	(7,318.8)	(7,318.8)
Purchase of redeemable noncontrolling interest	(436.0)	0.0	0.0	0.0	0.0	0.0	0.0	0.0
Capital lease obligations	(346.0)	(363.0)	(355.0)	0.0	0.0	0.0	0.0	0.0
Other	(396.0)	(271.0)	(242.0)	0.0	0.0	0.0	0.0	0.0
Total cash from financing activities	$(14,191.0)	$(12,028.0)	$(8,458.0)	$(12,663.5)	$(12,506.1)	$(12,348.7)	$(12,191.3)	$(12,033.9)
Effect of exchange rate on cash	194.0	66.0	(33.0)	194.0	66.0	(33.0)	194.0	66.0
Total change in cash and cash equivalents	$632.0	$(512.0)	$(845.0)	$587.6	$1,818.8	$1,903.6	$2,279.0	$3,172.3
Supplemental Data:								
Cash flow before debt pay-down				587.6	1,818.8	1,903.6	2,279.0	3,172.3

There's often a lot of confusion as to whether these line items should be added or subtracted. The best rule of thumb is to follow how the cash flow statement is making these adjustments. We are trying to replicate a form of cash flow, so if the cash flow statement is adding the item, we should also add it; if the cash flow statement is subtracting the item, we should subtract. According to a standard cash flow statement, the flow should be:

Net Income + D&A + Deferred Taxes + Other Noncash Items + Working Capital Changes − CAPEX + A/T Net Interest Expense

Yes, it is plus working capital changes, because the cash flow statement adds working capital changes to the net income to get to cash from operations. Many textbooks suggest subtracting working capital, but they are actually referring to subtracting the balance sheet working capital changes. In other words, if accounts receivable increased from $0 to $1,000, or if the balance sheet change is $1,000, then we know the cash flow change is −$1,000, because an increase in an asset reflects a cash outflow. However, if we take the actual working capital number directly from the cash flow statement, which is already represented as a negative (−$1,000), we just add it.

It is crucial to note that there can be other items in the investing activities other than capital expenditures (CAPEX) that could arguably be attributable to everyday operations. Although it's not explicitly defined in the unlevered free cash flow formula, the point of the entire analysis is to get to a number that reflects the cash we expect to be generated from the future operations of the business. Further, in the operating activities, there may be other adjustments that are not categorized within the standard unlevered free cash flow definition. It is important to step back and think about how these line items are affecting net income to decide if they should also be adjusted in the unlevered free cash flow. In other words, if these line items are actually noncash items that need to be adjusted to net income in order to get to a closer measure of cash from net income, then they should be included in the analysis. However, if these are truly nonrecurring events, and if we have already pulled them out of net income on the income statement, adjusting them here may not be correct. This is one example of how important it is to understand fully where unlevered free cash flow is coming from and why it is being used as opposed to just taking and using the formula as printed.

Now, the previous definition is not the most standard definition of unlevered free cash flow. Typically, we use EBIT as a starting point, not net income. It is easier to project an income statement from revenue down to

EBIT only, rather than all the way down to net income, especially since we are adding back so many items anyway. However, both ways will get you the same results. So if we had EBIT as a starting point, we still have to make the same core adjustments:

Unlevered Free Cash Flow	Unlevered Free Cash Flow
Net income	EBIT
+ Depreciation and amortization	+ Depreciation and amortization
+ Deferred taxes	+ Deferred taxes
+ Other noncash items	+ Other noncash items
+ Working capital changes	+ Working capital changes
− Capital expenditures	− Capital expenditures
+ A/T net interest expense	
= Total unlevered free cash flow	

Note here we have to double-check once again which line items we are (or are not) including as other noncash items, and for a different reason: If the particular noncash item was a net income adjustment for a line item that was below the EBIT line, which we didn't even include anyway, adjusting it here would be incorrect.

We still have to make one more adjustment: taxes. We do not need to adjust for interest expense, as EBIT is already before interest expense. But EBIT is also before taxes. So in order to adjust for taxes, we need to take EBIT × Tax Rate. It is important to note we do not take the taxes figure from the income statement, as that number includes the effects of interest.

Unlevered Free Cash Flow	Unlevered Free Cash Flow
Net income	EBIT
+ Depreciation and amortization	+ Depreciation and amortization
+ Deferred taxes	+ Deferred taxes
+ Other noncash items	+ Other noncash items
+ Working capital changes	+ Working capital changes
− Capital expenditures	− Capital expenditures
+ A/T net interest expense	− Taxes (EBIT × Tax %)
= Total unlevered free cash flow	= Total unlevered free cash flow

SHIPCO EXAMPLE (*Continued*)

For ShipCo, we have in Table 3.7 simple unlevered free cash flow projections. We have assumed EBIT will grow at 5 percent per year. We have kept the depreciation and amortization (D&A) expense, CAPEX, and working capital constant each year—this is just for simplification and illustration. We have also assumed a 40 percent tax rate. We will use these cash flows to determine the investor rate of return (IRR) for ShipCo.

It is important to note here the importance of understanding the derivation of unlevered free cash flow. In this ever-changing market environment with new and evolving business models, the standard textbook definition of unlevered free cash flow may need to be adjusted to be a true measure of value for a particular entity. Understanding the purpose of unlevered free cash flow as a measure of value will help us to create our own adjustments to get to the true value of an entity.

Step 2: Calculation of Exit Enterprise Value

Unlevered free cash flows contain EBIT and EBITDA. So, assuming we have used an EBIT or EBITDA multiple as our exit value method, we can apply that multiple to the exit year metric found in the unlevered free cash flow projections.

$$\text{EBITDA Multiple} \times \text{Exit Year EBITDA} = \text{Exit Enterprise Value}$$

Note that this gives us enterprise value. To calculate our return, we need equity value, so we need to remove the effects of debt.

SHIPCO EXAMPLE (*Continued*)

Looking at Table 3.7, we note the 2017E EBITDA is $6,381.4 + $400.0 (EBIT + D&A). So 5 times $6,781.4 gives us the exit value of $33,907.0.

TABLE 3.7 ShipCo Unlevered Free Cash Flow

Projected Free Cash Flow						
	2012A	2013E	2014E	2015E	2016E	2017E
EBIT	$5,000.0	$5,250.0	$5,512.5	$5,788.1	$6,077.5	$6,381.4
EBIT growth rate		*5.0%*	*5.0%*	*5.0%*	*5.0%*	*5.0%*
D&A	400.0	400.0	400.0	400.0	400.0	400.0
CAPEX	(1,000.0)	(1,000.0)	(1,000.0)	(1,000.0)	(1,000.0)	(1,000.0)
Changes in working capital	(100.0)	(100.0)	(100.0)	(100.0)	(100.0)	(100.0)
Taxes (40%)		(2,100.0)	(2,205.0)	(2,315.3)	(2,431.0)	(2,552.6)
Unlevered free cash flow		2,450.0	2,607.5	2,772.9	2,946.5	3,128.8

Step 3: Calculation of Exit Debt

Now that we have an exit value, we need to subtract year 5 net debt to determine that actual value retuned to us as investors. In order to calculate exit year debt, we need to take several things into consideration:

- We always begin with the amount of debt raised upon initial acquisition.
- We need to calculate interest incurred each year we own the business.
- Cash generated (unlevered free cash flow) can be used to pay down debt and interest.

So, the beginning value of debt raised upon initial acquisition (beginning debt) plus the interest incurred each year less cash generated is the exit debt, or:

$$\text{Beginning Debt} + \text{Total Interest} - \text{Total Cash} = \text{Exit Debt}$$

Total interest can be calculated by applying an interest rate to the amount of debt raised, multiplied by the number of years we have held the business, and multiplied by $(1 - \text{Tax } \%)$.

Or:

$$\text{Beginning Debt} \times \text{Interest Rate } \% \times \text{Years} \times (1 - \text{Tax } \%)$$

Should the company have more than one type of debt with different interest rates, interest should be calculated for each type of debt, then added together. Note that this is a quick analysis and is not designed to handle the fact that interest expense can be reduced if debt is paid down year after year. We are conservatively assuming the interest expense is held constant. We will see later that the ability to handle a more dynamic debt and interest pay-down schedule is a benefit of a full-scale leveraged buyout analysis.

Total cash is the sum of the unlevered free cash flows for the projected years.

Explanation of Adjusting Interest by $(1 - \text{Tax } \%)$ We often get questions on why we multiply the interest expense by $(1 - \text{Tax } \%)$. Interest is tax deductible. We will clarify with this example.

Net income including interest:

Interest × (1 − Tax %)	
EBIT	$5,000
Interest	1,000
EBT	4,000
Tax (40%)	1,600
Net income	2,400

This demonstrates net income of $2,400 contains the effects of $1,000 in interest. If we remove $1,000 in interest expense, we also need to adjust taxes.

Net income excluding interest:

Interest × (1 − Tax %)	
EBIT	$5,000
Interest	0
EBT	5,000
Tax (40%)	2,000
Net income	3,000

You can see that once the $1,000 interest is removed, the net income has increased from the $2,400 to $3,000. Notice that the increase was $600, not $1,000. This is because although interest expense is removed, taxes associated with that interest expense are also removed.

In other words, once that interest expense is removed, the EBT has in fact increased by $1,000 (from $4,000 to $5,000). Higher EBT means higher taxes. Consequently, the taxes have increased from $1,600 to $2,000. So, the real changes are: (1) an interest expense reduction of $1,000 and (2) tax expense increase of $400, or $1,000 − $400; this is the $600 net effect to net income.

Now the $1,000 is interest less the $400 (interest times the tax rate). So,

$$\text{Interest} - (\text{Interest} \times \text{Tax \%})$$

Using algebra, we can pull out interest so the formula will read:

$$\text{Interest} \times (1 - \text{Tax \%})$$

Step 4: Calculation of IRR

Once we have the exit enterprise value and the exit debt, we simply subtract to get exit equity value. This is the value returned to us as investors. With this value, we can calculate the IRR.

$$\text{IRR} = (\text{Exit Equity Value/Equity Invested}) \wedge (1/\text{Years}) - 1$$

where the equity invested is the value of equity the investors originally invested in the business (found in the sources of cash), and the years is the amount of time that we held the business.

SHIPCO EXAMPLE (*Continued*)

Looking at Table 3.4 (sources of cash), we notice we have raised $8,750.0 of bank debt and $6,250.0 of high yield debt. Let's assume the interest rates are 10 percent for the bank debt and 15 percent for the high yield debt. Note again that we are making oversimplifications to illustrate the LBO process; don't take these assumptions as being realistic. Once the method is understood, we will use the Heinz case for real-world application.

We now calculate total interest for each. Since the formula is:

$$\text{Beginning Debt} \times \text{Interest Rate } (\%) \times \text{Years} \times (1 - \text{Tax } \%)$$

we can plug in the assumptions to get:

$$\$8,750.0 \times 10\% \times 5 \times (1 - 40\%) = \$2,625.0$$

for bank debt and

$$\$6,250.0 \times 15\% \times 5 \times (1 - 40\%) = \$2,812.5$$

for high yield debt, totaling $5,437.5 in interest expense.

To calculate total cash, we just need to add up the cash flows from 2013E to 2017E from Table 3.7: $2,450.0 + $2,607.5 + $2,772.9 + $2,946.5 + $3,128.8 = $13,905.7.

$$\text{Exit Debt} = \text{Beginning Debt} + \text{Total Interest} - \text{Cash}$$

or

$$\$8,750.0 + \$6,250.0 + \$5,437.5 - \$13,905.7 = \$6,531.8$$

So, with an exit enterprise value of $33,907.0 and $6,531.8 of final debt, the exit equity value is $27,375.2 ($33,907.0 − $6,531.8). This is basically the net amount returned to us. We compare this with our initial investment to calculate the IRR. Our original equity investment is $10 million. This is found in the sources of cash, Table 3.4. So to calculate IRR,

$$(\$27,375.2/\$10,000) \wedge (1/5) - 1 = 22.3\%$$

That's it! This is the simple version of a leveraged buyout IRR analysis. Although 22.3 percent is not too bad a yearly return, some funds have minimum return requirements, such as 25 percent.

To strengthen your understanding of such an analysis, it is important to highlight some key variables affecting the IRR:

- *Purchase price.* Of course the purchase price plays a major role in determining the IRR. The higher the purchase price, the more costly the investment may be to the investor, and therefore the lower the IRR. A couple of exceptions here: We are assuming that a higher purchase price would mean the investor would have to put more equity into the initial investment. Also, a higher purchase price can be offset by a higher sale value, and if so, the IRR may not be affected.
- *Sources of cash.* The amount of debt that can be raised to make such an investment will also affect the IRR. The more debt we can raise, the less equity we have to put in, and so the higher our expected returns will be.
- *Interest rate.* A lower interest rate would lower our costs, which would increase our cash, which would allow us to pay down debt faster and increase the IRR.
- *Time frame.* Typically, a shorter time frame would produce a higher IRR. But be careful not to get fooled, as this is a compounded percentage. In other words, a 25 percent annual return over five years does not give us as high an overall return as 20 percent annually over 10 years. Take a $1,000 investment, for example.

$$\$1,000 \times (1+25\%) \wedge 5 = \$3,051.76$$

or

$$\$1,000 \times (1+20\%) \wedge 10 = \$6,191.74$$

Which would you prefer? Although the first example is showing a higher return of 25 percent, the overall exit value is only half of the second example.

- *Operations performance (EBITDA projections).* The more we can improve EBITDA, the higher our potential sale value, which would increase IRR. Also, a higher EBITDA would improve our cash flow.
- *Cash flow (UFCF projections).* Improved cash flow performance will allow us to pay down debt faster and will improve our IRR.
- *Exit multiple.* The higher our exit multiple (exit value), the higher our return.

These are the major variables that affect an IRR analysis. Keep these in mind when we continue with the Heinz case. Although such analyses are used as a quick estimate of investor return, there are several major flaws with such a brief analysis:

- *Lack of income statement.* We have no record of net income, and we may have overlooked some crucial expenses below the EBIT line that could potentially hinder business performance.
- *Lack of complete cash flow statement.* Although unlevered free cash flow as discussed earlier is a good measure of cash, without a complete cash flow statement we may overlook some other crucial cash flow line items that can hinder cash generation.
- *Lack of balance sheet.* Without a balance sheet we really don't know how much debt the business can take on. A complete model will help us better determine debt capacity.
- *Interest expense.* In this example we calculated interest expense by multiplying the interest rate by the amount of debt initially raised. We then multiplied the interest expense by the number of years we own the business. In doing so, we are assuming the interest expense is held flat each year. However, in reality debt could be paid down each year, thus reducing interest expense. Although keeping the interest expense the same each year can be seen as conservative, the ability to capture interest savings each year by paying down debt is a crucial component to a leveraged buyout analysis.
- *Goodwill/intangible assets.* We have not assumed benefits of amortizing intangible assets related to paying a premium above book value for the business. We will discuss this in Chapter 8.
- *Synergies.* We did not account for the effects of synergies or cost savings. Although we could have done this in the unlevered free cash flow analysis, it is better to project synergies directly in the income statement.

These are some of the many reasons why a full-scale leveraged buyout analysis provides a more accurate estimation of an effective investor return. However, such a quick analysis is helpful in highlighting the major concepts and drivers to a leveraged buyout analysis. In the next part we evaluate the leveraged buyout of Heinz completely as done on Wall Street.

TWO

Leveraged Buyout Full-Scale Model

If you have read the previous chapters several times, you have a good understanding of the leveraged buyout (LBO) theory. At the end of the last chapter we spoke about weaknesses of a simple leveraged buyout analysis, which warrant the need for a full-scale model. However, a simple analysis can be great for giving a rough indication of whether the investment is even worth looking at further.

A full-scale model does have major benefits:

- *Detailed projections.* If you are really serious about buying the business, there needs to be complete projections with every line item in the income statement, cash flow statement, and balance sheet broken out. This level of detail is helpful to really understand the business's finances.
- *Balance sheet adjustments.* We will soon discuss the importance of showing the balance sheet after the investment has been made including all the new debt and equity used to fund the purchase.
- *Debt schedule.* The fact that a full-scale model contains a debt schedule, which calculates interest expense and flows into the three statements, is key. We will prove its importance as we step through the Heinz case.

Recall Step 3 in the LBO simple analysis, the calculation of exit debt. A full-scale model that is properly linked completely through will contain a debt schedule that will handle the paying down and adjustments of debt and interest. So you will see that, when we have a full-scale model, we don't need to make all the debt, interest, and cash side calculations we have done in the simple analysis. In a full-scale model, to find our exit debt, we simply look up the total value of net debt found on the debt schedule or balance sheet. We can then subtract that from enterprise value to get our exit equity return.

These are just a few of the major benefits a full-scale model brings. A full-scale leveraged buyout model is built in nine parts:

1. Assumptions (purchase price, sources, and uses).
2. Income statement.
3. Cash flow statement.
4. Balance sheet adjustments.
5. Depreciation schedule.
6. Working capital schedule.
7. Balance sheet projections.
8. Debt schedule.
9. Investor rate of return (IRR).

In subsequent chapters, we will build out each section and explain how they link together to form a full-scale leveraged buyout model. We will use the model entitled "NYSF – Leveraged_Buyout_Model_Template.xls" found on the book's website. We recommend you download the model and build it out as we step through the construction of the Heinz case.

CHAPTER 4

Assumptions

The assumptions are the core drivers of the model. The major segments of the Assumptions tab include the Purchase Price, Uses of Funds, and Sources of Funds.

In order to use Heinz as a model for a complete leveraged buyout (LBO) analysis, we will build an Assumptions tab containing many possible drivers, even though they may not be needed in this particular case. Let's review the press release for the potential Heinz buyout:

Heinz Leveraged Buyout Press Release
PITTSBURGH & OMAHA, Neb. & NEW YORK--(BUSINESS WIRE)--H.J. Heinz Company (NYSE: HNZ) ("Heinz") today announced that it has entered into a definitive merger agreement to be acquired by an investment consortium comprised of Berkshire Hathaway and 3G Capital.

Under the terms of the agreement, which has been unanimously approved by Heinz's Board of Directors, Heinz shareholders will receive $72.50 in cash for each share of common stock they own, in a transaction valued at $28 billion, including the assumption of Heinz's outstanding debt. The per share price represents a 20% premium to Heinz's closing share price of $60.48 on February 13, 2013, a 19% premium to Heinz's all-time high share price, a 23% premium to the 90-day average Heinz share price and a 30% premium to the one-year average share price.

(Heinz Press Release, February 14, 2013)

The press release reads that "Heinz shareholders will receive $72.50 in cash for each share."

Before constructing the model, it is important to research various data sources for accurate information. I would recommend going to the company website and www.sec.gov for the most accurate information on the company. We have already found the February 14 press release from the investor relations section of the company website. To locate this press release, you can navigate to www.heinz.com. At the top right of the Heinz home page is an "Investor Relations" button. See Figure 4.1.

At the bottom of this page is the financial news section where the acquisition press release can be found.

U.S. Securities and Exchange Commission (SEC) filings can be the best resource for financial data on the company being acquired. A proxy statement contains an "Opinion of Financial Adviser" section, also known as a fairness opinion, where the financial advisers detail the valuation supporting the acquisition. The SEC Form S-4 and an 8-K are other examples of filings that may contain financial details on an acquisition. The company's annual report can also contain a paragraph discussing the merger.

We can navigate to the website at www.sec.gov.

At the top right of Figure 4.2 there is a "Company Filings" link. Clicking this link takes us to another page where we can type in "Heinz" in the "Company Name" search box, and click the "Search" button. This will reveal a list of public entities related to the name "Heinz." See Figure 4.3.

We can see there are a lot of entities with the name "Heinz" in them. The public company is entity number 0000046640, entitled "Heinz H J Co" at the top. Let's click this. The results are shown in Figure 4.4. You may need to scroll down to get to documents filed around the time of transaction announcement.

The 10-Q and 10-K reports are in this section and will be helpful to us. But more important, we want to detect filings related to the acquisition. Again it may take some clicking around to find public filings with useful information. However, the document description at the bottom of Figure 4.4 reads "Preliminary proxy statements relating to merger or acquisition," filed on March 4, 2013. So this is clearly related to the acquisition. Click this for useful preliminary information on the acquisition. The other documents do not contain as much information as the preliminary proxy to date, so we will build the model with preliminary proxy information. We can later update the model as more information becomes available. The proxy can also be found on the companion website labeled "Heinz_Preliminary_Proxy.pdf."

Finally, other information sources such as tender offers, news releases, or research reports are good resources that may contain financial information on a merger. But for now, we will use the annual report, the proxy document, and 10-Qs and 10-Ks to construct our leveraged buyout analysis.

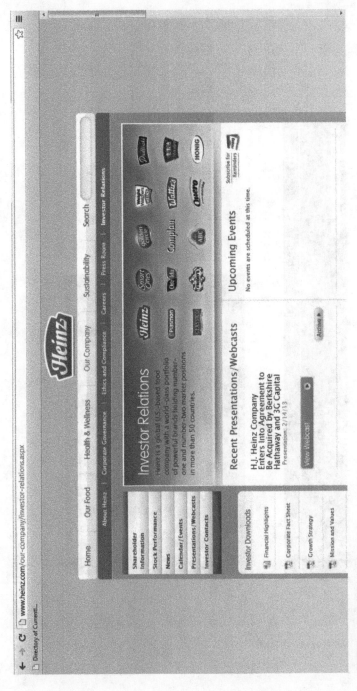

FIGURE 4.1 Heinz Website—Investor Relations

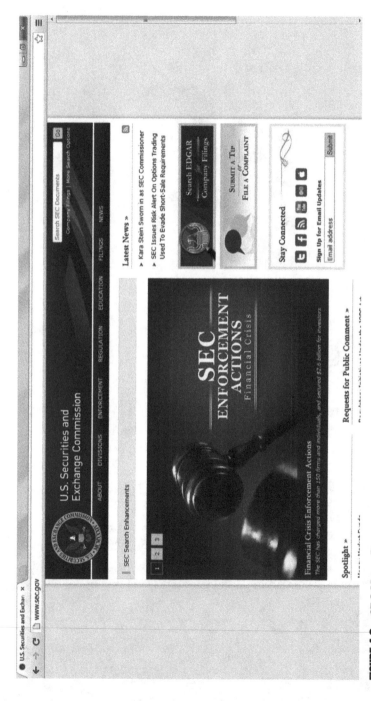

FIGURE 4.2   SEC Home Page

FIGURE 4.3 SEC Heinz Search Results

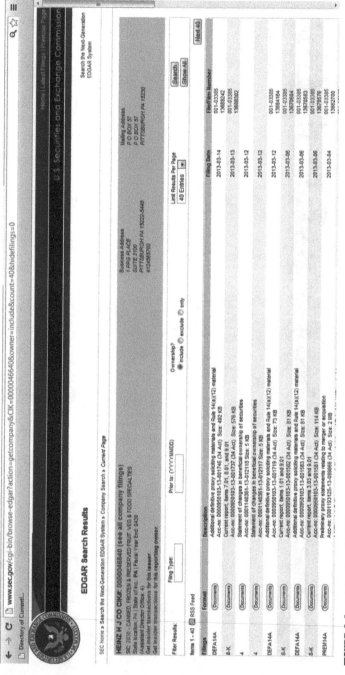

FIGURE 4.4 Heinz Public Filings

NOTE

At the time of writing this chapter, the proxy filed on March 3, 2013 was the latest and most relevant proxy document filed. However, by book completion, more proxy documents will have been filed revealing relevant information but also missing important core information found in this key preliminary proxy document. So as not to confuse matters by jumping back and forth among several proxy documents, we will run the initial analysis with just this core preliminary proxy information. This is so as not to complicate the instruction of major LBO drivers with minor details, yet still get to an expected return on investment for the business.

PURCHASE PRICE

As we discussed in Chapter 3, the February 14 press release stated Heinz will be purchased for $72.50 per share. In order to calculate the total purchase price based on $72.50 per share we need the total diluted share count for Heinz.

A company's shares outstanding reported on the income statement can be reported as basic or diluted. The basic share count is a count of the number of shares outstanding in the market. The diluted share count is the number of shares outstanding in the market plus any shares that would be considered outstanding today if all option and warrant holders who are in-the-money, meaning the options are exercisable because the stock price is above the exercise price, decide to exercise on their securities. The diluted share count is best thought of as a what-if scenario. If all the option and warrant holders who could exercise would, how many shares would be outstanding now? In an acquisition scenario, like in the Heinz situation, because shareholders are receiving a premium for their shares (20 percent according to the press release), it is very likely that all option and warrant holders will exercise their shares. So we need to calculate the purchase price based on diluted shares outstanding. Luckily for us, there is complete detail of the shares to be acquired in the proxy report. The bottom of the very first page of the proxy reads:

Aggregate number of securities to which transaction applies:
329,787,479 shares of common stock, which consists of:
(i) 320,959,712 shares of common stock issued and outstanding

as of February 27, 2013, (ii) 86,805 shares of common stock issuable upon the conversion of third cumulative preferred stock, $1.70 first series, as of February 27, 2013, (iii) 6,713,956 shares of common stock issuable upon the exercise of options to purchase shares of common stock outstanding as of February 27, 2013 and (iv) 2,027,006 shares of common stock subject to restricted share units and phantom shares as of February 27, 2013.

This is effectively saying there are 329,787,479 diluted shares outstanding as of February 27, 2013. We know this is a diluted number because it mentions the inclusion of options and other convertible shares. But we need to know how much each of these shares will convert at in order to calculate the total transaction value. If we read on, we find:

Per unit price or other underlying value of transaction computed pursuant to Exchange Act Rule 0-11 (set forth the amount on which the filing fee is calculated and state how it was determined):

In accordance with Section 14(g) of the Securities Exchange Act of 1934, as amended, the filing fee was determined by multiplying 0.00013640 by the underlying value of the transaction of $23,575,707,195.62, which has been calculated as the sum of: (a) the product of (i) 320,959,712 issued and outstanding shares of common stock as of February 27, 2013 and (ii) the merger consideration of $72.50 per share; plus (b) the product of (i) 86,805 shares of common stock issuable upon the conversion of third cumulative preferred stock, $1.70 first series, as of February 27, 2013 and (ii) the merger consideration of $72.50 per share; plus (c) the product of (i) 6,713,956 shares of common stock issuable upon the exercise of options to purchase shares of common stock outstanding as of February 27, 2013 and (ii) $22.77 per share (the difference between $72.50 per share and the weighted-average exercise price of such options of $49.73 per share); plus (d) the product of (i) 2,027,006 shares of common stock subject to restricted share units and phantom shares as of February 27, 2013 and (ii) the merger consideration of $72.50 per share.

This is basically saying the transaction value is $23,575,707,195.62, a value arrived at by multiplying the offer price ($72.50) by the number of basic shares (320,959,712), convertible preferred stock (86,805), and restricted common stock (2,027,006); (320,959,712 + 86,805 + 2,027,006) × $72.50 = $23,422,830,417.5. In addition, 6,713,956 is the number of stock options we multiply by the difference between the offer price of $72.50 and

TABLE 4.1 Total Purchase Price

Type of Shares	No. of Shares	Price per Share	Total Value
Basic shares outstanding	320,959,712	$72.50	$23,269,579,120.00
Convertible preferred stock	86,805	72.50	6,293,362.50
Restricted common stock	2,027,006	72.50	146,957,935.00
Stock options	6,713,956	22.77	152,876,778.12
Total purchase price			$23,575,707,195.62

the option exercise price of $49.73 ($72.50 − $49.73 = $22.77). So, $22.77 × 6,713,956 = $152,876,778.12. Adding this to $23,422,830,417.5 gives us the $23,575,707,195.62. This is the purchase price of the company. See Table 4.1.

This is how the proxy document lays out the purchase price. However, in modeling we prefer a different method—the treasury stock method.

The Treasury Method

We now know that if options are in-the-money, then technically these options could be exercised and should be included in our diluted share count. Now, the purchase price was $72.50, which was well above the average strike price of $49.73 indicated earlier. This means that if all options are exercised, they would all total a value of $333,885,031.88 ($49.73 × 6,713,956). Now there is a common method called the treasury method that states that the exercised options are bought back. So, if we divide the total value of options exercised by the purchase price ($333,885,031.88/$72.50), we would get 4,605,310.78 shares bought back. In other words, 6,713,956 options have been exercised, but 4,605,310.8 are bought back, giving us 2,108,645.22 new shares outstanding. We can add this number to the total number of shares of the other securities (320,959,712 + 86,805 + 2,027,006) to get 325,182,168.22. You may notice that 325,182,168.22 times $72.50 gets us the same purchase price of $23,575,707,195.62. (If you do this on paper there will be a slight rounding error. However, try it on a calculator or in Excel and the numbers will match.) The benefit of this method is that we can now present a total share count (325,182,168.22) in our model and one purchase price per share ($72.50) as opposed to the method done in the proxy document. Some argue that, as it does not make technical sense to produce a portion of a share, one should round share calculations to whole numbers. We did not done so here because if we had, the total purchase price would not exactly match to the purchase price reported on the proxy document. Either way, rounding or not rounding will not make any material difference to our overall analysis, and for what it's worth, we will round the share count to whole numbers when modeling the Heinz analysis.

You may also notice that the press release at the beginning of this chapter mentions that the transaction is valued at $28 billion. Although not yet 100 percent clear, the increase from $23.6 billion to $28 billion is most likely attributable to the Heinz debt and fees the buyers must allocate funds for. We will note that in the uses of cash section.

Target Share Price

Refer to the Assumptions tab in the model, and let's link up the purchase price section based on information in the press release and in Tables 4.1 and 4.2. You will notice at the top left of the tab the box entitled "Purchase Price." The first line item within that box is "Target share price." This refers to the current stock trading value of Heinz. In order to properly back into the numbers given in the press release, let's use the $60.48 value noted at the time of press release. We can hard-code "60.48" into Cell C6.

Before doing so, it is important to mention the first two important rules of modeling etiquette:

1. All hard-coded numbers and assumption drivers should be entered in blue font.
2. All formulas should be entered in black font.

TABLE 4.2   Diluted Share Calculation

Share price	$	72.50
Number of basic shares outstanding		320,959,712.00
Number of convertible preferred shares		86,805.00
Number of restricted common shares		2,027,006.00
Number of outstanding options (in-the-money)		6,713,956.00
Average option strike price	$	49.73
Total option proceeds	$	333,885,031.88
Treasury stock method shares repurchased		4,605,310.78
Additional shares outstanding (from exercise of options)		2,108,645.22
Total diluted shares outstanding		325,182,168.22
Total purchase price		$23,575,707,195.62

When we mention "hard-coded" numbers, we mean numbers that are typed directly into a cell—that is, not links or formulas. All other formulas in the model are dependent on hard codes, so should remain black. So, for example, the historical numbers we will now enter are hard-coded. These should be colored blue. But the formulas that are simply summing hard-coded numbers should be in black font, as those are formulas. This is a standard on the Street and makes a model easier to analyze. It is important to be able to quickly zero in on the numbers and assumptions that drive the model projections (the blue numbers).

Purchase Premium

The next line in the model is entitled "Purchase premium." This is the control premium paid above the current market share value. The press release mentions that the purchasing consortium actually offered $72.50 per share for the company. In most transactional models, it is important to hard-code the control premium into the model as the control premium is often used as an assumption driver. In other words, once the model is complete, we would like to be able to adjust the assumption driver (control premium) to see what effect it would have on the investor rate of return (IRR). The press release states $72.50 is a 20 percent premium to the current trading value of Heinz. However, the press release is most likely rounding that percentage. It is better to accurately calculate the premium directly into Cell C7. So in C7 we should hard-code "=72.5/60.48-1." This would give us a control premium of 19.9 percent.

We can now use the control premium to calculate the implied purchase price per share. This may seem a bit redundant as we already know the purchase price per share is $72.50. But we want to design the flexibility to adjust the model based on the control premium. We'll show you how this works. The formula for purchase price per share is:

$$\text{Current Share Price} \times (1 + \text{Control Premium})$$

So, in Cell C8, "Purchase price per share," we can:

Calculating Purchase Price per Share (Cell C8)

Excel Keystrokes	Description
Type "="	Enters into "formula" mode
Select Cell C6	Current share price
Type "*"	Multiplies

(continued)

Type "(1+"	Adds "1" to the control premium percentage
Select Cell C7	Control premium
Type ")"	Closes "1+Control Premium"
Hit Enter	End
Formula result	=C6*(1+C7)

Purchase Price

We will now use the purchase price per share to drive the actual purchase price. You should be beginning to see the benefit of having control premium as the driver. If we overwrite the 19.9 percent with a higher control premium percentage (you can try it now and then "undo"), the purchase price per share will increase and so will the total purchase price. If we lower the 19.9 percent, the purchase price will decrease. It is important that we have such drivers so that you can run various model sensitivities to test the boundaries of the calculated returns.

In Cell C9, we can hard-code the shares we had earlier identified as 325,182,168. (As mentioned previously we will round the share count to whole numbers.) However, note that shares are reported in actual numbers and in our model we would like to note dollar values in millions. (See top left Cell B3.) So, let's hard-code the shares in "millions" units. In Cell C9 we can type "=325.182168."

We can now calculate the total purchase price by multiplying the purchase price per share by the total shares outstanding, or:

Total Purchase Price (Cell C10)

Excel Keystrokes	Description
Type "="	Enters into "formula" mode
Select Cell C8	Purchase price per share
Type "*"	Multiplies
Select Cell C9	Diluted shares
Hit Enter	End
Formula result	=C8*C9

This should give us $23,575.7 million as the purchase price. Note this is not the $28 billion reported in the press release. The difference is most likely the net debt and transaction fees. We discuss this now.

SOURCES OF FUNDS

Because the preliminary proxy document gives us more information about the sources of funds than the uses of funds at this point in time (i.e., the preliminary proxy does not yet provide indication of net debt and transaction fees), we will begin with analyzing the sources of funds first. It is typically more common to fill out the uses of funds *before* the sources of funds, but we will soon see the preliminary proxy does not indicate what the exact uses will be. So we will look to the sources first and attempt to back-solve into the uses of funds. Remember that the total sources of funds must match the total uses of funds—so that will help us back-solve.

As discussed in Chapter 3, the sources of funds contain the various amounts of debt and equity necessary to fund the transaction. How will the transaction be financed? We can find information in the proxy report, recent news articles, and press releases. At the bottom of page 5 and top of page 6 of the preliminary proxy report we see the following:

> We *anticipate that the total funds needed to complete the merger, including the funds needed to:*
> ■ *pay our shareholders (and holders of our other equity-based interests) the amounts due to them under the merger agreement and pay related expenses, which would be approximately $[—] billion based upon the shares (and our other equity-based interests) outstanding as of [—], 2013; and*
> ■ *will be funded through a combination of:*
>   ■ *$4.12 billion in common equity contributed by 3G Capital;*
>   ■ *$12.12 billion in equity contributed by Berkshire Hathaway, composed of $4.12 billion in common equity and $8 billion in preferred equity with warrants;*
>   ■ *$10.5 billion in term loans under the senior secured credit facilities (along with a $1.5 billion revolving credit facility that will not be drawn to fund the merger); and*
>   ■ *the issuance of up to $2.1 billion aggregate principal amount of senior secured second lien notes (or, to the extent such notes are not issued at or prior to the closing of the merger, by a senior secured second lien bridge loan facility of up to $2.1 billion less the amount of any notes issued).*

Notice the first bullet point contains two blanks, "[—]." Those blanks are actually referring to the uses of cash. The first bullet point notes that the funds raised will be for paying the shareholders. The second bullet point explains additional funds need to be raised to pay Heinz debts.

Remember we discussed the need to pay down debt in Chapter 3. As Heinz is a public company, the buyer will be responsible for the debts. You certainly cannot leave that obligation with the shareholders. The first blank is due to the fact that the final purchase price and debt balance are most likely to change between now and deal closing. As the deal progresses, we will see additional proxy statements with more data. As per my note earlier, additional proxy documents may be filed, and if so, we can then go back and update the data with more relevant information. Of course, the point of this analysis is to best understand the structure and process behind a buyout. Once you have the proper tools, updating the data will be a simple process.

Equity

The next bullet points explain how funds will be raised. Reading the bullets indicates that $4.12 billion in common equity will be contributed by both 3G Capital and Berkshire Hathaway. However, in addition to the common equity, Berkshire will raise an additional $8 billion in preferred equity with warrants. The preferred equity will contain other benefits such as a dividend, which we will need to model out. We will do so in Chapter 15.

Debt

The last two bullet points explain the debt raised to fund the acquisition noting $10.5 billion in term loans (this is the bank debt), and an additional $1.5 billion revolving credit facility. They note the credit facility will not be drawn, so we will list it as 0 for now. They also mention $2.1 billion in additional notes.

Let's lay out this information in our sources of funds schedule in the model. See Table 4.3.

Notice that we've simply hard-coded the values in millions in each respective debt and equity source.

In Cell F15, for total sources of funds, we can total all of the previous values. So Cell F15 will read "=SUM(F8:F14)."

Total Sources of Funds (Cell F15)

Excel Keystrokes	Description
Type "="	Enters into "formula" mode
Type "SUM("	Begins "SUM" formula
Select Cell F8	Selects the first cell in series

Type ":"	Indicates we want to include all cells from the first cell to the last cell in series
Select Cell F14	Selects the last cell in series
Type ")"	Ends "SUM" formula
Hit Enter	End
Formula result	"=SUM(F8:F14)"

TABLE 4.3 Heinz Sources of Funds

	Amount	% of Total Capital	% Equity Ownership
Debt			
Revolving line of credit	$ 0.0		
Term facilities	10,500.0		
The notes	2,100.0		
Equity			
Berkshire Hathaway preferred	8,000.0		
Berkshire Hathaway common	4,120.0		
3G Capital common	4,120.0		
Total	$28,840.0		

Note that the total sources of funds actually add up to $28,840 million, slightly higher than the $28,000 million suggested in the press release. We will discuss this in the uses of funds section.

Percentage of Total Capital

It is important to calculate each source as a percentage of the total. This helps us better understand how much each piece of debt and equity is contributing to the total sources of funds. To calculate the percentage of total capital for each source of cash, we divide each individual source into the total sources of funds. So, for example, to calculate the revolver percentage of total capital, we divide the revolver amount into the total sources of funds.

Revolver% Total Capital (Cell G8)

Excel Keystrokes	Description
Type "="	Enters into "formula" mode
Select Cell F8	Revolver
Type "/"	Divides
Select Cell F15	Total capital
Hit F4	Adds "$" references
Hit Enter	End
Formula result	=F8/$F$15

Since the revolver is $0, this will result in 0 percent of total capital. Remember that these numbers will most likely change as the transaction comes to a close, so we want to be sure all formulas are properly constructed in the model to handle adjusting the scenarios. Also, notice we put dollar signs ("$") around the reference to Cell F15. This anchors the reference to the cell, so if we copy the formula in Cell G8 all the way down to G14, the reference to the numerator will change, but the denominator will always refer to the total sources of funds.

Anchoring Formula References As a guide, a cell with a formula such as "=B1" when copied to the right will change to "C1" in the second column and to "D1" in the third column, and so on (as shown in Figure 4.5).

◢	A	B	C	D
1	Value	10	20	30
2		40	50	60
3	Formula	=B1	=C1	=D1
4		=B2	=C2	=D2
5	Result	10	20	30
6		40	50	60

FIGURE 4.5 Unanchored Formulas

◢	A	B	C	D
1	Value	10	20	30
2		40	50	60
3	Formula	=$B1	=$B1	=$B1
4		=$B2	=$B2	=$B2
5	Result	10	10	10
6		40	40	40

FIGURE 4.6 Formulas with Anchored Columns

◢	A	B	C	D
1	Value	10	20	30
2		40	50	60
3	Formula	=$B$1	=$B$1	=$B$1
4		=$B$1	=$B$1	=$B$1
5	Result	10	10	10
6		10	10	10

FIGURE 4.7 Formulas with Anchored Columns and Rows

However, if we include a dollar sign before the "B" (i.e., "=$B1"), copying this formula to the right will leave the "B" reference intact (see Figure 4.6). So the formula will still read "=$B1" in the second and third columns. But we have anchored only the column reference, not the row reference. So, if we were to copy this formula down, the row reference will still change, reading "=$B2" in the second row.

We could have added a "$" to the row reference to keep this from happening. If we change the formula to "=$B$1," then we can copy this formula to the right and down and it will always read "=$B$1" (see Figure 4.7).

Now, in G15, we can total all of the previously given percentages to ensure that they do in fact add up to 100 percent. So Cell G15 will read "=SUM(G8:G14)."

Total Capital % (Cell G15)

Excel Keystrokes	Description
Type "="	Enters into "formula" mode
Type "SUM("	Begins "SUM" formula
Select Cell G8	Selects the first cell in series
Type ":"	Indicates we want to include all cells from the first cell to the last cell in series
Select Cell G14	Selects the last cell in series
Type ")"	Ends "SUM" formula
Hit Enter	End
Formula result	"=SUM(G8:G14)"

See Table 4.4.

Percentage of Equity Ownership

Percentage of Equity Ownership helps us determine the potential equity in the business that will be owned by each contributor. Remember, debt does not result in receiving an actual equity stake in the business; however, some sort of convertible or hybrid security may have an equity component attached to it. So, the revolving line of credit, the term facilities, and the notes will have 0 percent equity ownership. We hard-code "0%" in Cells H8 through H10.

It has been noted that Berkshire will receive a 30 percent stake for their investment in the business, and 3G will receive a 70 percent stake. This information has not been confirmed but we will use this for now. This percentage is important in calculating investment returns to each party. We will assume the 30 percent reported is inclusive of any equity component that may be attached to the Berkshire Hathaway preferreds. So let's hard-code "0%", "30%", and "70%" into Cells H12, H13, and H14 respectively, making sure they are in blue font.

In Cell H15, we can total all of these percentages to ensure that they do in fact add up to 100 percent. So Cell H15 is "=SUM(H8:H14)."

TABLE 4.4　Heinz Percentage of Total Capital

Sources		Amount	% of Total Capital	% Equity Ownership
Debt				
	Revolving line of credit	$ 0.0	0%	
	Term facilities	10,500.0	36%	
	The notes	2,100.0	7%	
Equity				
	Berkshire Hathaway preferred	8,000.0	28%	
	Berkshire Hathaway common	4,120.0	14%	
	3G Capital common	4,120.0	14%	
Total		**$28,840.0**	100%	

Total Equity % (Cell H15)

Excel Keystrokes	Description
Type "="	Enters into "formula" mode
Type "SUM("	Begins "SUM" formula
Select Cell H8	Selects the first cell in series
Type ":"	Indicates we want to include all cells from the first cell to the last cell in series
Select Cell H14	Selects the last cell in series
Type ")"	Ends "SUM" formula
Hit Enter	End
Formula result	"=SUM(H8:H14)"

See Table 4.5.

TABLE 4.5 Percentage of Equity Ownership

Sources		Amount	% of Total Capital	% Equity Ownership
Debt				
	Revolving line of credit	$ 0.0	0%	0%
	Term facilities	10,500.0	36%	0%
	The notes	2,100.0	7%	0%
Equity				
	Berkshire Hathaway preferred	8,000.0	28%	0%
	Berkshire Hathaway common	4,120.0	14%	30%
	3G Capital common	4,120.0	14%	70%
Total		$28,840.0	100%	100%

USES OF FUNDS

As discussed in Chapter 3, the uses of funds consist mainly of purchase price, the net debt, and transaction fees.

We already have calculated the $23,575.7 million purchase price.

Net Debt

The fundamental definition of net debt is a company's short-term debts plus long-term debts less cash and cash equivalents:

$$\text{Net Debt} = \text{Short-Term Debt} + \text{Long-Term Debt} - \text{Cash}$$

However, we want to represent all liabilities and obligations that the buyer needs to be responsible for upon acquisition. So, this definition could be expanded to include other liabilities as well, such as capital lease obligations. It is important to do some research to understand exactly what liabilities the buyers are responsible for paying off in order to arrive at the correct net debt number. We will later see that in a full-scale model, the net debt that we have calculated here needs to tie back to the balance sheet in order for our balance sheet adjustments to match. Ideally, the company will have a proxy report detailing its breakout of net debt. Unfortunately, the preliminary proxy report does not yet disclose that detail. So the best place to refer the net debt numbers is from the balance sheet we will create. However, since we do not have the balance sheet built out yet, let's make a simple assumption for now, knowing we will relink this once we have the balance sheet in the model completed.

Notice that the press release mentions:

*Under the terms of the agreement, which has been unanimously approved by Heinz's Board of Directors, Heinz shareholders will receive $72.50 in cash for each share of common stock they own, in a transaction **valued at $28 billion, including the assumption of Heinz's outstanding debt.***

The press release states that including debt the value of the purchase will be $28 billion. Again, we hope there will be a future proxy release that will give us more detail, and we will build out a balance sheet where we can link in our own net debt calculation. But until then, we can simply estimate the net debt assumed by $28 billion less the purchase price we've calculated.

Notice the "Uses of funds" box in the model beginning in Cell I6. Here we can pull the purchase price calculated in Cell C10 into Cell J6. Or Cell J6 will read "=C10." For now, in the net debt Cell J7, we can subtract $28 billion from that $23.6 billion in Cell J6. Or we can have Cell J7 read "=28000-J6," which gives us for now $4,423.3 (see Table 4.5). Once we have the balance sheet modeled out, we can relink this. It should not be too far off from this estimate.

Heinz Uses of Funds

Uses	
Purchase price (equity value)	$23,575.7
Net debt	4,424.3
Transaction fees	
% Fee	
Total	

Transaction Fees

We mentioned in Chapter 3 most types of transaction fees that could exist. In this case, it is too early to determine the exact transaction fees the company will pay in total.

Performing a word search on "fees" in the proxy report reveals several notes regarding fees, including the following found on page 59 of the preliminary proxy:

> The Heinz Board selected Centerview as its financial advisor be-
> cause it is a nationally recognized investment banking firm that
> has substantial experience in transactions similar to the merger.
> Centerview has acted as financial advisor to Heinz in connection
> with, and has participated in certain of the negotiations leading to,
> the merger. In consideration of Centerview's services, pursuant to
> a letter agreement, dated February 13, 2013, **Heinz has agreed to
> pay Centerview a fee of approximately $36 million, $4 million of**
> which was paid following the execution of the merger agreement,
> and the remainder of which will become payable upon the consum-
> mation of the merger. Heinz has also agreed to reimburse certain of
> Centerview's expenses arising, and to indemnify Centerview against
> certain liabilities that may arise, out of its engagement.

Another note on page 65 of the preliminary proxy report mentions expected fees paid to BofA Merrill Lynch:

> Heinz has agreed to pay BofA Merrill Lynch for its services in connec-
> tion with the merger an aggregate fee of approximately $21,000,000,
> $2,000,000 of which is payable in connection with its opinion and
> $19,000,000 of which is contingent upon the completion of the

merger. Heinz also has agreed to reimburse BofA Merrill Lynch for its expenses incurred in connection with BofA Merrill Lynch's engagement and to indemnify BofA Merrill Lynch, any controlling person of BofA Merrill Lynch and each of their respective directors, officers, employees, agents and affiliates against specified liabilities, including liabilities under the federal securities laws.

Although these notes are helpful in determining the fees paid to several of the investment banks, we do not have an indication of total fees paid to all, including lenders and lawyers, to name a few. In reality, the company may not even know at this point what the total transaction fees will amount to. We do have a clue, however, that can help us back into the fees. We realize the total sources of funds, $28,840 million, are greater than the $28,000 million we have so far as uses of funds. Knowing that the total sources of funds must match the total uses of funds, we can basically use the difference for now as an estimated measure of fees. So, in cell J8, we can back into the transaction fees by subtracting the purchase price and net debt from the total sources of funds.

Transaction Fees (Cell J8)

Excel Keystrokes	Description
Type "="	Enters into "formula" mode
Select Cell F15	Total sources of funds
Type "-"	Subtracts
Select Cell J7	Net debt
Type "-"	Subtracts
Select Cell J6	Purchase price
Hit Enter	End
Formula result	=F15-J7-J6

This gives us $840 million in transaction fees. Again, it's important to remember that this is not the most accurate way to calculate the fees. Quite often in modeling, fees can be estimated as an overall percentage of the purchase price. But, in the Heinz case, because the sources of funds were the only fixed data provided to us, and the uses of funds except for the purchase price were the unknown, we chose to plug into the unknowns (net debt and transaction fees) for now. We hope to get more information as the company starts to file more public data. Further, we will have a more accurate estimate of debt once we start constructing the balance sheet, leaving only the transaction fees as the largest unknown. Let's now look at the transaction fees as a percentage of the purchase price. We can calculate this by dividing the transaction fees into the purchase price.

Transaction Fee % of Purchase Price (Cell J9)

Excel Keystrokes	Description
Type "="	Enters into "formula" mode
Select Cell J8	Transaction fees
Type "/"	Divides
Select Cell J6	Purchase price
Hit Enter	End
Formula result	=J8/J6

This gives us 3.6 percent of the purchase price being paid out in transaction fees (see Heinz Uses of Funds table below). We now calculate the total uses by adding the purchase price, the net debt, and the total transaction fees. So, Cell J10 will read "=SUM(J6:J8)."

Total Uses of Funds (Cell J10)

Excel Keystrokes	Description
Type "="	Enters into "formula" mode
Type "SUM("	Begins "SUM" formula
Select Cell J6	Selects the first cell in series
Type ":"	Indicates we want to include all cells from the first cell to the last cell in series
Select Cell J8	Selects the last cell in series
Type ")"	Ends "SUM" formula
Hit Enter	End
Formula result	"=SUM(J6:J8)"

Heinz Uses of Funds

Uses	
Purchase price (equity value)	$23,575.7
Net debt	4,424.3
Transaction fees	840.0
% Fee	3.6%
Total	$28,840.0

And of course the total sources of funds match our total uses of funds. With our purchase price, total sources, and total uses properly laid out, we can now proceed to the income statement. There are a few other assumptions left to identify, but we will handle them as we build out the next statements.

In the following chapters we will briefly give a conceptual overview of each statement before going into the actual modeling. Feel free to skip right to the modeling if you do not need the overview.

CHAPTER 5

The Income Statement

The income statement measures a company's profit (or loss) over a specific period of time. A business is generally required to report and record the sales it generates for tax purposes. And, of course, taxes on sales made can be reduced by the expenses incurred while generating those sales. Although there are specific rules that govern when and how those expense reductions can be utilized, there is still a general concept:

$$Profit = Revenue - Expenses$$

A company is taxed on profit. So:

$$Net\ Income = Profit - Tax$$

However, income statements have grown to be quite complex. The multifaceted categories of expenses can vary from company to company. As analysts, we need to identify major categories within the income statement in order to facilitate proper analysis. For this reason, one should always categorize income statement line items into nine major categories:

1. Revenue (sales).
2. Cost of goods sold (COGS).
3. Operating expenses.
4. Other income.
5. Depreciation and amortization.
6. Interest.
7. Taxes.
8. Nonrecurring and extraordinary items.
9. Distributions.

No matter how convoluted an income statement is, a good analyst would categorize each reported income statement line item into one of these nine groupings. This will allow the analyst to easily understand the major categories that drive profitability in an income statement and can further allow him or her to compare the profitability of several different companies—an analysis very important in determining relative valuation. We will briefly recap the line items.

REVENUE

Revenue is the sales or gross income a company has made during a specific operating period. It is important to note that when and how revenue is recognized can vary from company to company and may be different from the actual cash received. Revenue is recognized when "realized and earned," which is typically when the products sold have been transferred or once the service has been rendered.

COST OF GOODS SOLD

Cost of goods sold (COGS) is the direct costs attributable to the production of the goods sold by a company. These are the costs most directly associated with the revenue. COGS is typically the cost of the materials used in creating the products sold, although some other direct costs could be included as well.

Gross Profit

Gross profit is not one of the nine categories listed, as it is a totaling item. Gross profit is the revenue less the cost of goods sold. It is often helpful to determine the net value of the revenue after the cost of goods sold is removed. One common metric analyzed is gross profit margin, which is the gross profit divided by the revenue. We will calculate these totals and metrics for Heinz later in the chapter.

A business that sells cars, for example, may have manufacturing costs. Let's say we sell each car for $20,000, and we manufacture the cars in-house. We have to purchase $5,000 in raw materials to manufacture the car. If we sell one car, $20,000 is our revenue and $5,000 is the cost of goods sold. That leaves us with $15,000 in gross profit, or a 75 percent gross profit margin. Now let's say in the first quarter of operations we sell 25 cars. That's 25 × $20,000 or $500,000 in revenue. Our cost of goods sold is 25 × $5,000, or $125,000, which leaves us with $375,000 in gross profit.

Car Co.	1Q 2012
Revenue	$500,000.0
COGS	125,000.0
Gross Profit	375,000.0
% Gross Profit Margin	75%

OPERATING EXPENSES

Operating expenses are expenses incurred by a company as a result of performing its normal business operations. These are the relatively indirect expenses related to generating the company's revenue and supporting its operations. Operating expenses can be broken down into several other major subcategories. The most common categories are:

- *Selling, general, and administrative (SG&A).* These are all selling expenses and all general and administrative expenses of a company. Examples are employee salaries and rents.
- *Advertising and marketing.* These are expenses relating to any advertising or marketing initiatives of the company. Examples are print advertising and Google Adwords.
- *Research and development (R&D).* These are expenses relating to furthering the development of the company's products or services.

Let's say in our car business we have employees who were paid $75,000 in total in the first quarter. We also had rents to pay of $2,500, and we ran an advertising initiative that cost us $7,500. Finally, let's assume we employed some R&D efforts to continue to improve the design of our car that cost roughly $5,000 in the quarter. Using the previous example, our simple income statement looks like this:

Car Co.	1Q 2012
Revenue	$500,000.0
COGS	125,000.0
Gross Profit	375,000.0
% Gross Profit Margin	75%
Operating Expenses	
SG&A	77,500.0
Advertising	7,500.0
R&D	5,000.0
Total Operating Expenses	90,000.0

OTHER INCOME

Companies can generate income that is not core to their business. As this income is taxable, it is recorded on the income statement. However, since it is not core to business operations, it is not considered revenue. Let's take the example of the car company. A car company's core business is producing and selling cars. However, many car companies also generate income in another way: financing. If a car company offers its customers the ability to finance the payments on a car, those payments come with interest. The car company receives that interest. That interest is taxable and is considered additional income. However, as that income is not core to the business, it is not considered revenue; it is considered other income.

Another common example of other income is income from noncontrolling interests, also known as income from unconsolidated affiliates. This is income received when one company has a noncontrolling interest investment in another company. So when a company (Company A) invests in another company (Company B) and receives a minority stake in Company B, Company B distributes a portion of its net income to Company A. Company A records those distributions received as other income.

EBITDA

Earnings before interest, taxes, depreciation, and amortization (EBITDA) is a very important measure among Wall Street analysts. We will see later its many uses as a fundamental metric in valuation and analysis. EBITDA can be calculated as Revenue − COGS − Operating Expenses + Other Income.

It is debatable whether other income should be included in EBITDA. There are two sides to the argument.

1. *Other income should be included in EBITDA.* If a company produces other income, it should be represented as part of EBITDA, and other income should be listed above our EBITDA total. The argument here is that other income, although not core to revenue, is still in fact operating and should be represented as part of the company's operations. There are many ways of looking at this. Taking the car example, we can perhaps assume that the financing activities, although not core to revenue, are essential enough to the overall profitability of the company to be considered as part of EBITDA.

2. *Other income should not be included in EBITDA.* If a company produces other income, it should not be represented as part of EBITDA, and other income should be listed below our EBITDA total. The argument here is that although it is a part of the company's profitability, it

is not core enough to the operations to be incorporated as part of the company's core profitability.

Determining whether to include other income as EBITDA is not simple and clear-cut. It is important to consider whether the other income is consistent and reoccurring. If it is not, the case can more likely be made that it should not be included in EBITDA. It is also important to consider the purpose of your particular analysis. For example, if you are looking to acquire the entire business, and that business will still be producing that other income even after the acquisition, then maybe it should be represented as part of EBITDA. Or maybe that other income will no longer exist after the acquisition, in which case it should not be included in EBITDA. As another example, if you are trying to compare this business's EBITDA with the EBITDA of other companies, then it is important to consider if the other companies also produce that same other income. If not, then maybe it is better to keep other income out of the EBITDA analysis, to make sure there is a consistent comparison among all of the company EBITDAs.

Different banks and firms may have different views on whether other income should be included in EBITDA. Even different industry groups' departments within the same firm have been found to have different views on this topic. As a good analyst, it is important to come up with one consistent defensible view, and to stick to it. Note that the exclusion of other income from EBITDA may also assume that other income will be excluded from earnings before interest and taxes (EBIT) as well.

Let's assume in our car example the other income will be part of EBITDA.

Car Co.	1Q 2012
Revenue	$500,000.0
COGS	125,000.0
Gross Profit	375,000.0
% Gross Profit Margin	*75%*
Operating Expenses	
SG&A	77,500.0
Advertising	7,500.0
R&D	5,000.0
Total Operating Expenses	90,000.0
Other Income	1,000.0
EBITDA	286,000.0
EBITDA Margin	*57%*

Notice we have also calculated EBITDA margin, which is calculated as EBITDA divided by revenue.

DEPRECIATION AND AMORTIZATION

Depreciation is the accounting for the aging and depletion of fixed assets over a period of time. Amortization is the accounting for the cost basis reduction of intangible assets (intellectual property such as patents, copyrights, and trademarks, for example) over their useful lives. It is important to note that not all intangible assets are subject to amortization. We discuss depreciation and amortization (D&A) in Chapter 9.

EBIT

Similar to EBITDA, EBIT is also utilized in valuation. EBIT is EBITDA less depreciation and amortization. So let's assume the example car company has $8,000 in D&A each quarter. So:

Car Co.	1Q 2012
EBITDA	$286,000.0
EBITDA Margin	57%
D&A	8,000.0
EBIT	278,000.0
EBIT Margin	56%

Notice we have also calculated EBIT margin, which is calculated as EBIT divided by revenue.

INTEREST

Interest is composed of interest expense and interest income. Interest expense is the cost incurred on debt that the company has borrowed. Interest income is commonly the income received from cash held in savings accounts, certificates of deposit, and other investments.

Let's assume the car company has taken out $1 million in loans and incurs 10 percent of interest per year on those loans. So the car company has $100,000 in interest expense per year, or $25,000 per quarter. We can also assume that the company has $50,000 of cash and generates 1 percent of interest income on that cash per year ($500), or $125 per quarter.

Often, the interest expense is netted against the interest income as net interest expense.

EBT

Earnings before taxes (EBT) can be defined as EBIT minus net interest.

Car Co.	1Q 2012
EBIT	$278,000.0
EBIT Margin	*56%*
Interest Expense	25,000.0
Interest Income	125.0
Net Interest Expense	24,875.0
EBT	253,125.0
EBT Margin	*51%*

Notice we have also calculated EBT margin, which is EBT divided by revenue.

TAXES

Taxes are the financial charges imposed by the government on the company's operations. Taxes are imposed on earnings before taxes as defined previously. In the car example, we can assume the tax rate is 35 percent.

Net Income

Net income is calculated as EBT minus taxes. The complete income statement follows.

Car Co.	1Q 2012
Revenue	$500,000.0
COGS	125,000.0
Gross Profit	375,000.0
% Gross Profit Margin	*75%*
Operating Expenses	
SG&A	77,500.0
Advertising	7,500.0
R&D	5,000.0

(continued)

Total Operating Expenses	90,000.0
Other Income	1,000.0
EBITDA	286,000.0
EBITDA Margin	*57%*
D&A	8,000.0
EBIT	278,000.0
EBIT Margin	*56%*
Interest Expense	25,000.0
Interest Income	125.0
Net Interest Expense	24,875.0
EBT	253,125.0
EBT Margin	*51%*
Tax	88,593.75
Tax Rate (%)	*35%*
Net Income	164,531.25

NONRECURRING AND EXTRAORDINARY ITEMS

Nonrecurring and extraordinary items or events are income or expenses that either are one-time or do not pertain to everyday core operations. Gains or losses on sales of assets or from business closures are examples of nonrecurring events. Such nonrecurring or extraordinary events can be scattered about in a generally accepted accounting principles (GAAP) income statement, so it is the job of a good analyst to identify these items and move them to the bottom of the income statement in order to have EBITDA, EBIT, and net income line items that represent everyday, continuous operations. We call this "clean" EBITDA, EBIT, and net income. However, we do not want to eliminate those nonrecurring or extraordinary items completely, so we move them to the section at the bottom of the income statement. From here on out we will refer to both nonrecurring and extraordinary items simply as "nonrecurring items" to simplify. We will see how this is dealt with in the case of Heinz later in this chapter.

DISTRIBUTIONS

Distributions are broadly defined as payments to equity holders. These payments can be in the form of dividends or noncontrolling interest payments, to name the major two types of distributions.

Noncontrolling interest is the portion of the company or the company's subsidiary that is owned by another outside person or entity. If another entity (Entity A) owns a noncontrolling interest in the company (Entity B), Entity B must distribute a portion of Entity B's earnings to Entity A. (We discuss noncontrolling interests in more detail in Chapter 7.)

Net Income (as Reported)

Because we have recommended moving some nonrecurring line items into a separate section, the net income listed in the previous example is effectively an adjusted net income, which is most useful for analysis, valuation, and comparison. However, it is important to still represent a complete net income with all adjustments included to match the original given net income. So it is recommended to have a second net income line, defined as net income minus nonrecurring events minus distributions, as a sanity check.

SHARES

A company's shares outstanding reported on the income statement can be reported as basic or diluted. The basic share count is a count of the number of shares outstanding in the market. The diluted share count is the number of shares outstanding in the market plus any shares that would be considered outstanding today if all option and warrant holders who are in-the-money decided to exercise on their securities. The diluted share count is best thought of as a what-if scenario. If all the option and warrant holders who could exercise would, how many shares would be outstanding now?

Earnings per Share (EPS)

Earnings per share (EPS) is defined as the net income divided by the number of shares outstanding. A company typically reports a basic EPS and a diluted EPS, divided by basic shares or diluted shares, respectively. It is important to note that each company may have a different definition of what exactly to include in net income when calculating EPS. In other words, is net income before or after noncontrolling interest payments? Or before or after dividends? For investors, it is common to use net income before dividends have been paid but after noncontrolling interest investors have been paid. However, we recommend backing into the company's EPS historically to identify the exact formula it is using. We illustrate this process with Heinz next.

Basic EPS = Net Income / Basic Shares
Diluted EPS = Net Income / Diluted Shares

HEINZ INCOME STATEMENT

There are several ways to obtain a public company's financial information. We would first recommend going to the company's website and locating the "Investor Relations" button. See Chapter 4 guiding you to the investor relations section for Heinz.

Both the annual report and the company 10-K should have a section containing financial statements. We note that the transaction was announced in February 2013. In order to get the most recent data in our model, it is ideal to use a combination of 10-Ks and 10-Qs to calculate most recent data. So, we will use Heinz's 2012 annual report and the Q3 quarterly report filed on February 21, 2013. There is a web version of these reports at www.sec.gov, or you can find "pdf" versions of the 2012 annual report and the quarterly report on the Heinz website. We have also posted the reports on this book's website. It is your choice which to use, but I would recommend the "pdf" so you can download a local version to your desktop.

Once you have downloaded the correct documents, scroll down to locate the income statement in the annual report. Make sure you have identified the company's complete income statement and not its "Financial Summary." If you continue to scroll down through the company's annual report, you will find the complete income statement on page 33. You will also notice that it is properly labeled as "Consolidated Statements of Income" (see Figure 5.1). We will use this income statement to analyze Heinz's historical financial position. It is standard to have three years of financials in a company model, so we will create a model from years 2010 to 2012.

Revenue

When looking at the income statement, you want to first identify all the major line items as referenced earlier in this chapter, beginning with sales (i.e., revenue). We can see that Heinz simply lists sales directly in the first line. Notice that the company has decided to report figures in "thousands" units. It is important to be very careful to stay consistent with units throughout the model to avoid errors. In the Assumptions tab, we had laid out our sources and uses in "millions." Although both are acceptable, let's stick with millions. I find it is easier to read with companies that have such large values. As a helpful rule, a model can get a bit too convoluted if there are more than seven digits in each cell (xxx,xxx.x is an ideal format, in my opinion). Also notice that the period end date is in April. The exact day changes from year to year. You can see this in each column at the top of the income statement in the annual report.

H.J. Heinz Company and Subsidiaries

Consolidated Statements of Income

	Fiscal Year Ended		
	April 29, 2012	April 27, 2011	April 28, 2010
	(52 1/2 Weeks)	(52 Weeks)	(52 Weeks)
	(In thousands, except per share amounts)		
Sales	$ 11,649,079	$ 10,706,588	$ 10,494,983
Cost of products sold	7,649,549	6,754,048	6,700,677
Gross profit	3,999,530	3,952,540	3,794,306
Selling, general, and administrative expenses	2,548,362	2,304,350	2,235,078
Operating income	1,451,168	1,648,190	1,559,228
Interest income	34,615	22,565	45,137
Interest expense	294,104	275,398	295,711
Other expense, net	(8,236)	(21,188)	(18,200)
Income from continuing operations before income taxes	1,183,443	1,374,169	1,290,454
Provision for income taxes	243,535	368,221	358,514
Income from continuing operations	939,908	1,005,948	931,940
Loss from discontinued operations, net of tax	—	—	(49,597)
Net income	939,908	1,005,948	882,343
Less: Net income attributable to the noncontrolling interest	16,749	16,438	17,451
Net income attributable to H.J. Heinz Company	$ 923,159	$ 989,510	$ 864,892
Income/(loss) per common share:			
Diluted			
Continuing operations attributable to H.J. Heinz Company common shareholders	$ 2.85	$ 3.06	$ 2.87
Discontinued operations attributable to H.J. Heinz Company common shareholders	—	—	(0.16)
Net income attributable to H.J. Heinz Company common shareholders	$ 2.85	$ 3.06	$ 2.71
Average common shares outstanding—diluted	323,321	323,042	318,113
Basic			
Continuing operations attributable to H.J. Heinz Company common shareholders	$ 2.87	$ 3.09	$ 2.89
Discontinued operations attributable to H.J. Heinz Company common shareholders	—	—	(0.16)
Net income attributable to H.J. Heinz Company common shareholders	$ 2.87	$ 3.09	$ 2.73
Average common shares outstanding—basic	320,686	320,118	315,948
Cash dividends per share	$ 1.92	$ 1.80	$ 1.68
Amounts attributable to H.J. Heinz Company common shareholders:			
Income from continuing operations, net of tax	$ 923,159	$ 989,510	$ 914,489
Loss from discontinued operations, net of tax	—	—	(49,597)
Net income	$ 923,159	$ 989,510	$ 864,892

FIGURE 5.1 Heinz Annual Income Statement

The end date for 2012 is April 29, whereas 2011's end date is April 27 and 2010's is April 28. It is for this reason that at the top of the model we have vaguely stated "Period Ending." Please refer to the Financials tab in the model.

We can enter the three years from the income statement in Figure 5.1. We will simply hard-code or type the numbers directly into the model as represented in the annual report. In Row 6, marked "Revenue," we can type in "10494.983," "10706.588," and "11649.079" for 2010, 2011, and

2012, respectively. Notice we have adjusted for the units by replacing the last comma with a decimal point. Also, remember to color the font of these blue as they are hard codes. Later, we will look to the company's historical trends as a clue to estimating projections. See Table 5.1. Now let's calculate the historical growth of the company's net sales. The formula for growth in a current year is:

$$\text{Current Year/Previous Year} - 1$$

We can calculate the 2011 revenue growth by entering the following into Cell E7:

Calculating 2011 Revenue Growth (Cell E7)

Excel Keystrokes	Description
Type "="	Enters into "formula" mode
Select Cell E6	2011 revenue
Type "/"	Divide
Select Cell D6	2010 revenue
Type "-1"	Subtracts 1
Hit Enter	End
Formula result	=E6/D6-1

This should give you a 2.0 percent revenue growth in 2011. This process can be repeated for the 2012 revenue. Or you can simply cut and paste the 2012 formula and copy it to the right. There are three ways to copy formulas over to the right:

1. Click and drag the 2011 formula over to 2012. With the mouse, you can select the bottom right corner of Cell E7, and while holding down the left mouse button, you can drag the formula over to Cell F7.
2. Highlight the 2011 revenue growth in Cell E7. Select "Copy" from the menu bar (or hit "Ctrl" + "C"). Then highlight or click the 2012 revenue growth cell (F7), and select "Paste" from the menu bar (or hit "Ctrl" + "V").
3. Preferred method:
   a. Highlight both the 2011 revenue growth in Cell E7 and the empty 2012 revenue growth in Cell F7. This can be done in either of two ways:
      i. With the mouse: by selecting Cell E7, making sure to select the center of the cell, not the bottom right corner, and while holding

TABLE 5.1   Heinz Historical Revenue

Consolidated Income Statements (in US$ millions except per share amounts)			
		Actuals	
Period Ending	2010A	2011A	2012A
Revenue	$10,495.0	$10,706.6	$11,649.1
Y/Y revenue growth (%)		*2.0%*	*8.8%*

           down the left mouse button, continue to move the mouse to the
           right, or,

   ii. With the keyboard: by selecting Cell E7, then holding down the
         "Shift" key while tapping the right arrow until the desired cells are
         selected.

  b. Type "Ctrl" + "R," which stands for copy right. Note there is also a
     hot key called "Ctrl" + "D," which stands for copy down. Unfortu-
     nately, there is not a hot key for copy left or copy up.

MODELING TIP

We strongly recommend you use keyboard hot keys (such as "Ctrl"
+ "R") as often as possible. The more comfortable you become with
using the keyboard as opposed to the mouse, the more efficient you
will become as a modeler. Note Appendix 3 for a list of helpful Excel
hot keys.

    The F9 key manually recalculates formulas in the model. Depending on
your settings, you may need to hit F9 to recalculate your cells. We will step
through how to change the recalculation settings when discussing circular
references later in the book (Chapter 12).

Getting to EBITDA

Below the sales line in the Heinz annual report we see "Cost of products
sold," "Gross profit," and "Selling, general, and administrative expenses."
When referencing the categories earlier in this chapter, we listed Category
2 as cost of goods sold and Category 3 as operating expenses. "Cost of
products sold" is a Category 2 (cost of goods sold) expense, and "Selling,

general, and administrative expenses" belong in Category 3 (operating expenses). Gross profit is a totaling item calculated as sales less cost of products sold. Ideally, there would be a more detailed breakout of the costs, and if there was such a breakout, I would recommend listing each cost line item separately within the operating expenses section. It is worth doing a quick word search on "expense" or "operating expense" in the annual report to see if there is a more detailed table listing the individual expenses.

Digging Up Depreciation and Amortization

When identifying all expenses on an income statement, it is important to also locate the depreciation and amortization expenses. Companies that have depreciating assets or intangible assets generally record associated depreciation and amortization as an expense to reduce taxes. So, if a company has depreciation and amortization, it should be represented on the income statement. However, not every company lists these expenses as separate line items. So a good analyst needs to do some more hunting to locate both depreciation and amortization if they exist. Heinz certainly depreciates its assets. If you are unsure if the company you are analyzing depreciates assets, you should research the company's assets. An easy way to begin is by performing a word search for "depreciation" and "amortization" on the company's annual report, or you can go to the cash flow statement to see if depreciation and amortization line items exist. Depreciation and amortization is located in several places in the company's annual report. We show in Figure 5.2 the table found on page 71 of the company annual report. This appears to be a financial breakout of the company's operating business units.

In Figure 5.2 we can see that depreciation and amortization for the consolidated business are $299,050, $298,660, and $342,793, for 2010, 2011, and 2012, respectively. It is also good to know that on page 38 of the annual report (Figure 5.3), the cash flow statement shows 2012 and 2011 depreciation and amortization of the exact same amounts as in Figure 5.2, although, they are listed as two separate line items. The sum of the two matches what we have in Figure 5.2. This is a good cross-check.

However, note that the 2010 depreciation number of $299,050 in Figure 5.2 is slightly different than the sum of the cash flow depreciation and amortization of $302,836 ($254,528 + $48,308) found on page 38 of the annual report (Figure 5.3). There can be advanced accounting rules that can cause differences between depreciation shown on the cash flow statement and in other sections of the company financials.

	Fiscal Year Ended					
	April 29, 2012	*April 27, 2011*	*April 28, 2010*	*April 29, 2012*	*April 27, 2011*	*April 28, 2010*
	(52 1/2 Weeks)	*(52 Weeks)*	*(52 Weeks)*	*(52 1/2 Weeks)*	*(52 Weeks)*	*(52 Weeks)*
			(In thousands)			
	Net External Sales			*Operating Income (Loss)*		
North American Consumer Products	$ 3,241,533	$ 3,265,857	$ 3,192,219	$ 812,056	$ 832,719	$ 771,497
Europe	3,441,282	3,236,800	3,332,619	608,829	581,148	554,300
Asia/Pacific	2,568,716	2,320,789	2,007,252	206,306	221,580	195,261
U.S. Foodservice	1,418,970	1,413,456	1,429,511	166,298	175,977	150,628
Rest of World	978,578	469,686	533,382	105,080	53,371	69,219
Nonoperating[a]	—	—	—	(223,084)	(216,605)	(158,989)
Productivity Initiatives[d]	—	—	—	(224,317)	—	(37,665)
Gain on Property Disposal in the Netherlands[e]	—	—	—	—	—	14,977
Consolidated Totals	$ 11,649,079	$ 10,706,588	$ 10,494,983	$ 1,451,168	$ 1,648,190	$ 1,559,228
	Depreciation and Amortization Expenses			*Capital Expenditures[b]*		
Total North America	$ 133,589	$ 123,817	$ 122,774	$ 103,958	$ 101,001	$ 88,841
Europe	98,384	91,222	105,684	113,420	97,964	74,095
Asia/Pacific	63,102	53,326	46,976	99,912	71,419	46,105
Rest of World	19,290	6,324	6,638	38,539	12,829	11,785
Nonoperating[a]	28,428	23,971	16,978	62,905	52,433	56,816
Consolidated Totals	$ 342,793	$ 298,660	$ 299,050	$ 418,734	$ 335,646	$ 277,642
	Identifiable Assets					
Total North America	$ 3,394,387	$ 3,633,276	$ 3,532,477			
Europe	4,158,349	4,398,944	3,815,179			
Asia/Pacific	2,544,332	2,424,739	1,869,591			
Rest of World	1,145,696	1,149,802	276,902			
Nonoperating[c]	740,529	623,884	581,562			
Consolidated Totals	$ 11,983,293	$ 12,230,645	$ 10,075,711			

[a] Includes corporate overhead, intercompany eliminations, and charges not directly attributable to operating segments.
[b] Excludes property, plant, and equipment obtained through acquisitions.
[c] Includes identifiable assets not directly attributable to operating segments.
[d] See Note 3 for further details on Fiscal 2012 productivity initiatives. Fiscal 2010 includes costs associated with targeted workforce reductions and asset write-offs that were part of a corporation-wide initiative to improve productivity. The asset write-offs relate to two factory closures and the exit of a formula business in the U.K.
[e] Includes payments received from the government in the Netherlands net of estimated costs to exit the facility. See Note 4 for additional explanation.

FIGURE 5.2 Heinz Operations by Segment

There is another table that contains depreciation on page A-7 in the annual report that explains the difference (see Figure 5.4). A note (1) referenced in the "Depreciation and amortization" line of the table that reads:

Amounts exclude operating results related to the Company's private label frozen desserts business in the U.K. as well as the Kabobs and Appetizers And, Inc. businesses in the U.S., which were divested in Fiscal 2010 and have been presented in discontinued operations.

	Fiscal Year Ended		
	April 29, 2012	April 27, 2011	April 28, 2010
	(52 1/2 Weeks)	(52 Weeks)	(52 Weeks)
		(In thousands)	
Operating activities:			
Net income	$ 939,908	$ 1,005,948	$ 882,343
Adjustments to reconcile net income to cash provided by operating activities:			
Depreciation	295,718	255,227	254,528
Amortization	47,075	43,433	48,308
Deferred tax (benefit)/provision	(94,816)	153,725	220,528
Net losses on divestitures	—	—	44,860
Pension contributions	(23,469)	(22,411)	(539,939)
Asset write-downs from Fiscal 2012 productivity initiatives	58,736	—	—
Other items, net	75,375	98,172	90,938
Changes in current assets and liabilities, excluding effects of acquisitions and divestitures:			
Receivables (includes proceeds from securitization)	171,832	(91,057)	121,387
Inventories	60,919	(80,841)	48,537
Prepaid expenses and other current assets	(11,584)	(1,682)	2,113
Accounts payable	(72,352)	233,339	(2,805)
Accrued liabilities	(20,008)	(60,862)	96,533
Income taxes	65,783	50,652	(5,134)
Cash provided by operating activities	$ 1,493,117	$ 1,583,643	$ 1,262,197

FIGURE 5.3   Heinz Cash Flow from Operations

This note suggests there is some additional depreciation and amortization that have been associated with a divested business and was therefore removed. It could be that this portion of depreciation and amortization was not adjusted in the cash flow statement, hence the difference. For such a small difference, and given that difference occurs only in 2010, it is not a big deal. The most important task is to ensure that our historical bottom-line numbers match what has been reported to be certain that all has been properly represented in our model.

We will see later, the company has separated out depreciation and amortization for good reason: depreciation, accounting for the aging of assets, is related to the company's property, plant, and equipment, whereas amortization is related to the company's intangible assets. Companies often combine depreciation and amortization as one, but since Heinz has separated them out, let's do the same here. So let's use the depreciation and amortization from the cash flow statement (Figure 5.3) since they have been separated out.

Now that we have identified depreciation and amortization, we have to determine where the depreciation and amortization expenses lie in the income statement. We have proven depreciation and amortization exists, and we assume it must be somewhere in the income statement although not directly shown. Be careful not to simply add these expenses to the income statement. The depreciation and amortization amount we have found is most likely buried in one of the expense items we have already identified. But how do we know which expense line item contains these expenses?

Five-Year Summary of Operations and Other Related Data
H.J. Heinz Company and Subsidiaries

(In thousands, except per share amounts)	2012	2011	2010	2009	2008
Summary of Operations:					
Sales[1]	$ 11,649,079	$ 10,706,588	$ 10,494,983	$ 10,011,331	$ 9,885,556
Cost of products sold[1]	$ 7,649,549	$ 6,754,048	$ 6,700,677	$ 6,442,075	$ 6,233,420
Interest expense[1]	$ 294,104	$ 275,398	$ 295,711	$ 339,635	$ 364,808
Provision for income taxes[1]	$ 243,535	$ 368,221	$ 358,514	$ 375,483	$ 372,587
Income from continuing operations attributable to H.J. Heinz Company common shareholders[1]	$ 923,159	$ 989,510	$ 914,489	$ 929,511	$ 846,623
Income from continuing operations per share attributable to H.J. Heinz Company common shareholders—diluted[1]	$ 2.85	$ 3.06	$ 2.87	$ 2.91	$ 2.62
Income from continuing operations per share attributable to H.J. Heinz Company common shareholders—basic[1]	$ 2.87	$ 3.09	$ 2.89	$ 2.95	$ 2.65
Other Related Data:					
Dividends paid:					
Common	$ 619,095	$ 579,606	$ 533,543	$ 525,281	$ 485,234
Per share	$ 1.92	$ 1.80	$ 1.68	$ 1.66	$ 1.52
Preferred	$ 9	$ 12	$ 9	$ 12	$ 12
Average common shares outstanding—diluted	323,320,668	323,041,725	318,113,131	318,062,977	321,717,238
Average common shares outstanding—basic	320,686,010	320,118,159	315,947,737	313,747,318	317,019,072
Number of employees	32,200	34,800	29,600	32,400	32,500
Capital expenditures	$ 418,734	$ 335,646	$ 277,642	$ 292,121	$ 301,588
Depreciation and amortization[1]	$ 342,793	$ 298,660	$ 299,050	$ 274,107	$ 281,467
Total assets	$ 11,983,293	$ 12,230,645	$ 10,075,711	$ 9,664,184	$ 10,565,043
Total debt	$ 5,026,689	$ 4,613,060	$ 4,618,172	$ 5,141,824	$ 5,183,654
Total H.J. Heinz Company shareholders' equity	$ 2,758,589	$ 3,108,962	$ 1,891,345	$ 1,219,938	$ 1,887,820
Return on average invested capital (ROIC)[2]	16.8%	19.3%	17.8%	18.4%	16.8%
Book value per common share	$ 8.61	$ 9.68	$ 5.95	$ 3.87	$ 6.06
Price range of common stock:					
High	$ 55.00	$ 51.38	$ 47.84	$ 53.00	$ 48.75
Low	$ 48.17	$ 40.00	$ 34.03	$ 30.51	$ 41.37

FIGURE 5.4 Heinz Five-Year Summary Operating Statistics

Unfortunately, in many cases, it may not be easy to tell. A word search on "depreciation" or "amortization" may reveal a note describing where that item is expensed on the income statement. In Heinz's case, it does not. Quite often depreciation and amortization is a part of cost of goods sold or sales, general, and administrative expenses, or spread out between the two. It is also often that one cannot identify exactly where these expenses are buried.

It should be comforting to know, however, that whether we end up extracting the depreciation and amortization expenses from cost of goods sold or from sales, general, and administrative expenses, or from both, it will not affect our EBITDA, which is most crucial for our valuation. So in this example let us assume they are a component of the cost of goods sold.

So assuming depreciation and amortization are a component of the cost of goods sold, we will reduce the amount of that expense by the depreciation and amortization values. So, for example, in 2012, the cost of goods sold expense will be reduced from $7,649,549 by the total of depreciation and amortization of $295,718 + $47,075 (from Figure 5.3) to get $7,306,756. We will do this in the model next.

We now have enough information to lay out a historical income statement for three years down to EBITDA.

Cost of Goods Sold

Heinz reports cost of goods sold (COGS) as cost of products sold, and records $6,700,677, $6,754,048, and $7,649,549, for 2010, 2011, and 2012, respectively. But, given the previous discussion, we have assumed the depreciation and amortization expenses are contained within the COGS. So in Row 8, we should hard-code the COGS less the depreciation and amortization expense, or in 2010, we should have "(6700.677-254.528-48.308)." Remember that we have agreed to use the depreciation and amortization reported on the cash flow statement, which is the same as the income statement reported depreciation and amortization except in 2010. We also have to convert from thousands to millions, so we replace the last comma with a decimal point. We can continue to hard-code in the COGS less the depreciation and amortization expenses in 2011 and 2012. See Table 5.2.

Notice that there is a metric, COGS as a percentage of revenue, in Row 9. We will discuss later how calculating an expense as a percentage of

TABLE 5.2   Heinz COGS

Consolidated Income Statements (in US$ millions except per share amounts)			
		Actuals	
Period Ending	2010A	2011A	2012A
Revenue	$10,495.0	$10,706.6	$11,649.1
Y/Y revenue growth (%)		2.0%	8.8%
Cost of goods sold	6,397.8	6,455.4	7,306.8
COGS as a % of revenue			

revenue may or may not be a good indicator of future performance. To best prepare us for that discussion, let's calculate this metric now. So the 2010 COGS as a percentage of revenue will be:

Calculating 2010 COGS as a % of Revenue (Cell D9)

Excel Keystrokes	Description
Type "="	Enters into "formula" mode
Select Cell D8	2010 COGS
Type "/"	Divides
Select Cell D6	2010 revenue
Hit Enter	End
Formula result	"=D8/D6"

This gives us 61.0 percent in 2010. We can now copy this formula to the right through 2012.

Gross Profit

Gross profit is revenue less cost of goods sold.

Calculating 2010 Gross Profit (Cell D10)

Excel Keystrokes	Description
Type "="	Enters into "formula" mode
Select Cell D6	2010 revenue
Type "-"	Subtracts
Select Cell D8	2010 COGS
Hit Enter	End
Formula result	"=D6-D8"

And we can calculate the gross profit margin as explained earlier in this chapter.

Calculating 2010 Gross Profit Margin (Cell D11)

Excel Keystrokes	Description
Type "="	Enters into "formula" mode
Select Cell D10	2010 gross profit
Type "/"	Divides
Select Cell D6	2010 revenue
Hit Enter	End
Formula result	"=D10/D6"

TABLE 5.3 Heinz Historical Gross Profit

Consolidated Income Statements (in US$ millions except per share amounts)			
		Actuals	
Period Ending	2010A	2011A	2012A
Revenue	$10,495.0	$10,706.6	$11,649.1
Y/Y revenue growth (%)		*2.0%*	*8.8%*
Cost of goods sold	6,397.8	6,455.4	7,306.8
COGS as a % of revenue	*61.0%*	*60.3%*	*62.7%*
Gross profit	$ 4,097.1	$ 4,251.2	$ 4,342.3
Gross profit margin (%)	*39.0%*	*39.7%*	*37.3%*

We can copy both formulas in Cells D10 and D11 to the right through 2012 and move on to operating expenses. See Table 5.3.

Selling, General, and Administrative Expenses

Heinz lists selling, general, and administrative expenses (SG&A) directly under gross profit. (See Figure 5.1.) So in Row 13, we should hard-code the $2,235,078, $2,304,350, and $2,548,362 for 2010, 2011, and 2012, respectively. Remember to hard-code these in millions units, not thousands. We can then calculate these expenses as a percentage of revenue as we have done with the cost of goods sold.

Calculating 2010 SG&A % of Revenue (Cell D14)

Excel Keystrokes	Description
Type "="	Enters into "formula" mode
Select Cell D13	2010 SG&A
Type "/"	Divides
Select Cell D6	2010 revenue
Hit Enter	End
Formula result	"=D13/D6"

We can copy Cell D14 to the right through 2012.

Fund Management Fee

You may notice Row 15, "Fund Management Fee," in the model. Often, investment funds charge themselves an annual fee (for example 1.0x or 1.5x a CEO's salary) while owning the business. This is one of several ways such funds make money. If such a fee will exist for the Heinz buyout, it will not occur until after the buyers actually own the business, so the value will be $0 for the historical years. We can hard-code "0" in Cells D15, E15, and F15.

Cost Savings

Cost savings, also known as cost synergies, are cost reductions due to operating improvements implemented after the purchase. We will discuss cost savings in more detail when calculating the projections. Since they do not affect the historical metrics, we can hard-code "0" in Cells D16, E16, and F16.

We can now total the operating expenses in Row 18 by adding Rows 13, 15, and 16, or Cell D18 should be "=D13 + D15 + D16."

Calculating 2010 Total Operating Expense (Cell D18)

Excel Keystrokes	Description
Type "="	Enters into "formula" mode
Select Cell D13	2010 SG&A
Type "+"	Adds
Select Cell D15	2010 fund management fee
Type "+"	Subtracts
Select Cell D16	2010 cost savings
Hit Enter	End
Formula result	"=D13 + D15 + D16"

We can copy Cell D18 to the right through 2012.

Other Income

We note that Heinz does not have any "other income" line items separated out. We will hard-code other income as "0" in Row 20.

EBITDA

We can now calculate EBITDA as gross profit less the total operating expenses.

Calculating 2010 EBITDA (Cell D21)

Excel Keystrokes	Description
Type "="	Enters into "formula" mode
Select Cell D10	2010 gross profit
Type "-"	Subtracts
Select Cell D18	2010 total operating expenses

(continued)

Type "-"	Subtracts
Select Cell D20	2010 other income
Hit Enter	End
Formula result	"=D10-D18-D20"

And we can calculate the EBITDA margin as explained earlier in this chapter.

Calculating 2010 EBITDA Margin (Cell D22)

Excel Keystrokes	Description
Type "="	Enters into "formula" mode
Select Cell D21	2010 EBITDA
Type "/"	Divides
Select Cell D6	2010 revenue
Hit Enter	End
Formula result	"=D21/D6"

We can copy both formulas in cells D21 and D22 to the right through 2012 (see Table 5.4).

TABLE 5.4   Heinz Historical EBITDA

Consolidated Income Statements (in US$ millions except per share amounts)			
		Actuals	
Period Ending	2010A	2011A	2012A
Revenue	$10,495.0	$10,706.6	$11,649.1
Y/Y revenue growth (%)		2.0%	8.8%
Cost of goods sold	6,397.8	6,455.4	7,306.8
COGS as a % of revenue	61.0%	60.3%	62.7%
Gross profit	$ 4,097.1	$ 4,251.2	$ 4,342.3
Gross profit margin (%)	39.0%	39.7%	37.3%
Operating expenses			
Selling, general, and administrative	2,235.1	2,304.4	2,548.4
SG&A as a % of revenue	21.3%	21.5%	21.9%
Fund management fee	0.0	0.0	0.0
Cost savings	0.0	0.0	0.0
Cost savings as a % of SG&A			
Total operating expenses	$ 2,235.1	$ 2,304.4	$ 2,548.4
Other income			
Equity in earnings of unconsolidated affiliates	0.0	0.0	0.0
EBITDA	$ 1,862.1	$ 1,946.9	$ 1,794.0
EBITDA margin (%)	17.7%	18.2%	15.4%

Beyond EBITDA

Once we have EBITDA, we can continue identifying the rest of Heinz's income statement line items.

Depreciation and Amortization

We have already identified the depreciation as $254,528, $255,227, and $295,718 for 2010, 2011, and 2012, respectively (from Figure 5.3). We can hard-code these in millions units into Row 23. We can also hard-code the amortization of $48,308, $43,433, and $47,075 into row 24.

There is one more line item here that is a transaction adjustment: amortization of identifiable intangible assets. We will discuss and link these through when we discuss intangible assets and debt in the balance sheet adjustments section, Chapter 8. These transaction adjustments will not affect our historical financials, so let's hard-code them as "0" in years 2010 to 2012.

We can now total the depreciation and amortization in Row 26 by adding Rows 23, 24, and 25, or Cell D26 should be "=D23 + D24 + D25." We can copy these formulas to the right.

Calculating 2010 Total Depreciation and Amortization (Cell D26)

Excel Keystrokes	Description
Type "="	Enters into "formula" mode
Select Cell D23	2010 depreciation
Type "+"	Adds
Select Cell D24	2010 amortization
Type "+"	Subtracts
Select Cell D25	2010 amortization of identifiable intangible assets
Hit Enter	End
Formula result	"=D23 + D24 + D25"

EBIT

EBIT is EBITDA less depreciation and amortization. We can calculate EBIT.

Calculating 2010 EBIT (Cell D27)

Excel Keystrokes	Description
Type "="	Enters into "formula" mode
Select Cell D21	2010 EBITDA
Type "-"	Subtracts
Select Cell D26	2010 total depreciation and amortization
Hit Enter	End
Formula result	"=D21-D26"

TABLE 5.5   Heinz Historical EBIT

Consolidated Income Statements (in US$ millions except per share amounts)

		Actuals	
Period Ending	2010A	2011A	2012A
EBITDA	$1,862.1	$1,946.9	$1,794.0
EBITDA margin (%)	*17.7%*	*18.2%*	*15.4%*
Depreciation	254.5	255.2	295.7
Amortization	48.3	43.4	47.1
Amortization of identifiable intangible assets	0.0	0.0	0.0
Total depreciation and amortization	$ 302.8	$ 298.7	$ 342.8
EBIT	1,559.2	1,648.2	1,451.2
EBIT margin (%)	*14.9%*	*15.4%*	*12.5%*

And we can also calculate the EBIT margin.

Calculating 2010 EBIT Margin (Cell D28)

Excel Keystrokes	Description
Type "="	Enters into "formula" mode
Select Cell D27	2010 EBIT
Type "/"	Divides
Select Cell D6	2010 revenue
Hit Enter	End
Formula result	"=D27/D6"

We can copy cells D27 and D28 to the right through 2012. See Table 5.5.

Interest

Heinz has two lines of interest: interest expense and interest income. Note that even though both interest expense and interest income are listed as positive numbers, interest income is actually increasing EBIT whereas interest expense is decreasing EBIT. This is an example of how one needs to make sure the income statement line items are flowing properly. It is not always clear in an income statement if a line item is adding or subtracting from the totals. We will, at the end of the income statement, make sure we can match the net income we calculate to Heinz's net income to ensure all is flowing properly.

So, we can hard-code the interest expense and the interest income items into Rows 30 and 31, respectively. The net interest expense is the interest

TABLE 5.6   Heinz Historical Net Interest Expense

Consolidated Income Statements (in US$ millions except per share amounts)

	Actuals		
Period Ending	2010A	2011A	2012A
EBIT	$1,559.2	$1,648.2	$1,451.2
EBIT margin (%)	14.9%	15.4%	12.5%
Interest			
Interest expense	295.7	275.4	294.1
Interest income	45.1	22.6	34.6
Net interest expense	$ 250.6	$ 252.8	$ 259.5

expense less the interest income, so in Row 32, we will subtract Row 31 from Row 30, or D32 will read "=D30-D31." We can copy Cell D32 to the right through 2012. See Table 5.6.

Calculating 2010 Net Interest Expense (Cell D32)

Excel Keystrokes	Description
Type "="	Enters into "formula" mode
Select Cell D30	2010 interest expense
Type "-"	Subtracts
Select Cell D31	2010 interest income
Hit Enter	End
Formula result	"=D30-D31"

Other Expense, Net

Heinz does report one other expense line item listed as "Other expense, net" (see Figure 5.1). Further research reveals the following note on page 14 of the annual report.

> *Net interest expense increased $7 million, to $259 million, reflecting a $19 million increase in interest expense, partially offset by a $12 million increase in interest income. The increase in interest income is mainly due to earnings on short-term investments and the increase in interest expense is largely due to interest rate mix in the Company's debt portfolio and acquisitions made last fiscal year. Other expenses, net, decreased $13 million, to $8 million, primarily due to currency gains this year compared to currency losses in the prior year.*

> (Heinz Annual Report, page 14)

Here is another note referring to "Other expense, net" found on page 68 of the Heinz annual report:

> *As of April 29, 2012, the Company is hedging forecasted transactions for periods not exceeding 3 years. During the next 12 months, the Company expects $1.7 million of net deferred gains reported in accumulated other comprehensive loss to be reclassified to earnings, assuming market rates remain constant through contract maturities. Hedge ineffectiveness related to cash flow hedges, which is reported in current period earnings as other expense, net, was not significant for the years ended April 29, 2012, April 27, 2011 and April 28, 2010. Amounts reclassified to earnings because the hedged transaction was no longer expected to occur were not significant for the years ended April 29, 2012, April 27, 2011 and April 28, 2010.*

(Heinz Annual Report, page 68)

These are two of quite a few notes relating to "Other expense, net." For our purposes, we need to determine if this line item should be considered in our operating income statement, or if it should be moved to the extraordinary or nonrecurring events section. These two notes indicate that this line item is related to currency losses and cash flow hedges. It does not sound like these are line items related directly to Heinz's core business of selling food products. So I would recommend keeping this line item below our operations.

Let's hard-code these "Other expense, net" line items into Row 39 as extraordinary items in millions units. We note that we will have to make some tax adjustments to these numbers later on. Once that is complete, we can then calculate EBT.

EBT

Remember that EBIT less interest is EBT.

Calculating 2010 EBT (Cell D33)

Excel Keystrokes	Description
Type "="	Enters into "formula" mode
Select Cell D27	2010 EBIT
Type "-"	Subtracts
Select Cell D32	2010 net interest expense
Hit Enter	End
Formula result	"=D27-D32"

TABLE 5.7 Heinz Income Tax

Consolidated Income Statements (in US$ millions except per share amounts)			
		Actuals	
Period Ending	2010A	2011A	2012A
EBT	$1,308.7	$1,395.4	$1,191.7
EBT margin (%)	12.5%	13.0%	10.2%
Income tax expense	363.6	373.9	245.2
All-in effective tax rate (%)	27.8%	26.8%	20.6%

EBT margin is EBT divided by revenue.

Calculating 2010 EBT Margin (Cell D34)

Excel Keystrokes	Description
Type "="	Enters into "formula" mode
Select Cell D33	2010 EBT
Type "/"	Divides
Select Cell D6	2010 revenue
Hit Enter	End
Formula result	"=D33/D6"

We can copy cells D33 and D34 to the right through 2012. See Table 5.7.

Taxes

In 2012 we see that Heinz paid $243,535 in taxes as per its annual report (see Figure 5.1). But because we had removed an expense ("Other expense, net") from above the "Net income" line, we need to adjust this tax number. If we effectively move a line item from above the "Net income" line to below, the taxes associated with that item should go with it. We also make this adjustment assuming that it is more important to back into the implied tax rate actually incurred by Heinz as opposed to the actual taxes reported. It is the historical tax rates that will help us gauge appropriate taxes to pay in the future. We suggest handling this by calculating the effective tax rate paid in a given period, then using that tax rate to recalculate the adjusted tax paid. So, if the company had paid $243,535 in 2012 taxes, based on a $1,183,443 EBT (line item "Income from continuing operations before income taxes"), the company had an implied tax rate of 20.6 percent (243,535/1,183,443). So we recommend directly in the tax percent row, to hard-code in the calculation behind the 20.6 percent tax rate, and to footnote it. So, in Cell F36, for example, we should have "=243535/1183443". We could have adjusted these numbers for the change in units, but it would not change the percentage calculated. We do the same for 2011 and 2010. See Table 5.7.

We can then simply multiply the EBT times the new rate to get the implied taxes incurred if the nonrecurring expense was not included above the "Net income" line.

Calculating 2010 Income Tax Expense (Cell D35)

Excel Keystrokes	Description
Type "="	Enters into "formula" mode
Select Cell D33	2010 EBT
Type "*"	Multiplies
Select Cell D36	2010 tax rate
Hit Enter	End
Formula result	"=D33*D36"

We can copy this formula to the right through 2012.

Net Income (Adjusted)

Remember that EBT less taxes equals net income.

Calculating 2010 Net Income (Cell D37)

Excel Keystrokes	Description
Type "="	Enters into "formula" mode
Select Cell D33	2010 EBT
Type "-"	Subtracts
Select Cell D35	2010 income taxes
Hit Enter	End
Formula result	"=D33-D35"

We can copy this formula to the right through 2012.

Nonrecurring Events and Extraordinary Items

In addition to the "Other expense, net" that we had brought down to this section, Heinz has another nonrecurring event, "Loss from discontinued operations, net of tax" (see Figure 5.1). This has happened only in 2010. Again, we have to make sure we check in which direction this line item affects net income. In this case it is reducing our net income despite the fact that it is listed in parentheses. Some analysts prefer to reverse the logic by flipping the signs from negative to positive and vice versa. There is no absolutely correct way, as long as the total net income at the bottom of the income statement matches what is reported in the annual report.

Typically, we have positive numbers listed as expenses reducing net income. So, let's hard-code the "(49,597)" as a positive number to be consistent with our logic. Be sure to hard-code this in millions units into Cell D40 (so, "49.597"). We can hard-code "0" in 2011 and 2012.

Now we need to make one adjustment to the "Other expense, net" line item (Row 39). Each expense you have moved from above EBT to below should be tax affected (there may be several advanced exceptions). So in 2010, for example, the $18.2 million charge needs to be tax affected by multiplying by 1 – tax rate.

Adjusting 2010 Other Expense, Net (Cell D39)

Excel Keystrokes	Description
Type "="	Enters into "formula" mode
Type "18.2"	The original pretax expense
Type "*"	Multiplies
Type "(1-"	Begins 1 – tax % formula
Select Cell D36	2010 tax rate (%)
Type ")"	Closes 1 – tax % formula
Hit Enter	End
Formula result	"=18.2*(1-D36)"

This ensures we have properly moved the tax savings associated with that expense from the tax line to the nonrecurring events line. In order to match the same total amount of taxes initially reported by Heinz, we need to use the same tax rate calculated in the effective tax rate line of that period, so it is best if we just link up to that exact cell. This should give you $13.1 in 2010. We need to do this for 2011 and 2012. Be careful—we cannot just copy this formula to the right, as the pretax "Other expense, net" ("18.2" in 2010) is different each year.

Note: We do not need to make this tax adjustment for the "Loss from discontinued operations" line item because it is already net of tax. First it states "net of tax" directly in the line item, and second the line item is located after the tax line.

We can keep the other nonrecurring events as $0, and calculate the total nonrecurring events in row 43 and copy to the right through 2012. See the results in Table 5.8.

TABLE 5.8   Historical Heinz Nonrecurring Events

Consolidated Income Statements (in US$ millions except per share amounts)

	Actuals		
Period Ending	2010A	2011A	2012A
Nonrecurring events			
Other expense, net	$13.1	$15.5	$6.5
Loss from discontinued operations, net of tax	49.6	0.0	0.0
Effect of accounting changes	0.0	0.0	0.0
Extraordinary items, net of tax	0.0	0.0	0.0
Total nonrecurring events	$62.7	$15.5	$6.5

MODELING TIP

There is a quick way to sum up several rows at once. Holding down "Alt" and "=" at the same time will automatically suggest a SUM formula to use. You can hit Enter to accept the formula as is or you can first make adjustments to the formula and save. Appendix 3 has a list of many popular hot keys that can be utilized to make your modeling skills more efficient.

Net Income (After Nonrecurring Events)

We can now calculate the net income (after nonrecurring events), which is net income less nonrecurring events. It is this net income that should match the "Net income" line in the Heinz annual report. Note the difference between this net income and net income (adjusted) from earlier. Net income (adjusted) excludes the nonrecurring and extraordinary events. That is important to get a more normalized net income indicative of standard operations. But it is still important to be able to match Heinz's bottom-line numbers despite our adjustments. See Table 5.9.

Calculating 2010 Net Income (After Nonrecurring Events) (Cell D44)

Excel Keystrokes	Description
Type "="	Enters into "formula" mode
Select Cell D37	2010 net income (adjusted)
Type "-"	Subtracts
Select Cell D43	2010 nonrecurring events
Hit Enter	End
Formula result	"=D37-D43"

We can copy this formula to the right through 2012. See Table 5.9.

Distributions

Heinz's line item, "Net income attributable to noncontrolling interest" is effectively noncontrolling interests. See Figure 5.1. We can hard-code this into Row 45 in millions units. See Table 5.9.

Net Income (as Reported)

We can now calculate the net income (as reported) as net income (after nonrecurring events) minus noncontrolling interests.

Calculating 2010 Net Income (As Reported) (Cell D46)

Excel Keystrokes	Description
Type "="	Enters into "formula" mode
Select Cell D44	2010 net income (after nonrecurring events)
Type "-"	Subtracts
Select Cell D45	2010 net income attributable to noncontrolling interests
Hit Enter	End
Formula result	"=D44-D45"

We can copy Cell D46 to the right through 2012. These totals should tie with the "Net income attributable to H.J. Heinz Company" line item. See Figure 5.1 and Table 5.9.

Shares and EPS

We can hard-code in the basic and diluted shares that Heinz has reported into Rows 51 and 52 before calculating earnings per share (EPS). You can locate the diluted shares a few lines below "Net income attributable to H.J. Heinz Company" (see Figure 5.1); the line reads "Average common shares outstanding—diluted." Basic shares are a few lines below the diluted shares; that line reads "Average common shares outstanding—basic." Be sure to hard-code these numbers in millions units. See Table 5.9.

We can then calculate the basic EPS by dividing the net income (as reported) by the number of basic shares outstanding, and can calculate the diluted EPS by dividing the net income (as reported) by the number of diluted shares outstanding. The purpose of calculating EPS here is to ensure we have metrics that match what the company had reported for accuracy in our analysis. It is, however, common to calculate EPS using our adjusted net income, depending on the purpose of the analysis.

Calculating 2010 Basic EPS (Cell D48)

Excel Keystrokes	Description
Type "="	Enters into "formula" mode
Select Cell D46	2010 net income (as reported)
Type "/"	Divides
Select Cell D51	2010 shares
Hit Enter	End
Formula result	"=D46/D51"

We repeat the same process for the diluted EPS, using diluted shares in place of basic shares.

Calculating 2010 Diluted EPS (Cell D49)

Excel Keystrokes	Description
Type "="	Enters into "formula" mode
Select Cell D46	2010 net income (as reported)
Type "/"	Divides
Select Cell D52	2010 diluted shares
Hit Enter	End
Formula result	"=D46/D52"

We can copy Cells D48 and D49 to the right through 2012. See Table 5.9. Note: If you compare our results with those from the Heinz annual report, it seems that the company has in all cases rounded the EPS down. I have not rounded down, but rather expanded the EPS calculation to three decimal places so we can see how close it comes to the Heinz numbers.

TABLE 5.9   Heinz Historical Income Statement

Consolidated Income Statements (in US$ millions except per share amounts)			
		Actuals	
Period Ending	2010A	2011A	2012A
Revenue	$10,495.0	$10,706.6	$11,649.1
Y/Y revenue growth (%)		2.0%	8.8%
Cost of goods sold	6,397.8	6,455.4	7,306.8
COGS as a % of revenue	61.0%	60.3%	62.7%
Gross profit	$ 4,097.1	$ 4,251.2	$ 4,342.3
Gross profit margin (%)	39.0%	39.7%	37.3%
Operating expenses			
Selling, general, and administrative	2,235.1	2,304.4	2,548.4
SG&A as a % of revenue	21.3%	21.5%	21.9%
Fund management fee	0.0	0.0	0.0

TABLE 5.9 (*Continued*)

Consolidated Income Statements (in US$ millions except per share amounts)			
		Actuals	
Period Ending	2010A	2011A	2012A
Cost savings	0.0	0.0	0.0
Cost savings as a % of SG&A			
Total operating expenses	$ 2,235.1	$ 2,304.4	$ 2,548.4
Other income			
Equity in earnings of unconsolidated affiliates	0.0	0.0	0.0
EBITDA	$ 1,862.1	$ 1,946.9	$ 1,794.0
EBITDA margin (%)	17.7%	18.2%	15.4%
Depreciation	254.5	255.2	295.7
Amortization	48.3	43.4	47.1
Amortization of identifiable intangible assets	0.0	0.0	0.0
Total depreciation and amortization	$ 302.8	$ 298.7	$ 342.8
EBIT	1,559.2	1,648.2	1,451.2
EBIT margin (%)	14.9%	15.4%	12.5%
Interest			
Interest expense	295.7	275.4	294.1
Interest income	45.1	22.6	34.6
Net interest expense	$ 250.6	$ 252.8	$ 259.5
EBT	$ 1,308.7	$ 1,395.4	$ 1,191.7
EBT margin (%)	12.5%	13.0%	10.2%
Income tax expense	363.6	373.9	245.2
All-in effective tax rate (%)	27.8%	26.8%	20.6%
Net income (adjusted)	$ 945.1	$ 1,021.5	$ 946.4
Nonrecurring events			
Other expense, net	13.1	15.5	6.5
Loss from discontinued operations, net of tax	49.6	0.0	0.0
Effect of accounting changes	0.0	0.0	0.0
Extraordinary items, net of tax	0.0	0.0	0.0
Total nonrecurring events	$ 62.7	$ 15.5	$ 6.5
Net income (after nonrecurring events)	$ 882.3	$ 1,005.9	$ 939.9
Net income attributable to noncontrolling interests	17.5	16.4	16.7
Net income (as reported)	864.9	989.5	923.2
Earnings per share (EPS)			
Basic	2.737	3.091	2.879
Diluted	2.719	3.063	2.855
Average common shares outstanding			
Basic	315.9	320.1	320.7
Diluted	318.1	323.0	323.3

LAST TWELVE MONTHS (LTM)

Before going on to make Heinz projections, it is important to consider the timing of financial metrics. Heinz reports annual financials as of April. With a transaction announcement date of February 14, much time has passed from the previous April to the announcement date. For purposes of this case, it is important to represent the company financials as close to the announcement date as possible. The reality of the situation is that many months can pass from transaction announcement to the actual close of the transaction, and in theory we can project the model out on a stand-alone basis several months before simulating the acquisition. But that does get quite a bit convoluted, and we do want to tie back to the numbers represented in the announcement press release as we don't have any more data to run the analysis with. So for now, we will make the assumption that the transaction is run on announcement date. Although we know the transaction has not yet closed, this still gives us an understanding of what the potential investment opportunity is to Berkshire and 3G, which is the goal of this analysis. It is common practice on Wall Street to construct the model first on announcement date, and then periodically update the model as the transaction close date approaches.

Before calculating the metrics, it is important to understand last twelve months (LTM) calculations. The LTM is a method to calculate the most recent financials based on combining annual reports (10-Ks) with quarterly reports (10-Qs). When going back to the Heinz investor relations section of its website, we notice the company has produced three additional quarterly reports since its annual report. So, it not only has financial data from April 28, 2011, to April 29, 2012, but it has a "Q1" report showing financial results from April 30, 2012, to July 29, 2012; a "Q2" report showing financial results from July 30, 2012, to October 28, 2012; and a "Q3" report showing financial results from October 29, 2012, to January 27, 2013.

So, technically, we can get Heinz financial results for the last 12 months up to January 27, 2013. This is not financial information at the exact announcement date but it is very close.

Annual 2012	Q1 2013	Q2 2013	Q3 2013
4/28/2011– 4/29/2012	4/30/2012– 7/29/2012	7/30/2012– 10/28/2012	10/29/2012– 1/27/2013

We note Q1 and Q2 as 2013 even though both quarters end in 2012. This is because they are the first and second quarters of the Heinz fiscal calendar, which will end in April 2013.

In order to use this information to get 12 months of financials through January 27, 2013, we can first add the annual report financials to the Q1,

Q2, and Q3 financials. When we say "add," we mean (taking revenue, for example) adding the 2012 revenue from the annual report to the Q1, Q2, and Q3 revenue. This gives us 21 months of financials (from April 28, 2011, to January 27, 2013), so we now need to subtract nine months of financials or three quarters (from April 28, 2011, to January 25, 2012) in order to get a representation of 12 months of revenue through January 27, 2013.

Annual 2012			Q1 2013	Q2 2013	Q3 2013
4/28/2011–4/29/2012			4/30/2012–7/29/2012	7/30/2012–10/28/2012	10/29/2012–1/27/2013
Q1 2012	Q2 2012	Q3 2012			
4/28/2011–7/27/2011	7/28/2011–10/26/2011	10/27/2011–1/25/2012			

So, in other words, if we take the 2012 annual report numbers, add the Q1 2013, Q2 2013, and Q3 2013 numbers, and subtract the Q1 2012, Q2 2012, and Q3 2012 numbers, we will get financials from January 26, 2012, to January 27, 2013:

$$\text{LTM} = \text{Annual } 2012 + \text{Q1 } 2013 + \text{Q2 } 2013 +$$
$$\text{Q3 } 2013 - \text{Q1 } 2012 - \text{Q2 } 2012 - \text{Q3 } 2012$$

We should now build out LTM financials for Heinz. First notice that the Heinz Q3 report (found on the Wiley website in "Heinz_Quarterly_ Report_Q3.pdf," on the Heinz website, or on the Securities and Exchange Commission website at www.sec.gov) contains a set of financials representing the total of Q1, Q2, and Q3 to date. If you scroll down to page 3 of the Heinz Q3 report, you will see financials representing nine months ended January 27, 2013, and January 25, 2012. See Figure 5.5.

There may be some benefits to actually laying out the model quarter by quarter, but for our purposes, we can use these consolidated nine-month financials to calculate our LTM.

So we will first lay out the income statement exactly as we had done for the annual financials. We will then calculate the Heinz LTM using the following formula:

$$\text{Heinz LTM} = \text{Annual } 2012 + 9 \text{ Mo. } 2013 - 9 \text{ Mo. } 2012$$

If you notice in the model, Columns G and H are set up for the nine-month 2012 and 2013 income statements, respectively. We won't go into stepping you through the construction of this line by line, as it is exactly the same as the method we used for the annual historical financials. I recommend

H.J. Heinz Company and Subsidiaries Consolidated Statements of Income

		Nine Months Ended	
		January 27, 2013 FY 2013	January 25, 2012 FY 2012
		(Unaudited) (In thousands, Except per Share Amounts)	
Sales	$	8,538,315	$ 8,495,904
Cost of products sold		5,416,840	5,511,796
Gross profit		3,121,475	2,984,108
Selling, general, and administrative expenses		1,841,487	1,814,210
Operating income		1,279,988	1,169,898
Interest income		22,295	25,626
Interest expense		213,069	218,104
Other expense, net		(18,098)	(3,289)
Income from continuing operations before income taxes		1,071,116	974,131
Provision for income taxes		169,957	191,904
Income from continuing operations		901,159	782,227
Loss from discontinued operations, net of tax		(72,079)	(19,893)
Net income		829,080	762,334
Less: Net income attributable to the noncontrolling interest		12,063	14,517
Net income attributable to H.J. Heinz Company	$	817,017	$ 747,817
Income/(loss) per common share:			
Diluted			
Continuing operations attributable to H.J. Heinz Company common shareholders	$	2.75	$ 2.37
Discontinued operations attributable to H.J. Heinz Company common shareholders		(0.22)	(0.06)
Net income attributable to H.J. Heinz Company common shareholders	$	2.53	$ 2.31
Average common shares outstanding—diluted		323,048	323,538
Basic			
Continuing operations attributable to H.J. Heinz Company common shareholders	$	2.77	$ 2.39
Discontinued operations attributable to H.J. Heinz Company common shareholders		(0.22)	(0.06)
Net income attributable to H.J. Heinz Company common shareholders	$	2.55	$ 2.32
Average common shares outstanding—basic		320,523	320,850
Cash dividends per share	$	1.545	$ 1.44
Amounts attributable to H.J. Heinz Company common shareholders:			
Income from continuing operations, net of tax	$	889,096	$ 767,710
Loss from discontinued operations, net of tax		(72,079)	(19,893)
Net income	$	817,017	$ 747,817

(Per share amounts may not add due to rounding)

FIGURE 5.5   Heinz Nine-Month Income Statements

using Figure 5.5 and the solution in Table 5.10 as guides. Remember to hard-code everything in millions units. Also, the total formula calculations can be copied across from the formulas we already calculated in Column F. Note five adjustments:

1. Revenue growth (%) does not apply in the nine-month financials. You can leave that out.
2. Remember you need to locate depreciation and amortization in the 10-Q and remove it from the COGS as we had done in the annual financials. In the Q3 report, depreciation is found on page 8 of the cash flow statement. (See Figure 5.6.) So, for example, in 2013 you will hard-code "221.519" into Cell H23 and "34.890" into Cell H24. You will also need to subtract these values from the COGS line.

	Nine Months Ended	
	January 27, 2013 FY 2013	January 25, 2012 FY 2012
	(Unaudited) (In thousands)	
Cash Flows from Operating Activities:		
Net income	$ 829,080	$ 762,334
Adjustments to reconcile net income to cash provided by operating activities:		
Depreciation	221,519	217,620
Amortization	34,890	33,965

FIGURE 5.6   Heinz Q3 Depreciation

3. We will again remove the "Other expense, net" from above the "Net income" line and move it down to the nonrecurring and extraordinary events section. So, we will need to make the same tax adjustments we had done in the annual financials. I would recommend that you reread that section and treat this as a self-test to make sure you fully understand why we are making such adjustments. So, we will back into the implied tax rate by dividing the reported provision for income taxes into the income from continuing operations before income taxes. So, for example, in 2013 we will hard-code "169.957/1071.116" into Cell H36. This gives us the implied tax rate. So we can then calculate the new taxes by multiplying this rate by the EBT we have calculated. For this we can just copy the annual income tax formula (Cell F35) across into Columns G and H.

4. "Other expense, net" will be hard-coded into Row 39 just as we had done in the annual financials. However, remember to apply (1 − Tax %).

5. Note the other nonrecurring item in the quarterly financials, "Loss from discontinued operations, net of tax." As this is "net of tax" (i.e., already after the income tax line), we do not need to apply the (1 − Tax %) as we had done with the "Other expense, net" line item. We can just hard-code the reported number into the nonrecurring events section without any further adjustments.

The rest of the financials should be hard-coded as we had done in the annual reports. Notice the EPS at the end is slightly off. I can only attribute this to the fact that some of the income statement numbers have been rounded which results in slight EPS differences. See Table 5.10.

We can now make appropriate adjustments to calculate the LTM data in Column I. We discussed earlier in this chapter that the adjustments to get the LTM data are:

Heinz LTM = Annual 2012 − 9 Mo. 2012 + 9 Mo. 2013

TABLE 5.10   Heinz Nine-Month Historical Financials

Consolidated Income Statements (in US$ millions except per share amounts)

	Last Twelve Months (LTM)		
Period Ending	9 Mo. 2012	9 Mo. 2013	LTM
Revenue	$8,495.9	$8,538.3	
Y/Y revenue growth (%)			
Cost of goods sold	5,260.2	5,160.4	
COGS as a % of revenue	*61.9%*	*60.4%*	
Gross profit	$3,235.7	$3,377.9	
Gross profit margin (%)	*38.1%*	*39.6%*	
Operating expenses			
Selling, general, and administrative	1,814.2	1,841.5	
SG&A as a % of revenue	*21.4%*	*21.6%*	
Fund management fee	0.0	0.0	
Cost savings	0.0	0.0	
Cost savings as a % of SG&A			
Total operating expenses	$1,814.2	$1,841.5	
Other income			
Equity in earnings of unconsolidated affiliates	0.0	0.0	
EBITDA	$1,421.5	$1,536.4	
EBITDA margin (%)	*16.7%*	*18.0%*	
Depreciation	217.6	221.5	
Amortization	34.0	34.9	
Amortization of identifiable intangible assets	0.0	0.0	
Total depreciation and amortization	$ 251.6	$ 256.4	
EBIT	1,169.9	1,280.0	
EBIT margin (%)	*13.8%*	*15.0%*	
Interest			
Interest expense	218.1	213.1	
Interest income	25.6	22.3	
Net interest expense	$ 192.5	$ 190.8	
EBT	977.4	1,089.2	
EBT margin (%)	*11.5%*	*12.8%*	
Income tax expense	192.6	172.8	
All-in effective tax rate (%)	*19.7%*	*15.9%*	
Net income (adjusted)	$ 784.9	$ 916.4	

TABLE 5.10　(*Continued*)

Consolidated Income Statements (in US$ millions except per share amounts)

Period Ending	Last Twelve Months (LTM)		
	9 Mo. 2012	9 Mo. 2013	LTM
Nonrecurring events			
Other expense, net	2.6	15.2	
Loss from discontinued operations, net of tax	19.9	72.1	
Effect of accounting changes	0.0	0.0	
Extraordinary items, net of tax	0.0	0.0	
Total nonrecurring events	$ 22.5	$ 87.3	
Net income (after nonrecurring events)	$ 762.3	$ 829.1	
Net income attirbutable to noncontrolling interests	14.5	12.1	
Net income (as reported)	747.8	817.0	
Earnings per share (EPS)			
Basic	2.331	2.549	
Diluted	2.311	2.529	
Average common shares outstanding			
Basic	320.9	320.5	
Diluted	323.5	323.0	

So we can apply this formula to the LTM column (Column I). Let's take revenue, for example:

Calculating LTM Revenue (Cell I6)

Excel Keystrokes	Description
Type "="	Enters into "formula" mode
Select Cell F6	2012 revenue
Type "-"	Subtracts
Select Cell G6	9 Mo. 2012 revenue
Type "+"	Adds
Select Cell H6	9 Mo. 2013 revenue
Hit Enter	End
Formula result	"=F6-G6 + H6"

This should give you $11,691.5 in revenue. Note that this is a formula, so it should be in black font. Now we want to copy this formula down for every line item in the Heinz LTM column. However, take care to note the following adjustments (refer to Table 5.11). You may want to reference the "solution" files found on the Wiley website to more illustration on how these formulas have been constructed:

- Make sure to continue calculating "Totaling" line items top-down as we did with the historical financials. In other words, gross profit (a "total") should be calculated as one normally would by taking revenue minus COGS. You can just copy these formulas over to the right from Column H.
- We can leave percent Growth empty.
- Make sure to also calculate the percentage of revenue and margin numbers as we had done in the historical financials. For example, COGS as a percentage of revenue can be calculated as COGS/revenue in the LTM column. You can just copy these formulas over to the right from Column H.
- The "Income tax expense" line item should be calculated like revenue, COGS, or any other expense line item using the LTM formula. (You can just copy that down.) We can then back into the implied tax rate by dividing the income tax calculated into the EBT.

Calculating LTM Tax Rate (%) (Cell I36)

Excel Keystrokes	Description
Type "="	Enters into "formula" mode
Select Cell I35	LTM tax expense
Type "/"	Divides
Select Cell I33	LTM EBT
Hit Enter	End
Formula result	"=I35/I33"

- E.P.S. can be calculated as we did in the historical financials. You can just copy these formulas over to the right from Column H.
- The shares outstanding is an outstanding balance item. This is the total number of shares outstanding at a specific date. In other words, this is not an item that is reported over a period, where LTM adjustments would apply. So, we can just take the last reported balance (the nine-month). Or I51 would read "=H51," and I52 would read "=H52." See Table 5.11.

TABLE 5.11   Heinz LTM Income Statement

Consolidated Income Statements (in US$ millions except per share amounts)			
	Last Twelve Months (LTM)		
Period Ending	9 Mo. 2012	9 Mo. 2013	LTM
Revenue	$8,495.9	$8,538.3	$11,691.5
Y/Y revenue growth (%)			
Cost of goods sold	5,260.2	5,160.4	7,207.0
COGS as a % of revenue	*61.9%*	*60.4%*	*61.6%*
Gross profit	$3,235.7	$3,377.9	$ 4,484.5
Gross profit margin (%)	*38.1%*	*39.6%*	*38.4%*
Operating expenses			
Selling, general, and administrative	1,814.2	1,841.5	2,575.6
SG&A as a % of revenue	*21.4%*	*21.6%*	*22.0%*
Fund management fee	0.0	0.0	0.0
Cost savings	0.0	0.0	0.0
Cost savings as a % of SG&A			
Total operating expenses	$1,814.2	$1,841.5	$ 2,575.6
Other income			
Equity in earnings of unconsolidated			
affiliates	0.0	0.0	0.0
EBITDA	$1,421.5	$1,536.4	$ 1,908.9
EBITDA margin (%)	*16.7%*	*18.0%*	*16.3%*
Depreciation	217.6	221.5	299.6
Amortization	34.0	34.9	48.0
Amortization of identifiable			
intangible assets	0.0	0.0	0.0
Total depreciation and amortization	$ 251.6	$ 256.4	$ 347.6
EBIT	1,169.9	1,280.0	1,561.3
EBIT margin (%)	*13.8%*	*15.0%*	*13.4%*
Interest			
Interest expense	218.1	213.1	289.1
Interest income	25.6	22.3	31.3
Net interest expense	$ 192.5	$ 190.8	$ 257.8
EBT	977.4	1,089.2	1,303.5
EBT margin (%)	*11.5%*	*12.8%*	*11.1%*
Income tax expense	192.6	172.8	225.5
All-in effective tax rate (%)	*19.7%*	*15.9%*	*17.3%*
Net income (adjusted)	$ 784.9	$ 916.4	$ 1,078.0

(continued)

TABLE 5.11 (*Continued*)

Consolidated Income Statements (in US$ millions except per share amounts)			
	Last Twelve Months (LTM)		
Period Ending	9 Mo. 2012	9 Mo. 2013	LTM
Nonrecurring events			
Other expense, net	2.6	15.2	19.1
Loss from discontinued operations, net of tax	19.9	72.1	52.2
Effect of accounting changes	0.0	0.0	0.0
Extraordinary items, net of tax	0.0	0.0	0.0
Total nonrecurring events	$ 22.5	$ 87.3	$ 71.3
Net income (after nonrecurring events)	762.3	829.1	1,006.7
Net income attributable to noncontrolling interests	14.5	12.1	14.3
Net income (as reported)	747.8	817.0	992.4
Earnings per share (EPS)			
Basic	2.331	2.549	3.096
Diluted	2.311	2.529	3.072
Average common shares outstanding			
Basic	320.9	320.5	320.5
Diluted	323.5	323.0	323.0

INCOME STATEMENT—PROJECTIONS

Now that we have completed our LTM adjustments, we need to project the income statement out five years. Although the equity investors in Heinz have stated they are interested in holding the business for many years to come, they have most likely constructed a short-term LBO analysis to at least determine the potential returns their investment could have. This is a good indication of investment value. We could have constructed a seven-year model or longer, but as the business uncertainty increases as our projections go further out into the future, so does the uncertainty of our model.

For our projections, we will project off of the LTM metrics. We are taking the perspective that we will purchase the company on announcement date and so will project the business five years from announcement. In reality, there will be at least 6 to 12 months' time from announcement to closing. Some analysts have the theory that one should first build a model projecting the 6 or 12 months until transaction close and then model the potential buyout. However, in this case, there is just too much uncertainty surrounding the Heinz close date, and the point of our analysis is to determine what value the equity investors see in this potential buyout today. Or, better, when the deal was announced, what value did they see in the business on that day? As time goes on and we get closer to the close date, we can just simply update the model with new numbers as they are reported. So, since our LTM end date is January 2013, the next projected year (year 1 of the transaction) will be January 2014, and so on.

Making projections is no easy task. One needs to spend much time understanding and researching the core business model, how it generates revenue, its cost structure, and beyond to best get a handle on the next years of its performance. Ideally, a Wall Street research analyst will have had years of experience following and keeping close watch on the business and would have a good handle on its future trends in order to make good projections. That being said, there are methods to make fair generalizations, albeit broad, but strong enough to use as tools to assess overall company valuation. Remember, a good model is a functional and flexible one—one that is designed to be adjusted easily, to grow, and to evolve as we gain more knowledge and insight into the inner workings of the business, therefore slowly homing in on a perfect valuation.

Revenue

Revenue, for example, can be quite difficult to predict. Heinz posted $11,649.1 million in 2012 revenue, an 8.8 percent increase from 2011. How will we know what revenue will be in 2013? Or 2014? The truth is, it is almost impossible to be 100 percent sure. We will need to make an assumption with the understanding that that assumption will come with a degree of uncertainty, and may therefore change.

So how can we best make rational predictions for the next years? It is important to research and understand the company's business model, gathering as much information as we can to make our own best judgment. Revenue, for example, is almost always driven by a product of pricing and volume. So, when thinking about projecting revenue, our research should focus on understanding the company's pricing and volume. What initiatives are the new buyers going to take to increase its volume in the next years? Will they be increasing advertising? Will they continue to acquire other businesses or customers? Will they pursue efforts to find synergies and reduce costs? In addition to the previous research, we recommend the following five sources to better understand the business model:

1. *Investor presentations.* Try to look for a recent investor presentation in the investor relations section of the company website. These presentations

are typically designed to explain recent and future performance to existing or future investors in the company's stock. These presentations can contain high-level projections.

2. *Earnings calls.* One can easily find when the next earnings call will be in the investor relations section of the website. During the earnings call you can listen to the management speak about the company's most recent performance. Management sometimes gives guidance on the company's future performance.

3. *Wall Street research.* If you can get your hands on an equity research report, written by a Wall Street analyst who has followed the company for several years, that report would contain estimated future performance.

4. *Fairness opinions.* Company proxy reports may contain what is called a fairness opinion, which is a valuation of the business by a third-party source such as an investment bank. Such fairness opinions contain a business model, which should have projections. We illustrate this in Chapter 13.

5. *Data sources.* Yahoo! Finance, Thomson First Call, and Bloomberg are examples of data sources that contain Wall Street consensus estimates. Yahoo! Finance is a free resource, so, if you do not have access to a paid service, this can serve as a good reference.

These are just a few examples of where one can get guidance. We recommend not depending on any single source of information, but gathering as many sources as you can and cross-checking with your research to make the strongest educated estimates possible.

For purposes of this analysis, and knowing that the research can take a considerable amount of time, we can make a first guess assumption and leave the detailed research for once the model is complete. We can, for example, assume the revenue will continue to grow at its historical rates. Notice that the Heinz revenue has grown at 8.8 percent from 2011 to 2012. How has the growth been for the next nine months to date? We can look at the revenue growth from 2012 to LTM as a rough indicator.

Calculating LTM Revenue Growth (Cell I7)

Excel Keystrokes	Description
Type "="	Enters into "formula" mode
Select Cell I6	LTM revenue
Type "/"	Divide
Select Cell F6	2012 revenue
Type "-1"	Subtracts 1
Hit Enter	End
Formula result	=I6/F6-1

This gives us 0.4 percent growth. That's very low compared to the year before. This is quite unusual and would warrant further research to see why the growth has reduced.

We can get an indication of what other Wall Street analysts say about the future performance of Heinz. An easy and free data source is Yahoo! Finance. One can, for example, go to http://finance.yahoo.com and type in "HNZ," the ticker for Heinz, in the "Finance Search" bar. There is a lot of great information here that can be used as a first cut. It is not the best source, but it is a free source, so it is a good starting point. On the left, we can select "Analyst Estimates." Note that once the acquisition closes, the company will be private and public company information may no longer exist. If that is the case, please refer to Figure 5.7.

This data is a consensus by several Wall Street analysts who follow Heinz. The second box from the top, entitled "Revenue Est," gives us the consensus revenue. On the far right, we can see that the average revenue estimate for next year is $11.73 billion. Note that our LTM data is not from the same exact time frame that the analysts are referring to, but the analyst estimates do give us an indication that even Wall Street is not expecting the high growth seen in prior years. If you look to the bottom of the revenue estimates table, there is an average estimated sales growth assumption. For the current year, that assumption is 0.7 percent, much lower than the previous year's 8.8 percent.

We can also look at the latest quarterly press release to see if it discusses year-to-date statistics. In the investor relations section of the Heinz website, there is a menu option for "Press Room." If we scroll down, we see several press releases, including this one, dated February 21, 2013:

Heinz Reports Third-Quarter EPS from Continuing Operations, Excluding Special Items, of $0.99 ($0.95 Reported)

(http://news.heinz.com/press-release/finance/heinz-reports-third-quarter-eps-continuing-operations-excluding-special-items-)

This can also be found on the book's website. I would recommend spending a few minutes reading that press release. You should find the following section key to understanding year-to-date performance.

Heinz Q3 Press Release
Year-to-Date—Continuing Operations
For the nine months ended January 27, 2013, sales of $8.54 billion increased 0.5% on a reported basis and 3.7% on an organic basis.

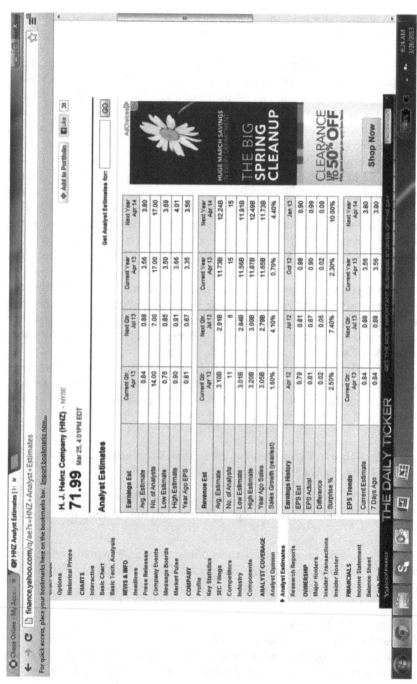

FIGURE 5.7 Yahoo! Finance HNZ Estimates

Operating income was $1.28 billion, an increase of 9.4%. Excluding special items, operating income was $1.29 billion, up 0.9%. Net income from continuing operations was $889 million, up 15.8%. Excluding special items, net income from continuing operations was $901 million, an increase of 6.8%.

The year-to-date tax rate was 15.9% versus 19.7% last year. Heinz reported diluted earnings per share from continuing operations of $2.75, an increase of 16.0%. Excluding special items, diluted earnings per share from continuing operations was $2.79, an increase of 7.3%.

EPS in the first nine months of this year was reduced by $0.06 from unfavorable foreign currency translation.

Including discontinued operations, Heinz reported total Company net income of $817 million and EPS of $2.53 in the first nine months of this year.

So, interestingly enough, Heinz states year-to-date revenue growth has been only 0.5 percent.

Now let's take a look at 2014. The 2014 average Street estimated revenue growth (see Figure 5.7), is 4.4 percent. However, look at the low and high estimate range. The low is $11.81 billion and the high is $12.49 billion. It's interesting to note that the $11.81 billion low estimate is 0.7 percent greater than the 2013 estimate of $11.73 billion. It looks, then, like some analysts are not expecting growth to improve, whereas others are expecting an improvement. In comparison, the low and high estimated range for 2013 was not as wide as the 2014 range.

We can take either the LTM growth rate of 0.4 percent or the Street range from the low of 0.7 percent to a high of 6.5 percent (12.49Bn / 11.73Bn − 1). Let's stay conservative and keep our estimates at the LTM level for now. It could be wise to create conservative and aggressive revenue scenarios that are adjustable to see how an increase in revenue would impact model results.

We can enter our estimated 0.4 percent assumptions into the model. Let's type "0.4%" into Cell J7; "0.4%" is a hard code and an assumption driver, so remember to color the font blue. This percent will drive the actual 2014 revenue projection. We want the 2014 revenue to be driven off of our assumption, or:

$$\text{2014 Revenue} = \text{LTM Revenue} \times (1 + \text{2014 Revenue Growth Assumption})$$

TABLE 5.12   Heinz Projected Revenue

Consolidated Income Statements (in US$ millions except per share amounts)					
			Estimates		
Period Ending	2014E	2015E	2016E	2017E	2018E
Revenue	$11,738.3	$11,785.2	$11,832.3	$11,879.7	$11,927.2
Y/Y revenue					
growth (%)	0.4%	0.4%	0.4%	0.4%	0.4%

Calculating 2014 Revenue (Cell J6)

Excel Keystrokes	Description
Type "="	Enters into "formula" mode
Select Cell I6	LTM revenue
Type "*"	Multiplies
Type "(1 + "	Begins the (1 + x%) portion of the formula
Select Cell J7	2014 revenue growth assumption
Type ")"	Closes the (1 + x%) portion of the formula
Hit Enter	End
Formula result	"=I6*(1 + J7)"

This will give us 2014 revenue of $11,738.3.

Let's assume the growth will be the same for now to keep the model simple. But we will make adjustments once the model is complete. So, we can copy Cells J6 and J7 to the right all the way through 2018. See Table 5.12.

Cost of Goods Sold

Next let's look at the costs. Again, fully understanding and researching each cost is important in best estimating its future performance. However, such detail may be as difficult to project as the revenue. It is first important to consider whether the costs are fixed or variable. A fixed cost is relatively static and may grow a certain percentage year over year. Rent, for example, can be considered a fixed cost as it may increase only 5 to 10 percent each year, independent of the growth in revenue. In contrast, a variable cost will increase in direct proportion to the growth of the business, most commonly determined by the revenue growth. In other words, if the revenue is increasing by 10 percent, the variable costs will also increase by 10 percent. If the revenue decreases by 4 percent, the variable costs will also decrease by 4 percent.

Quite often cost of goods sold is considered a variable cost. If your revenue is declining, you are most likely selling less product, so your costs should also be decreasing. Or conversely, if your revenue is increasing, you are most likely selling more product, so cost of goods sold should be increasing in direct proportion to the revenue. There are, however, exceptions. For example, revenue increase could be due to an increase in pricing, not because more product has been sold. In this case maybe costs should not be increasing at all; there is no change in volume. Or, a further twist, maybe the company is raising its prices because the manufacturer that is providing raw materials has raised its prices, so effectively both revenue and costs should be increasing at the same rate. This is where a deeper understanding of the company's business model and cost structure comes in handy.

Historical trends can help us determine how best to make initial projections, with the knowledge that we can later tweak as we build a more fundamental understanding of the business. If we analyze the historical cost of goods sold as a percentage of revenue over the past three years, we notice the costs have been around 60 percent to 63 percent of revenue each year. This consistent trend is a strong indicator that the cost of goods sold could be variable, growing at the same rate as revenue. If the percentages had not been consistent over the past three years, further research would need to be done to better understand the reasons for the variability. The company could have significantly changed its business model or taken other initiatives to significantly increase or decrease its costs in relation to its revenue. In that case, one could listen to the last earnings call or earnings release to get management's views on whether cost of goods sold is expected to increase or to decrease.

Since we have readjusted our financials, I prefer to take the LTM rate as long as it is still within the historical range. So let's take 61.6 percent as the projection for 2014 to 2018. We can hard-code "61.6%" into Cell J9 as our assumption driver. The formula for projecting cost of goods sold in 2014 will be:

$$2014 \text{ COGS} = 2014 \text{ COGS as a \% of Revenue} \times 2014 \text{ Revenue}$$

Calculating 2014 COGS (Cell J8)

Excel Keystrokes	Description
Type "="	Enters into "formula" mode
Select Cell J9	2014 COGS as a % of revenue
Type "*"	Multiplies
Select Cell J6	2014 revenue
Hit Enter	End
Formula result	"=J9*J6"

TABLE 5.13 Heinz Projected Gross Profit

(in US$ millions except per share amounts)					
			Estimates		
Period Ending	2014E	2015E	2016E	2017E	2018E
Revenue	$11,738.3	$11,785.2	$11,832.3	$11,879.7	$11,927.2
Y/Y revenue growth (%)	0.4%	0.4%	0.4%	0.4%	0.4%
Cost of goods sold	7,230.8	7,259.7	7,288.7	7,317.9	7,347.2
COGS as a % of revenue	61.6%	61.6%	61.6%	61.6%	61.6%
Gross profit	$ 4,507.5	$ 4,525.5	$ 4,543.6	$ 4,561.8	$ 4,580.0
Gross profit margin (%)	38.4%	38.4%	38.4%	38.4%	38.4%

This will give us 2014 COGS of $7,230.8. We can copy Cells J8 and J9 to the right all the way through 2018. We can also calculate future gross profit and the gross profit margin. We have already calculated these formulas in the LTM column, so we can just copy Cells I10 and I11 through 2018 as well. See Table 5.13.

Operating Expenses

This same procedure can be repeated for each cost on the income statement: conducting adequate research, analyzing the historical trends, and considering whether each cost is fixed or variable in order to best determine which of the five methods should be used to project the costs forward.

Let's analyze the company's operating (selling, general, and administrative) expenses. If we look at the historical expense as a percentage of revenue over the past three years, we notice the costs were 21.3 percent, 21.5 percent, 21.9 percent, and 22.0 percent for 2010, 2011, and 2012, and LTM, respectively. Again, we can take the LTM percentage as our future assumption for 2014 to 2018.

Note that I am recommending hard-coding "22.0%" directly into Cell J14. Some people like to link Cell J14 directly to Cell I14 (i.e., J14 = "I14"). If you do so you will have slightly different numbers due to rounding. So for purposes of clarity I am recommending just simply hard-coding "22.0%."

2014 SG&A = 2014 SG&A as a % of Revenue × 2014 Revenue

Calculating 2014 SG&A (Cell J13)

Excel Keystrokes	Description
Type "="	Enters into "formula" mode
Select Cell J14	2014 SG&A as a percentage of revenue
Type "*"	Multiplies
Select Cell J6	2014 revenue
Hit Enter	End
Formula result	"=J14*J6"

This gives us $2,582.4 in 2014. We can copy Cells J13 and J14 to the right.

Fund Management Fee

We mentioned earlier that the fund management fee is the annual fee investment funds charge themselves (for example, 1.0x or 1.5x a CEO's salary) while owning the business. We have no indication yet of what type of management fee (if any) 3G or Berkshire Hathaway will charge, and if they do, it will most likely be a nominal amount in relation to the over $2Bn of EBITDA the company is producing. This amount could be more significant in smaller buyouts, but it's important to mention this potential charge for instructional purposes. Let's leave it $0 for now.

Cost Savings

Cost savings, also known as cost synergies, are cost reductions due to operating improvements implemented after the purchase. As of now we have no indication of what cost reductions are planned to be achieved. Cost savings are very difficult to predict and even harder to realize. In smaller businesses they are scrutinized line item by line item. For example, if after an acquisition a CEO's salary will be reduced by half, you would naturally incorporate that adjustment into the model. But for larger businesses whose cost savings can span many different areas of operations, it may be more efficient to assume a small percentage of operating expenses or SG&A (0.5 percent to 3 percent, for example). This depends on not only how much cost savings you believe will be needed, but how much can actually be implemented.

We could be extremely conservative and assume $0 cost savings, but incorporating a modest amount will illustrate the use of such cost reductions. So, although we have absolutely no indication of cost savings at this point, let's assume that 1 percent of SG&A will be reduced. So, we can hard-code "1%" into Cell J17. We can then multiply by the SG&A to get a measure of cost reductions. However, since these reductions are reducing our expenses, we want to show these values as a negative.

Calculating 2014 Cost Savings (Cell J16)

Excel Keystrokes	Description
Type "="	Enters into "formula" mode
Type "-"	Negates the result
Select Cell J17	2014 cost savings as a % of SG&A
Type "*"	Multiplies
Select Cell J13	2014 SG&A
Hit Enter	End
Formula result	"=-J17*J13"

This gives us $25.8 million in expected cost savings. Again, we can adjust this if we hear more news about potential improvements. We can copy Cells J16 and J17 to the right through 2018.

We can also copy the total operating expenses formula from Cell I18 to the right through 2018.

Other Income

We mentioned earlier that Heinz does not separate other income into a separate line item and we have no further detail on such income. So, we can continue to hard-code this forward as zero through 2018.

We can copy the EBITDA and EBITDA margin percent formulas, Cells J21 and J22, to the right through 2018 as well. We now have a Heinz model complete up through EBITDA (see Table 5.14).

Depreciation and Amortization

When building a complete financial model, it is recommended to leave projected depreciation and amortization empty for now. We will build a depreciation schedule, which will contain projected depreciation and amortization expenses to be linked in here. We will also discuss the amortization of intangible assets later in Chapter 8, "Balance Sheet Adjustments." We can, however, copy the total depreciation and amortization, EBIT, and EBIT margin percent formulas, Cells I26, I27, and I28, to the right through 2018.

Interest Income

When building a complete financial model, it is recommended to leave projected interest expense and interest income empty. We will build a debt schedule, which will help us better project interest expense and interest income to be linked in here. We can, however, copy the net interest expense, EBT, and EBT margin percent formulas, Cells I32, I33, and I34, to the right through 2018.

TABLE 5.14 Heinz Projected EBITDA

Consolidated Income Statements (in US$ millions except per share amounts)

Period Ending	Estimates				
	2014E	2015E	2016E	2017E	2018E
Revenue	$11,738.3	$11,785.2	$11,832.3	$11,879.7	$11,927.2
Y/Y revenue growth (%)	0.4%	0.4%	0.4%	0.4%	0.4%
Cost of goods sold	7,230.8	7,259.7	7,288.7	7,317.9	7,347.2
COGS as a % of revenue	61.6%	61.6%	61.6%	61.6%	61.6%
Gross profit	$ 4,507.5	$ 4,525.5	$ 4,543.6	$ 4,561.8	$ 4,580.0
Gross profit margin (%)	38.4%	38.4%	38.4%	38.4%	38.4%
Operating expenses					
Selling, general, and administrative	2,582.4	2,592.7	2,603.1	2,613.5	2,624.0
SG&A as a % of revenue	22.0%	22.0%	22.0%	22.0%	22.0%
Fund management fee	0.0	0.0	0.0	0.0	0.0
Cost savings	(25.8)	(25.9)	(26.0)	(26.1)	(26.2)
Cost savings as a % of SG&A	1.0%	1.0%	1.0%	1.0%	1.0%
Total operating expenses	$ 2,556.6	$ 2,566.8	$ 2,577.1	$ 2,587.4	$ 2,597.7
Other income	0.0	0.0	0.0	0.0	0.0
Equity in earnings of unconsolidated affiliates					
EBITDA	$ 1,950.9	$ 1,958.7	$ 1,966.5	$ 1,974.4	$ 1,982.3
EBITDA margin (%)	16.6%	16.6%	16.6%	16.6%	16.6%

Taxes

We can take a look at the historical tax percentages to estimate our projections. Our implied LTM tax rate calculated was 17.3 percent and in 2012, Heinz paid 20.6 percent in taxes. These tax rates do seem low. It is helpful to take a look at the tax rates in 2010 and 2011, which were 27.8 percent and 26.8 percent, respectively. So, it does look like 2012 was unusually low. What adds more complexity to this situation is that once Heinz potentially is purchased, the entity will change; it will become a private entity. This may affect the way that entity is taxed.

Further research reveals the following note found in the Heinz annual report:

> The effective tax rate for Fiscal 2012 was 20.6 percent. Excluding charges for productivity initiatives, the effective tax rate was 21.7 percent in the current year compared to 26.8 percent last year. The decrease in the effective tax rate is primarily the result of the increased benefits from the revaluation of the tax basis of foreign assets, the reversal of an uncertain tax position liability due to the expiration of the statute of limitations in a foreign tax jurisdiction, the beneficial resolution of a foreign tax case, and lower tax on the income of foreign subsidiaries primarily resulting from a statutory tax rate reduction in the U.K. These benefits were partially offset by the current year expense for changes in valuation allowances.

(Heinz Annual Report, page 14)

The note reveals that there were some benefits that resulted in a lower tax rate. But we are still unsure if these benefits will remain in the newly restructured entity. Further research reveals another helpful table from page 47 of the annual report. See Figure 5.8.

The differences between the U.S. federal statutory tax rate and the Company's consolidated effective tax rate on continuing operations are as follows:

	2012	2011	2010
U.S. federal statutory tax rate	35.0%	35.0%	35.0%
Tax on income of foreign subsidiaries	(8.7)	(5.6)	(4.3)
Changes in valuation allowances	2.6	(0.2)	0.2
Earnings repatriation	2.1	3.0	1.2
Tax-free interest	(5.6)	(4.2)	(4.6)
Effects of revaluation of tax basis of foreign assets	(3.3)	(1.6)	(0.5)
Audit settlements and changes in uncertain tax positions	(2.1)	—	(1.3)
Other	0.6	0.4	2.1
Effective tax rate	20.6%	26.8%	27.8%

FIGURE 5.8   Heinz Annual Income Tax

Figure 5.8 explains the breakdown of how Heinz arrived at the 20.6 percent rate from the standard 35 percent rate. According to this table, if we removed the "Effects of revaluation of tax basis of foreign assets" 3.3 percent reduction and the apparently one-off "Audit settlements and changes in uncertain tax positions" of 2.1 percent, we would get a 26.0 percent tax rate.

The highest rate we have is the 2010 rate of 27.8 percent. This is similar to the 26.0 percent rate. We could take the 35 percent U.S. federal statutory tax rate, but that may be too conservative. Some of the aforementioned deductions may carry into the new entity. Let's use the 27.8 percent rate, as it is the maximum rate we had calculated in the model. So it is the most conservative from our historical analysis, but not as conservative as the 35 percent federal rate. At the end of the analysis, you can always see how increasing the tax rate to 35 percent can affect the analysis results. Let's hard-code "27.8%" into Cell J36.

Calculating 2014 Income Tax Expense (Cell J35)

Excel Keystrokes	Description
Type "="	Enters into "formula" mode
Select Cell J36	2014 tax rate percent
Type "*"	Multiplies
Select Cell J33	2014 EBT
Hit Enter	End
Formula result	"=J36*J33"

This gives us an income tax expense of $542.3. We can copy Cells J35 and J36 to the right through 2018.

Cell I37, net income (adjusted) can also be copied through 2018.

Nonrecurring Events and Extraordinary Items

These items are either extraordinary or nonrecurring. If they are nonrecurring, they will likely not exist in the future. If they are extraordinary, we may still want to project them; however, we note they are not core to the business's operations.

Other expense includes items such as currency adjustments that do seem to be recurring. Projecting such "other" line items may be difficult, especially if it is unclear exactly what these items are made up of. This happens more often in the cash flow statement, and in Chapter 6 we discuss more structured methods to project such "other" line items. We recommend a conservative approach, so let's assume the greatest expense of the previous years in our analysis will be next year's expenses. It just so happens that the greatest expense is also the 19.1 we calculated for the LTM. Let's hard-code "19.1" as our assumption for the years 2014 through 2018.

The loss from discontinued operations occurred only in the nine-month 2012 and 2013 quarterly reports and not in the 2012 annual report, which is a bit odd. This could mean that the reporting was different in the annual report than in the quarterly report. We have tried researching further but have found no other disclosure. We also do not see it in 2011, but it does occur in 2010. Let's assume for now this is not a recurring expense and hard-code it "0." This is something that could be investigated further, but it does not have a huge impact on the overall net income, so let's leave it at "0" for now.

We can also continue to leave Rows 41 and 42 as zero.

Cells I43 and I44, total nonrecurring events and net income (after non-recurring events), can be copied through 2018.

Noncontrolling Interest, Shares, and Earnings per Share

Because in a leveraged buyout analysis the company is taken private, all equity holders will be bought out. There is a possibility that noncontrolling interest holders will be carried over to the new business, but the nature of their equity will most likely be renegotiated and will change. We had conducted some preliminary research and it appears some of the minority holders may be carried over to the new entity, but it is uncertain and the effects to the net income are quite small. So let's not consider projecting these items in the future right now. We will also see the returns to Berkshire and 3G (the goal of this case) won't be heavily affected by these less significant line items. We can simply leave them out or hard-code them "0." We are done here. See Table 5.15.

Also note that Appendix 1 lists out detailed model-building steps in a leveraged buyout analysis. Refer to Appendix 1 often to ensure you are following the model building path.

TABLE 5.15 Heinz Projected Income Statement

Consolidated Income Statements (in US$ millions except per share amounts)

			Estimates			
Period Ending	2014E	2015E	2016E	2017E	2018E	
Revenue	$11,738.3	$11,785.2	$11,832.3	$11,879.7	$11,927.2	
Y/Y revenue growth (%)	*0.4%*	*0.4%*	*0.4%*	*0.4%*	*0.4%*	
Cost of goods sold	7,230.8	7,259.7	7,288.7	7,317.9	7,347.2	
COGS as a % of revenue	*61.6%*	*61.6%*	*61.6%*	*61.6%*	*61.6%*	
Gross profit	$4,507.5	$4,525.5	$4,543.6	$4,561.8	$4,580.0	
Gross profit margin (%)	*38.4%*	*38.4%*	*38.4%*	*38.4%*	*38.4%*	
Operating expenses						
Selling, general, and administrative	2,582.4	2,592.7	2,603.1	2,613.5	2,624.0	
SG&A as a % of revenue	*22.0%*	*22.0%*	*22.0%*	*22.0%*	*22.0%*	
Fund management fee	0.0	0.0	0.0	0.0	0.0	
Cost savings	(25.8)	(25.9)	(26.0)	(26.1)	(26.2)	
Cost savings as a % of SG&A	*1.0%*	*1.0%*	*1.0%*	*1.0%*	*1.0%*	
Total operating expenses	$2,556.6	$2,566.8	$2,577.1	$2,587.4	$2,597.7	
Other income						
Equity in earnings of unconsolidated affiliates	0.0	0.0	0.0	0.0	0.0	
EBITDA	$1,950.9	$1,958.7	$1,966.5	$1,974.4	$1,982.3	
EBITDA margin (%)	*16.6%*	*16.6%*	*16.6%*	*16.6%*	*16.6%*	
Depreciation						
Amortization						
Amortization of identifiable intangible assets						
Total depreciation and amortization	$ 0.0	$ 0.0	$ 0.0	$ 0.0	$ 0.0	
EBIT	1,950.9	1,958.7	1,966.5	1,974.4	1,982.3	
EBIT margin (%)	*16.6%*	*16.6%*	*16.6%*	*16.6%*	*16.6%*	

(continued)

TABLE 5.15 (Continued)

Consolidated Income Statements (in US$ millions except per share amounts)

Period Ending	Estimates				
	2014E	2015E	2016E	2017E	2018E
Interest					
Interest expense					
Interest income					
Net interest expense	$ 0.0	$ 0.0	$ 0.0	$ 0.0	$ 0.0
EBT	1,950.9	1,958.7	1,966.5	1,974.4	1,982.3
EBT margin (%)	16.6%	16.6%	16.6%	16.6%	16.6%
Income tax expense	542.3	544.5	546.7	548.9	551.1
All-in effective tax rate (%)	27.8%	27.8%	27.8%	27.8%	27.8%
Net income (adjusted)	$ 1,408.5	$ 1,414.2	$ 1,419.8	$ 1,425.5	$ 1,431.2
Nonrecurring events					
Other expense, net	19.1	19.1	19.1	19.1	19.1
Loss from discontinued operations, net of tax	0.0	0.0	0.0	0.0	0.0
Effect of accounting changes	0.0	0.0	0.0	0.0	0.0
Extraordinary items, net of tax	0.0	0.0	0.0	0.0	0.0
Total nonrecurring events	$ 19.1	$ 19.1	$ 19.1	$ 19.1	$ 19.1
Net income (after nonrecurring events)	$ 1,389.4	$ 1,395.1	$ 1,400.7	$ 1,406.4	$ 1,412.1
Net income attributable to noncontrolling interests	0.0	0.0	0.0	0.0	0.0
Net income (as reported)					
Earnings per share (EPS)					
Basic					
Diluted					
Average common shares outstanding					
Basic					
Diluted					

CHAPTER 6

The Cash Flow Statement

The cash flow statement is a measure of how much cash a company has produced or spent over a period of time. Although an income statement shows profitability, that profit may or may not result in actual cash gain. This is because many income statement items that are recorded do not necessarily result in an effect on cash. For example, when a sale is made, a customer can pay in cash or on credit. If a company has $10 million in sales and all customers have paid in cash, then the company has actually generated $10 million in cash. But if a company has $10 million in sales on credit, then although the revenue has been recorded on the income statement, cash has not been received. The cash flow statement aims to determine how much cash the company actually generated, which is broken out into three segments:

1. Cash from operating activities.
2. Cash from investing activities.
3. Cash from financing activities.

The sum of all the cash generated (or spent) from operating activities, from investing activities, and from financing activities results in the total amount of cash spent or received in a given period.

CASH FLOW FROM OPERATING ACTIVITIES

Cash flow from operating activities is a representation of how much cash has been generated from net income or profit. We explained earlier how revenue could be received in cash or on credit. As revenue is a source of income, if a portion of that revenue is on credit, we need to make an adjustment to net income based on how much of that revenue is actually cash. Similarly, expenses recorded on the income statement could be cash expenses (they have been paid) or noncash expenses (they have not been paid). Let's take a billing invoice on an operating expense such as office supplies as an example. Once the invoice is received (a bill we have to pay), we would need to record this on the income statement, even if we had not actually paid that bill yet. Having this expense on our income statement would bring our profitability down. But, when looking at cash available, that bill should not be included, as we have not paid it. So, for cash flow from operations, we would add that expense back to the net income, effectively reversing the expense effects.

Example:

Income Statement	
Revenue (collected in cash)	$10,000,000.0
SG&A (invoice we did not pay)	2,000,000.0
Net Income	8,000,000.0
Cash Flow	
Net Income	$ 8,000,000.0
Add back SG&A	2,000,000.0
Cash from Operations	10,000,000.0

This should make logical sense. We've collected $10 million in cash from our sales; we received an invoice of $2 million, but we did not pay that invoice. The invoice is expensed properly on the income statement, but we do not want to include that in our cash analysis, as it did not yet affect our cash. So, we add that expense back to the net income. The cash from operations rightfully shows that we still have $10 million in cash.

Now, let's say of the $10 million in revenue, only $8 million was cash sales, and $2 million was sold on credit. The income statement looks exactly the same, but the cash flow statement is different. If we had collected only $8 million of that $10 million of revenue in cash, then we would need to subtract the $2 million of revenue we did not collect from the net income. So:

Income Statement	
Revenue (only $8MM collected in cash)	$10,000,000.0
SG&A (invoice we did not pay)	2,000,000.0
Net Income	8,000,000.0
Cash Flow	
Net Income	$ 8,000,000.0
Subtract revenue we did not collect in cash	(2,000,000.0)
Add back SG&A we did not pay	2,000,000.0
Cash from Operations	8,000,000.0

This analysis may seem trivial, but it is important to understand the methodology as we apply this to more complex income statements. In general, cash from operating activities is generated by taking net income and removing all the noncash items.

Or, in its most fundamental form, cash from operations as demonstrated is:

Net Income + Expenses we did not pay – Revenue we did not receive

But it gets slightly more complex. To understand this completely, let's take a look at all of the components of an income statement and determine which items can be considered cash and which are noncash.

Revenue

As we had explained previously, if revenue is received on credit, this would be removed from net income. The portion of revenue received on credit is called **accounts receivable**.

Cost of Goods Sold

Cost of goods sold (COGS) is the inventory costs related to the item sold. If it costs $50 to make a chair, for example, and we sell that chair for $100, then for each chair sold, we will record a $50 expense related to the manufacturing cost of the product; this is cost of goods sold. However, we must also reduce our inventory balance by $50 for each chair sold. A reduction in inventory results in a positive cash inflow in the cash from operations section on the cash flow statement. We will illustrate examples of this in the next section.

Operating Expenses

As explained previously with the $2 million invoice, if an expense received had not been paid, this would be added back to net income. The portion of operating expenses that has not been paid is called **accrued expenses**.

Depreciation

Depreciation is an expense that is never actually paid. As described earlier, it is accounting for the aging of assets. So, like any expense that is not cash, we add it back to net income when calculating cash flow from operations.

Interest

Interest expense is almost always paid in cash. There can be certain complex debt instruments that are exceptions, but if a company cannot pay its interest, then generally it is considered defaulting on its debt. So, for this reason, we almost always consider interest as cash. Therefore, we would not add it back to net income in the cash flow statement.

Taxes

Taxes can be deferred in some situations, which will be discussed later. The portion of taxes that we expensed but did not yet pay is referred to as deferred taxes.

Table 6.1 summarizes the most common income statement line items and the related accounts if they can be deferred.

TABLE 6.1   Most Common Income Statement Line Items

Net Income Line Item	Possible Deferrable Items?	Effect on Cash from Operations
Revenue	Yes	Changes in accounts receivable
Cost of Goods Sold	Yes	Changes in inventory Changes in accounts payable
Operating Expenses	Yes	Changes in accrued expenses Changes in prepaid expenses
Depreciation	Yes	Depreciation
Interest	No	None (some exceptions)
Taxes	Yes	Deferred taxes

Keeping with the theme demonstrated previously, where we adjust the related revenue and expense items we did not pay or receive in cash from net income to get a measure of cash generated or spent, we can generalize this table toward cash flow from operating activities:

Cash from Operating Activities = Net Income + Changes in Accounts Receivable + Changes in Inventory + Changes in Accounts Payable + Changes in Accrued Expenses + Changes in Prepaid Expenses+ Depreciation + Deferred Taxes

Although we will discuss this later, there is a definition for Changes in Accounts Receivable + Changes in Inventory + Changes in Accounts Payable + Changes in Accrued Expenses + Changes in Prepaid Expenses called **changes in operating working capital,** so we can rework the formula:

Cash from Operating Activities = Net Income + Depreciation + Deferred Taxes + Changes in Operating Working Capital

Note the actual changes in each individual line item could be positive or negative. This will be explained in Chapter 10, Working Capital.

To be complete, cash from operating activities should include adjustments based on any and all income statement line items that are noncash. So, you may see "+ Other Noncash Items" toward the end of the formula to capture those adjustments.

Cash from Operating Activities = Net Income + Depreciation + Deferred Taxes + Other Noncash Items + Changes in Operating Working Capital

The important lesson here is to gain the conceptual understanding of how cash from operating activities is derived from the income statement. As we get into more complex case studies and analyses, and for due diligence purposes, you will learn that it is important to understand cash flow as derived from individual income statement line items, rather than memorizing a standard formula. This is especially important in leveraged buyouts when analyzing smaller private companies that maybe do not have a complete set of financials. The ability to derive an operating working capital schedule and cash flow from operations from an income statement will be useful. This is just the fundamental beginning of such analyses.

CASH FLOW FROM INVESTING ACTIVITIES

Now that we have a measure of cash generated from our operations, there are two other areas from which cash can be generated or spent: investing activities and financing activities. Cash flow from investing activities is cash generated or spent from buying or selling assets, businesses, or other investments or securities. More specifically, the major categories are:

- Capital expenditures (investments in property, plant, and equipment).
- Buying or selling assets.
- Buying, selling, spinning off, or splitting off businesses or portions of business entities.
- Investing in or selling marketable and nonmarketable securities.

CASH FLOW FROM FINANCING ACTIVITIES

Cash flow from financing activities is defined as cash generated or spent from equity or debt. More specifically:

- Raising or buying back equity or preferred securities.
- Raising or paying back debt.
- Distributions to equity holders (noncontrolling interests and dividends).

The sum of the cash flow from operating activities, cash flow from investing activities, and cash flow from financing activities gives us a total measure of how much cash is generated or has been spent over a given period.

FINANCIAL STATEMENT FLOWS EXAMPLE

Let's take a second, slightly deeper example walking through a complete sale process. We are a new company interested in selling chairs, so we open up a local retail shop. We will sell each chair for $100. It will cost approximately $50 in raw material to create one chair. So the first thing we will do is purchase enough raw material to build 10 chairs ($500). The simple flows are:

Cash Flow			Balance Sheet	
Net Income		0.0	Cash	(500.0)
Changes in Inventory (Purchase of Chairs)	(500.0)		Inventory	500.0
Total Changes in Cash		(500.0)		

No income has been generated. Cash is negative, as we have spent money to pay for the inventory. An inventory asset has been created on the balance sheet. We will discuss the balance sheet in its entirety later.

Now the cash balance in the balance sheet is –$500. We clearly do not have cash to pay for these raw materials, but the vendor is allowing us to defer the money owed to him until we are able to come up with the cash. So, we incur a liability to the vendor called **accounts payable**.

The new flows will be:

Cash Flow			Balance Sheet	
Net Income		0.0	Cash	0.0
Changes in Inventory (Purchase of Chairs)	(500.0)		Inventory	500.0
Changes in Accounts Payable	500.0		Accounts Payable	500.0
Total Changes in Cash		0.0		

At the end of the transaction, the cash balance is zero, we have an asset of $500 in inventory, and we have a liability of $500 in payables due to the vendor.

Now, let's say one chair is sold for $100. Two things happen on the income statement:

1. Revenue is recorded for $100.
2. COGS is incurred of $50.

Let's walk through how each of these transactions flows through the income statement, cash flow statement, and balance sheet. It is recommended to focus on one transaction at a time, making sure each completely flows through all three statements before moving on to the next transaction.

If revenue is recorded at $100, then taxes are affected at, let's say, 40 percent; so taxes are $40, and the net income effect is $60:

Income Statement	
Revenue	100.0
Taxes (@ 40%)	(40.0)
Net Income	**60.0**

Next we move to the cash flow statement. Net income begins the cash flow statement, which is the $60 change. Nothing else on the cash flow statement is affected at this point, so the total cash change is $60. On the balance sheet, the change in cash will affect our cash balance, which is an asset. And the net income change, we will later learn, affects our retained earnings.

Cash Flow	
Net Income	60.0
Total Changes in Cash	**60.0**

Balance Sheet	
Cash	60.0
Inventory	500.0
Accounts Payable	500.0
Retained Earnings (Net Income)	60.0

Now let's look at the COGS, which incurs a cost of $50. Let's examine the financial statement adjustments based on the COGS to get a complete representation of the sale. So, in the income statement, we will incur an expense of $50. As expenses are tax deductible, taxes will be reduced by $20, resulting in a net income reduction of $30:

Income Statement	
COGS	(50.0)
Taxes (@ 40%)	20.0
Net Income	**(30.0)**

Next, we move to the cash flow statement, which starts with net income. COGS is related to inventory. We need to reduce the inventory asset on the balance sheet to reflect the $50 of raw materials that have been sold, which results in a positive cash adjustment. So we will add a "Changes in Inventory" line of $50:

Cash Flow	
Net Income	**(30.0)**
Changes in Inventory	50.0
Total Changes in Cash	**20.0**

Balance Sheet Adjustments	
Cash	20.0
Inventory	(50.0)
Retained Earnings (Net Income)	(30.0)

For the balance sheet, the cash change from before will increase the cash asset balance. Inventory will be reduced by $50 to reflect the raw materials sold. And the retained earnings will decrease by the net income change of –$30.

We can now combine this balance sheet adjustment with the total balance sheet.

Balance Sheet Adjustments	
Cash	20.0
Inventory	(50.0)
Retained Earnings (Net Income)	(30.0)

Balance Sheet	
Cash	80.0
Inventory	450.0
Accounts Payable	500.0
Retained Earnings (Net Income)	30.0

We will learn later what it means when we say the balance sheet balances. Here, it does balance, as the sum of the assets (80 + 450 = 530) less the liabilities (500) equals the shareholders' equity (30).

If you have little accounting experience, some of these adjustments may seem a bit confusing. Don't worry about this just yet. As you proceed through the next few chapters, especially Chapter 7, you will gain a clearer understanding of the balance sheet.

The previous sale was a cash sale. Let's now say that we have sold another chair, but this time the sale was on credit.

Income Statement	
Revenue	100.0
Taxes (@ 40%)	(40.0)
Net Income	**60.0**

Notice that the income statement looks the same whether the sale was made in cash or on credit. The cash flow statement will be a little different. If the customer pays on credit, then we need to make an adjustment to the cash flow statement, as we did not yet receive that cash. Effectively, we need to subtract the portion of revenue we did not yet receive in cash, and we will create an accounts receivable asset account in the cash flow statement and balance sheet to represent the money owed to us.

Cash Flow	
Net Income	60.0
Changes in Accounts Receivable	(100.0)
Total Changes in Cash	**(40.0)**

Balance Sheet Adjustments	
Cash	(40.0)
Accounts Receivable	100.0
Retained Earnings (Net Income)	60.0

Notice the total cash change is –$40, which reflects the taxes owed on the sale. Because we have recorded the sale, even though we did not receive the cash on that sale yet, we still incur and pay taxes on that sale.

We need to add these adjustments to the original balance sheet, giving us:

Balance Sheet Adjustments	
Cash	(40.0)
Accounts Receivable	100.0
Retained Earnings (Net Income)	60.0

Balance Sheet	
Cash	40.0
Inventory	450.0
Accounts Receivable	100.0
Accounts Payable	500.0
Retained Earnings (Net Income)	90.0

So the cash balance, which was previously $80, has been reduced to $40, an accounts receivable account has been created, and the retained earnings increase from $30 to $90.

We can now make the adjustments to the COGS and inventory.

Income Statement	
COGS	(50.0)
Taxes (@ 40%)	20.0
Net Income	**(30.0)**

Cash Flow	
Net Income	**(30.0)**
Changes in Inventory	50.0
Total Changes in Cash	**20.0**

Balance Sheet Adjustments	
Cash	20.0
Inventory	(50.0)
Retained Earnings (Net Income)	(30.0)

And we can update the balance sheet:

Balance Sheet Adjustments	
Cash	20.0
Inventory	(50.0)
Retained Earnings (Net Income)	(30.0)

Balance Sheet	
Cash	60.0
Inventory	400.0
Accounts Receivable	100.0
Accounts Payable	500.0
Retained Earnings (Net Income)	60.0

Notice that the COGS movements are also the same whether the purchase was made in cash or on credit. The balance sheet balances, as the sum of the assets (60 + 400 + 100 = 560) less the liabilities (500) equals the shareholders' equity (60).

Now let's say we have sold the remaining eight chairs, four of which have been sold on credit. The income statement is:

Income Statement	
Revenue	800.0
Taxes (@ 40%)	(320.0)
Net Income	**480.0**

Since four of the chairs were sold on credit, we need to remove the $400 from net income on the cash flow statement and adjust for the balance sheet.

Cash Flow			Balance Sheet Adjustments	
Net Income	480.0		Cash	80.0
Changes in Accounts Receivable	(400.0)		Accounts Receivable	400.0
Total Changes in Cash	**80.0**		Retained Earnings (Net Income)	480.0

So adding these balance sheet adjustments to the total balance sheet gives us:

Balance Sheet Adjustments			Balance Sheet	
Cash	80.0		Cash	140.0
Accounts Receivable	400.0		Inventory	400.0
Retained Earnings (Net Income)	480.0		Accounts Receivable	500.0
			Accounts Payable	500.0
			Retained Earnings (Net Income)	540.0

We can now make the adjustments for the COGS and inventory associated with the sale, which is $400. Remember, regardless of whether the sale is made in cash or on credit, we still need to adjust for the COGS and removal of inventory.

Income Statement	
COGS	(400.0)
Taxes (@ 40%)	160.0
Net Income	**(240.0)**

Now we need to remove the $400 from inventory, which results in a positive cash adjustment on the cash flow statement. For the balance sheet we need to adjust the inventory and cash accordingly.

Cash Flow			Balance Sheet Adjustments	
Net Income	**(240.0)**		Cash	160.0
Changes in Inventory	400.0		Inventory	(400.0)
Total Changes in Cash	**160.0**		Retained Earnings (Net Income)	(240.0)

Adding these balance sheet adjustments to the total balance sheet gives us:

Balance Sheet Adjustments			Balance Sheet	
Cash	160.0		Cash	300.0
Inventory	(400.0)		Inventory	0.0
Retained Earnings (Net Income)	(240.0)		Accounts Receivable	500.0
			Accounts Payable	500.0
			Retained Earnings (Net Income)	300.0

So now we have sold our entire inventory. Notice that we have $500 in payables due, but only $300 in cash. If we had collected on the accounts receivable from our customers, we would not have this situation. So, let's assume we finally collect on all the accounts receivables and we can pay down the payables.

We collect $500 in accounts receivable:

Cash Flow		Balance Sheet Adjustments	
Net Income	0.0	Cash	500.0
Accounts Receivable	500.0	Accounts Receivable	(500.0)
Total Changes in Cash	**500.0**	Retained Earnings (Net Income)	0.0

The receivable asset goes away and cash is collected. So adding these balance sheet adjustments to the total balance sheet gives us:

Balance Sheet Adjustments		Balance Sheet	
Cash	500.0	Cash	800.0
Accounts Receivable	(500.0)	Inventory	0.0
Retained Earnings (Net Income)	0.0	Accounts Receivable	0.0
		Accounts Payable	500.0
		Retained Earnings (Net Income)	300.0

Notice we did not make any changes to the income statement, as we did not create any income-generating event here. We simply converted an asset into cash. We now have $800 in cash, enough to pay down our liabilities.

We pay $500 in liabilities:

Cash Flow		Balance Sheet Adjustments	
Net Income	0.0	Cash	(500.0)
Accounts Payable	(500.0)	Accounts Payable	(500.0)
Total Changes in Cash	**(500.0)**	Retained Earnings (Net Income)	0.0

Adding these balance sheet adjustments to the main balance sheet gives us:

Balance Sheet Adjustments		Balance Sheet	
Cash	(500.0)	Cash	300.0
Accounts Payable	(500.0)	Inventory	0.0
Retained Earnings (Net Income)	0.0	Accounts Receivable	0.0
		Accounts Payable	0.0
		Retained Earnings (Net Income)	300.0

We have collected all our assets and paid down all our liabilities. Notice that at $100 per chair and a cost of $50 per chair, selling 10 chairs nets us ($1,000 – $500) $500 pretax profit. At a 40 percent tax rate, tax is $200, so the net profit on that sale is $300 ($500 – $200), exactly the amount of cash and net income we have in the balance sheet.

Don't get discouraged if you did not understand this example completely. As you read on and gain a more fundamental understanding of the underlying concepts involved, the example will become clearer. I recommend revisiting this example a few times as you continue reading on.

HEINZ CASH FLOW STATEMENT

As done with the income statement, let's lay out the historical numbers for Heinz's cash flow before making projections. We want not only three years of historical numbers, but the last twelve months (LTM) numbers as well. Let's lay out the historical numbers first, and then go back and hard-code in the nine-month numbers as we had done with the income statement. The cash flow statement in the model begins in Row 53.

In the income statement, we have regrouped several of the line items, and extracted some other line items, to get to comparable metrics Wall Street analysts use for analysis such as earnings before interest, taxes, depreciation, and amortization (EBITDA). For the cash flow statement, it is recommended to lay out each item line by line. There may be a couple of line items we will make adjustments to later for more complex reasons, but at this point, keeping with this general rule is best. We will take the time to explain individual line items next. Heinz's cash flow statement can be found on page 38 of the Heinz annual report (see Figure 6.1).

Cash Flow from Operating Activities

As mentioned earlier, cash flow from operating activities is:

Cash flow from Operating Activities = Net Income +
Depreciation + Deferred Taxes + Other Noncash Items +
Changes in Operating Working Capital

We can certainly identify the top line item shown in Figure 6.1 as net income. The net income used in the cash flow statement is typically net income before dividend payments or noncontrolling interest distributions. The reason for this is that the cash flow from the financing activities section contains line items for removing such distributions. We need to start with net income before these distributions so as not to double-count removing those line items. Let's hard-code the net income into Row 58. We could have also just linked the net income numbers in from the income statement,

	Fiscal Year Ended		
	April 29, 2012	April 27, 2011	April 28, 2010
	(52 1/2 Weeks)	(52 Weeks)	(52 Weeks)
	(In thousands)		
Operating activities:			
Net income	$ 939,908	$ 1,005,948	$ 882,343
Adjustments to reconcile net income to cash provided by operating activities:			
Depreciation	295,718	255,227	254,528
Amortization	47,075	43,433	48,308
Deferred tax (benefit)/provision	(94,816)	153,725	220,528
Net losses on divestitures	—	—	44,860
Pension contributions	(23,469)	(22,411)	(539,939)
Asset write-downs from Fiscal 2012 productivity initiatives	58,736	—	—
Other items, net	75,375	98,172	90,938
Changes in current assets and liabilities, excluding effects of acquisitions and divestitures:			
Receivables (includes proceeds from securitization)	171,832	(91,057)	121,387
Inventories	60,919	(80,841)	48,537
Prepaid expenses and other current assets	(11,584)	(1,682)	2,113
Accounts payable	(72,352)	233,339	(2,805)
Accrued liabilities	(20,008)	(60,862)	96,533
Income taxes	65,783	50,652	(5,134)
Cash provided by operating activities	1,493,117	1,583,643	1,262,197
Investing activities:			
Capital expenditures	(418,734)	(335,646)	(277,642)
Proceeds from disposals of property, plant, and equipment	9,817	13,158	96,493
Acquisitions, net of cash acquired	(3,250)	(618,302)	(11,428)
Proceeds from divestitures	3,828	1,939	18,637
Sale of short-term investments	56,780	—	—
Change in restricted cash	(39,052)	(5,000)	192,736
Other items, net	(11,394)	(5,781)	(5,353)
Cash (used for)/provided by investing activities	(402,005)	(949,632)	13,443
Financing activities:			
Payments on long-term debt	(1,440,962)	(45,766)	(630,394)
Proceeds from long-term debt	1,912,467	229,851	447,056
Net payments on commercial paper and short-term debt	(42,543)	(193,200)	(427,232)
Dividends	(619,104)	(579,618)	(533,552)
Purchases of treasury stock	(201,904)	(70,003)	—
Exercise of stock options	82,714	154,774	67,369
Acquisition of subsidiary shares from noncontrolling interests	(54,824)	(6,338)	(62,064)
Other items, net	1,321	27,791	(9,099)
Cash used for financing activities	(362,835)	(482,509)	(1,147,916)
Effect of exchange rate changes on cash and cash equivalents	(122,147)	89,556	(17,616)
Net increase in cash and cash equivalents	606,130	241,058	110,108
Cash and cash equivalents at beginning of year	724,311	483,253	373,145
Cash and cash equivalents at end of year	$ 1,330,441	$ 724,311	$ 483,253

See Notes to Consolidated Financial Statements

FIGURE 6.1 Heinz Cash Flow Statement

but we need to be sure they are the exact same numbers. So for 2010 net income, we will hardcode "882.343" (a decimal point, not a comma because we want thousands units) into Cell D58, and continue to hard-code in the 2011 net income and the 2012 net income. See Table 6.2.

Next are the noncash adjustments starting with "depreciation" and "amortization." Hard-code both the numbers directly into Rows 59 and 60. So, for example, in 2010 we will hard-code "254.528" into Cell D59 and "48.308" into Cell D60. We can do the same in 2011 and 2012. See Table 6.2.

The next line in our model, "amortization of identifiable intangible assets" does not exist in the Heinz historical financials. This line item we added for leveraged buyout (LBO) transaction purposes and will be used for projections once we add our transaction adjustments into the model. We can hard-code "0" for the historical years.

Next, Heinz lists "Deferred tax (benefit)/provision," which falls in line with our depreciation, deferred taxes, and other noncash items from our cash flow from operations formula. We can hard-code these as shown in Figure 6.1.

"Net losses on divestitures" are the operational losses realized when divesting portions of the business. "Pension contributions" are monies contributed to the pension fund to support an increasing liability. We can simply hard-code these two line items into the cash flow statement as shown in Figure 6.1.

"Asset write-downs from Fiscal 2012 productivity initiatives" is an extraordinary item connected to the closure of factories in 2012. There is a note on page 57 on the annual report to explain this:

The Company recognized $58.7 million of non-cash asset write-downs during Fiscal 2012 related to eight factory closures. These factory closures are directly linked to the Company's Fiscal 2012 productivity initiatives (see Note 3). These charges reduced the Company's carrying value in the assets to the estimated fair value, the remainder of which is not material.

(From the Heinz Annual Report, page 57)

"Other items, net" are not clearly defined but they certainly need to be included. Quite often you will come across these "other" line items that will not be clearly identified. Later we will discuss how best to project such items; we will define each item as we project it, but for now, let's hard-code them into the model as they are listed in the annual report.

Finally, there are six line items under the heading "Changes in current assets and liabilities, excluding effects of acquisitions and divestitures"; these are the operating working capital items that we will discuss later on.

Again, for the historical section, we can just list the line items exactly as Heinz has done, but we will label the particular section more standard as "Changes in operating working capital." See Table 6.2.

We can now total the net changes in operating working capital. So, in D74 we can sum the six operating working capital line items, D68 through D73.

Total Net Changes in Working Capital (Cell D74)

Excel Keystrokes	Description
Type "="	Enters into "formula" mode
Type "SUM("	Begins "SUM" formula
Select Cell D68	Selects the first cell in series
Type ":"	Indicates we want to include all cells from the first cell to the last cell in series
Select Cell D73	Selects the last cell in series
Type ")"	Ends the "SUM" formula
Hit Enter	End
Formula result	=SUM(D68:D73)

We can then total the cash flows from the operating activities line, which is a sum of all the line items in the cash flows from operating activities section, cells D58 through D73. We can use the SUM formula just as we had done with the net changes in operating working capital.

Total Cash from Operating Activities (Cell D75)

Excel Keystrokes	Description
Type "="	Enters into "formula" mode
Type "SUM("	Begins "SUM" formula
Select Cell D58	Selects the first cell in series
Type ":"	Indicates we want to include all cells from the first cell to the last cell in series
Select Cell D73	Selects the last cell in series
Type ")"	Ends the "SUM" formula
Hit Enter	End
Formula result	=SUM(D58:D73)

These totals should match the totals presented in the Heinz annual report. We can copy Cells D74 and D75 to the right. See Table 6.2.

TABLE 8.2 Heinz Historical Cash Flow from Operating Activities

Consolidated Statements of Cash Flows (in US$ millions except per share amounts)			
		Actuals	
Period Ending	2010A	2011A	2012A
Cash flows from operating activities			
Net income	$ 882.3	$1,005.9	$ 939.9
Depreciation	254.5	255.2	295.7
Amortization	48.3	43.4	47.1
Amortization of identifiable intangible assets	0.0	0.0	0.0
Deferred tax (benefit)/provision	220.5	153.7	(94.8)
Net losses on divestitures	44.9	0.0	0.0
Pension contributions	(539.9)	(22.4)	(23.5)
Asset write-downs from Fiscal 2012 productivity initiatives	0.0	0.0	58.7
Other items, net	90.9	98.2	75.4
Changes in operating working capital			
Changes in receivables	121.4	(91.1)	171.8
Changes in inventories	48.5	(80.8)	60.9
Changes in prepaid expenses and other current assets	2.1	(1.7)	(11.6)
Changes in accounts payable	(2.8)	233.3	(72.4)
Changes in accrued liabilities	96.5	(60.9)	(20.0)
Changes in accrued income taxes	(5.1)	50.7	65.8
Net changes in operating working capital	$ 260.6	$ 49.5	$ 194.6
Total cash provided by (used for) operating activities	$1,262.2	$1,583.6	$1,493.1

Cash Flow from Investing Activities

The cash from the investing activities line items can also be laid out one by one. "Capital expenditures (CAPEX)" are investments in property, plant, and equipment. This is found in the first line of the cash from investing activities section. "Proceeds from disposals of property, plant, and equipment" are the monies received from the disposal of assets. "Acquisitions, net of cash acquired" are acquisitions of businesses that Heinz has made. Page 45, Note 5, in the Heinz annual report gives more detail on the exact investments made. "Proceeds from divestitures" are the monies received from the sale or divestment of businesses. "Sale of short-term investments" is the monies received from selling off company investments.

"Change in restricted cash" is funds added to or removed from the restricted cash account. Restricted cash is cash held by the company in a separate account in order not to be utilized for the company's day-to-day operations. Heinz invests in swaps, securities for which the company must maintain a certain balance of cash in a separate account for collateral. As the values of the swaps fluctuate based on market swings, so does the level of maintenance cash needed. If that restricted cash balance needs to be increased for some reason, money has to be put into that account. This would result in a cash outflow.

"Other items, net" are not clearly defined, but this line item certainly needs to be included. Quite often you will come across these "other" line items that will not be clearly identified. Later we will discuss how best to project such items.

We can list each line item line by line as Heinz has done on the annual report (see Table 6.3). We can then total line items in Cells D77 through D83 in the "Total cash flow from investing activities" line.

Total Cash flow from Investing Activities (Cell D84)

Excel Keystrokes	Description
Type "="	Enters into "formula" mode
Type "SUM("	Adds the "SUM" formula
Select Cell D77	Selects the first cell in series
Type ":"	Indicates we want to include all cells from the first cell to the last cell in series
Select Cell D83	Selects the last cell in series
Type ")"	Ends the "SUM" formula
Hit Enter	End
Formula result	=SUM(D77:D83)

We can copy this formula to the right through 2012.

Cash Flow from Financing Activities

Cash flow from financing activities consists of three major categories: raising or buying back equity, raising or buying back debt, and distributions. Because we want to prepare this model for the new capital structure after the acquisition, we want to include rows to reflect all the debt and equity being raised to fund the acquisition. Notice that each line item in Rows 86 to 90 reflects the capital raised as per the sources of funds. These line items will be "0" before the acquisition. After the acquisition, we can handle any additional increase or reduction of capital in these line items. So for now, let's hard-code Rows 86 to 90 as "0" for 2010, 2011, and 2012.

TABLE 6.3 Heinz Historical Cash Flow from Investing Activities

Consolidated Statements of Cash Flows (in US$ millions except per share amounts)			
		Actuals	
Period Ending	2010A	2011A	2012A
Cash flows from investing activities			
Capital expenditures (CAPEX)	$(277.6)	$ (335.6)	$(418.7)
Proceeds from disposals of property, plant, and equipment	96.5	13.2	9.8
Acquisitions, net of cash acquired	(11.4)	(618.3)	(3.3)
Proceeds from divestitures	18.6	1.9	3.8
Sale of short-term investments	0.0	0.0	56.8
Change in restricted cash	192.7	(5.0)	(39.1)
Other items, net	(5.4)	(5.8)	(11.4)
Total cash provided by (used for) investing activities	$ 13.4	$ (949.6)	$(402.0)

Now for the rest of this section, we want to lay out each item line by line as Heinz has done—with one exception. Quite often companies list the payments of debt instruments and the issuance of debt instruments as two separate line items. It will be much simpler if we combine the issuances and payments of like debt instruments together. This will make the model flow more smoothly as we link information from the debt schedule into this section. The first two lines, titled "Payments on long-term debt" and "Proceeds from long-term debt," are both related to long-term debt. Payments of long-term debt are monies used to pay down debt, and proceeds from long-term debt are monies received from issuing or raising new long-term debt. For this reason I would combine these two line items as one in Row 91. Again, we will see how those two line items combined as one will make the flow from the debt schedule into this section easier. So in 2010, in Cell D91, we will have "=-630.394+447.056", and so on for 2011 and 2012. See Table 6.4.

The next line item, "Net payments on commercial paper and short-term debt," is short-term debt. The line after, "Dividends," reflects dividend payouts to shareholders. "Purchases of treasury stock" are stock bought back by the company. "Exercise of stock options" is the funds increased from stock options being exercised. "Acquisition of subsidiary shares from noncontrolling interests" is Heinz buying back a small portion of its noncontrolling interests (or minority stakes). It's important here to note the difference between buying securities of other companies, which would be an investing activity, and buying back securities of its own company, which would be a financing activity. "Other items, net" is again, like most "other" line items, not clearly defined, but it certainly needs to be included. It is

TABLE 6.4 Heinz Historical Cash Flow from Financing Activities

Consolidated Statements of Cash Flows (in US$ millions except per share amounts)			
		Actuals	
Period Ending	2010A	2011A	2012A
Cash flows from financing activities			
Revolver borrowings (repayments)	$ 0.0	$ 0.0	$ 0.0
Term facilities borrowings (repayments)	0.0	0.0	0.0
The notes borrowings (repayments)	0.0	0.0	0.0
Common equity	0.0	0.0	0.0
Preferred equity	0.0	0.0	0.0
Proceeds (payments) of long-term debt	(183.3)	184.1	471.5
Net payments on commercial paper and short-term debt	(427.2)	(193.2)	(42.5)
Dividends	(533.6)	(579.6)	(619.1)
Purchases of treasury stock	0.0	(70.0)	(201.9)
Exercise of stock options	67.4	154.8)	82.7
Acquisitions of subsidiary shares from noncontrolling interests	(62.1)	(6.3)	(54.8)
Other items, net	(9.1)	27.8	1.3
Total cash provided by (used for) financing activities	$(1,147.9)	$(482.5)	$(362.8)

worth conducting some more research to see if there is additional information on these items. Unfortunately, in this case there is not. Let's list out all of these line items as Heinz has done in the annual report. We will discuss the more significant of these line items in more detail as we project them. For now, we just want to lay everything out. See Table 6.4.

We can total line items in Rows 86 through 97 in the "Total cash flow from financing activities" line (see Table 6.4).

Total Cash flow from Financing Activities (Cell D98)

Excel Keystrokes	Description
Type "="	Enters into "formula" mode
Type "SUM("	Adds the "SUM" formula
Select Cell D86	Selects the first cell in series
Type ":"	Indicates we want to include all cells from the first cell to the last cell in series
Select Cell D97	Selects the last cell in series
Type ")"	Ends the "SUM" formula
Hit Enter	End
Formula result	=SUM(D86:D97)

We can copy this formula to the right.

Notice in the Heinz cash flow statement there is a line entitled "Effect of exchange rate changes on cash and cash equivalents," which is an adjustment made on foreign currency due to the company's international subsidiaries. This does come up in multinational companies. So, we need to add this line item after the financing activities section in the cash flow statement as Heinz has done. Once we have hard-coded in the numbers for the effect of exchange rate changes on cash and cash equivalents into row 99, we can calculate the total change in cash by adding the cash flow from operating activities, cash flow from investing activities, cash flow from financing activities, and this effect of exchange rate changes on cash and cash equivalents line item.

Total Change in Cash and Cash Equivalents (Cell D100)

Excel Keystrokes	Description
Type "="	Enters into "formula" mode
Select Cell D75	Selects the total cash from operating activities
Type "+"	Adds
Select Cell D84	Selects the total cash from investing activities
Type "+"	Adds
Select Cell D98	Selects the total cash from financing activities
Type "+"	Adds
Select Cell D99	Selects the effect of exchange rates on cash and cash equivalents
Hit Enter	End
Formula result	=D75+D84+D98+D99

We can copy this formula to the right through 2012.

We should now have all the cash flow statement line items laid out for the three historical years (see Table 6.5).

TABLE 6.5   Heinz Historical Cash Flow

Consolidated Statements of Cash Flows (in US$ millions except per share amounts)

	Actuals		
Period Ending	2010A	2011A	2012A
Cash flows from operating activities			
Net income	$ 882.3	$1,005.9	$ 939.9
Depreciation	254.5	255.2	295.7
Amortization	48.3	43.4	47.1
Amortization of identifiable intangible assets	0.0	0.0	0.0
Deferred tax (benefit)/provision	220.5	153.7	(94.8)
Net losses on divestitures	44.9	0.0	0.0
Pension contributions	(539.9)	(22.4)	(23.5)
Asset write-downs from Fiscal 2012			
productivity initiatives	0.0	0.0	58.7
Other items, net	90.9	98.2	75.4

TABLE 6.5 (*Continued*)

Consolidated Statements of Cash Flows (in US\$ millions except per share amounts)			
		Actuals	
Period Ending	2010A	2011A	2012A
Changes in operating working capital			
Changes in receivables	121.4	(91.1)	171.8
Changes in inventories	48.5	(80.8)	60.9
Changes in prepaid expenses and other current assets	2.1	(1.7)	(11.6)
Changes in accounts payable	(2.8)	233.3	(72.4)
Changes in accrued liabilities	96.5	(60.9)	(20.0)
Changes in accrued income taxes	(5.1)	50.7	65.8
Net changes in operating working capital	\$ 260.6	\$ 49.5	\$ 194.6
Total cash provided by (used for) operating activities	\$ 1,262.2	\$1,583.6	\$1,493.1
Cash flows from investing activities			
Capital expenditures (CAPEX)	(277.6)	(335.6)	(418.7)
Proceeds from disposals of property, plant, and equipment	96.5	13.2	9.8
Acquisitions, net of cash acquired	(11.4)	(618.3)	(3.3)
Proceeds from divestitures	18.6	1.9	3.8
Sale of short-term investments	0.0	0.0	56.8
Change in restricted cash	192.7	(5.0)	(39.1)
Other items, net	(5.4)	(5.8)	(11.4)
Total cash provided by (used for) investing activities	\$ 13.4	\$ (949.6)	\$ (402.0)
Cash flows from financing activities			
Revolver borrowings (repayments)	0.0	0.0	0.0
Term facilities borrowings (repayments)	0.0	0.0	0.0
The notes borrowings (repayments)	0.0	0.0	0.0
Common equity	0.0	0.0	0.0
Preferred equity	0.0	0.0	0.0
Proceeds (payments) of long-term debt	(183.3)	184.1	471.5
Net payments on commercial paper and short-term debt	(427.2)	(193.2)	(42.5)
Dividends	(533.6)	(579.6)	(619.1)
Purchases of treasury stock	0.0	(70.0)	(201.9)
Exercise of stock options	67.4	154.8	82.7
Acquisitions of subsidiary shares from noncontrolling interests	(62.1)	(6.3)	(54.8)
Other items, net	(9.1)	27.8	1.3
Total cash provided by (used for) financing activities	\$(1,147.9)	\$ (482.5)	\$ (362.8)
Effect of exchange rate changes on cash and cash equivalents	(17.6)	89.6	(122.1)
Total change in cash and cash equivalents	110.1	241.1	606.1

HEINZ LAST TWELVE MONTHS (LTM) CASH FLOW

Before going on to make Heinz projections, we also need to make the same LTM adjustments as we had done for the income statement. Use the nine-month cash flow statement found on page 8 of the Heinz 3Q quarterly report. See Figure 6.2.

We will first lay out the cash flow statement exactly as we had done for the annual financials. We will then calculate the Heinz cash flow LTM using

H.J. Heinz Company and Subsidiaries Condensed
Consolidated Statements of Cash Flows

	Nine Months Ended	
	January 27, 2013 FY 2013	January 25, 2012 FY 2012
	(Unaudited) (In thousands)	
Cash Flows from Operating Activities:		
Net income	$ 829,080	$ 762,334
Adjustments to reconcile net income to cash provided by operating activities:		
Depreciation	221,519	217,620
Amortization	34,890	33,965
Deferred tax benefit	(59,718)	(71,533)
Net loss on divestitures	19,765	—
Impairment on assets held for sale	36,000	—
Pension contributions	(53,251)	(15,490)
Other items, net	22,654	87,859
Changes in current assets and liabilities, excluding effects of acquisitions and divestitures:		
Receivables (includes proceeds from securitization)	(148,132)	46,128
Inventories	(158,456)	(126,627)
Prepaid expenses and other current assets	5,699	(13,705)
Accounts payable	(42,852)	(182,333)
Accrued liabilities	(5,406)	(76,976)
Income taxes	(24,871)	82,272
Cash provided by operating activities	676,921	743,514
Cash Flows from Investing Activities:		
Capital expenditures	(259,187)	(274,498)
Proceeds from disposals of property, plant, and equipment	17,335	6,926
Proceeds from divestitures	16,783	664
Acquisitions, net of cash acquired	—	(3,250)
Sale of short-term investments	—	47,976
Change in restricted cash	3,994	(39,052)
Other items, net	(10,276)	(9,396)
Cash used for investing activities	(231,351)	(270,630)
Cash Flows from Financing Activities:		
Payments on long-term debt	(216,972)	(831,553)
Proceeds from long-term debt	202,332	1,310,903
Net proceeds/(payments) on commercial paper and short-term debt	31,068	(56,943)
Dividends	(499,678)	(464,901)
Exercise of stock options	96,111	74,518
Purchase of treasury stock	(139,069)	(201,904)
Acquisitions of subsidiary shares from noncontrolling interest	(80,132)	(54,824)
Earn-out settlement	(44,547)	—
Other items, net	1,602	5,479
Cash used for financing activities	(649,285)	(219,225)
Effect of exchange rate changes on cash and cash equivalents	(26,037)	(129,059)
Net (decrease)/increase in cash and cash equivalents	(229,752)	124,600
Cash and cash equivalents at beginning of year	1,330,441	724,311
Cash and cash equivalents at end of period	$ 1,100,689	$ 848,911

See Notes to Condensed Consolidated Financial Statements.

FIGURE 6.2   Heinz Nine-Month Cash Flow Statement

the same formula as we used when calculating the LTM for the income statement:

$$\text{Heinz LTM} = \text{Annual 2012} - \text{9-Mo. 2012} + \text{9-Mo. 2013}$$

If you notice in the model, Columns G and H are already set up for the nine-month 2012 and 2013 cash flow statements, respectively. We won't go into stepping you through the construction of this line by line, as it is almost exactly the same as the method we used for the annual historical financials. I recommend using Figure 6.2 and the solution in Table 6.6 as guides. This is great practice to see how much you have retained from this section. You may want to reread the earlier part of this chapter again for more practice.

Note seven adjustments:

1. Remember that amortization of identifiable intangible assets was added by us to handle transaction adjustments. They will be hard-coded as "0" for now.
2. There is a line item labeled "Impairment on assets held for sale" that did not exist in the annual report. We need to add a row and input this value. So let's add a row above Row 64 in the cash flow statement by holding down Shift and hitting the space bar. This highlights the row. Let go of those keys, and hit "Ctrl" + "Shift" + "=" at the same time (or you may just have to type "Ctrl" + "+" if you have a single "+" key because "Shift" + "=" is the same as a "+"). This will add a row, which we can now call "Impairment on assets held for sale" and make the 2010, 2011, 2012, and 9-Mo. 2012 annual historical values "0." We can then hard-code "36.0" into Cell H64. See Table 6.6.
3. There is no line item in the quarterly cash flow referring to "Asset write-downs from Fiscal 2012 productivity initiatives," so we will hard-code this as "0."
4. Continue to hard-code the new financing line items in the Cash from Financing activities Rows 87 to 91 as zero.
5. Remember to combine the line items "Payments on long-term debt" with "Proceeds from long-term debt" as we had done with the annual data.
6. There is a line item labeled "Earn-out settlement" in the cash flow from financing activities that does not exist in the annual report, so we need to add a row and input this value. So let's add a row above Row 98 in the cash flow statement just as we had done in the operating activities section. We can label the new row "Earn-out settlement" and make the 2010, 2011, 2012, and 9-Mo. 2012 annual historical values "0." We can then hard-code "-44.547" (negative) into Cell H98. See Table 6.6.
7. All the "Totals" formulas can be copied to the right from Column F.

TABLE 6.6 Heinz Nine-Month Historical Cash Flow Financials

Consolidated Statements of Cash Flows (in US$ millions except per share amounts)		
	Last Twelve Months (LTM)	
Period Ending	**9-Mo. 2012**	**9-Mo. 2013**	**LTM**
Cash flows from operating activities		
Net income	$ 762.3	$ 829.1
Depreciation	217.6	221.5
Amortization	34.0	34.9
Amortization of identifiable intangible assets	0.0	0.0
Deferred tax (benefit)/provision	(71.5)	(59.7)
Net losses on divestitures	0.0	19.8
Impairment on assets held for sale	0.0	36.0
Pension contributions	(15.5)	(53.3)
Asset write-downs from Fiscal 2012		
productivity initiatives	0.0	0.0
Other items, net	87.9	22.7
Changes in operating working capital		
Changes in receivables	46.1	(148.1)
Changes in inventories	(126.6)	(158.5)
Changes in prepaid expenses and other		
current assets	(13.7)	5.7
Changes in accounts payable	(182.3)	(42.9)
Changes in accrued liabilities	(77.0)	(5.4)
Changes in accrued income taxes	82.3	(24.9)
Net changes in operating working capital	$(271.2)	$(374.0)
Total cash provided by (used for) operating		
activities	$ 743.5	$ 676.9
Cash flows from investing activities		
Capital expenditures (CAPEX)	(274.5)	(259.2)
Proceeds from disposals of property, plant,		
and equipment	6.9	17.3
Acquisitions, net of cash acquired	0.7	16.8
Proceeds from divestitures	(3.3)	0.0
Sale of short-term investments	48.0	0.0
Change in restricted cash	(39.1)	4.0
Other items, net	(9.4)	(10.3)
Total cash provided by (used for) investing		
activities	$(270.6)	$(231.4)
Cash flows from financing activities		
Revolver borrowings (repayments)	0.0	0.0
Term facilities borrowings (repayments)	0.0	0.0
The notes borrowings (repayments)	0.0	0.0

TABLE 6.8 (*Continued*)

Consolidated Statements of Cash Flows (in US$ millions except per share amounts)			
	Last Twelve Months (LTM)		
Period Ending	9-Mo. 2012	9-Mo. 2013	LTM
Common equity	0.0	0.0	
Preferred equity	0.0	0.0	
Proceeds (payments) of long-term debt	479.4	(14.6)	
Net payments on commercial paper and short-term debt	(56.9)	31.1	
Dividends	(464.9)	(499.7)	
Purchases of treasury stock	74.5	96.1	
Exercise of stock options	(201.9)	(139.1)	
Acquisitions of subsidiary shares from noncontrolling interests	(54.8)	(80.1)	
Earn-out settlement	0.0	(44.5)	
Other items, net	5.5	1.6	
Total cash provided by (used for) financing activities	$(219.2)	$(649.3)	
Effect of exchange rate changes on cash and cash equivalents	(129.1)	(26.0)	
Total change in cash and cash equivalents	$ 124.6	$(229.8)	

We can now make appropriate adjustments to calculate the LTM data in Column I. We discussed earlier in Chapter 5 the adjustments to get LTM data as:

Heinz LTM = Annual 2012 – 9-Mo. 2012 + 9-Mo. 2013

So we can apply this formula to the LTM column (Column I). Let's take net income for example:

Calculating LTM Net Income (Cell I58)

Excel Keystrokes	Description
Type "="	Enters into "formula" mode
Select Cell F58	2012 net income
Type "-"	Subtracts
Select Cell G58	9-Mo. 2012 net income
Type "+"	Adds
Select Cell H58	9-Mo. 2013 net income
Hit Enter	End
Formula result	"=F58-G58+H58"

This should give you $1,006.7 in LTM net income. This is a formula, so it should be in black font. We now want to copy this formula down for every line item in the Heinz LTM column. However, make sure to continue to calculate "Total" line items as we had done with the historicals. In other words, total net operating working capital should be calculated as one normally would by taking the sum of rows 69 to 74. You can just copy these formulas over to the right from Column H. See Table 6.7.

The supplemental line item at the bottom of the cash flow statement entitled "Cash flow before debt pay-down" is a line item utilized for the debt schedule. So we will leave it empty for now and discuss that line item in the debt schedule section.

TABLE 6.7   Heinz LTM Cash Flow Statement

Consolidated Statements of Cash Flows (in US$ millions except per share amounts)			
	Last Twelve Months (LTM)		
Period Ending	9-Mo. 2012	9-Mo. 2013	LTM
Cash flows from operating activities			
Net income	$ 762.3	$ 829.1	$1,006.7
Depreciation	217.6	221.5	299.6
Amortization	34.0	34.9	48.0
Amortization of identifiable intangible assets	0.0	0.0	0.0
Deferred tax (benefit)/provision	(71.5)	(59.7)	(83.0)
Net losses on divestitures	0.0	19.8	19.8
Impairment on assets held for sale	0.0	36.0	36.0
Pension contributions	(15.5)	(53.3)	(61.2)
Asset write-downs from Fiscal 2012 productivity initiatives	0.0	0.0	58.7
Other items, net	87.9	22.7	10.2
Changes in operating working capital			
Changes in receivables	46.1	(148.1)	(22.4)
Changes in inventories	(126.6)	(158.5)	29.1
Changes in prepaid expenses and other current assets	(13.7)	5.7	7.8
Changes in accounts payable	(182.3)	(42.9)	67.1
Changes in accrued liabilities	(77.0)	(5.4)	51.6
Changes in accrued income taxes	82.3	(24.9)	(41.4)
Net changes in operating working capital	$(271.2)	$(374.0)	$ 91.8
Total cash provided by (used for) operating activities	$ 743.5	$ 676.9	$1,426.5

TABLE 6.7 (*Continued*)

Consolidated Statements of Cash Flows (in US$ millions except per share amounts)			
	Last Twelve Months (LTM)		
Period Ending	9-Mo. 2012	9-Mo. 2013	LTM
Cash flows from investing activities			
Capital expenditures (CAPEX)	(274.5)	(259.2)	(403.4)
Proceeds from disposals of property, plant, and equipment	6.9	17.3	20.2
Acquisitions, net of cash acquired	0.7	16.8	12.9
Proceeds from divestitures	(3.3)	0.0	7.1
Sale of short-term investments	48.0	0.0	8.8
Change in restricted cash	(39.1)	4.0	4.0
Other items, net	(9.4)	(10.3)	(12.3)
Total cash provided by (used for) investing activities	$(270.6)	$(231.4)	$ (362.7)
Cash flows from financing activities			
Revolver borrowings (repayments)	0.0	0.0	0.0
Term facilities borrowings (repayments)	0.0	0.0	0.0
The notes borrowings (repayments)	0.0	0.0	0.0
Common equity	0.0	0.0	0.0
Preferred equity	0.0	0.0	0.0
Proceeds (payments) of long-term debt	479.4	(14.6)	(22.5)
Net payments on commercial paper and short-term debt	(56.9)	31.1	45.5
Dividends	(464.9)	(499.7)	(653.9)
Purchases of treasury stock	74.5	96.1	(180.3)
Exercise of stock options	(201.9)	(139.1)	145.5
Acquisitions of subsidiary shares from noncontrolling interests	(54.8)	(80.1)	(80.1)
Earn-out settlement	0.0	(44.5)	(44.5)
Other items, net	5.5	1.6	(2.6)
Total cash provided by (used for) financing activities	$(219.2)	$(649.3)	$ (792.9)
Effect of exchange rate changes on cash and cash equivalents	$(129.1)	$ (26.0)	$ (19.1)
Total change in cash and cash equivalents	$ 124.6	$(229.8)	$ 251.8

CASH FLOW STATEMENT PROJECTIONS

When making projections, many cash flow statement line items come from supporting schedules: the depreciation schedule, working capital schedule, and debt schedule. So, cash flow statement projections cannot be complete without building those supporting schedules. Further, because this is a leveraged buyout, and because said supporting schedules are based largely on balance sheet information, we need to first create an adjusted balance sheet, portraying what the balance sheet will look like after transaction close, before constructing these auxiliary schedules. It is with that adjusted balance sheet that we can create the supporting schedules and then complete the cash flow statement.

So we will first project as much of the cash flow statement as we can, and then we will move on to the balance sheet adjustments, which will allow us to create depreciation and working capital schedules. We can then link the appropriate line items back into the cash flow statement. The debt schedule should always be done last. See Appendix 1 for the order of building a full-scale model.

Cash Flow from Operating Activities

Cash from operating activities begins with net income, which we have on the income statement. So, for our projections, we should pull net income into the cash flow statement from the income statement. It is important to ensure we are pulling the correct net income from the income statement. As a general rule, you should always select net income before distributions (dividends, noncontrolling interests). We can look to the historical net income and see which net income from the income statement matches the cash flow statement net income as a check. In this case it looks like the 2012 $939.9 is the net income before "net income attributable to noncontrolling interests." In our model that is income statement Row 44.

We can link that row into our cash flow, starting by selecting "=" in Cell J58 of our cash flow statement. We can now select the correct net income on the income statement (J44) and hit Enter. We can then copy the cash flow statement J58 formula to the right through 2018.

Most of the next lines come from other schedules, which means we will skip over them and leave them empty for now. "Depreciation," "Amortization," and "Deferred tax (benefit) / provision" all come from the depreciation schedule.

The transactional line item "amortization of identifiable intangible assets" was added by us to handle transaction adjustments. We will explain how to handle these when discussing the balance sheet adjustments. Let's also leave this row empty for now.

The six working capital items in Rows 69 to 74 will come from the working capital schedule. So we can skip these line items for now and link them in once we complete those schedules.

Nonrecurring Items

Several items in cash flow from operations appear to be occurring only one time. "Net losses on divestitures," for example, have happened in 2010, and again in the latest nine months, but do not seem to be constant. Let's project this as "0" as it appears that this is a one-time item. Of course, further research could give us a better indication of what may happen in the future. This value does not seem to be very significant, so we believe it is okay to hard-code this as "0" in the future. "Impairment on assets held for sale" also seems to be nonrecurring. Unfortunately, we could not find any more information on this item, but it has happened only once, so our best guess is to consider it a one-time item. It is also conservative to assume the previous cash inflow will not repeat, so let's hard-code this "0." "Asset write-downs from Fiscal 2012 productivity initiatives" also appears to be a one-time item. Conducting further research reveals the following note found on page 57 of the Heinz annual report:

> *The Company recognized $58.7 million of non-cash asset write-downs during Fiscal 2012 related to eight factory closures. These factory closures are directly linked to the Company's Fiscal 2012 productivity initiatives (see Note 3). These charges reduced the Company's carrying value in the assets to the estimated fair value, the remainder of which is not material.*

This suggests a unique situation that does not come with a guarantee that it will occur again. So let's also hard-code this as "0." "Pension contributions" and "Other items, net," however, do seem to be recurring, so we need to think through how to project these with slightly more detail.

The Seven Methods of Projections

Some "other" line items (i.e., line items that are not standard, but are reoccurring) can be difficult to define, and more difficult to project. In such instances, we recommend seven possible methods to project such line items:

1. Conservative (the minimum of the past three years).
2. Aggressive (the maximum of the past three years).
3. Average (the average of the past three years).
4. Last year (recent performance).
5. Repeat the cycle.

6. Year-over-year growth.
7. Project out as a percentage of an income statement or balance sheet line item.

   1. Conservative. In a cash flow statement, we assume money spent is more conservative than money received. So, taking the minimum amount from the past three years may not be the most accurate method, but it is a conservative approach. You can use the "minimum" formula in Excel. For example "=min(x,y,z)" will give you the lowest amount of x, y, and z. We also sometimes consider an "absolute conservative" approach where if the past three years were positive numbers (cash inflows) we would go even below the minimum of the past three years by assuming 0.

   2. Aggressive. This is probably not the most recommended method, but it is a possible method, so we will note it. Assuming more money received is more aggressive, we would take the maximum amount from the past three years. You can use the "maximum" formula in Excel; "=max(x,y,z)" will give you the maximum amount of x, y, and z.

   3. Average. This is a popular method, but be warned that quite often the average of the past three years does not give the best indication of next year's performance, especially if one of the past three years was unusual. We mention this specifically because we see many analysts using the average method as the safety method. We recommend that it is better to go through all the various methods carefully before considering the average method. You can use the "average" formula in Excel; "=average(x,y,z)" will give you the average amount of x, y, and z.

   4. Last year. This is based on the underlying assumption that the company's performance last year is most indicative of its future performance. If one does not know the business or the specific line item well, it may not be easy to determine if this is the correct method to use. However, a combination of this method and the "conservative" method is a quite useful indicator. In other words, if last year's performance also happens to be the most conservative of the past three years, then we have two supporting methodologies that point to the same number. The more support we have, the better.

   5. Repeat the cycle. Quite often the past three years' numbers will be quite volatile, swinging from positive to negative or from a very small value to a large value. Although it is often difficult to identify exactly why, some companies can plan more significant cash flow events every second or third year. For example, companies can make larger capital expenditure investments every third year, and smaller investments in the other years. In this case, you may want to continue this trend.

The easiest way to do this is to have the projected 2013 year equal to the first historical year (2010). This way, when copied correctly, 2014 will equal the 2011 value, 2015 will equal the 2012 value, and so on.

6. **Year-over-year growth.** Here we can assume some year-over-year growth rate to project the line item going forward. The growth rate can be dependent on what exactly that "other" line item is. If it is rent, for example, we can assume that the rent will increase by a standard 5 percent each year. You can also take a look at the historical trends much like what we had done with revenue and apply those trends to the projections.

7. **Project out as a percentage of an income statement or balance sheet line item.** "Other" line items can sometimes grow dependent on another income statement or balance sheet line item. For example, if the "other" item is made up of employee salaries, you may want to project this line item based on a percentage of selling, general, and administrative (SG&A) expense. One way to determine if this can be an appropriate method is by looking at the historical percentage of SG&A. If the percentages have been fairly consistent over the past three years, then this could be a good indication.

MODEL TIP

It is always important to add comments in Excel describing the exact method you are using. A good analyst should always add explicit detail and explanations of assumptions to the model for clarity.

It is not easy to determine exactly which method to use. But it is important to note that quite often these "other" items are insignificant to the overall analysis. To prove this, choose one of the seven methods, and highlight that "other" line item to be revisited once the model is complete. Then, try to change your assumptions using one of the seven methods and see if it significantly changes your analysis. If it does, it is worth further research.

To give you a good idea as to the thought process, let's walk through how to analyze the "Other items, net" line item in Row 67. We still need to project out "Pension contributions," but "Other items, net" better illustrates how to handle "other" line items. We will come back to the pension contributions.

One should always first perform research to see if there is more detail on that line item. Unfortunately, in this case there is little additional detail. So let's step through all the possibilities. In this model, we will analyze

2010, 2011, 2012, and also our LTM numbers. We should compare all four 12-month metrics:

1. *Conservative.* The conservative method, the minimum of all years, would give us 10.2 from the LTM column. We like conservative models, so this may be the way to go, but we should first consider all options.
2. *Aggressive.* An aggressive approach is not recommended. So let's cross this one out.
3. *Average.* The average method could work, but there is a decline from 2011 to 2012, and a major drop in the LTM year. If this drop reflects a trend, maybe the average would give us a number that is too high. But let's not cross this off entirely yet.
4. *Last year.* The past year's value (which we will consider is the LTM) of 10.2 also happens to be the most conservative value. Having two methods in favor of the same value is good reference.
5. *Repeat the cycle.* Repeating the cycle would be a method to consider, but we don't see a cycle here. We see a drop or decline.
6. *Year-over-year growth.* There is a sharp decline, not a steady one. So there is no strong basis to calculate a trend for a future decline in our opinion.
7. *Project out as a percentage of an income statement or balance sheet line item.* First, if it is unclear exactly what "other" is referring to, it is difficult to know what other line item we can base this number on. We can suggest it must be an income statement line item, as this line is in the operating activities section of the cash flow statement (operating suggests income); however, we still don't know which exact income statement line item it would refer to. Second, we don't see many line items in the income statement that are reducing as significantly as this line item, so even if we did find a relatable item to calculate a percentage, it would not give us a smooth enough historical trend to base projections on. Therefore, we should also cross this one off.

So, we are left with the "average," the "conservative," and the "last year" approaches. Given that the "conservative" method gives us the same results as the "last year" method, we like two methods that support each other, and we like conservative models, let's go with the conservative approach. We can also highlight this, and once the model is done, try using the "average" or "repeat the cycle" approach to see if it makes a major difference in our analysis. This will make the process 100 percent thorough.

So we can have Cell J67 link from Cell I67, or Cell J67 would read "=I67." We can then copy this to the right through 2018.

Now let's take a look at pension contributions. We first note a paragraph found in the Heinz annual report, which reads:

The Company recognized pension expense related to defined benefit programs of $25 million, $27 million, and $25 million for fiscal years 2012, 2011, and 2010, respectively, which reflected expected return on plan assets of $235 million, $229 million, and $211 million, respectively. The Company contributed $23 million to its pension plans in Fiscal 2012 compared to $22 million in Fiscal 2011 and $540 million in Fiscal 2010. The Company expects to contribute approximately $80 million to its pension plans in Fiscal 2013.

(Heinz Annual Report, page 26)

So this mentions that the company expects an $80 million contribution in 2013, significantly higher than the $22 million and $23 million contributed in 2011 and 2012, yet not as significant as the $540 million in 2010. So what is the basis for identifying how to project this into the future? We really do not know for sure, but if the company provides future guidance, which is rare, we should use it; that should supersede all of the seven methods. Let's use the $80 million for now. We can hard-code "-80" (negative) into Cell J65, and we can copy this to the right.

We can also copy the net changes in operating working capital and the total cash flow from operating activities formulas, Cells I75 and I76, through to 2018. This is all we can complete for now in the cash flow from operating activities section. See Table 6.8.

MODEL TIP

We strongly recommend saving deeper research for once the model is completely linked through. I have often seen analysts one or two days after receiving a model assignment still researching the company to hone their revenue and cost assumptions. When asked to see the model, it is not excusable to mention to your superior that you are still conducting research and there is no model to review. It is preferable to have a completely linked model first, with even the most general assumptions, and then later go back to tweak and hone assumptions.

TABLE 6.8 Heinz Projected Cash Flow from Operating Activities

Consolidated Statements of Cash Flows (in US$ millions except per share amounts)

Period Ending	Estimates				
	2014E	2015E	2016E	2017E	2018E
Cash flows from operating activities					
Net income	$1,389.4	$1,395.1	$1,400.7	$1,406.4	$1,412.1
Depreciation					
Amortization					
Amortization of identifiable intangible assets					
Deferred tax (benefit)/provision					
Net losses on divestitures	0.0	0.0	0.0	0.0	0.0
Impairment on assets held for sale	0.0	0.0	0.0	0.0	0.0
Pension contributions	(80.0)	(80.0)	(80.0)	(80.0)	(80.0)
Asset write-downs from Fiscal 2012 productivity initiatives	0.0	0.0	0.0	0.0	0.0
Other items, net	10.2	10.2	10.2	10.2	10.2
Changes in operating working capital					
Changes in receivables					
Changes in inventories					
Changes in prepaid expenses and other current assets					
Changes in accounts payable					
Changes in accrued liabilities					
Changes in accrued income taxes					
Net changes in operating working capital	$ 0.0	$ 0.0	$ 0.0	$ 0.0	$ 0.0
Total cash provided by (used for) operating activities	$1,319.6	$1,325.3	$1,330.9	$1,336.6	$1,342.3

Cash Flow from Investing Activities

Capital expenditures (CAPEX) are one of the few line items that management often gives guidance on. By performing a word search on "capital expenditures" in the Heinz annual report, we reveal the following note:

> Cash used for investing activities totaled $402 million compared to $950 million of cash last year. Capital expenditures totaled $419 million (3.6% of sales) compared to $336 million (3.1% of sales) in the prior year, which is in-line with planned levels. Higher

capital spending reflects increased investments in Project Keystone, capacity projects in emerging markets and productivity initiatives. The Company expects capital spending as a percentage of sales to be approximately 4% in Fiscal 2013.

(From the Heinz Annual Report, page 18)

The company did not provide an exact number, but suggested basing it on 4 percent of sales. So, let's project CAPEX as a percentage of sales. We should add a line underneath the CAPEX row 78 and label it "CAPEX % of revenue." We can then hard-code "4 %" into Cell J79. We can copy the 4 percent to the right through 2018 and project the CAPEX.

Note: Be sure that the 4 percent is labeled in blue font and is in the proper percent format. When hard-coding 4.0 percent, make sure you have formatted the cells into percentages. If your cells have not been formatted as percentages and you type in 4.0 percent, Excel will convert that percentage into the decimal 0.04, which may appear as 0.0 in the cell if it is rounding to one decimal place. Selecting "Ctrl" + "1" while Cell J79 is highlighted is a quick way to open up the "Format Cells" box. Here you can select "Percentage" as an option.

2014 CAPEX (Cell J78)

Excel Keystrokes	Description
Type "="	Enters into "formula" mode
Type "-"	CAPEX should be negative—a cash outflow
Select Cell J79	2014 CAPEX % of revenue
Type "*"	Multiplies
Select Income Statement Cell J6	2014 revenue
Hit Enter	End
Formula result	=-J79*J6

This gives us –$469.5 in 2014. We can now copy Cell J78 to the right through 2018. See Table 6.9.

TABLE 6.9 Heinz Projected CAPEX

Consolidated Statements of Cash Flows (in US$ millions except per share amounts)					
	Estimates				
Period Ending	2014E	2015E	2016E	2017E	2018E
Cash flows from investing activities					
Capital expenditures (CAPEX)	$(469.5)	$(471.4)	$(473.3)	$(475.2)	$(477.1)
CAPEX % of revenue	4.0%	4.0%	4.0%	4.0%	4.0%

Proceeds from Disposals of Property, Plant, and Equipment

This line item is related to a company selling off or disposing of portions of its property, plant, or equipment. It is unclear what exactly the company is disposing of, but it is most likely selling old equipment it is planning on replacing. Note that this can also be related to the sale of equipment from portions of businesses the company has closed or is planning on closing. This is clearly an unknown and is difficult to project without further company guidance. We continue to recommend being conservative here. However, given the nonrecurring nature of disposals, we can argue that taking a minimum of the past three years is not conservative enough. Being most conservative could mean there are no more disposals. If we want to be most conservative, we can assume this will be zero in the future. Further, as Heinz will be bought out, it is unclear how such items will be managed in the future. Given such uncertainty, we recommend the absolutely conservative approach. Let's hard-code this as "0."

Acquisitions, Net of Cash Acquired

This line item is related to the purchase of business entities. We can make the same argument for most of the other investing activity line items that we made with the proceeds from disposals of property, plant, and equipment. These items not only are extremely uncertain, but in a leveraged buyout scenario, may be seen as superfluous when cash should be conserved to pay down debt. Although it is mentioned that the strategy for the Heinz acquisition is to be a platform for other acquisitions, it is too aggressive at this stage to model out several acquisitions. As a priority, to understand the investment returns, we will assume cash will be used to pay down debts. Let's also hard-code this "0"—the absolutely conservative method.

Proceeds from Divestitures

This item is related to the sale or divestiture of businesses entities. Again, we can be extremely conservative and assume we will not be divesting assets any further. Let's hard-code this "0"—the absolutely conservative method. This is not to say that there will never be divestitures again, but we believe it is too risky to assume we will receive cash benefits from divestitures at this point in time.

Sale of Short-Term Investments

This item looks nonrecurring, as it has appeared only in 2012. So, we can assume this is "0."

Change in Restricted Cash

Heinz invests in swaps, securities in which the company must maintain a certain balance of cash in a separate account for collateral. As the values of the swaps fluctuate based on market swings, so does the level of maintenance cash needed. This item is recurring, but given its relationship to market volatility, it becomes very difficult to predict. This line item contains positive swings as well as negative ones, so assuming this is "0" is not the most conservative approach. Going back to the seven methods:

1. *Conservative.* The conservative method, the minimum of all years, would give us –39.1. We like conservative models, so this may be the way to go, but we should first consider all options.
2. *Aggressive.* An aggressive approach is not recommended, as this would result in a high positive cash flow of 192.7. So let's cross this one out.
3. *Average.* The average method could work, but the unusually high 2010 value of 192.7 would skew the average results.
4. *Last year.* The last year's value (which we will consider is the LTM) of 4.0 could be okay. It is not the most conservative, nor the most aggressive, but the small number close to 0 can be a good balance: an average of sorts.
5. *Repeat the cycle.* Repeat the cycle would be a method to consider, but we don't see a cycle here.
6. *Year-over-year growth.* Given the volatility in connection with the market, there is no strong basis in our opinion.
7. *Project out as a percentage of an income statement or balance sheet line item.* As this line item is based largely on securities, and therefore market volatility, it is unlikely that this should be based on some operating performance. We should also cross this one off.

So it looks like the "conservative" or the "last year" method works the best here. This is a tough call. I like conservative models, but –39.1 may be too conservative. Let's, however, use that for now. This line item is quite insignificant when compared to other cash flow line items so it is doubtful that either method would greatly affect the overall analysis. Although not necessary, I like to actually put in a "minimum" formula, so anyone else looking at the model can better understand why we have decided to use the assumption we chose by looking at the formula structure.

2014 Change in Restricted Cash (Cell J84)

Excel Keystrokes	Description
Type "="	Enters into "formula" mode
Type "min("	Starts minimum formula
Select Cell I84	LTM change in restricted cash
Type ","	Adds a comma to get ready for the next value
Select Cell F84	2012 change in restricted cash
Type ","	Adds a comma to get ready for the next value

(continued)

Select Cell E84	2011 change in restricted cash
Type ","	Adds a comma to get ready for the next value
Select Cell D84	2010 change in restricted cash
Type ")"	Ends minimum formula
Hit Enter	End
Formula result	=MIN(I84,F84,E84,D84)

This gives us –39.1, the minimum amount. For 2015, take care not to copy the same formula to the right. Doing so will shift all the cell references and change the output. Assuming we want to keep the projected 2014 number constant, we simply want to have our 2015 projection equal to our 2014 projection. So, we want Cell K84 to read "=J84", or type "=" in Cell K84, tap the left arrow key once to select Cell J84, and hit Enter. It is the formula in Cell K84 that we can copy over to the right through 2018 (see Table 6.10).

TABLE 6.10   Heinz Projected Change in Restricted Cash

Change in restricted cash	2010 A	2011 A	2012 A	9Mo. 2012	9Mo. 2013	LTM	2014 E	2015 E	2016 E	2017 E	2018 E
	192.7	(5.0)	(39.1)	(39.1)	4.0	4.0	(39.1)	(39.1)	(39.1)	(39.1)	(39.1)
Formula	192.7	(5.0)	(39.1)	(39.1)	4.0	=F84-G84+H84	=MIN(I84, F84,E84,D84)	=J84	=K84	=L84	=M84

Other Items, Net

Like most "other" items, it is difficult to define exactly what "Other items, net" is made up of. Using the seven methods approach as before, we have decided to use the "last year" method, as it also happens to be the "conservative" method as well. We can use the "minimum" formula as before to illustrate use of the conservative method, or we can simply have J85 read "=I85" to illustrate the use of the last year method. We did the latter. We can copy cell J85 to the right through 2018.

Now we need to redo our "total cash from investing activities" formula, because we had added the line "CAPEX % of revenue," which we do not want included in our total.

Total Cash from Investing Activities (Cell D86)

Excel Keystrokes	Description
Type "="	Enters into "formula" mode
Select Cell D78	Selects the first row
Type "+SUM("	Adds the "SUM" formula
Select Cell D80	Selects the first cell in series
Type ":"	Indicates we want to include all cells from the first cell to the last cell in series

Select Cell D85	Selects the last cell in series
Type ")"	Ends the "SUM" formula
Hit Enter	End
Formula result	=D78+SUM(D80:D85)

We can now copy this formula through 2018 (see Table 6.11).

Cash Flow from Financing Activities

Remember to think of the financing activities in three major sections.

1. Raising or buying back equity.
2. Raising or paying down debt.
3. Distributions.

All items relating to new debts we will leave empty for now. These projected line items will ultimately come from the debt schedule, which will be

TABLE 6.11 Heinz Projected Cash Flow from Investing Activities

Consolidated Statements of Cash Flows (in US$ millions except per share amounts)					
	Estimates				
Period Ending	2014E	2015E	2016E	2017E	2018E
Cash flows from investing activities					
Capital expenditures (CAPEX)	$(469.5)	$(471.4)	$(473.3)	$(475.2)	$(477.1)
CAPEX % *of revenue*	4.0%	4.0%	4.0%	4.0%	4.0%
Proceeds from disposals of property, plant, and equipment	0.0	0.0	0.0	0.0	0.0
Acquisitions, net of cash acquired	0.0	0.0	0.0	0.0	0.0
Proceeds from divestitures	0.0	0.0	0.0	0.0	0.0
Sale of short-term investments	0.0	0.0	0.0	0.0	0.0
Change in restricted cash	(39.1)	(39.1)	(39.1)	(39.1)	(39.1)
Other items, net	(12.3)	(12.3)	(12.3)	(12.3)	(12.3)
Total cash provided by (used for) investing activities	$(520.9)	$(522.7)	$(524.6)	$(526.5)	$(528.4)

discussed later. This includes revolver borrowings (repayments), term facilities borrowings (repayments), and notes borrowings (repayments).

All items relating to new equity we can hard-code as "0." This includes common equity and preferred equity (Rows 91 and 92). You will understand this better once we start linking the projected cash flow into the balance sheet, but adding a value for common equity in 2014 means the investors will put in more funds beyond the original investment. We will assume the investors will not be reinvesting into the business yet.

All items related to old debts are gone. We assume the debts of the business have been paid down. Remember in the uses of cash in the Assumptions tab, we illustrate that additional funds need to be raised to pay down the old debts. So these items will not exist anymore. This includes proceeds (payments) of long-term debt, and net payments on commercial paper and short-term debt (Rows 93 and 94). These will all be "0." We will solidify this when we explain the balance sheet adjustments after the transaction.

All items related to old equity are gone. The equity of the business has been bought out. So these items will not exist anymore. This includes dividends, purchases of treasury stock, exercise of stock options, and acquisitions of subsidiary shares (Rows 95 to 98). These will all be "0." We will solidify this when we explain the balance sheet adjustments after a transaction. See Table 6.12.

Earn-Out Settlement

The earn-out settlement was a settlement related to Foodstar that occurred in the third quarter of 2013. We found a note in the 3Q report that briefly explains the situation:

The Company acquired Foodstar, a manufacturer of soy sauces and fermented bean curd in China, in Fiscal 2011. Consideration for this acquisition included a potential earn-out payment in Fiscal 2014 contingent upon certain net sales and EBITDA (earnings before interest, taxes, depreciation and amortization) targets during Fiscals 2013 and 2014. The fair value of the earn-out was estimated using a discounted cash flow model and was based on significant inputs not observed in the market and thus represented a Level 3 measurement. Key assumptions in determining the fair value of the earn-out included the discount rate, and revenue and EBITDA projections for Fiscals 2013 and 2014. During the third quarter of Fiscal 2013, the Company renegotiated the terms of the earn-out agreement in order to give the Company additional flexibility in the future for growing its business in China, one of its largest and most important emerging markets. This renegotiation resulted in *the settlement of the earn-out for a cash payment of $60.0 million, of which $15.5 million was reported in cash from operating activities and $44.5 million was reported in cash from financing activities on the consolidated cash flow statement for the nine months ended January 27, 2013. In addition, the Company incurred a $12.1 million charge in the third quarter ended January 27, 2013, which was recorded in SG&A on the consolidated income statement and in the Non-Operating segment, for the difference between the settlement amount and current carrying value of the earn-out as reported on the Company's balance sheet at the date of this transaction.*

(Heinz 3Q Report, page 20)

So this earn-out is nonrecurring and should be hard-coded "0" in the future.

The note mentions that the earn-out has affected other financials, including the SG&A portion of the income statement. If you wish to be completely accurate, you may want to remove the $12.1 million charge from the nine-month 2013 SG&A and consider that as part of the nonrecurring events. We will leave the SG&A as is for now; we do not want to complicate the book with back-and-forth adjustments. And this particular adjustment is so relatively small, it will not affect the overall analysis. It is important, however, to understand that such adjustments can be made to normalize income statement items such as EBIT and EBITDA.

Other Items, Net

Again, here is another "other" item that is difficult to define. Using the seven methods approach as before, we have decided to use the conservative method. However, there are several other methods we could have used. If this number had been significantly negative, we would have considered a different method. Note that these values are particularly small when compared to the total cash flow of the business, so we did not spend too much time deliberating over the alternative methods, as we would have with a cash flow item that has larger flows. To illustrate use of the conservative method, we have used the "minimum" formula:

2014 Other Items, Net (Cell J100)

Excel Keystrokes	Description
Type "="	Enters into "formula" mode
Type "MIN("	Starts minimum formula
Select Cell I100	LTM other items, net
Type ","	Adds a comma to get ready for the next value
Select Cell F100	2012 other items, net
Type ","	Adds a comma to get ready for the next value

(continued)

Select Cell E100	2011 other items, net
Type ","	Adds a comma to get ready for the next value
Select Cell D100	2010 other items, net
Type ")"	Ends minimum formula
Hit Enter	End
Formula result	=MIN(I100,F100,E100,D100)

This results in the −9.1 from 2010. Remember, when using the "minimum" formula take care to not copy the same formula to the right for 2015. Doing so will shift all the cell references and change our answer. Assuming we want to keep the projected 2014 number constant, we simply want to have our 2015 projection equal to our 2014 projection. So, type "=" in Cell K100, tap the left arrow key once to select Cell J100, and hit Enter. It is the formula in Cell K100 that we can copy over to the right through 2018.

We can now copy the total formula from I101 over to 2018. See Table 6.12.

TABLE 6.12 Heinz Projected Cash flow from Financing Activities

Consolidated Statements of Cash Flows (in US$ millions except per share amounts)

		Estimates			
Period Ending	2014E	2015E	2016E	2017E	2018E
Cash flows from financing activities					
Revolver borrowings (repayments)					
Term facilities borrowings (repayments)					
The notes borrowings (repayments)					
Common equity	0.0	0.0	0.0	0.0	0.0
Preferred equity	0.0	0.0	0.0	0.0	0.0
Proceeds (payments) of long-term debt	0.0	0.0	0.0	0.0	0.0
Net payments on commercial paper and short-term debt	0.0	0.0	0.0	0.0	0.0
Dividends	0.0	0.0	0.0	0.0	0.0
Purchases of treasury stock	0.0	0.0	0.0	0.0	0.0
Exercise of stock options	0.0	0.0	0.0	0.0	0.0
Acquisitions of subsidiary shares from noncontrolling interests	0.0	0.0	0.0	0.0	0.0
Earn-out settlement	0.0	0.0	0.0	0.0	0.0
Other items, net	(9.1)	(9.1)	(9.1)	(9.1)	(9.1)
Total cash provided by (used for) financing activities	$(9.1)	$(9.1)	$(9.1)	$(9.1)	$(9.1)

Effect of Exchange Rates on Cash

This line item is volatile. Let's use the "conservative" method given the volatility, although other methods could work here as well. Here, maybe we are being too conservative, but in my opinion, it's better to be conservative and pleasantly surprised if the outcome is more positive than predicted. We will again use the "minimum" formula:

2014 Effect of Exchange Rates on Cash (Cell J102)

Excel Keystrokes	Description
Type "="	Enters into "formula" mode
Type "MIN("	Starts minimum formula
Select Cell I102	LTM effect of exchange rates on cash
Type ","	Adds a comma to get ready for the next value
Select Cell F102	2012 effect of exchange rates on cash
Type ","	Adds a comma to get ready for the next value
Select Cell E102	2011 effect of exchange rates on cash
Type ","	Adds a comma to get ready for the next value
Select Cell D102	2010 effect of exchange rates on cash
Type ")"	Ends minimum formula
Hit Enter	End
Formula result	=MIN(I102,F102,E102,D102)

This results in the −122.1 from 2012. Remember to have our 2015 projection equal to our 2014 projection. So, type "=" in Cell K102, tap the left arrow key once to select Cell J102 and hit Enter. This is the formula, Cell J100 that we can copy over to the right through 2018 (see Table 6.13).

Our cash flow projections are complete and we can now copy the Total cash and cash equivalents formula from I103 over to the right through 2018.

There is a line at the bottom of the cash flow statement entitled "Cash flow before debt pay-down." As discussed when inputting the historicals, this line item is utilized for the debt schedule. So we will leave that line item empty for now and discuss in the debt schedule section.

It is now time to discuss and create the adjusted balance sheet. With the adjusted balance sheet we can build the depreciation and operating working capital schedules, which will be used to complete these cash flow projections. Refer to Appendix 1 to ensure you are following the model building path.

TABLE 6.13 Heinz Projected Cash Flow Statement

Consolidated Statements of Cash Flows (in US$ millions except per share amounts)

Period Ending	2014E	2015E	Estimates 2016E	2017E	2018E
Cash flows from operating activities					
Net income	$1,389.4	$1,395.1	$1,400.7	$1,406.4	$1,412.1
Depreciation					
Amortization					
Amortization of identifiable intangible assets					
Deferred tax (benefit) / provision					
Net losses on divestitures	0.0	0.0	0.0	0.0	0.0
Impairment on assets held for sale	0.0	0.0	0.0	0.0	0.0
Pension contributions	(80.0)	(80.0)	(80.0)	(80.0)	(80.0)
Asset write-downs from Fiscal 2012 productivity initiatives	0.0	0.0	0.0	0.0	0.0
Other items, net	10.2	10.2	10.2	10.2	10.2
Changes in operating working capital					
Changes in receivables					
Changes in inventories					
Changes in prepaid expenses and other current assets					
Changes in accounts payable					
Changes in accrued liabilities					
Changes in accrued income taxes					
Net changes in operating working capital	$ 0.0	$ 0.0	$ 0.0	$ 0.0	$ 0.0
Total cash provided by (used for) operating activities	$1,319.6	$1,325.3	$1,330.9	$1,336.6	$1,342.3

Cash flows from investing activities					
Capital expenditures (CAPEX)	(469.5)	(471.4)	(473.3)	(475.2)	(477.1)
CAPEX % of *revenue*	4.0%	4.0%	4.0%	4.0%	4.0%
Proceeds from disposals of property, plant, and equipment	0.0	0.0	0.0	0.0	0.0
Acquisitions, net of cash acquired	0.0	0.0	0.0	0.0	0.0
Proceeds from divestitures	0.0	0.0	0.0	0.0	0.0
Sale of short-term investments	0.0	0.0	0.0	0.0	0.0
Change in restricted cash	(39.1)	(39.1)	(39.1)	(39.1)	(39.1)
Other items, net	(12.3)	(12.3)	(12.3)	(12.3)	(12.3)
Total cash provided by (used for) investing activities	$ (520.9)	$ (522.7)	$ (524.6)	$ (526.5)	$ (528.4)
Cash flows from financing activities					
Revolver borrowings (repayments)	0.0	0.0	0.0	0.0	0.0
Term facilities borrowings (repayments)	0.0	0.0	0.0	0.0	0.0
The notes borrowings (repayments)	0.0	0.0	0.0	0.0	0.0
Common equity	0.0	0.0	0.0	0.0	0.0
Preferred equity	0.0	0.0	0.0	0.0	0.0
Proceeds (payments) of long-term debt	0.0	0.0	0.0	0.0	0.0
Net payments on commercial paper and short-term debt	0.0	0.0	0.0	0.0	0.0
Dividends	0.0	0.0	0.0	0.0	0.0
Purchases of treasury stock	0.0	0.0	0.0	0.0	0.0
Exercise of stock options	0.0	0.0	0.0	0.0	0.0

(continued)

TABLE 6.13 (Continued)

Consolidated Statements of Cash Flows (in US$ millions except per share amounts)

Period Ending		Estimates				
	2014E	2015E	2016E	2017E	2018E
Acquisitions of subsidiary shares from noncontrolling interests	0.0	0.0	0.0	0.0	0.0
Earn-out settlement	0.0	0.0	0.0	0.0	0.0
Other items, net	(9.1)	(9.1)	(9.1)	(9.1)	(9.1)
Total cash provided by (used for) financing activities	$ (9.1)	$ (9.1)	$ (9.1)	$ (9.1)	$ (9.1)
Effect of exchange rate changes on cash and cash equivalents	(122.1)	(122.1)	(122.1)	(122.1)	(122.1)
Total change in cash and cash equivalents	$ 667.5	$ 671.3	$ 675.0	$ 678.8	$ 682.6
Supplemental Data:					
Cash flow before debt pay-down					

CHAPTER 7

The Balance Sheet

The balance sheet is a measure of a company's financial position at a specific point in time. The balance sheet's performance is broken up into three major categories: assets, liabilities, and shareholders' equity; the company's total value of assets must always equal the sum of its liabilities and shareholders' equity.

$$\text{Assets} = \text{Liabilities} + \text{Shareholders' Equity}$$

ASSETS

An asset is a resource held to produce some economic benefit. Examples of assets are cash, inventory, accounts receivable, and property. Assets are separated into two categories: current assets and noncurrent assets.

Current Assets

A current asset is an asset whose economic benefit is expected to come within one year. Examples of common current assets follow.

Cash and Cash Equivalents
Cash is currency on hand. Cash equivalents are assets that are readily convertible into cash, such as money market holdings, short-term government bonds or Treasury bills, marketable securities, and commercial paper. Cash equivalents are often considered as cash because they can be easily liquidated when necessary.

Accounts Receivable
Accounts receivable (AR) are sales made on credit. The revenue for the sale has been recognized, but the customer did not pay for the sale in cash. An asset is recorded for the amount of the sale and remains until the customer has paid. If AR increases by $100, for example, then we must have booked a sale. So, revenue increases by $100.

Income Statement	
Revenue	$100.0
Taxes (@ 40%)	(40.0)
Net Income	**60.0**

The resulting net income increase of $60 flows to the cash flow statement. We then need to remove the $100 in AR, as an increase in AR of $100 results in an operating working capital cash outflow of $100. Combined with the net income increase of $60, we have a total cash change of –$40.

Cash Flow		Balance Sheet	
Net Income	60.0	Cash	(40.0)
Changes in Accounts Receivable	(100.0)	Accounts Receivable	100.0
Total Changes in Cash	**(40.0)**	Retained Earnings (Net Income)	60.0

In the balance sheet, cash is reduced by $40, AR increases by $100, and retained earnings increases by $60. Note the relationship between the changes in accounts receivable on the cash flow statement and accounts receivable on the balance sheet: cash down, asset up. The balance sheet balances; total assets (–$40 + $100 = $60) less liabilities ($0) equals retained earnings ($60).

When the customer finally pays, cash is received and the AR on the balance sheet is removed.

Cash Flow		Balance Sheet	
Net Income	**0.0**	Cash	100.0
Changes in Accounts Receivable	100.0	Accounts Receivable	(100.0)
Total Changes in Cash	**100.0**	Retained Earnings (Net Income)	0.0

Inventory

Inventory is the raw materials and the goods that are ready for sale. When raw materials are acquired, inventory is increased by the amount of material purchased. Once goods are sold and recorded as revenue, the value of the inventory is reduced and a cost of goods sold (COGS) expense is recorded. Let's say, for example, we are selling chairs.

If inventory increases by $50, then we have most likely purchased inventory, resulting in a cash outflow. Cash is reduced by $50 and an inventory asset is created. Note the relationship between the changes in inventory on the cash flow statement and inventory on the balance sheet: cash down, asset up.

Cash Flow		Balance Sheet	
Net Income	**0.0**	Cash	(50.0)
Changes in Inventory	(50.0)	Inventory	50.0
Total Changes in Cash	**(50.0)**	Retained Earnings (Net Income)	0.0

If inventory decreases by $50, it is most likely related to a sale of that inventory, which is expensed as COGS. Note that the additional expense affects taxes and the resulting net income is –$30. An asset sold results in a cash increase; when added to the –$30 of net income, it gives us a total $20 change in cash.

Income Statement	
COGS	(50.0)
Taxes (@ 40%)	20.0
Net Income	(30.0)

Cash Flow			Balance Sheet	
Net Income	(30.0)		Cash	20.0
Changes in Inventory	50.0		Inventory	(50.0)
Total Changes in Cash	20.0		Retained Earnings (Net Income)	(30.0)

Inventory is reduced by 50. Net income affects retained earnings. The balance sheet balances; total assets ($20 – $50 = –$30) less liabilities ($0) equals retained earnings (–$30).

Prepaid Expense

Prepaid expense is an asset created when a company pays for an expense in advance of when it is billed or incurred. Let's say we decide to prepay rent expense by $100. Cash goes into a prepaid expense account. Note the relationship between the changes in prepaid expense on the cash flow statement and prepaid expense on the balance sheet: cash down, asset up.

Cash Flow			Balance Sheet	
Net Income	0.0		Cash	(100.0)
Changes in Prepaid Expense	(100.0)		Prepaid Expense	100.0
Total Changes in Cash	(100.0)		Retained Earnings (Net Income)	0.0

When the expense is actually incurred, it is then expensed in the selling, general, and administrative (SG&A) account; after tax we get –$60 in net income.

Income Statement	
SG&A	$(100.0)
Taxes (@ 40%)	40.0
Net Income	(60.0)

The –$60 in net income flows into retained earnings on the balance sheet. The prepaid expense asset is reduced, causing a change in prepaid expense inflow.

Cash Flow	
Net Income	(60.0)
Changes in Prepaid Expense	100.0
Total Changes in Cash	**40.0**

Balance Sheet	
Cash	40.0
Prepaid Expense	(100.0)
Retained Earnings (Net Income)	(60.0)

The balance sheet balances: the total assets ($40 – $100 = –$60) less liabilities ($0) equals shareholders' equity (–$60).

Noncurrent Assets

Noncurrent assets are not expected to be converted into cash within one year. Some examples of noncurrent assets follow.

Property, Plant, and Equipment (PP&E)

Property, plant, and equipment are assets purchased in order to further the company's operations. Also known as fixed assets, examples of PP&E are buildings, factories, and machinery.

Intangible Assets

An intangible asset is an asset that cannot be physically touched. Intellectual property, such as patents, trademarks, and copyrights, along with goodwill and brand recognition are all examples intangible assets.

LIABILITIES

A liability is any debt or financial obligation of a company. There are current liabilities and noncurrent liabilities.

Current Liabilities

Current liabilities are company debts or obligations that are owed within one year. Some examples of current liabilities follow.

Accounts Payable

Accounts payable are obligations owed to a company's suppliers. If a company, for example, purchases $500 in raw materials from its supplier on credit, the company incurs a $500 account payable. The company increases the accounts payable by $500 until it pays the supplier.

Cash Flow	
Net Income	0.0
Changes in Accounts Payable	500.0
Total Changes in Cash	500.0

Balance Sheet	
Cash	500.0
Accounts Payable	500.0
Retained Earnings (Net Income)	0.0

Once the supplier is paid, the accounts payable is reduced by $500, and cash on the balance sheet goes down by $500. Note the relationship between the changes in accounts payable on the cash flow statement and accounts payable on the balance sheet: cash up, liability up.

Accrued Liabilities

Accrued liabilities are expenses that have been incurred but have not yet been paid. If a company receives a utility bill of $1,000, for example, which is expensed under SG&A, an accrued liabilities account is also recorded for $1,000 in the balance sheet.

Income Statement	
SG&A	$(1,000.0)
Taxes (@ 40%)	400.0
Net Income	(600.0)

After taxes, the net income effect is –$600, which flows to cash flow. Note the relationship between the changes in accrued liabilities on the cash flow statement and accrued liabilities on the balance sheet: cash up, liability up.

Cash Flow			Balance Sheet	
Net Income	(600.0)		Cash	400.0
Changes in Accrued Liabilities	1,000.0		Accrued Liabilities	1,000.0
Total Changes in Cash	400.0		Retained Earnings (Net Income)	(600.0)

Once the bill has been paid, the accrued liabilities is reduced, and cash in the balance sheet goes down by $1,000.

Cash Flow			Balance Sheet	
Net Income	0.0		Cash	(1,000.0)
Changes in Accrued Liabilities	(1,000.0)		Accrued Liabilities	(1,000.0)
Total Changes in Cash	(1,000.0)		Retained Earnings (Net Income)	0.0

Short-Term Debts

Short-term debts are debts that come due within one year.

Noncurrent Liabilities

Noncurrent liabilities are company debts or obligations due beyond one year. Some examples of noncurrent liabilities follow.

Long-Term Debts
Long-term debts are debts due beyond one year.

Deferred Taxes
Deferred taxes result from timing differences between net income recorded for generally accepted accounting principles (GAAP) purposes and net income recorded for tax purposes. Deferred taxes can act as a liability or an asset. We discuss deferred taxes in Chapter 9.

HEINZ BALANCE SHEET

We should now hard-code in the historical balance sheet numbers for Heinz. It is first important to note timing. Since we are performing the analysis as of January 2013, we would like a balance sheet snapshot as of that date. Remember, a balance sheet is a snapshot, a current overall standing of assets, liabilities, and equity; so we do not need to make last twelve months (LTM) adjustments as we had done in the income statement and cash flow statement. Pages 6 and 7 of the Heinz 3Q quarterly report contain the most current balance sheet information. See Figures 7.1 and 7.2.

Heinz's balance sheet line items can be listed as the company has done—there will be a few adjustments we will make here, but we should go through them line by line. Let's just hard-code in the latest balance sheet—no prior

H.J. Heinz Company and Subsidiaries
Condensed Consolidated Balance Sheets

	January 27, 2013 FY 2013 (Unaudited) (In thousands)	April 29, 2012* FY 2012
Assets		
Current Assets:		
Cash and cash equivalents	$ 1,100,689	$ 1,330,441
Trade receivables, net	896,415	815,600
Other receivables, net	202,358	177,910
Inventories:		
Finished goods and work-in-process	1,135,509	1,082,317
Packaging material and ingredients	312,845	247,034
Total inventories	1,448,354	1,329,351
Prepaid expenses	173,045	174,795
Other current assets	88,011	54,139
Total current assets	3,908,872	3,882,236
Property, plant, and equipment	5,319,307	5,266,561
Less accumulated depreciation	2,891,133	2,782,423
Total property, plant, and equipment, net	2,428,174	2,484,138
Goodwill	3,104,527	3,185,527
Trademarks, net	1,050,856	1,090,892
Other intangibles, net	383,043	407,802
Other noncurrent assets	1,053,632	932,698
Total other noncurrent assets	5,592,058	5,616,919
Total assets	$ 11,929,104	$ 11,983,293

FIGURE 7.1   Heinz Historical 3Q Balance Sheet—Assets

H.J. Heinz Company and Subsidiaries
Condensed Consolidated Balance Sheets

		January 27, 2013 FY 2013	April 29, 2012* FY 2012
		(Unaudited)	
		(In thousands)	
Liabilities and Equity			
Current Liabilities:			
Short-term debt	$	14,747	$ 46,460
Portion of long-term debt due within one year		1,038,511	200,248
Trade payables		1,129,651	1,202,398
Other payables		158,143	146,414
Accrued marketing		320,052	303,132
Other accrued liabilities		623,962	647,769
Income taxes		91,283	101,540
Total current liabilities		3,376,349	2,647,961
Long-term debt		3,930,592	4,779,981
Deferred income taxes		776,660	817,928
Nonpension postretirement benefits		230,919	231,452
Other noncurrent liabilities		504,760	581,390
Total long-term liabilities		5,442,931	6,410,751
Redeemable noncontrolling interest		28,706	113,759
Equity:			
Capital stock		107,834	107,835
Additional capital		608,820	594,608
Retained earnings		7,877,440	7,567,278
		8,594,094	8,269,721
Less:			
Treasury stock at cost (110,445 shares at January 27, 2013, and 110,870 shares at April 29, 2012)		4,675,844	4,666,404
Accumulated other comprehensive loss		887,669	844,728
Total H.J. Heinz Company shareholders' equity		3,030,581	2,758,589
Noncontrolling interest		50,537	52,233
Total equity		3,081,118	2,810,822
Total liabilities and equity	$	11,929,104	$ 11,983,293

FIGURE 7.2   Heinz Historical 3Q Balance Sheet—Liabilities and Equity

historicals. We are going to use this balance sheet to make adjustments reflecting the purchase. You can choose to hard-code the prior year's numbers, but it is not so important in this case as we are not going to analyze balance sheet trends; rather, we will create an adjusted balance sheet based on transaction assumptions.

We are going to hard-code the Heinz balance sheet directly in the consolidated balance sheet adjustments section beginning in Row 106. Once we have hard-coded in the Heinz balance sheet, we are going to adjust and project what the balance sheet will look like after the transaction. It is the posttransaction (or pro forma) balance sheet we will use to make our future projections. Refer to the high-level model overview in Appendix 1 to ensure you have a good understanding of where we are in the overall process of building this full-scale model.

Current Assets

"Cash and cash equivalents," "Trade receivables, net," and "Other receivables, net" we can hard-code in. So we can enter the "1,100.689," "896.415," and "202.358" into Cells E112, E113, and E114, respectively, remembering to adjust each value into millions of units. (See Table 7.1.)

Inventories have been separated into two separate line items. Although we could technically break out the inventory components as Heinz has done, we are really just concerned about the total balance. The cash flow statement is a clue here. We will later see how the cash flow statement is used to drive our balance sheet forward. So if the cash flow statement does not separate out types of inventory, we should not. So let's just hard-code the total, "1448.354," into Cell E115. The idea of looking to the cash flow statement to align and project balance sheet items is very important to modeling and will be discussed in Chapter 11.

We can continue by hard-coding in the "Prepaid expenses" as Heinz has it, but in millions of units, into Cell E116. Unfortunately, we could not find much detail on exactly what "Other current assets" is made up of, but regardless we need to present it as Heinz has, so we can hard-code "88.011" into Cell E117. (See Table 7.1.)

We can easily total up the historical current assets in Cell E118 as "=SUM(E112:E17)." By now you should be familiar with how to create a SUM formula. The "Alt" + "=" hot key can also work well here.

TABLE 7.1   Heinz Historical Current Assets

Consolidated Balance Sheet Adjustments (in US$ millions except per share amounts)	
	Actuals
On January 27, 2013	LTM
Assets	
Current assets:	
Cash and cash equivalents	$1,100.7
Trade receivables, net	896.4
Other receivables, net	202.4
Total inventories	1,448.4
Prepaid expenses	173.0
Other current assets	88.0
Total current assets	$3,908.9

Noncurrent Assets

Property, plant, and equipment are noncurrent assets. You may often see the property, plant, and equipment line items separated from the accumulated depreciation line items as Heinz has done here. Let's just focus on the net PP&E number. Although the additional detail is good to have, we do not recommend having those items broken out within the balance sheet. You will later see that it will disturb the flow when making projections. If you feel it is necessary, you may want to have a separate schedule separating out the gross PP&E from the accumulated depreciation, but for now let's just focus on the "Total property, plant, and equipment, net." Let's hard-code "2428.174" into Cell E119.

Goodwill
Goodwill is an intangible asset that typically arises as a result of an acquisition. We discuss the importance of goodwill in the next chapter. Let's list this as a separate item; we can hard-code "3104.527" into Cell E120.

Intangible Assets
Although trademarks are a type of intangible asset, Heinz separates out the trademarks asset from all other intangible assets. More detail can be found on page 12 of the Heinz quarterly report. (See Figure 7.3.)

Because trademarks and other intangible assets are all considered intangible assets, we could group these line items together. For now, let's continue with hard-coding everything in line-by-line fashion. See Table 7.2.

Other Noncurrent Assets
Other noncurrent assets we can also list separately. Although it is not 100 percent clear what this line item is made up of, further research does mention other noncurrent assets in several notes, including:

> *The amounts recognized for pension benefits as other non-current assets on the Company's condensed consolidated balance sheets were $492.4 million as of January 27, 2013 and $399.9 million as of April 29, 2012.*

> (From Heinz annual report, page 14)

We also get Figure 7.4, from page 21 of the Heinz quarterly report, suggesting that derivatives such as foreign exchange contracts and interest rate contracts are among the other noncurrent assets.

So, we can hard-code the "1053.632" into Cell E123.

We can then total the assets section of the balance sheet. In Cell E124 we should have "=SUM(E118:E123)." See Table 7.2.

	January 27, 2013			April 29, 2012		
	Gross	Accum Amort	Net	Gross	Accum Amort	Net
			(In thousands)			
Trademarks	$ 286,554 $	(90,953) $	195,601 $	282,937 $	(87,925) $	195,012
Licenses	208,186	(168,234)	39,952	208,186	(163,945)	44,241
Recipes/processes	87,189	(37,107)	50,082	89,207	(35,811)	53,396
Customer-related assets	211,482	(75,360)	136,122	216,755	(69,244)	147,511
Other	46,476	(26,388)	20,088	48,643	(25,442)	23,201
	$ 839,887 $	(398,042) $	441,845 $	845,728 $	(382,367) $	463,361

FIGURE 7.3   Heinz Trademarks and Other Intangible Assets

	January 27, 2013			April 29, 2012		
	Foreign Exchange Contracts	Interest Rate Contracts	Cross-Currency Interest Rate Swap Contracts	Foreign Exchange Contracts	Interest Rate Contracts	Cross-Currency Interest Rate Swap Contracts
			(In thousands)			
Assets:						
Derivatives designated as hedging instruments:						
Other receivables, net	$ 23,131	$ 5,146	$ —	$ 17,318	$ 6,851	$ 18,222
Other noncurrent assets	11,912	27,365	—	8,188	29,393	4,974
	35,043	32,511	—	25,506	36,244	23,196
Derivatives not designated as hedging instruments:						
Other receivables, net	4,023	—	—	5,041	—	—
Other noncurrent assets	—	389	—	—	234	—
	4,023	389	—	5,041	234	—
Total assets	$ 39,066	$ 32,900	$ —	$ 30,547	$ 36,478	$ 23,196
Liabilities:						
Derivatives designated as hedging instruments:						
Other payables	$ 4,240	$ —	$ 22,389	$ 10,653	$ —	$ 2,760
Other noncurrent liabilities	—	—	25,274	14	—	—
	4,240	—	47,663	10,667	—	2,760
Derivatives not designated as hedging instruments:						
Other payables	1,516	—	—	1,952	—	—
Total liabilities	$ 5,756	$ —	$ 47,663	$ 12,619	$ —	$ 2,760

FIGURE 7.4　Heinz Derivative Instruments and Other Intangible Assets

TABLE 7.2　Heinz Historical Total Assets

Consolidated Balance Sheet Adjustments (in US$ millions except per share amounts)

	Actuals
On January 27, 2013	**LTM**
Assets	
Current assets:	
Cash and cash equivalents	$ 1,100.7
Trade receivables, net	896.4
Other receivables, net	202.4
Total inventories	1,448.4
Prepaid expenses	173.0
Other current assets	88.0
Total current assets	$ 3,908.9
Property, plant, and equipment, net	2,428.2
Goodwill	3,104.5
Trademarks, net	1,050.9
Other intangibles, net	383.0
Other noncurrent assets	1,053.6
Total assets	$11,929.1

Current Liabilities

We can now continue listing out the historical values for liabilities.

"Short-term debt" and the "Portion of long-term debt due within one year" we should hard-code as given in the Heinz quarterly report. Portion of long-term debt due within one year is the portion of the long-term debt that needs to be paid this year. Notice the "Revolver" line in Row 129. We had added this in order to handle the potential revolving line of credit that will be raised once the company has been purchased. We will discuss this in further detail when creating the balance sheet adjustments in the next chapter. For now, we will hard-code the revolver as "0" as it does not exist in the Heinz historical statements. See Table 7.3.

"Trade payables" and "other payables" can also be hard-coded as Heinz has them. Further research reveals "Other payables" on page 21 of the Heinz quarterly report, suggesting that derivatives are among the other payables. See Figure 7.4.

"Accrued marketing" is an accrued liability most likely related to marketing and advertising. We can hard-code this line item in as Heinz has done. We unfortunately do not get any detail on what "Other accrued liabilities" are made up of. However, let's also hard-code this directly into the model. "Income taxes" are taxes that Heinz has deferred. We will discuss this further in the Working Capital Chapter 10. For now, let's hard-code this in as Heinz has it. We can now total all current liabilities, so Cell E135 will read "=SUM(E127:E134). See Table 7.3.

TABLE 7.3 Heinz Historical Current Liabilities

Consolidated Balance Sheet Adjustments (in US$ millions except per share amounts)	
	Actuals
On January 27, 2013	**LTM**
Liabilities	
Current liabilities:	
Short-term debt	$ 14.7
Portion of long-term debt due within one year	1,038.5
Revolving line of credit	0.0
Trade payables	1,129.7
Other payables	158.1
Accrued marketing	320.1
Other accrued liabilities	624.0
Income taxes	91.3
Total current liabilities	$3,376.3

Noncurrent Liabilities

Notice in the first two rows (136 and 137), we have added placeholders for the debt raised to fund the purchase for the term facilities and for the notes. As with the revolving line of credit, let's hard-code this as "0" for now. We will discuss in the balance sheet adjustments chapter the significance of these rows and how to use them to create the pro forma balance sheet.

The Heinz long-term debt of $3,930,592 should be hard-coded in Cell E138 as "3930.592."

Deferred Taxes

We will also list out the deferred taxes. See Table 7.4. We discuss deferred taxes in Chapter 9.

Nonpension Postretirement Benefits

Nonpension postretirement benefits are typically benefits other than pensions paid to employees during their retirement years. Most postretirement benefits include life insurance and medical plans. Although these benefits are mostly employer-paid, retired employees often share in the cost of these benefits through co-payments, payment of deductibles, and making employee contributions to the plan when required.

Unfortunately, further research in the quarterly report does not reveal any additional information on exactly what the Heinz postretirement benefits are. However, we found the following note in page 58 of the Heinz annual report:

> *Other Postretirement Benefit Plans:*
> *The Company provides health care and life insurance benefits for retired employees and their eligible dependents. Certain of the Company's U.S. and Canadian employees may become eligible for such benefits. The Company currently does not fund these benefit arrangements until claims occur and may modify plan provisions or terminate plans at its discretion.*

So, let's hard-code the $230,919 in millions into Cell E140.

Other Noncurrent Liabilities

Other noncurrent liabilities we can also list separately. Although it is not 100 percent clear what this line item is made up of, further research does reveal the table, from page 21 of the Heinz quarterly report, suggesting that derivatives, including cross-currency interest rate swaps, are among the other noncurrent liabilities. (See Figure 7.4.)

So let's hard-code "504.760" into Cell E141.

Redeemable Noncontrolling Interest

To explain redeemable noncontrolling interest, it is first important to explain exactly what noncontrolling interest is.

> *The noncontrolling interest is the portion of equity (net assets) in a subsidiary not attributable, directly or indirectly, to a parent [ASC 810-10-45-15; IAS 27R.4]. Only financial instruments issued by a subsidiary that are classified as equity in the subsidiary's financial statements for financial reporting purposes can be noncontrolling interest in the consolidated financial statements [ASC 810-10-45-17]. A financial instrument that a subsidiary classifies as a liability is not a noncontrolling interest in the consolidated financial statements. However, not all financial instruments that are issued by a subsidiary and classified as equity will be recognized as a noncontrolling interest within equity in consolidation. For example, certain preferred stock, warrants, puts, calls, and options may not form part of noncontrolling interest within equity in consolidation by the parent company. For more information on the guidance to determine whether such instruments are considered noncontrolling interests in consolidation, see BCG 6.2.*

> (Pricewaterhouse Coopers, "A Global Guide to Accounting for Business Combinations and Noncontrolling Interests," page 57)

In other words, this is a portion of the company's subsidiary that is not owned by the company itself. For example, if Company A acquires 75 percent of Company B, Company A must consolidate all of Company B's financials into Company A's (because Company A had acquired greater than 50 percent of Company B). But the 25 percent of Company B that Company A does not own is recorded separately on Company A's balance sheet as noncontrolling interest. According to GAAP rules, this is recorded in the equity section of the balance sheet. Further, 25 percent of Company B's net income is reported as noncontrolling interest on the income statement for distribution to the owner(s) of the 25 percent stake of Company B. Let's look at the following example.

Income Statement—Company A	
Revenue	$10,000.0
Expenses	(7,000.0)
Taxes (@ 40%)	(1,200.0)
Net Income	1,800.0

Income Statement—Company B	
Revenue	$1,500.0
Expenses	(250.0)
Taxes (@ 40%)	(500.0)
Net Income	750.0

After the 75 percent acquisition, Company A will fully consolidate with Company B, showing a total net income of $2,550, which is Company A's net income of $1,800 plus Company B's net income of $750. However, at the bottom of the income statement, the portion of Company B's net income that Company A does not own is removed (25% × $750).

Income Statement—Company A + B	
Revenue	$11,500.0
Expenses	(7,250.0)
Taxes (@ 40%)	(1,700.0)
Net Income	2,550.0
Noncontrolling Interest	(187.5)
Net Income after NCI	2,362.5

Now the balance sheets are slightly different.

Balance Sheet—Company A	
Total Assets	$25,000.0
Total Liabilities	17,500.0
Shareholders' Equity	7,500.0

Balance Sheet—Company B	
Total Assets	$3,500.0
Total Liabilities	2,250.0
Shareholders' Equity	1,250.0

In the balance sheet the total assets and total liabilities are 100 percent consolidated. However, the equity is treated a bit differently. The shareholders' equity is 100 percent of Company A + 75 percent of Company B. A separate line (noncontrolling interest) is created representing the 25 percent of Company B. So the Assets – Liabilities = Equity formula will still hold (in this case equity as opposed to shareholders' equity).

Balance Sheet - Company A + B	
Total Assets	$28,500.0
Total Liabilities	19,750.0
Shareholders' Equity	8,437.5
Noncontrolling interest	312.5
Total Equity	8,750.0

The shareholders' equity is $7,500 + 75% × $1,250, and the non-controlling interest is 25% × $1,250.

Heinz separates out a portion of its noncontrolling interest and labels it "redeemable noncontrolling interest."

A note from the Heinz quarterly report explains the specific situation:

Redeemable Noncontrolling Interest
The minority partner in Coniexpress has the right, at any time, to exercise a put option to require the Company to purchase their equity interest at a redemption value determinable from a specified formula based on a multiple of EBITDA (subject to a fixed minimum linked to the original acquisition date value). The Company also has a call right on this noncontrolling interest exercisable at any time and subject to the same redemption price. The put and call options cannot be separated from the noncontrolling interest and the combination of a noncontrolling interest and the redemption feature require classification of the minority partner's interest as a redeemable noncontrolling interest in the condensed consolidated balance sheet.

So Heinz has the right to buy back this portion of the noncontrolling holder's stake at a specified price as per the note. Or the noncontrolling holder has the right to require that Heinz buy the stake at a specific price. Notice Heinz has classified this outside of the long-term liabilities section. This is a slightly tricky situation, as noncontrolling interests are, as per the latest accounting rules, classified as equity. This suggests the $28,706 thousand is being treated as some sort of mezzanine or hybrid between debt and equity. This is further defined as follows:

U.S. GAAP companies with securities that are redeemable upon the occurrence of an event that is not solely within the control of the issuer are subject to the guidance issued in ASC 480-10-S99-3A. Therefore, U.S. GAAP companies would continue to classify these securities as mezzanine equity in the consolidated financial statements but still consider these securities a noncontrolling interest.

(Pricewaterhouse Coopers, "A Global Guide to Accounting for Business Combinations and Noncontrolling Interests," page 58)

So, noncontrolling interests that can still be redeemed are classified as such. Even though Heinz does not have it listed this way, let's include this in our total liabilities within the long-term liabilities section. So, we can list Heinz's redeemable noncontrolling interest directly in Cell E142.

In conclusion, after listing out the Heinz balance sheet line items, we can total them in Cell E143, taking care also to include the total current liabilities, or "=SUM(E135:E142)" (see Table 7.4).

TABLE 7.4 Heinz Historical Total Liabilities

Consolidated Balance Sheet Adjustments (in US$ millions except per share amounts)	
	Actuals
On January 27, 2013	LTM
Liabilities	
Current liabilities:	
Short-term debt	$ 14.7
Portion of long-term debt due within one year	1,038.5
Revolving line of credit	0.0
Trade payables	1,129.7
Other payables	158.1
Accrued marketing	320.1
Other accrued liabilities	624.0
Income taxes	91.3
Total current liabilities	$3,376.3
Term facilities	0.0
The notes	0.0
Long-term debt	3,930.6
Deferred income taxes	776.7
Nonpension postretirement benefits	230.9
Other noncurrent liabilities	504.8
Redeemable noncontrolling interest	28.7
Total liabilities	$8,848.0

Equity and Shareholders' Equity

The shareholders' equity section of the balance sheet can be thought of in two major segments:

1. *Equity*. This can include common stock, preferred stock, or treasury stock.
2. *Earnings*. This can include:
   - *Retained earnings*—the portion of net income of the business that has not been distributed out to equity holders.
   - *Other comprehensive income or losses*—the unrealized gains or losses not included in standard net income. These unrealized gains and losses can be due to securities available for sale, derivatives, foreign currency

adjustments due to foreign subsidiaries, or pension adjustments, to name a few possibilities.

Common Stock and Additional Paid-In Capital

The first two equity line items in Figure 7.2, "Capital stock" and "Additional capital," we recommend combining as one. Shares are assigned a par value representing some base value the shares are initially worth. This par value is quite nominal, for example $0.10 per share. Once the shares are issued in the market, the price issued less this par value is the "capital in excess of par value." For example, let's say we want to raise 500 shares in the market. If we issue the shares into the market at $20 per share, the total value of funds raised is $20 × 500, or $10,000. However, if our shares had a $0.10 par value, we record this issuance in the shareholders' equity on the balance sheet in two lines: the par value at $50 (500 × $0.10) and the difference between the par value and the funds raised ($9,950) under "capital in excess of par value." This is also commonly known as additional paid-in capital (APIC), or Heinz labels this as Additional Capital.

For modeling purposes, it is just as easy to combine these line items as long as both the par value and the APIC are referring to the same type of security. So in our balance sheet we will have "=107.834 + 608.820" for capital stock, Cell E146.

Notice in the next two rows (147 and 148), we have added placeholders for the equity raised to fund the purchase, common equity (raised by both 3G and Berkshire Hathaway), and preferred equity (raised by Berkshire Hathaway). Like with the revolver and the term loans, let's hard-code this as "0" for now. We will discuss in the balance sheet adjustments chapter the significance of these rows and how to use them to create the pro forma balance sheet.

Retained Earnings, Treasury Stock, and Accumulated Other Comprehensive Loss

Retained earnings, treasury stock, and accumulated other comprehensive loss we will list as is on the balance sheet. Notice that treasury stock and accumulated other comprehensive loss have been separated out in a "Less:" section, indicating that these items are reducing the shareholders' equity. Because they are all part of the shareholders' equity section, we would prefer to list all such line items together in one group, but list the items that reduce shareholders' equity as negative. This is how it is more often done. However, there is no harm in creating the "Less:" section as Heinz has done. Let's hard-code "7877.440," "-4675.844," and "-887.699" into Cells E149, E150, and E151, respectively. Notice we converted the treasury stock and accumulated other comprehensive loss values to negative.

Noncontrolling Interest

Notice that the noncontrolling interest is listed separately from the rest of the shareholders' equity. Total equity is the shareholders' equity plus the noncontrolling interests. So we will first total shareholders' equity in Cell E152, summing Cells E146 through E151. Cell E152 is "=SUM(E146:E151)." We can then hard-code the noncontrolling interest into Cell E153. Our total equity is the sum of Cells E152 and E153. So in Cell E154 we will have "=E152+E153."

Our total liabilities and equity is the sum of Cells E154 and E143, so in Cell E155 we will have "=E154+E143." Notice the "match" Row 157, which tests to be sure the total assets equals the sum of the total liabilities and equity. The match should read "Y" at this point (see Table 7.5).

Refer to Appendix 1 to ensure you are following the model building path.

TABLE 7.5   Heinz Historical Balance Sheet

Consolidated Balance Sheet Adjustments (in US$ millions except per share amounts)	
	Actuals
On January 27, 2013	LTM
Assets	
Current assets:	
Cash and cash equivalents	$ 1,100.7
Trade receivables, net	896.4
Other receivables, net	202.4
Total inventories	1,448.4
Prepaid expenses	173.0
Other current assets	88.0
Total current assets	$ 3,908.9
Property, plant, and equipment, net	2,428.2
Goodwill	3,104.5
Trademarks, net	1,050.9
Other intangibles, net	383.0
Other noncurrent assets	1,053.6
Total assets	$11,929.1
Liabilities	
Current liabilities:	
Short-term debt	14.7
Portion of long-term debt due within one year	1,038.5
Revolving line of credit	0.0

TABLE 7.5 (*Continued*)

Consolidated Balance Sheet Adjustments (in US$ millions except per share amounts)

On January 27, 2013	Actuals LTM
Trade payables	1,129.7
Other payables	158.1
Accrued marketing	320.1
Other accrued liabilities	624.0
Income taxes	91.3
Total current liabilities	$ 3,376.3
Term facilities	0.0
The notes	0.0
Long-term debt	3,930.6
Deferred income taxes	776.7
Nonpension postretirement benefits	230.9
Other noncurrent liabilities	504.8
Redeemable noncontrolling interest	28.7
Total liabilities	$ 8,848.0
Total Equity	
Shareholders' equity	
Capital stock	716.7
Common equity investment	0.0
Preferred equity investment	0.0
Retained earnings	7,877.4
Treasury stock	(4,675.8)
Accumulated other comprehensive loss	(887.7)
Total shareholders' equity	3,030.6
Noncontrolling interest	50.5
Total equity	$ 3,081.1
Total liabilities and equity	$11,929.1
Supplemental Data: Balance? (Y/N)	Y

CHAPTER 8

Balance Sheet Adjustments

It is now time to revisit the transaction at hand. We have just hard-coded the latest reported Heinz balance sheet. However, what will the balance sheet look like after the transaction? It is important to properly represent what the balance sheet will look like after the purchase in order to make proper projections.

First let's recap what happens when a buyer comes into the business.

THE BUYER IS PAYING FOR

- *Shareholders' equity at a premium (purchase price):* The price negotiated for a transaction can represent the book value of the business (which is identified by shareholder's equity on the balance sheet). However, it is common for a buyer to pay a higher value for the business than what is stated as its book value. First, companies can have a public market value that most likely trades at a premium to book value (see Chapter 2 on valuation). Second, to properly incentivize the seller, a buyer typically pays a premium to the market value. This is called a control premium. That premium can be represented as goodwill. We may make additional adjustments to goodwill but this is a conceptual beginning. We will discuss such adjustments in the Goodwill section of this chapter.
- *Net debt (short-term + long-term – cash) and other obligations:* Refer to the discussion in Chapter 3 where we gave an initial overview of the buyout process. The buyer is responsible for the net debt only under certain conditions. Because Heinz is a public company, the buyer may be responsible for raising additional funds to pay down the debt. Or, based on the debt contracts, it may be okay to keep the debt on the balance sheet. If the company were private, it could be possible for the seller to be responsible for the debt. In addition, the buyer may also be responsible for equity holders of the business, including minority interest holders and other obligations such as capital leases. These all need to be taken into consideration when determining what aspects of the business need to be funded versus carried over to the new company's balance sheet.

THE BUYER IS RECEIVING

- *Total assets (excluding cash):* So to name the major items for example:
  - Accounts receivable.
  - Inventory.
  - Prepaid expense.
  - Property, plant, and equipment (PP&E).
- *Total liabilities (excluding net debt and other obligations):* To name the major items for example:
  - Accrued expenses.
  - Accounts payable.

So, in an acquisition a buyer is receiving target company line items, excluding items that deal with shareholders' equity or net debt. This is because we are paying off the shareholders (shareholders' equity is gone), and we are paying down the net debt (net debt is gone assuming we are responsible for paying down the net debt).

Additionally, three major categories of items are created upon the acquisition.

1. Goodwill (and other related adjustments to be discussed in the Goodwill section).
2. New debt (if debt is raised to fund the acquisition).
3. New equity (if equity is used to fund the acquisition).

GOODWILL

Goodwill is an intangible asset that typically arises as a result of an acquisition. In U.S. GAAP accounting rules, the price paid for a business above the book value (shareholders' equity) is generally defined as goodwill. But several other adjustments are often made based on tangible and intangible assets and deferred taxes, which will affect our amount of purchase price over book value allocated to goodwill.

> *Goodwill arising from a transaction is calculated as the total purchase price minus the sum of the fair values of the acquired tangible and intangible assets, liabilities, contingent liabilities and deferred taxes.*

> **(From "Intangible Assets and Goodwill in the Context of Business Combinations," KPMG, 2010, page 6, www.kpmg.com/PT/pt/ IssuesAndInsights/Documents/Intangible-assets-and-goodwill.pdf)**

More specifically these adjustments are:

Step-Up of Existing Assets

Notice the quote mentions the *fair values* of the acquired tangible and intangible assets. So, commonly pursuant to an acquisition, all of the assets are reevaluated and can be adjusted accordingly to their fair market values. This adjustment is called a "step-up" of assets. Note that a step-up of assets could result in additional deferred taxes. (See Chapter 9 for more on deferred tax.)

New Intangible Assets

Often in an acquisition a portion of the purchase price above book value can be allocated to new intangible assets. The conceptual idea is that the reason an acquirer could pay more for the company than what is stated on the book value is because they are paying for some intangible assets (branding, intellectual property, for example) that had not previously been identified and accounted for. It is beneficial to allocate as much of the purchase price over book value to intangible assets because, according to U.S. GAAP rules, intangible assets can be amortized. And of course, amortization is an income statement expense that reduces taxes.

The ability to amortize these items in general depends on how the business will be acquired and whether we are reporting for GAAP or Tax purposes. (Review Table 3.1 titled "Types of Acquisitions" in Chapter 3.) Note that goodwill itself, in contrast, is not amortized under U.S. GAAP accounting. It can be reevaluated (written down) every year, but gets no amortization.

One needs to also assess the actual value of the intangible assets and even determine if intangible assets exist. This indeed is a very difficult task, even for the professionals. See the following note from page 6 of "Intangible Assets and Goodwill in the Context of Business Combinations" by KPMG on the method and difficulty of valuing intangible assets.

> *Typically, due to their unique characteristics, the market price for intangible assets cannot be determined. In practice, the fair value to be attributed is therefore mainly determined by income oriented valuation methods. In this approach, the value of an asset is estimated as the present value of the future cash flows generated by the asset as at the date of acquisition (or "the valuation date"), which accrue to the acquiring company over the asset's remaining useful economic life or, if applicable, from the disposal of the asset. As part of this methodology, data such as the useful economical life or future expected spreads have to be determined and, with each industry having its own competition structure, principles and value drivers, industry specific knowledge is vital.*

(From "Intangible Assets and Goodwill in the Context of Business Combinations," KPMG, 2010, page 6, www.kpmg.com/PT/pt/ IssuesAndInsights/Documents/Intangible-assets-and-goodwill.pdf)

Page 11 of the KPMG report (see Figure 8.1) shows valuable statistics on the percentage of a purchase price that is allocated to intangible assets for historical transactions broken out by industry. This chart can be useful in order to guesstimate how much of the purchase price over book value can be allocated to goodwill versus intangible assets. It is interesting to note that the consumer products and services sector shows 57.0 percent. Remember

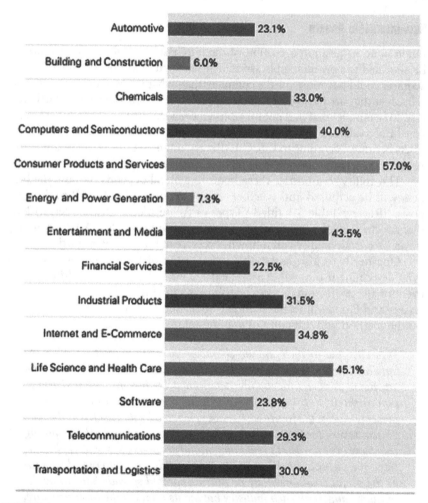

Industry	Percentage
Automotive	23.1%
Building and Construction	6.0%
Chemicals	33.0%
Computers and Semiconductors	40.0%
Consumer Products and Services	57.0%
Energy and Power Generation	7.3%
Entertainment and Media	43.5%
Financial Services	22.5%
Industrial Products	31.5%
Internet and E-Commerce	34.8%
Life Science and Health Care	45.1%
Software	23.8%
Telecommunications	29.3%
Transportation and Logistics	30.0%

FIGURE 8.1   Percentage Allocation of Purchase Price to Intangible Assets by Industry (Median)
Source: "Intangible Assets and Goodwill in the Context of Business Combinations," KPMG, 2010, 11.

that a buyer would most likely prefer a high allocation of intangibles to receive a tax deduction. In reality professionals such as intangible asset appraisers are brought in to analyze and value how much of the purchase price over book value can be allocated to intangible assets.

Deferred Tax Adjustments

In a purchase it is possible that a company's preexisting deferred tax assets and deferred tax liabilities will be adjusted or wiped out altogether. If that is the case, this will affect the amount of purchase price over book value allocated to Goodwill. And again, a tangible asset step or new intangible assets could result in additional deferred taxes created. (See the deferred tax section in Chapter 9.)

In summary:

Purchase Price – Book Value = Goodwill + Intangible Assets + Step-Up of Existing Assets + Deferred Tax Adjustments

For modeling purposes, let's assume 25 percent of the price paid above book is attributed to intangible assets. This is much more conservative than the 57.0 percent in Figure 8.1. We have often seen 25 percent used as a quick conservative assumption. Let's also conservatively assume no additional asset step-ups, or deferred tax adjustments, so the remainder is a goodwill asset. Here is an example:

An independent investor would like to buy a distribution business. The business has a book value of $20,000. The investor offers $30,000 for the company. This reflects a premium of $10,000 ($30,000 – $20,000 of shareholders' equity) of the purchase price over book value. The new balance sheet will have a shareholders' equity value of $30,000, reflecting the price paid. The investor estimates 25 percent of the $10,000 premium is attributable to intangible assets (e.g., the brand name "John's Trucks") and will be amortized for 15 years. The remainder is goodwill. The new balance sheet looks like Table 8.1.

So the high-level concept is a potential acquisition has four components that can be translated into a specific road map to make adjustments to a balance sheet in order to estimate an appropriate balance sheet after the purchase:

1. Paying off shareholders, net debt, and other obligations.
2. Receiving all other assets and liabilities.
3. Creating new goodwill, new intangible assets, stepping up assets, and deferring tax adjustments.
4. Creating new debt and new equity.

TABLE 8.1   Sample Balance Sheet Before and After LBO

John's Trucking Company (in $US thousands 000s)		
	Before	After
Assets		
Cash	$ 0.0	$ 0.0
Intangible Assets	0.0	2.5
Goodwill	0.0	7.5
Truck	20.0	20.0
Total Assets	$20.0	$30.0
Liabilities		
Debt	$ 0.0	$ 0.0
Shareholders' Equity	$20.0	$30.0

We recommend looking at the uses and sources of funds, our assumptions, to help justify appropriate transaction adjustments to be made. Just as cash drives the balance sheet, uses and sources of funds here drive our balance sheet adjustments.

Here we note the most common of uses:

- Purchase price.
- Net debt (and other obligations if necessary).
- Transaction fees.

TABLE 8.2   Balance Sheet Adjustments

Uses	Additions (+)	Subtractions (−)
Purchase price	Assets	
Target book value		
Goodwill		
Intangible assets		
Net debt	Liabilities	
Target short-term debt		
Target long-term debt		
(Target cash)		
Transaction fees	Shareholders' Equity	
Sources		
Debt		
Equity		

And we note the most common sources:

- Debt (term loans, high yield debt, and mezzanine debt as common examples).
- Equity (common or preferred).

Purchase Price Balance Sheet Adjustment

These sources and uses can be utilized to track exactly which transaction adjustments we should make. But we first need to translate our sources and uses items into balance sheet line items. For example, the purchase price is not directly a balance sheet item. However, we know that purchase price is measured against the target company's equity. And we know that if the purchase price is greater than the target company's equity, that difference is some combination of goodwill, intangible assets, and possibly a step-up of assets or deferred tax adjustments. For ease in conceptualizing this illustration let's just assume the purchase price over book is made up of just goodwill and intangible assets; there is no asset step-up or deferred tax adjustments in this illustration (See Table 8.2.)

So, the way to conceptualize this is that the funds allocated to the purchase price are used to pay down the shareholders' equity. But in order to keep the balance sheet in balance, if the purchase price is greater than the shareholders' equity, those extra funds go into a combination of a goodwill asset and an intangible asset account.

In Table 8.3 the arrows indicate where the specific adjustments to the purchase price should happen in the balance sheet. First, all components of the target book value are removed. This is the entire shareholders' equity section of the balance sheet. Old shareholders are gone, so that value is eliminated. New goodwill is created, and so are new intangible assets.

TABLE 8.3 Purchase Price Adjustment to Balance Sheet

Uses	Additions (+)	Subtractions (−)
Purchase price	Assets	
Target book value		
Goodwill	→ New goodwill	
Intangible assets	→ New intangible assets	
Net debt	Liabilities	
Target short-term debt		
Target long-term debt		
(Target cash)		
Transaction fees	Shareholders' Equity	
Sources		
Debt		
Equity		→ Target book value

TABLE 8.4   Net Debt Adjustment to Balance Sheet

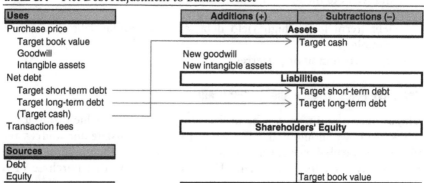

Net Debt Balance Sheet Adjustment

Next, we can look at net debt. (See Table 8.4.) For simplicity, to illustrate the process, we assumed the buyer is responsible for paying down the debts and the only obligations are the long-term and short-term debt. If the buyer is required to pay down the debts, the debts will be removed from the target balance sheet. Note we use "Net debt," as is often the case. If cash still exists on the target balance sheet, we will assume that will be used to pay down obligations as well. We list "Target cash" in parentheses to illustrate that this will net against the debt values.

Sources Balance Sheet Adjustment

Any funds sourced to meet the acquisition cost would become a new line item on the balance sheet. In this simple example we have raised some debt to fund the acquisition and have also raised some equity, so we draw lines to reflect that. See Table 8.5. In the Heinz case or other more complex cases,

TABLE 8.5   Sources Adjustments to Balance Sheet

Uses	Additions (+)	Subtractions (−)
Purchase price	**Assets**	
Target book value		Target cash
Goodwill	New goodwill	
Intangible assets	New intangible assets	
Net debt	**Liabilities**	
Target short-term debt		Target short-term debt
Target long-term debt		Target long-term debt
(Target cash)		
Transaction fees	**Shareholders' Equity**	
	New debt	
Sources	New equity	
Debt		
Equity		Target book value

TABLE 8.6   Transaction Fee Adjustments to Balance Sheet

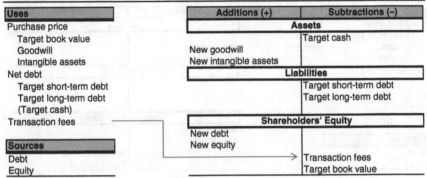

Uses		Additions (+)	Subtractions (−)
Purchase price		**Assets**	
Target book value			Target cash
Goodwill		New goodwill	
Intangible assets		New intangible assets	
Net debt		**Liabilities**	
Target short-term debt			Target short-term debt
Target long-term debt			Target long-term debt
(Target cash)			
Transaction fees		**Shareholders' Equity**	
		New debt	
Sources		New equity	
Debt			Transaction fees
Equity			Target book value

we just have more variations of debt and equity raised. Either way, each will become a new balance sheet line item.

Transaction Fees Balance Sheet Adjustment

Finally, we need to make adjustments based on the transaction fees. This is a bit tricky, as transaction fees are typically paid on the acquisition date. We know that we have raised a combination of debt and equity (sources) to help fund transaction fees, which are contained in our uses. But what is the balancing item to adjust for fees? We can make the adjustment directly in the shareholders' equity section of the balance sheet, reducing retained earnings other comprehensive income by the amount of transaction fees. See Table 8.6.

All the changes are laid out in Table 8.7. If you can conceptualize the balance sheet adjustments in this way—that is, the adjustments are based on the sources and uses of funds—the pro forma balance sheet must balance.

TABLE 8.7   Total Balance Sheet Adjustments

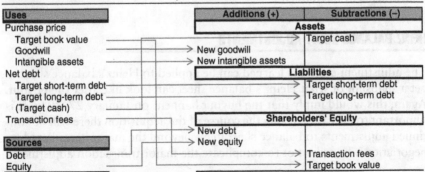

Uses		Additions (+)	Subtractions (−)
Purchase price		**Assets**	
Target book value			Target cash
Goodwill		New goodwill	
Intangible assets		New intangible assets	
Net debt		**Liabilities**	
Target short-term debt			Target short-term debt
Target long-term debt			Target long-term debt
(Target cash)			
Transaction fees		**Shareholders' Equity**	
		New debt	
Sources		New equity	
Debt			Transaction fees
Equity			Target book value

TABLE 8.8   Balance Sheet Adjustments—No Debt Pay-Down

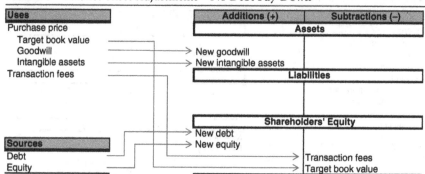

As sources of funds match the uses of funds, and assuming the starting balance sheet you are working with actually balances, funds coming into the balance sheet adjusted by the uses of funds should still produce a balancing balance sheet.

It is also important to conceptualize the adjustments this way because you may face unusual or more complex transactions where these standard adjustments do not apply, or where additional adjustments need to be made. You should have the tools to draw your own road map from the sources and uses as we have done. As a simple example, what if the buyer does not have to pay down debts and rather is able to keep the debt on the balance sheet? Well, if the buyer does not have to raise additional funds to pay down debt, then the debt will no longer be a part of the uses. And if that's the case, then there would be no need to make debt adjustments to the balance sheet. See Table 8.8.

Similarly, if additional sources or uses are added, you would need to think through how those items would transfer into balance sheet items, and adjust accordingly. Let's take a look now at how to actually make such adjustments in the model.

HEINZ BALANCE SHEET ADJUSTMENTS

The adjustment concepts learned can be applied to Heinz's balance sheet to get a snapshot of what Heinz's balance sheet can look like after the buyout. Again, this would imply that the buyout happens on January 27, 2013. It is important to note that during the course of the acquisition there will be continued adjustments to balance sheet items beyond the major items based on negotiations. In order not to complicate the major transaction adjustments with such one-off adjustments as asset write-ups or write-downs and deferred taxes, we have not included such adjustments. For instructional purposes, it is important to highlight the major adjustments that are transferrable to most acquisitions. Once the transaction is closed, we hope to see such a proxy document with all relative adjustments and the reasons for each. The lack of such detailed adjustments should not have a large effect on the overall returns analysis.

Net Debt

Before actually making the balance sheet adjustments, there are a few assumptions we need to complete back on the Assumptions tab in the model. If you recall in the uses section of the balance sheet, we had made a simplifying assumption backing into the net debt of Heinz because earlier on we had not evaluated the Heinz balance sheet. Now that we have evaluated and hard-coded in the Heinz balance sheet, we can use this information for our net debt in the uses section. So, in the Assumptions tab in the model we want to replace the formula in Cell K7 to now link directly from the balance sheet the total value of all debts less cash. This will include:

- Long-term debt.
- Portion of long-term debt due within one year.
- Short-term debt.
- Cash.

So cell J7 in the Assumptions tab will be: "=Financials!E138+Financials!E128+Financials!E127-Financials!E112."

This should give us $3,883.2 thousand in net debt, which is not too far off from our prior assumption. Notice, however, this net debt reduction has increased the transaction fees to $1,381.1 thousand, 5.9 percent of the purchase price. This is very high and a bit unrealistic. However, the preliminary proxy gave us an indication of sources of funds totaling $28,840 thousand and our uses of funds must match our sources of funds. In reality, I predict the buyers may reduce the amount of debt or equity raised. This would effectively bring the transaction fee numbers down to something more reasonable. For example, if we reduce the term facilities by $1Bn, hardcoding "9500" into F9, we see the transaction fees reduce to 1.6 percent of the purchase price—more reasonable. However, let's continue to stick to the numbers reported on the preliminary proxy despite the high fees. It is more conservative this way; we can always make adjustments at the end; this should not affect the overall returns too much.

Goodwill and Intangible Assets

It is also important now to calculate goodwill and intangible assets, which will also be used in our balance sheet adjustments. Beginning in Cell J12 in the Assumptions tab, we would need to pull in the Heinz purchase price. We can take this from Cell J6, so in Cell J12 we will have "=J6."

The next line, target book value, we will take from the Heinz balance sheet. Since the purchase price represents the value of the common stock, option holders, preferred holders, and restricted stockholders (not the non-controlling interest holder in this case), we need to compare this purchase price with just the shareholders' equity, not the total equity. So, in Cell J13 we will link in Cell E152 from the Financials tab.

The price over book, J14, represents the total premium paid over book value, or the purchase price less the book value. So J14 will be "=J12-J13."

Because the Heinz acquisition is a stock acquisition (see the "Types of Acquisitions" section in Chapter 3), not all of the purchase price above book value can be considered amortizable. Further, as discussed in the Goodwill section, it is almost impossible to separate out the potential intangible assets from the goodwill. But we can at least use a conservative assumption taking 25 percent of the purchase price above book value.

We also need to establish a useful life for the intangible assets. For new intangible assets, it is common practice to use 15 years. So, we can hard-code "25%" into Cell J15 and "15" into Cell J17. We can always adjust these assumptions if we get more clarity as to the purchase structure. The value of the new intangible assets can now be calculated by multiplying the 25 percent by the purchase price over book. Or, in Cell J16 we will have "=J14*J15."

We can now calculate the new amortization created from the new intangible assets. Assuming a 15-year amortization life, J18 will simply be "=J16/J17." See Table 8.9. This expense will be linked into the income statement

TABLE 8.9 Heinz Goodwill and Intangible Assets

Goodwill and Intangible Assets	
Purchase price (equity value)	$23,575.7
Target book value	3,030.6
Price over book	20,545.1
% book to amortization	25%
New Intangible Assets	5,136.3
Amortization (years)	15
Amortization ($/year)	342.4
Adjustments:	
Step-up of PP&E	0.0
Deferred tax adjustments	0.0
Goodwill	15,408.8

and cash flow statement. We will do that together in the depreciation and amortization chapter, Chapter 9, although it is technically possible to go ahead and link that through now.

Until we have more information, we will conservatively assume no step-up in PP&E and no deferred tax adjustments, so we can hardcode "0" in cells J20 and J21.

Finally, the goodwill, what is then left over, can be calculated by subtracting the new intangible assets, step-up in PP&E, and deferred tax adjustments from the purchase price over book value. Or, in J22 we will have "=J14-J16-J20-J21." These values will be used in the transaction adjustments.

Balance Sheet Adjustments

We can now go back to the Financials tab and start linking in the adjustments. Beginning in Row 110, you may notice Columns F and G labeled "Additions" and "Subtractions," respectively. We will use these columns to place our adjustments based on the theories discussed in the prior section.

Note that it is common practice, instead of using additions and subtractions, to make "T-accounting" adjustments using debits and credits. In other words, a debit would increase an asset, but decrease a liability; a credit would decrease an asset, but increase a liability. Although this method may more accurately represent balance sheet changes as per the methods of T-accounting, it is confusing and does not ultimately change how the adjustments are actually being made. It is easier and more straightforward simply to have additions and subtractions.

Before making the actual adjustments, let's set up the "Total" column in Column H. Each line item in the Total column will be equal to the LTM balance sheet line item plus the additions and minus the subtractions, or:

$$\text{Total} = \text{LTM} + \text{Additions} - \text{Subtractions}$$

So, for example, in H112 we should have "=E112+F112-G112."

We want to do this for every line item except the totals. In other words, the total current assets, Row 118, should be adding top down as total current assets normally do. So we can copy the formula in H112 down to H117 by highlighting everything from H112 through H117 and hitting "Ctrl + D." We can then recalculate the sum formula in H118 or we can hit "Alt" + "=" or we can copy and paste the same total formula from Cell E118 over to H118. If done correctly, the Total column values should be identical to the LTM column values. See Table 8.10.

We can continue this throughout the entire Total column, using the same adjustment formula used in Cells H112 to H117 for each line item except for the totals in the Total column. We can copy Cell H117, for example, and paste it into Rows 119 to 123. We can then recalculate total assets or simply copy the formula in E124 into H124.

TABLE 8.10   Setting Up the Asset Balance Sheet Adjustments

Consolidated Balance Sheet Adjustments (in US$ millions except per share amounts)				
		Pro Forma		
	Actuals	Additions	Subtractions	
On January 27, 2013	LTM	(+)	(−)	Total
Assets				
Current assets:				
Cash and cash equivalents	$1,100.7			$1,100.7
Trade receivables, net	896.4			896.4
Other receivables, net	202.4			202.4
Total inventories	1,448.4			1,448.4
Prepaid expenses	173.0			173.0
Other current assets	88.0			88.0
Total current assets	$3,908.9			$3,908.9

We can continue with the liabilities and equity sections copying the formula from H123 into H127 to H134, H136 to H142, H146 to H151, and H153. We can then take the total formulas from E135, E143, E152, E154, and E155, and copy them over to the H column. See Table 8.11.

It is important that the formulas are calculating correctly at this point so when we input our adjustments, they will properly flow into the Total column.

We can now start making adjustments as per the prior section's discussion. With the understanding that the purchase price can be represented as Shareholders' Equity + Goodwill + Intangible Assets + Step-Up to PP&E + Deferred Tax Adjustments, we can make adjustments to the balance sheet removing the target shareholders' equity, and adding the new goodwill and other items created. So, let's first remove all the components of the shareholders' equity. Column G is the "Subtraction" column, so to remove the shareholders' equity component, we can link cells in this column from the LTM column. In other words, we can have Cell G146 be "=E146." This will link the value "761.7" into Cell E146, which will make the total capital stock read "0." It is important to have the adjustments link this way so that if we ever need to change the original balance sheet numbers everything will still flow through properly.

We want to continue removing the other components of shareholders' equity, including:

■ Common equity investment.
■ Preferred equity investment.
■ Retained earnings.

TABLE 8.11 Setting Up the Balance Sheet Adjustments

Consolidated Balance Sheet Adjustments (in US$ millions except per share amounts)

On January 27, 2013	Actuals LTM	Pro Forma Additions (+)	Pro Forma Subtractions (−)	Total
Assets				
Current assets:				
Cash and cash equivalents	$ 1,100.7			$ 1,100.7
Trade receivables, net	896.4			896.4
Other receivables, net	202.4			202.4
Total inventories	1,448.4			1,448.4
Prepaid expenses	173.0			173.0
Other current assets	88.0			88.0
Total current assets	$ 3,908.9			$ 3,908.9
Property, plant, and equipment, net	2,428.2			2,428.2
Goodwill	3,104.5			3,104.5
Trademarks, net	1,050.9			1,050.9
Other intangibles, net	383.0			383.0
Other noncurrent assets	1,053.6			1,053.6
Total assets	$ 11,929.1			$11,929.1
Liabilities				
Current liabilities:				
Short-term debt	14.7			14.7
Portion of long-term debt due within one year	1,038.5			1,038.5
Revolving line of credit	0.0			0.0
Trade payables	1,129.7			1,129.7
Other payables	158.1			158.1
Accrued marketing	320.1			320.1
Other accrued liabilities	624.0			624.0

(continued)

TABLE 8.11 (Continued)

Consolidated Balance Sheet Adjustments (in US$ millions except per share amounts)

On January 27, 2013	Actuals LTM	Pro Forma Additions (+)	Subtractions (−)	Total
Income taxes	91.3			91.3
Total current liabilities	**$ 3,376.3**			**$ 3,376.3**
Term facilities	0.0			0.0
The notes	0.0			0.0
Long-term debt	3,930.6			3,930.6
Deferred income taxes	776.7			776.7
Nonpension postretirement benefits	230.9			230.9
Other noncurrent liabilities	504.8			504.8
Redeemable noncontrolling interest	28.7			28.7
Total liabilities	**$ 8,848.0**			**$ 8,848.0**
Total Equity				
Shareholders' equity				
Capital stock	716.7			716.7
Common equity investment	0.0			0.0
Preferred equity investment	0.0			0.0
Retained earnings	7,877.4			7,877.4
Treasury stock	(4,675.8)			(4,675.8)
Accumulated other comprehensive loss	(887.7)			(887.7)
Total shareholders' equity	**3,030.6**			**3,030.6**
Noncontrolling interest	50.5			50.5
Total equity	**$ 3,081.1**			**$ 3,081.1**
Total liabilities and equity	**$ 11,929.1**			**$11,929.1**
Supplemental Data: Balance? (Y/N)	Y			Y

TABLE 8.12 Target Shareholder's Equity Adjustment

| | Actuals | Pro Forma | | |
	LTM	Additions (+)	Subtractions (−)	Total
Shareholders' equity				
Capital stock	$ 716.7		$ 716.7	$ 0.0
Common equity investment	0.0		0.0	0.0
Preferred equity investment	0.0		0.0	0.0
Retained earnings	7,877.4		7,877.4	0.0
Treasury stock	(4,675.8)		(4,675.8)	0.0
Accumulated other comprehensive loss	(887.7)		(887.7)	0.0
Total shareholders' equity	3,030.6			0.0
Noncontrolling interest	50.5			50.5
Total equity	$ 3,081.1			$ 50.5
Total liabilities and equity	$11,929.1			$8,898.5
Balance? (Y/N)	Y			N

- Treasury stock.
- Accumulated other comprehensive loss.

Or we can simply copy Cell G146 down through Cell G151, zeroing out the shareholders' equity section. See Table 8.12.

Now we can add the goodwill and intangible assets into the assets section of the adjustments. Column F handles additions into the balance sheet. Both goodwill and intangible assets will be linked in from the Assumptions tab. So, F120 will read "=Assumptions!J22" and F122 will be "=Assumptions!J16." We are assuming the intangible assets created based on the acquisition will be categorized under "Other intangibles" as opposed to the narrower "Trademarks," although it would not make much difference either way in the analysis. Although we assumed the step-up or PP&E and deferred tax adjustments were 0, we can still link them in. So, F119 will read "=Assumptions!J20" and G139 will be "=Assumptions!J21." Notice that we linked the step-up in PP&E as an asset addition and the deferred tax adjustment as a liability reduction. There could also be deferred tax asset adjustments, which could have been listed separately in the asset section of the balance sheet or more simply netted against the liability here.

Next we can adjust out the components of net debt. Again we will use Column G to subtract out the following line items:

Line Item	Cell	Formula
Cash	G112	"=E112"
Short-term debt	G127	"=E127"
Portion of long-term debt due within one year	G128	"=E128"
Long-term debt	G138	"=E138"

Next we can link in all of the sources of funds. The sources of funds we have are:
- Revolving line of credit.
- Term facilities.
- The notes.
- Common equity (we have combined 3G and Berkshire Hathaway's common equity).
- Preferred equity.

We can use Column F to add in adjustments in line with the following:

Line Item	Cell	Formula
Revolving line of credit	F129	"=Assumptions!F8" (even though the value is "0" for now, we should link it in case we end up using the revolver)
Term facilities	F136	"=Assumptions!F9"
The notes	F137	"=Assumptions!F10"
Common equity	F147	"=Assumptions!F13+Assumptions!F14"
Preferred equity	F148	"=Assumptions!F12"

The final adjustment we need to make is with the transaction fees. Remember that transaction fees will be affected in the shareholders' equity section, so we will make an adjustment in Cell G149, retained earnings. Cell G149 already contains a formula for adjusting out the shareholders' equity, so we need to append this formula to include the transaction fees; the formula will change from "=E149" to "=E149+Assumptions!J8." Note that we could have also made the transaction fee adjustment in the "Accumulated other comprehensive loss" line as well. It really does not make much difference as it will affect the total Shareholder's Equity the same.

Once this last adjustment is made, the new pro forma balance sheet should be in balance. You should see a "Y" in Cell H157. If you do not, there may be a problem with the structure of formulas in the Total column or the total formulas in the total columns. See Table 8.13 to compare.

It is important to note the benefit of balance sheet transaction adjustments in conducting due diligence. If shareholders' equity, net debt, and other obligations are eliminated from a target balance sheet, we are left with several important items (taking the Heinz balance sheet as the example):

- Trade receivables, net.
- Other receivables, net.
- Total inventories.
- Prepaid expenses.
- Other current assets.
- Property, plant, and equipment, net.
- Goodwill.
- Trademarks, net.
- Other intangibles, net.
- Other noncurrent assets.
- Trade payables and other payables.
- Accrued marketing and other liabilities.
- Income taxes.
- Deferred income taxes.
- Nonpension postretirement benefits.
- Other noncurrent liabilities.
- Minority interests.

The current assets and current liabilities here can be reworked as operating working capital. So simplifying the preceding gives us:

- PP&E.
- Goodwill.
- Trademarks.
- Other intangibles.
- Other noncurrent assets.
- Deferred income taxes.
- Nonpension postretirement benefits.
- Other noncurrent liabilities.
- Working capital.
- Minority interests.

These are the very items that need extensive due diligence, as it is the value of these items that you are paying for. Should the nonpension postretirement benefits be an obligation to the buyer? How large is the future liability? What is the true value of the PP&E? What is the true value of goodwill and other intangibles? How sound are the deferred income taxes,

TABLE 8.13 Heinz Balance Sheet Adjustments

Consolidated Balance Sheet Adjustments (in US$ millions except per share amounts)

On January 27, 2013	Actuals LTM	Pro Forma Additions (+)	Subtractions (−)	Total
Assets				
Current assets:				
Cash and cash equivalents	$ 1,100.7		$1,100.7	$ 0.0
Trade receivables, net	896.4			896.4
Other receivables, net	202.4			202.4
Total inventories	1,448.4			1,448.4
Prepaid expenses	173.0			173.0
Other current assets	88.0			88.0
Total current assets	**$ 3,908.9**			**$ 2,808.2**
Property, plant, and equipment, net	2,428.2	0.0		2,428.2
Goodwill	3,104.5	$15,408.8		18,513.4
Trademarks, net	1,050.9			1,050.9
Other intangibles, net	383.0	5,136.3		5,519.3
Other noncurrent assets	1,053.6			1,053.6
Total assets	**$11,929.1**			**$31,373.5**
Liabilities				
Current liabilities:				
Short-term debt	14.7		14.7	0.0
Portion of long-term debt due within one year	1,038.5		1,038.5	0.0
Revolving line of credit	0.0	0.0		0.0
Trade payables	1,129.7			1,129.7
Other payables	158.1			158.1
Accrued marketing	320.1			320.1

Other accrued liabilities	624.0	624.0
Income taxes	91.3	91.3
Total current liabilities	**$ 3,376.3**	**$ 2,323.1**
Term facilities	0.0	10,500.0
The notes	0.0	2,100.0
Long-term debt	3,930.6	0.0
Deferred income taxes	776.7	776.7
Nonpension postretirement benefits	230.9	230.9
Other noncurrent liabilities	504.8	504.8
Redeemable noncontrolling interest	28.7	28.7
Total liabilities	**$ 8,848.0**	**$16,464.1**
Total Equity		
Shareholders' equity		
Capital stock	716.7	0.0
Common equity investment	0.0	8,240.0
Preferred equity investment	0.0	8,000.0
Retained earnings	7,877.4	(1,381.1)
Treasury stock	(4,675.8)	0.0
Accumulated other comprehensive loss	(887.7)	0.0
Total shareholders' equity	**3,030.6**	**14,858.9**
Noncontrolling interest	50.5	50.5
Total equity	**$ 3,081.1**	**$14,909.4**
Total liabilities and equity	**$11,929.1**	**$31,373.5**
Supplemental Data:		
Balance? (Y/N)	**Y**	**Y**

and when will they come due? How much is working capital changing on a day-to-day basis, and will there be a major difference between now and the actual close? What is the status with the minority interest holder? Can we negotiate a buyout of his or her interest? These are some of the many questions that need to be asked in order to truly understand the value of the assets and liabilities the buyer will soon own.

We have often seen situations where a company looks and sounds like a good purchase, but after running this balance sheet analysis we have uncovered hidden liabilities that render the transaction unprofitable. In such situations, had the buyer gone through with the deal, he or she would be left with a hugely unprofitable situation. Peering into the balance sheet and the balance sheet adjustments also helps understand what are the important pieces of the business that need further examination in the due diligence process. If this were a private business, a buyer might find other hidden liabilities this way that he or she may not want. If so, the buyer may use such unwanted liabilities to negotiate a lower purchase price, or can try to negotiate to leave the liabilities with the seller. The cash generated or spent from working capital from the time the purchase price has been established to acquisition close is also a heavily contested topic. If working capital is being produced during that time frame, who receives the cash? Technically, the purchase price should be adjusted if the company's cash balance changes. Would the cash go to the buyer? To the seller? Or would it be split 50/50? Or what happens if the working capital illustrates a cash need? Each of these items needs to be discussed and negotiated in the due diligence process.

Now that we have a pro forma balance sheet, we can proceed with completing the model and determining the potential returns on this investment. Refer to Appendix 1 to ensure you are following the model building path.

CHAPTER 9

Depreciation Schedule

Depreciation is accounting for the aging of assets.

> *Depreciation is an income tax deduction that allows a taxpayer to recover the cost or other basis of certain property. It is an annual allowance for the wear and tear, deterioration, or obsolescence of the property.*
>
> *Most types of tangible property (except land), such as buildings, machinery, vehicles, furniture, and equipment are depreciable. Likewise, certain intangible property, such as patents, copyrights, and computer software is depreciable.*

(From www.irs.gov)

In other words, as a company owns and utilizes an asset, its value will most likely decrease. As discussed in the balance sheet chapter, if an asset value decreases, there must be another change to one of the other line items in the balance sheet to offset the asset reduction. Accounting rules state that the reduction in asset value can be expensed, with the idea being that the asset's aging or wear and tear is partly due to utilization of the asset to produce or generate revenue. If the item is expensed, net income is reduced, which in turn will reduce the retained earnings in the shareholders' equity section of the balance sheet.

Let's take an example of an asset that has a depreciation expense of $5,000. Depreciation expense reduces net income after taxes, as shown. Net income drives the cash flow statement, but since depreciation is a noncash expense it is added back to cash.

Income Statement		Cash Flow	
Depreciation	(5,000.0)	Net Income	(3,000.0)
Taxes (@ 40%)	2,000.0	Depreciation	5,000.0
Net Income	(3,000.0)	Total Changes in Cash	2,000.0

In the balance sheet, net income drives retained earnings. Depreciation will lower the value of the asset being depreciated (the plant, property, and equipment [PP&E]).

Cash Flow		Balance Sheet Adjustments	
Net Income	(3,000.0)	Cash	2,000.0
Depreciation	5,000.0	PP&E	(5,000.0)
Total Changes in Cash	2,000.0	Retained Earnings (Net Income)	(3,000.0)

There are several methods allowed to depreciate assets. Each has its benefits under certain conditions. In this chapter we will learn about the most popular methods and how they are utilized. The two major categories are:

1. Straight-line depreciation.
2. Accelerated depreciation.

STRAIGHT-LINE DEPRECIATION

The straight-line method of depreciation evenly ages the asset by the number of years that asset is expected to last—it's useful life. For example, if we purchase a car for $50,000 and that car has a useful life of 10 years, the depreciation would be $5,000 per year. So next year the asset will have depreciated by $5,000 and its value would be reduced to $45,000. In the following year, the asset will be depreciated by another $5,000 and be worth $40,000. By year 10, the asset will be worth $0 and have been fully depreciated.

One can also assign a residual value (also known as scrap value) to an asset, which is some minimal value an asset can be worth after the end of its useful life. So, for example, if the car after year 10 can be sold for $1,000 for spare parts, then $1,000 is the residual value. In this case, by year 10, the value of the car should be $1,000, not $0. In order to account for residual value in the depreciation formula, we need to depreciate the value of the car less this residual value, or $50,000 minus $1,000, which is $49,000. The depreciation will now be $4,900 per year, which means the next year the value of the car will be $44,100. And by year 10, the final value of the car will be $1,000. So the definition for straight-line depreciation is:

Depreciation = (Fair Value of Asset − Residual Value)/Useful Life

ACCELERATED DEPRECIATION

Accelerating depreciation allows a greater depreciation expense earlier in the life of the asset, and a lower depreciation in the later years. The most common reason for accelerating depreciation is that a higher depreciation expense will produce a lower taxable net income, and therefore lower taxes. There are several methods of accelerating depreciation, the most common of which are:

- Declining balance.
- Sum of the year's digits.
- Modified Accelerated Cost Recovery System (MACRS).

Declining Balance

The declining balance method takes a percentage of the net property balance each year. The net property balance is reduced each year by the depreciation expensed in that particular year.

The percentage applied is calculated by dividing 1 by the life of the asset times an accelerating multiplier:

$$1/\text{Useful Life} \times \text{Accelerating Multiplier}$$

The multiplier is most commonly 2.0 or 1.5.

In the car example, the asset has a life of 10 years. If we assume 2.0 as the accelerating multiplier then the declining balance percentage is:

$$1/10 \times 2 = 20\%$$

We will apply 20 percent to the net property balance each year to calculate the accelerated depreciation of the car. So, 20 percent of $50,000 is $10,000. The net balance is $40,000 ($50,000 − $10,000). In year 2 we will apply 20 percent to the $40,000, which gives us $8,000. The new net balance is $32,000 ($40,000 − $8,000). And in year 3, we will apply 20 percent to the $32,000 to get $6,400. See Table 9.1.

TABLE 9.1 Declining Balance Example

Period Ending December 31					
	2013E	2014E	2015E	2016E	2017E
Net property, plant, and equipment	$50,000.0	$40,000.0	$32,000.0	$25,600.0	$20,480.0
Accelerated depreciation (%)	20%	20%	20%	20%	20%
Depreciation expense	$10,000.0	$ 8,000.0	$ 6,400.0	$ 5,120.0	$ 4,096.0

Sum of the Year's Digits

To use the sum of the year's digits method, we first take the sum of the digits from 1 to the life of the asset. For example, an asset with a useful life of 10 years will have a sum of 55: $1 + 2 + 3 + 4 + 5 + 6 + 7 + 8 + 9 + 10$. For year 1, the percentage will be 10/55 or 18.18 percent (rounded to the hundredth place). For year 2, the percentage will be 9/55 or 16.36 percent. For year 3 it is 8/55 or 14.55 percent, and so on. This percentage is applied to the base value of the asset and is not reduced by the depreciation each year like in the declining balance method.

Year 1 depreciation = $50,000 × 18.18% or $9,090

Year 2 depreciation = $50,000 × 16.36% or $8,180

Year 3 depreciation = $50,000 × 14.55% or $7,275

Year 4 depreciation = $50,000 × 12.73% or $6,365

Year 5 depreciation = $50,000 × 10.91% or $5,455

Notice in Table 9.2 that we are basing the future depreciation on the original balance each year. This differs from the declining balance method, where we calculate depreciation on the net property balance each year (property net of depreciation).

Modified Accelerated Cost Recovery System (MACRS)

The Modified Accelerated Cost Recovery System (MACRS) is the U.S. tax method of depreciation.

The MACRS method is a predefined set of percentages based on the asset's useful life. These percentages are applied to the base value of the asset each year (you can look up these percentages at www.irs.gov). There are several

TABLE 9.2 Sum of the Year's Digits Example

Period Ending December 31					
	2013E	2014E	2015E	2016E	2017E
Net property, plant, and equipment	$50,000.0				
Accelerated depreciation (%)	18.18%	16.36%	14.55%	12.73%	10.91%
Depreciation expense	$ 9,090.0	$8,180.0	$7,275.0	$6,365.0	$5,455.0

TABLE 9.3   MACRS Half-Year Convention

Year	Depreciation Rate for Recovery Period					
	3-year	**5-year**	**7-year**	**10-year**	**15-year**	**20-year**
1	33.33%	20.00%	14.29%	10.00%	5.00%	3.750%
2	44.45	32.00	24.49	18.00	9.50	7.219
3	14.81	19.20	17.49	14.40	8.55	6.677
4	7.41	11.52	12.49	11.52	7.70	6.177
5		11.52	8.93	9.22	6.93	5.713
6		5.76	8.92	7.37	6.23	5.285
7			8.93	6.55	5.90	4.888
8			4.46	6.55	5.90	4.522
9				6.56	5.91	4.462
10				6.55	5.90	4.461
11				3.28	5.91	4.462
12					5.90	4.461
13					5.91	4.462
14					5.90	4.461
15					5.91	4.462
16					2.95	4.461
17						4.462
18						4.461
19						4.462
20						4.461
21						2.231

conventions used, each with a different set of calculated percentages, including the half-year convention and the midquarter convention. The differences in conventions are dependent on when exactly the asset is placed in service and starts depreciating. The half-year convention, shown in Table 9.3, assumes that the asset is not placed in service and does not begin depreciating until midyear.

When looking at the "3-year" percentages, notice that the first percentage is actually lower (33.33 percent) than the next year's percentage (44.45 percent), which is not really accelerating. The half-year convention assumes the asset is not placed in service, and so does not start depreciating until midyear, so an adjustment had been made to that first percentage.

The midquarter convention, shown in Table 9.4, assumes that the asset starts depreciating in the middle of the first quarter. So here the starting percentage of 58.33 percent is higher than that of the half-year convention. Because the asset is placed in service in the first quarter rather than at midyear, the asset will begin depreciating earlier, and will therefore have a greater depreciation expense by the end of the first year.

There are also midquarter convention tables where the asset is placed in service in the second, third, and fourth quarters.

TABLE 9.4   MACRS Midquarter Convention Placed in Service in First Quarter

Year	Depreciation Rate for Recovery Period					
	3-year	**5-year**	**7-year**	**10-year**	**15-year**	**20-year**
1	58.33%	35.00%	25.00%	17.50%	8.75%	6.563%
2	27.78	26.00	21.43	16.50	9.13	7.000
3	12.35	15.60	15.31	13.20	8.21	6.482
4	1.54	11.01	10.93	10.56	7.39	5.996
5		11.01	8.75	8.45	6.65	5.546
6		1.38	8.74	6.76	5.99	5.130
7			8.75	6.55	5.90	4.746
8			1.09	6.55	5.91	4.459
9				6.56	5.90	4.459
10				6.55	5.91	4.459
11				0.82	5.90	4.459
12					5.91	4.460
13					5.90	4.459
14					5.91	4.460
15					5.90	4.459
16					0.74	4.460
17						4.459
18						4.460
19						4.459
20						4.460
21						0.565

Determining which table to use really depends on when the assets are placed in service, which is often unobtainable information. So, by default, we typically use the midquarter convention where the asset is placed in service in the first quarter, as it results in the greatest depreciation expense in the first year. It is always recommended that you consult an asset appraiser and a tax professional to be sure you are using the correct methods of depreciation.

For an asset with a 10-year useful life, using Table 9.4, we would apply 17.50 percent to the value of the asset to get Year 1 depreciation expense. For year 2, the percentage will be 16.50 percent. See Table 9.5 for the first five years' depreciation calculations for an asset originally worth $50,000.

Note that quite often there are differences between the income statement reported for U.S. generally accepted accounting principles (GAAP) purposes and the income statement for tax purposes. One of the major differences can be the method of depreciation. Common depreciation methods under U.S. GAAP include straight-line, declining balance, and sum of the year's digits. Tax accounting uses the Modified Accelerated Cost Recovery

TABLE 9.5 Modified Accelerated Cost Recovery System

Period Ending December 31					
	2013E	2014E	2015E	2016E	2017E
Net property, plant, and equipment	$50,000.0				
Accelerated depreciation (%)	17.50%	16.50%	13.20%	10.56%	8.45%
Depreciation expense	$ 8,750.0	$8,250.0	$6,600.0	$5,280.0	$4,225.0

System (MACRS). The differences in the net income caused by using a different depreciation method when filing GAAP reports versus tax statements can cause a deferred tax liability. We discuss this in more detail next.

DEFERRED TAXES

A deferred tax asset is defined as an asset on a company's balance sheet that may be used to reduce income tax expense. A deferred tax asset is most commonly created after receiving a net operating loss (NOL), which occurs when a company's expenses exceed its sales. The IRS allows a company to offset the loss against taxable income in another year. The NOL can be carried back two to five years or carried forward up to 20 years. Note that the amount of years a company can carry back or carry forward a loss depends on several business factors that need to be considered by the IRS on a case-by-case basis. More information on the specific criteria can be found at www.irs.gov. It is always strongly recommended to verify treatment of NOLs with a certified accountant or tax professional.

NOL Carryback Example

Income Statement	2010	2011	2012
EBT	$750.0	$1,500.0	$(1,000.0)
Taxes (@ 40%)	(300.0)	(600.0)	0.0
Net Income	450.0	900.0	(1,000.0)

The company in this example has suffered a net loss in 2012. So, it files for a two-year carryback, which allows the company to offset the 2012 loss by receiving a refund on taxes paid in the prior two years. So that $1,000 loss becomes a balance from which taxes can be deducted in other years.

NOL Applied to 2010	
Beginning Balance	$1,000.0
Taxable Income	750.0
Tax Refund (@ 40%)	300.0
NOL Balance	250.0

We first apply the $1,000 loss to the $750 of taxable income in 2010, which results in a $300 refund. This leaves us with $250 ($1,000 − $750) of NOLs left to apply to 2011.

NOL Applied to 2011	
Beginning Balance	$ 250.0
Taxable Income	1,500.0
Tax Refund (@ 40%)	100.0
NOL Balance	0.0

In 2011, we have $1,500 of taxable income. However, with only $250 in NOLs left, we can receive a refund on only $250 of the $1,500. So that's a $100 refund ($250 × 40%). Combined with the $300 refund, we have a total of $400 refunded.

If the company had little or no taxable income in the prior years, it can elect to carry forward the net operating losses for up to 20 years depending on various considerations. Let's take another example, where, after the two-year carryback credits have been applied, an NOL balance still exists.

Income Statement	2010	2011	2012
EBT	$100.0	$200.0	$(1,000.0)
Taxes (@ 40%)	(40.0)	(80.0)	0.0
Net Income	60.0	120.0	(1,000.0)

The company in this example has also suffered a net loss in 2012. The company files for a two-year carryback, which allows it to offset the 2012 loss by receiving a refund on taxes paid in the prior two years.

NOL Applied to 2010	
Beginning Balance	$1,000.0
Taxable Income	100.0
Tax Refund (@ 40%)	40.0
NOL Balance	900.0

We first apply the $1,000 loss to the $100 taxable income in 2010, which results in a $40 refund. This leaves us with $900 ($1,000 – $100) of NOLs left to apply to 2011.

NOL Applied to 2011	
Beginning Balance	$900.0
Taxable Income	200.0
Tax Refund (@ 40%)	80.0
NOL Balance	700.0

In 2011, we have $200 of taxable income. Applying the NOL will result in an $80 refund, or $120 in total refunds when combined with the 2010 tax refund. But notice we still have $700 in NOLs left. These can be used to offset future taxes. This $700 balance becomes a deferred tax asset until it is used or is no longer usable.

Deferred Tax Liability

A deferred tax liability is caused by temporary accounting differences between the income statement filed for GAAP purposes and the income statement for tax purposes. One common cause of a deferred tax liability is having differing methods of depreciation in a GAAP income statement versus that in a tax income statement. A company can produce a GAAP set of financials using straight-line depreciation, for example, yet have a tax set of financials using the MACRS method of depreciation. This causes a deferred tax liability, reducing taxes in the short term.

Let's take a simple example of a company with $100,000 in earnings before interest, taxes, depreciation, and amortization (EBITDA). For GAAP purposes let's assume we will use the straight-line depreciation of $5,000 ($50,000/10). Let's also say we have decided to accelerate the depreciation for tax purposes using the MACRS method of depreciation. For an asset with a 10-year useful life, the depreciation is $8,750 (17.5% × $50,000). This will create the income statements shown in Table 9.6 for GAAP purposes and for tax purposes.

The GAAP income statement in the left column shows a lower depreciation expense and shows $95,000 in earnings before taxes (EBT). The right column, however, the tax income statement, shows a higher depreciation expense because it has been accelerated. This creates a lower EBT of $91,250, and results in $1,500 ($38,000 – $36,500) of lower taxes. Now, the GAAP reported taxes of $38,000, which is the larger amount, is the tax number we see in a company's annual report or 10-K. The lower amount of

TABLE 9.6   Income Statements for GAAP and Tax Purposes

Income Statement	GAAP (Straight-Line Depreciation)	Tax (MACRS Depreciation)
EBITDA	$100,000.0	$100,000.0
Depreciation	(5,000.0)	(8,750.0)
EBIT	95,000.0	91,250.0
Interest	0.0	0.0
EBT	95,000.0	91,250.0
Taxes (@ 40%)	(38,000.0)	(36,500.0)
Net Income	$ 57,000.0	$ 54,750.0

taxes filed for tax purposes is the amount of taxes filed to the IRS that the company actually has to pay this year. So, the difference between the taxes reported and the taxes paid ($1,500) becomes a noncash item. Just like any expense that the company did not yet pay in cash, this noncash portion of taxes is added back to net income in the cash flow statement. This is a deferred tax liability.

Note that this is a great method to use in order to free up cash in the short term. The deferred tax amount of $1,500 calculated previously can also be calculated by subtracting the accelerated depreciation expense from the straight-line depreciation and multiplying by the tax rate.

Deferred Tax Liability = (Accelerated Depreciation –
Straight-Line Depreciation) × Tax Percent

or

($8,750 – $5,000) × 40% = $1,500

In modeling, we build a projected straight-line depreciation schedule and, if needed, an accelerated depreciation schedule. We then subtract the projected straight-line depreciation from the accelerated depreciation and multiply by the tax rate to estimate deferred tax. However, in a leveraged buyout (LBO) analysis, when the company is taken private, there may not be a need to produce GAAP financial reports. Thus there may be no difference calculated between straight-line and accelerated depreciation; that is, no deferred tax liability created from the depreciation of assets. In the Heinz case, we will not model out deferred tax liability in this way, but the concepts are still important to touch upon. Please see the book *Financial Modeling and Valuation* for a step-through of how this is done.

PROJECTING DEPRECIATION

The benefit of having a depreciation schedule is to lay out and project depreciation on not only the company's current assets but future planned property (CAPEX). It is however uncertain whether Heinz, after the buyout, will depreciate its assets on a straight-line basis or on an accelerated basis. Given the tax benefits of accelerating depreciation, no doubt that would be the preferred choice if the company is able to do so. We also know that the MACRS method of accelerating is the U.S. tax method of depreciating assets. However, we realize Heinz also operates in other countries. So, we are not sure what the buyers' plan is for the depreciation of Heinz's assets. The buyers themselves may not even know at this early stage of the transaction. Because the straight-line method is more universal and better demonstrates the core uses of depreciating assets, we will first build the Heinz model using the straight-line method. It is more important to understand the overall purpose of depreciation and how the depreciation schedule fits as a necessary piece in an LBO model. In the more advanced Part Three, we will construct an accelerated method of depreciation and build a switch illustrating how to toggle from one method to another. This way, we can test both methods and see if the difference will affect the overall return.

Straight-Line Depreciation

We need to consider depreciation on both the assets the company currently owns and its future property improvements that it is projecting to build (capital expenditures, or CAPEX). This will result in a tiered schedule with depreciation stacking each time a new CAPEX improvement occurs.

We begin with the company's last reported net property, plant, and equipment (PP&E) amount, the net value of its assets. We can find Heinz's last twelve months (LTM) net PP&E in the balance sheet. We'd like to work with the latest pro forma numbers, so the $2,428.2 value found in Cell H119, the balance sheet adjustments section, is the most current net PP&E balance we have in our model. So in Cell J210 we can link in the net PP&E number found in Cell H119. Cell J210 should read "=H119."

We now need to project depreciation for this net property value. Unfortunately there is difficulty here, as the reported property value is a combination of many different asset classes with different useful lives. The best way to project future depreciation requires a list of every asset that the company owns, the useful life of each asset, each asset's original purchase value, and the year each asset was purchased. However, it is almost impossible to get this information.

One suggested method to project depreciation is to take a weighted average of the company net asset value separated by asset class and the useful lives of each asset class, but there is a problem: We do not know when these assets were actually purchased. When performing a word search on "property" in the Heinz quarterly report, we do not find much additional information. Often more detail can be found in the annual reports. We find the following note in the Heinz annual report:

> *Land, buildings and equipment are recorded at cost. For financial reporting purposes, depreciation is provided on the straight-line method over the estimated useful lives of the assets, which generally have the following ranges: buildings—40 years or less, machinery and equipment—15 years or less, computer software—3 to 7 years, and leasehold improvements—over the life of the lease, not to exceed 15 years. Accelerated depreciation methods are generally used for income tax purposes. Expenditures for new facilities and improvements that substantially extend the capacity or useful life of an asset are capitalized. Ordinary repairs and maintenance are expensed as incurred. When property is retired or otherwise disposed, the cost and related accumulated depreciation are removed from the accounts and any related gains or losses are included in income. The Company reviews property, plant and equipment, whenever circumstances change such that the recorded value of an asset may not be recoverable. Factors that may affect recoverability include changes in planned use of the asset and the closing of facilities. The Company's impairment review is based on an undiscounted cash flow analysis at the lowest level for which identifiable cash flows exist and are largely independent. When the carrying value of the asset exceeds the future undiscounted cash flows, an impairment is indicated and the asset is written down to its fair value.*

> **(Heinz Annual Report, page 39)**

This does mention the different types of property the company owns and their respective useful lives. But it gives us a large range from three years to as long as 40 years, which is not enough information from which to choose an accurate useful life assumption.

The next best method is to analyze the historical depreciation trends. We know from row 23 in the income statement (or Table 9.13), there was a small jump in depreciation from 2011 to 2012, which is out of the ordinary compared to the other years. The latest depreciation levels were at $295.7 and $299.6 in 2012 and LTM, respectively. We should continue to see similar levels of future depreciation as it is unusual to see huge drops in depreciation unless the company has written down assets or sold assets, or unless a large portion of its assets has been fully depleted. Conversely, it is unusual to see a huge increase in depreciation unless the company has purchased a business or assets. With that noted, we should do some research to ensure that there has not been any such significant events with regard to the company's assets.

Let's begin modeling out the depreciation.

We discussed previously the wide range of useful lives for the assets that make up the PP&E for Heinz. Let's take the midpoint, which is approximately 20, for now; we will adjust this later. There are two rows of useful life years, Rows 213 and 214, for the PP&E and CAPEX, respectively. We can enter our assumption of 20 into Cell J213.

We will lay out the projected depreciation for PP&E in Row 215. As the formula for depreciation is Asset/Useful life, we can take the PP&E and divide it by our assumed useful life of 20.

PP&E Depreciation (Cell J215)

Excel Keystrokes	Description
Type "="	Enters into "formula" mode
Select J210	Net PP&E
Type "/"	Divides
Select J213	2014 PP&E depreciation years
Hit Enter	End
Formula result	=J210/J213

This will give us $121.4, which will be our depreciation each year over the life of the asset.

Notice if we copy this formula to the right, as we had done with most formulas on the income statement and cash flow statement, we will receive an error message. This is because, as expected, the cell references also shift to the right as we copy our formula to the right. In other words, the formula "=J210/J213" becomes "=H210/H213" and so on. However, in this case we do not want the cell references to change. We want to be able to copy the formula to the right without changing the cell references. We can do this by adding a "$" before the column references in the original formula. The "$" anchors the cell references. So we can add "$" to each column reference, changing the formula from "=J210/J213" to "=$J210/$J213." Hitting F4 while in edit mode of a cell is a quick way to add the "$" into these formulas. We can now copy this formula to the right.

Notice we have not, but could have, included the "$" before the row number as well, producing "=$J$210/$J$213." Doing so would have anchored the row references, but it would not make much difference here, as we are not going to copy this formula to other rows.

After copying the depreciation formula to the right, the depreciation schedule should look like Table 9.7.

Now we can start inputting our CAPEX assumptions and CAPEX depreciation. Remember, we have already projected CAPEX in our cash flow statement, so we can use those projections and link them into the depreciation schedule. Notice the CAPEX projections in our cash flow statement are negative. When linking them in, we want to reverse the signs so they are represented as positive numbers on the depreciation schedule. We want these formulas to be inserted into Row 211, so in Cell J211 we can type "=–" (notice the "–" sign after the "=" sign); on the cash flow statement select the CAPEX in year 2014, cash flow statement Cell J78, and hit Enter. We should now have the 2014 projected CAPEX as a positive number in our depreciation schedule. We can copy this formula to the right. We do not want the "$" here, as we want those cell column references to shift to the right as we copy the formula to the right.

We can now depreciate each CAPEX beginning with 2014. It is important to consider timing here. We are assuming the CAPEX will be built and completed in early 2014 and that there will be a full year of depreciation by the end of that year. We now need to make an assumption for the useful life of the CAPEX. Again, as per the note on page 39 of the annual report, the depreciation range of property is extremely wide. We tried researching

TABLE 9.7   Heinz PP&E Depreciation

			Estimates		
	2014E	2015E	2016E	2017E	2018E
Property, plant, and equipment beginning of year	$2,428.2				
Capital expenditures beginning of year					
Years (PP&E)	20				
Years (CAPEX)					
Existing PP&E	121.4	121.4	121.4	121.4	121.4
2014 CAPEX					
2015 CAPEX					
2016 CAPEX					
2017 CAPEX					
2018 CAPEX					
Total book depreciation					

"capital expenditures" on both the quarterly report and the annual report, but did not find any further detail that would help us home in on a better useful life. So, let's take the midpoint of approximately 20 as we had done with the PP&E, and we can adjust later from there.

Row 214 is reserved for our CAPEX useful life, so, let's input 20 into Cell J214. We can then create our 2014 CAPEX depreciation formula in Row 216.

2014 CAPEX Depreciation (Cell J216)

Excel Keystrokes	Description
Type "="	Enters into "formula" mode
Select J211	2014 CAPEX
Hit F4	Adds "$" to cell
Type "/"	Divides
Select J214	2014 CAPEX years
Hit F4	Adds "$" to cell
Hit Enter	End
Formula result	=$J$211/$J$214

This gives us $23.5 in depreciation from the 2014 CAPEX. This depreciation will of course occur every year for 20 years, so we need to copy this formula to the right through 2018 (see Table 9.8).

TABLE 9.8   Heinz 2014 CAPEX Depreciation

Depreciation and Amortization (in US$ millions except per share amounts)					
		Estimates			
Period Ending	2014E	2015E	2016E	2017E	2018E
Property, plant, and equipment beginning of year	$2,428.2				
Capital expenditures beginning of year	469.5	471.4	473.3	475.2	477.1
Straight-line depreciation					
Years (PP&E)	20				
Years (CAPEX)	20				
Existing PP&E	121.4	121.4	121.4	121.4	121.4
2014 CAPEX	23.5	23.5	23.5	23.5	23.5
2015 CAPEX					
2016 CAPEX					
2017 CAPEX					
2018 CAPEX					
Total book depreciation					

We can now continue this process for the 2015 CAPEX. Note that as the 2015 CAPEX will not begin until 2015, the depreciation will not start until 2015; so there will be no depreciation in 2014, or no formula in Cell J217. We will begin in Cell K217. Let's continue to assume the CAPEX spend will go toward the same type of property, so we will use 20 again for now. But it is important to keep this assumption separate from the useful life of the previous CAPEX in case we need to adjust the assumption later.

Let's input 20 into Cell K214. We can then create our 2015 CAPEX depreciation formula in Row 217.

2015 CAPEX Depreciation (Cell K217)

Excel Keystrokes	Description
Type "="	Enters into "formula" mode
Select K211	2015 CAPEX
Hit F4	Adds "$" to cell
Type "/"	Divides
Select K214	2015 CAPEX years
Hit F4	Adds "$" to cell
Hit Enter	End
Formula result	=$K$211/$K$214

This depreciation will of course occur every year for 20 years, so we need to copy this formula to the right (see Table 9.9).

TABLE 9.9   Heinz 2015 CAPEX Depreciation

Depreciation and Amortization (in US$ millions except per share amounts)					
		Estimates			
Period Ending	2014E	2015E	2016E	2017E	2018E
Property, plant, and equipment beginning of year	$2,428.2				
Capital expenditures beginning of year	469.5	471.4	473.3	475.2	477.1
Straight-line depreciation					
Years (PP&E)	20				
Years (CAPEX)	20	20			
Existing PP&E	121.4	121.4	121.4	121.4	121.4
2014 CAPEX	23.5	23.5	23.5	23.5	23.5
2015 CAPEX		23.6	23.6	23.6	23.6
2016 CAPEX					
2017 CAPEX					
2018 CAPEX					
Total book depreciation					

TABLE 9.10 Heinz 2016 CAPEX Depreciation

Depreciation and Amortization (in US$ millions except per share amounts)					
		Estimates			
Period Ending	2014E	2015E	2016E	2017E	2018E
Property, plant, and equipment beginning of year	$2,428.2				
Capital expenditures beginning of year	469.5	471.4	473.3	475.2	477.1
Straight-line depreciation					
Years (PP&E)	20				
Years (CAPEX)	20	20	20		
Existing PP&E	121.4	121.4	121.4	121.4	121.4
2014 CAPEX	23.5	23.5	23.5	23.5	23.5
2015 CAPEX		23.6	23.6	23.6	23.6
2016 CAPEX			23.7	23.7	23.7
2017 CAPEX					
2018 CAPEX					
Total book depreciation					

This pattern should continue for 2016 CAPEX, keeping 20 as the useful life assumption in Cell L214.

2016 CAPEX Depreciation (Cell L218)

Excel Keystrokes	Description
Type "="	Enters into "formula" mode
Select L211	2016 CAPEX
Hit F4	Adds "$" to cell
Type "/"	Divides
Select L214	2016 CAPEX years
Hit F4	Adds "$" to cell
Hit Enter	End
Formula result	=$L$211/$L$214

We copy this formula to the right (see Table 9.10).

And for 2017 CAPEX we keep the useful life assumption at 20 in Cell M214.

2017 CAPEX Depreciation (Cell M219)

Excel Keystrokes	Description
Type "="	Enters into "formula" mode
Select M211	2017 CAPEX
Hit F4	Adds "$" to cell

(continued)

Type "/"	Divides
Select M214	2017 CAPEX years
Hit F4	Adds "$" to cell
Hit Enter	End
Formula result	=$M$211/$M$214

We copy this formula to the right (see Table 9.11).

And for 2018 CAPEX we keep the useful life assumption at 20 in Cell N214.

2018 CAPEX Depreciation (Cell N220)

Excel Keystrokes	Description
Type "="	Enters into "formula" mode
Select N211	2018 CAPEX
Hit F4	Adds "$" to cell
Type "/"	Divides
Select N214	2018 CAPEX years
Hit F4	Adds "$" to cell
Hit Enter	End
Formula result	=$N$211/$N$214

TABLE 9.11 Heinz 2017 CAPEX Depreciation

Depreciation and Amortization (in US$ millions except per share amounts)					
			Estimates		
Period Ending	2014E	2015E	2016E	2017E	2018E
Property, plant, and equipment beginning of year	$2,428.2				
Capital expenditures beginning of year	469.5	471.4	473.3	475.2	477.1
Straight-line depreciation					
Years (PP&E)	20				
Years (CAPEX)	20	20	20	20	
Existing PP&E	121.4	121.4	121.4	121.4	121.4
2014 CAPEX	23.5	23.5	23.5	23.5	23.5
2015 CAPEX		23.6	23.6	23.6	23.6
2016 CAPEX			23.7	23.7	23.7
2017 CAPEX				23.8	23.8
2018 CAPEX					
Total book depreciation					

TABLE 9.12 Heinz Total Book Depreciation

Depreciation and Amortization (in US$ millions except per share amounts)					
	Estimates				
Period Ending	2014E	2015E	2016E	2017E	2018E
Property, plant, and equipment beginning of year	$2,428.2				
Capital expenditures beginning of year	469.5	471.4	473.3	475.2	477.1
Straight-line depreciation					
Years (PP&E)	20				
Years (CAPEX)	20	20	20	20	20
Existing PP&E	121.4	121.4	121.4	121.4	121.4
2014 CAPEX	23.5	23.5	23.5	23.5	23.5
2015 CAPEX		23.6	23.6	23.6	23.6
2016 CAPEX			23.7	23.7	23.7
2017 CAPEX				23.8	23.8
2018 CAPEX					23.9
Total book depreciation	$ 144.9	$168.5	$192.1	$215.9	$239.7

We can now total the depreciation expense in each year by summing Rows 215 through 220; in Cell J221 we will have "=SUM(J215:J220)" (see Table 9.12). We can copy this formula to the right.

This gives us a 2014 total book depreciation of $144.9. We can now analyze how this compares to the historical depreciation. See Table 9.13.

It looks like there was a small jump in depreciation from 2011 to 2012, which is out of the ordinary compared to the other years. The latest depreciation levels were at $295.7 and $299.6 in 2012 and LTM, respectively. Unless there have been major write-downs or divestitures, we should continue to see similar levels of future depreciation. Our 2014 projected value

TABLE 9.13 Heinz Depreciation and Amortization Growth

Depreciation and Amortization (in US$ millions except per share amounts)				
	Actuals			
Period Ending	2010A	2011A	2012A	LTM
Depreciation	254.5	255.2	295.7	299.6
% growth		0.3%	15.9%	1.3%
Amortization	48.3	43.4	47.1	48.0
% growth		–10.1%	8.4%	2.0%

of $144.9 is too low, so we need to make adjustments to our useful life assumptions to represent a number that reflects a more consistent trend. There are two major variables we can adjust, the useful life of the net PP&E and the useful life of the CAPEX. The depreciation of our net PP&E makes up the greater portion of the 2014 total book depreciation, so we would recommend trying to adjust downward the useful life of the PP&E first. If we adjust it (Cell J213) down to 10, we get $266.3 in depreciation, which is still too low. If we bring it down further to 5, we get $509.1, which is now too high. If we increase the useful life to 7, this gives us $370.4, still a bit too high. If we try 9, we get $293.3, a bit lower than the expected range of around $295 to $300, but very close. Let's stick with this for now.

The next problem is the 2015 depreciation. With 9 as the useful life for PP&E and 20 as the useful life for CAPEX, we have $316.8 in 2015 depreciation. This represents an 8 percent increase from the 2014 depreciation, too large compared to the ~1 percent to 1.5 percent growth we noticed in the LTM year. In order to approach a 1 to 1.5 percent increase, we need to increase our CAPEX useful life assumption. However, if we increase the 2014 CAPEX assumption, it is only appropriate to adjust every CAPEX useful life assumption accordingly, as we are assuming that the company is building or improving the same type of asset every year. So if we increase the useful life for every CAPEX from 2014 to 2018 up to 30 from 20, the 2014 depreciation growth decreases from 7 to 8 percent a year to 5 to 6 percent. If we increase the useful life further to 40, the growth decreases to 4 percent, which is still not as low as 1 to 1.5 percent, but we cannot increase the useful life further; based on the depreciation notes we found earlier, the maximum depreciation was 40. Also notice that our total depreciation in 2014 has lowered further to $281.5, slightly outside of the ~$295 to $300 range we defined earlier. So we should now tweak the PP&E CAPEX further. Adjusting this down to 8 gives us $315.3, a bit too high. If we use 8.5, we get $297.4. This works. So, after tweaking the assumptions, we have decided on using 8.5 in Cell J213, and hardcoding 40 in each cell from Cell J214 through N214. See Table 9.14.

This process has illustrated that adjusting the useful life for the net PP&E affects the overall balance of depreciation. So, if our depreciation is significantly low or high, we should first adjust the net PP&E useful life assumption. The CAPEX useful life affects the rate at which depreciation increases, so if the total depreciation is increasing too fast or too slow in the future, we should adjust the CAPEX useful life. It does take some practice to get comfortable with these drivers. We want to reiterate that this is not the most accurate way to project depreciation. The most accurate way is to have detailed data on all assets purchased—the cost, date purchased, and useful life of each. Given that this information is very difficult to obtain, we need to focus on the larger trends.

PROJECTING AMORTIZATION

Amortization is the accounting for the cost basis reduction of intangible assets (intellectual property such as patents, copyrights, and trademarks, for example) over their useful lives. As Heinz separates amortization from its depreciation, we need to make projection assumptions for amortization.

We found a note in the Heinz annual report:

Amortization expense for trademarks and other intangible assets was $31.8 million, $29.0 million and $28.2 million for the fiscal years ended April 29, 2012, April 27, 2011 and April 28, 2010, respectively. The remaining reduction in net trademarks and other intangible assets, subject to amortization expense, since April 27, 2011 is primarily due to translation adjustments. Based upon the amortizable intangible assets recorded on the balance sheet as of April 29, 2012, amortization expense for each of the next five fiscal years is estimated to be approximately $30 million.

(From Heinz Annual Report, pages 46–47)

Note the last sentence: Heinz estimates ~$30 million of amortization expense for each of the next five years. So it is safe enough for us to simply hard-code this value in as our future projections. It is often the case, since amortization does not come with yearly CAPEX improvements, that the future amortization is more predictable. So it is wise to do some quick research hoping to find company estimates on future amortization before trying to back into historical trends. We can hard-code "30" into Cell J222 and copy to the right through 2018.

Row 223 is reserved for the new intangible assets created from the buy-out. We can link this in from the Assumptions tab. So Cell J223 can read "=Assumptions!$J$18." Note that we anchored the reference to J18, so that we can easily copy this formula to the right and still refer to J18. Finally, we can total the depreciation and amortization in Row 224. J224 can read "=J221+J222+J223." We can copy Cells J223 and J224 to the right to complete the depreciation schedule. See Table 9.14.

We can now link our straight-line total book depreciation into our income statement. So, on the income statement, where we had left the projected depreciation empty (Cell J23), we can type "=" and then scroll back down to the depreciation schedule, select Cell J221, and hit Enter. We can do the same for the amortization, linking Cell J24 in from Cell J222, and the amortization of identifiable intangible assets, linking Cell J25 in from Cell J223.

TABLE 8.14   Total Heinz Projected Depreciation and Amortization

Depreciation and Amortization (in US$ millions except per share amounts)					
	Estimates				
Period Ending	2014E	2015E	2016E	2017E	2018E
Property, plant, and equipment beginning of year	$2,428.2				
Capital expenditures beginning of year	469.5	471.4	473.3	475.2	477.1
Straight-line depreciation					
Years (PP&E)	8.5				
Years (CAPEX)	40	40	40	40	40
Existing PP&E	285.7	285.7	285.7	285.7	285.7
2014 CAPEX	11.7	11.7	11.7	11.7	11.7
2015 CAPEX		11.8	11.8	11.8	11.8
2016 CAPEX			11.8	11.8	11.8
2017 CAPEX				11.9	11.9
2018 CAPEX					11.9
Total book depreciation	$ 297.4	$309.2	$321.0	$332.9	$344.8
Amortization	30.0	30.0	30.0	30.0	30.0
Amortization of identifiable intangible assets	342.4	342.4	342.4	342.4	342.4
Total depreciation and amortization	$ 669.8	$681.6	$693.4	$705.3	$717.2

We can then copy income statement Cells J23, J24, and J25 to the right through 2018.

Table 9.15 is the updated income statement projections with our depreciation linked in.

We can also link the straight-line depreciation into the cash flow statement. We recommend linking the cash flow statement depreciation from the income statement depreciation, as opposed to linking the cash flow statement depreciation from the depreciation schedule. Although this produces the same results, linking the depreciation from the income statement holds better to the concept that you are backing the very depreciation amount that has been expensed on the income statement, as that depreciation is noncash.

In the cash flow statement Cell J59, type "="; then select Cell J23, hit Enter, and copy to the right. We can do the same with Cell J60, linking in from J24, and with Cell J61, linking in from J25.

TABLE 9.15 Heinz Income Statement Projections with Depreciation Expense

Consolidated Income Statements (in US$ millions except per share amounts)

Period Ending	2014E	2015E	2016E	Estimates 2017E	2018E
Revenue	$11,738.3	$11,785.2	$11,832.3	$11,879.7	$11,927.2
Y/Y revenue growth (%)	*0.4%*	*0.4%*	*0.4%*	*0.4%*	*0.4%*
Cost of goods sold	7,230.8	7,259.7	7,288.7	7,317.9	7,347.2
COGS as a % of revenue	*61.6%*	*61.6%*	*61.6%*	*61.6%*	*61.6%*
Gross profit	$ 4,507.5	$ 4,525.5	$ 4,543.6	$ 4,561.8	$ 4,580.0
Gross profit margin (%)	*38.4%*	*38.4%*	*38.4%*	*38.4%*	*38.4%*
Operating expenses					
Selling, general, and administrative	2,582.4	2,592.7	2,603.1	2,613.5	2,624.0
SG&A as a % of revenue	*22.0%*	*22.0%*	*22.0%*	*22.0%*	*22.0%*
Fund management fee	0.0	0.0	0.0	0.0	0.0
Cost savings	(25.8)	(25.9)	(26.0)	(26.1)	(26.2)
Cost savings as a % of SG&A	*1.0%*	*1.0%*	*1.0%*	*1.0%*	*1.0%*
Total operating expenses	$ 2,556.6	$ 2,566.8	$ 2,577.1	$ 2,587.4	$ 2,597.7
Other income					
Equity in earnings of unconsolidated affiliates	0.0	0.0	0.0	0.0	0.0
EBITDA	$ 1,950.9	$ 1,958.7	$ 1,966.5	$ 1,974.4	$ 1,982.3
EBITDA margin (%)	*16.6%*	*16.6%*	*16.6%*	*16.6%*	*16.6%*
Depreciation	297.4	309.2	321.0	332.9	344.8
Amortization	30.0	30.0	30.0	30.0	30.0
Amortization of identifiable intangible assets	342.4	342.4	342.4	342.4	342.4
Total depreciation and amortization	669.8	681.6	693.4	705.3	717.2
EBIT	1,281.1	1,277.1	1,273.1	1,269.1	1,265.1
EBIT margin (%)	*10.9%*	*10.8%*	*10.8%*	*10.7%*	*10.6%*

PROJECTING DEFERRED TAXES

Finally, we need to consider deferred taxes. As mentioned earlier, we often calculate deferred taxes as per GAAP versus tax accounting differences. However, as the company may be reporting only one set of financials, these differences may not exist. So it is uncertain in reality how the company will treat deferred taxes in the future. They can potentially go away altogether; we just don't know. It is possible to use that deferred tax method, but we feel it is best, as this is an unknown, to take the most conservative approach, which is also close to the "last year" approach, of the "Seven methods of projections" from Chapter 6. The LTM value of –$83 million is not as large as the –$94.8 million in 2012, but it's very close. So carrying the LTM value over is a quite conservative projection method. It is safe to say this deferred tax line does not have a large impact on the overall transaction, so we can keep this assumption for now and tweak as the transaction comes to a close and we have more information on the deferred taxes. We can further, at the end of the analysis, try different approaches, and see if any of them changes the overall return to determine if it is even worthwhile belaboring the assumption. Let's have J62 be "=I62," and we can copy this to the right through 2018. (See Table 9.16.)

We can now proceed to the working capital schedule, which will help us complete the cash flow statement. Refer to Appendix 1 to ensure that you are following the model building path.

TABLE 9.16 Heinz Cash Flow Statement Projections with Depreciation Expense

Consolidated Statements of Cash Flows (in US$ millions except per share amounts)

Period Ending	Estimates				
	2014E	2015E	2016E	2017E	2018E
Cash flows from operating activities					
Net income	$ 905.8	$ 903.0	$ 900.1	$ 897.2	$ 894.3
Depreciation	297.4	309.2	321.0	332.9	344.8
Amortization	30.0	30.0	30.0	30.0	30.0
Amortization of identifiable intangible assets	342.4	342.4	342.4	342.4	342.4
Deferred tax	(83.0)	(83.0)	(83.0)	(83.0)	(83.0)
Net losses on divestitures	0.0	0.0	0.0	0.0	0.0
Impairment on assets held for sale	0.0	0.0	0.0	0.0	0.0
Pension contributions	(80.0)	(80.0)	(80.0)	(80.0)	(80.0)
Asset write-downs from Fiscal 2012 productivity initiatives	0.0	0.0	0.0	0.0	0.0
Other items, net	10.2	10.2	10.2	10.2	10.2
Changes in operating working capital					
Changes in receivables					
Changes in inventories					
Changes in prepaid expenses and other current assets					
Changes in accounts payable					
Changes in accrued liabilities					
Changes in accrued income taxes					
Net changes in operating working capital	0.0	0.0	0.0	0.0	0.0
Total cash provided by (used for) operating activities	$1,422.8	$1,431.7	$1,440.7	$1,449.7	$1,458.7
Cash flows from investing activities					
Capital expenditures (CAPEX)	(469.5)	(471.4)	(473.3)	(475.2)	(477.1)
CAPEX % of revenue	4.0%	4.0%	4.0%	4.0%	4.0%
Proceeds from disposal of property, plant, and equipment	0.0	0.0	0.0	0.0	0.0

(continued)

TABLE 9.16 (Continued)

Consolidated Statements of Cash Flows (in US$ millions except per share amounts)

Period Ending	Estimates				
	2014E	2015E	2016E	2017E	2018E
Acquisitions net of cash acquired	0.0	0.0	0.0	0.0	0.0
Proceeds from divestitures	0.0	0.0	0.0	0.0	0.0
Sale of short-term investments	0.0	0.0	0.0	0.0	0.0
Change in restricted cash	(39.1)	(39.1)	(39.1)	(39.1)	(39.1)
Other items, net	(12.3)	(12.3)	(12.3)	(12.3)	(12.3)
Total cash provided by (used for) investing activities	$ (520.9)	$ (522.7)	$ (524.6)	$ (526.5)	$ (528.4)
Cash flows from financing activities					
Revolver borrowings (repayments)	0.0	0.0	0.0	0.0	0.0
Term facilities borrowings (repayments)	0.0	0.0	0.0	0.0	0.0
The notes borrowings (repayments)	0.0	0.0	0.0	0.0	0.0
Common equity	0.0	0.0	0.0	0.0	0.0
Preferred equity	0.0	0.0	0.0	0.0	0.0
Proceeds (payments) of long-term debt	0.0	0.0	0.0	0.0	0.0
Net payments on commercial paper and short-term debt	0.0	0.0	0.0	0.0	0.0
Dividends	0.0	0.0	0.0	0.0	0.0
Purchases of treasury stock	0.0	0.0	0.0	0.0	0.0
Exercise of stock options	0.0	0.0	0.0	0.0	0.0
Acquisitions of subsidiary shares from noncontrolling interests	0.0	0.0	0.0	0.0	0.0
Earn-out settlement	0.0	0.0	0.0	0.0	0.0
Other items, net	(9.1)	(9.1)	(9.1)	(9.1)	(9.1)
Total cash provided by (used for) financing activities	$ (9.1)	$ (9.1)	$ (9.1)	$ (9.1)	$ (9.1)
Effect of exchange rate on cash and cash equivalents	(122.1)	(122.1)	(122.1)	(122.1)	(122.1)
Total change in cash and cash equivalents	$ 770.7	$ 777.8	$ 784.8	$ 791.9	$ 799.0
Supplemental Data:					
Cash flow before debt pay-down					

CHAPTER 10

Working Capital

Working capital is a measure of a company's current assets less its current liabilities.

Working Capital = Current Assets – Current Liabilities

Review Chapter 7 for definitions of assets and liabilities. But in summary:

ASSET

An asset is a resource held to produce some economic benefit. Examples of assets are cash, inventory, accounts receivable, and property.

Current Asset

A current asset is an asset whose economic benefit is expected to come within one year. Examples of current assets are cash, inventory, and accounts receivable.

LIABILITY

A liability is any debt or financial obligation of a company. Examples of liabilities are accounts payable, accrued expenses, long-term debt, and a deferred tax liability.

Current Liability

A current liability is a debt or financial obligation that is due within one year. Examples of current liabilities are accounts payable and accrued expenses.

The working capital, or the current assets less the current liabilities, helps us determine if cash coming in from our current assets will cover the liabilities that are coming due in the next 12 months. If working capital is positive, meaning current assets are greater than the current liabilities, we will potentially have more than enough funds to cover our liabilities coming due. If the working capital is negative, meaning current assets are less than the current liabilities, we do not have enough resources to pay our current liabilities—a working capital deficit. For this reason, working capital is regarded as a measure of a company's near-term liquidity.

OPERATING WORKING CAPITAL

For modeling purposes, we focus on a narrower definition of working capital called operating working capital (OWC). Operating working capital is also defined as current assets less current liabilities. However, OWC does not include cash and cash equivalents as part of current assets, and does not include debts as part of current liabilities.

Cash equivalents are assets that are readily convertible into cash, such as money market holdings, short-term government bonds and Treasury bills, marketable securities, and commercial paper. Cash equivalents are often considered as cash because they can be easily liquidated when necessary.

So, removing cash and cash equivalents, we are left with the following for current assets:

- Accounts receivable.
- Inventory.
- Prepaid expenses.

And removing debts, we are left with the following for current liabilities:

- Accounts payable.
- Accrued expenses.

Note that there are other possible current assets or current liabilities; the aforementioned are just a few of the most common examples.

Each of these line items is most closely related to the company's operations. For example, accounts receivable is the portion of revenue we did not collect in cash, and accrued expenses is the portion of expenses we did not yet pay in cash. For this reason, operating working capital is a good measure of how much cash is coming in from the day-to-day operations. Another way to look at this is: Operating working capital helps track how well a company is managing its cash generating from day-to-day operations. In contrast, working capital, because it includes cash, cash equivalents, and debts, may not give the clearest measure of just the day-to-day operations.

How do we know if the individual operating working capital items are really performing well? If we see accounts receivable, for example, increasing year over year, this could mean we have an ever-growing collections problem. However, this could also mean that the receivables are growing because the revenue is growing, which would be a good indicator of strong business growth. So it is not enough to look at these operating working capital line items independently in order to determine their performance; we need to compare these line items to some related income statement line item. We use a measure called "days" to track how well we are collecting our receivables or paying our payables. Days are measured by dividing the receivable or payable by their related income statement item and multiplying by 360.

For example, let's say in 2013 the accounts receivable balance is $25,000 and the revenue is $100,000.

Income Statement		Operating Working Capital	
Revenue	$100,000.0	Accounts Receivable	$25,000.0
COGS	10,000.0	Inventory	7,500.0
Operating Expenses	85,000.0	Prepaid Expenses	1,000.0
EBITDA	5,000.0	Accounts Payable	12,500.0
		Accrued Expenses	15,000.0
		Net OWC	6,000.0

The accounts receivable divided by the revenue gives us 25 percent. So, 25 percent of our 2013 revenue has not yet been collected. We multiply this percentage by the number of days in one year to get an equivalent number representing how many days these receivables have been left outstanding; 25% × 360 = 90, so of the 2013 revenue, 90 days are outstanding. As a rule of thumb, many companies require customer receipts to be paid within 30 days. However, depending on the business, 60, 90, or even more days could be acceptable. Ninety could be considered high or it could be okay, depending on the business model and the product sold. Notice that we have used 360 days instead of 365. Either way is acceptable; however, we more commonly use 360 because this is divisible by 12, which would make the modeling simpler if we ever wanted to break the year column down into 12 months.

$$\text{Accounts Receivable Days} = \frac{\text{Accounts Receivable}}{\text{Revenue}} \times 360$$

It is important to note that we have made a simplifying assumption in this formula for clarity. We took the last year's accounts receivable balance as the numerator in the calculation. In the actual analysis, it is important to take an average of the ending balances from the year being analyzed and the previous year. Because balance sheet items are balances at a specific point in time, averaging the current year's and previous year's performances gives a better indicator of measurement for the entire year. Income statement and cash flow items actually give us total performance over an entire period, so averaging does not apply. The complete formula for accounts receivable days in 2013 is:

2013 Accounts Receivable Days

$$= \frac{\text{Average}(2013 \text{ Accounts Receivable}, 2012 \text{ Accounts Receivable})}{2013 \text{ Revenue}}$$

Let's take another example using a liability, accrued expenses. Let's say the accrued expenses balance in 2013 is $15,000, and is made up of unpaid office rent. The 2013 income statement expense is $85,000. The accrued expenses of $15,000 divided by $85,000 gives us 17.6 percent. So, 17.6 percent of our 2013 expenses have not yet been paid. We multiply this percentage by the number of days in one year to get an equivalent number representing how many days these payables have been left outstanding. 17.6% × 360 = 63.4, so of the 2013 expense, 63.4 days are still outstanding, which could be considered too high in this case, especially considering that rent should typically be paid every 30 days.

$$\text{Accrued Expenses Days} = \frac{\text{Accrued Expenses}}{\text{Operating Expenses}} \times 360$$

We again simplified the example for purposes of instruction. When performing the actual analysis, we take the average of the accrued expenses balance in the year being analyzed and in the prior year.

2013 Accrued Expenses Days

$$= \frac{\text{Average }(2013 \text{ Accrued Expenses}, 2012 \text{ Accrued Expenses})}{2013 \text{ Operating Expenses}} \times 360$$

HEINZ'S OPERATING WORKING CAPITAL

Let's now take a look at Heinz's working capital line items. We use Heinz's balance sheet from the Heinz third quarter report to identify which are the proper current asset and current liability line items. See Figures 7.1 and 7.2 back in Chapter 7.

Starting from the top of the balance sheet, we know cash is not included in operating working capital. The next two line items, "Trade receivables" and "Other receivables," are operating working capital line items. Heinz has broken out "Inventories" into segments, but as discussed in Chapter 7, we will just consider the total inventories line. This is a working capital line item. The next line item, "Prepaid expenses," is also a working capital line item. "Other current assets," despite further research in the quarterly and annual reports, are not clearly defined. Since it is a current asset, it is more likely than not related to an operating item, so let's assume this is a working capital item.

On the liabilities side, there are "Short-term debt" and "Portion of long-term debt due within one year," which are not operating working capital line items, as they are debts. The next three line items, "Trade payables," "Other payables," and "Accrued marketing," are operating working capital line items. We will also assume that "Other accrued liabilities" is an operating working capital line item. Despite the vagueness of this line item being "other," if it is an accrued liability, it is most likely an expense that has not "income taxes," which we assume are accrued income taxes, we believe is also an operating working capital item. See the box for an explanation.

ACCRUED INCOME TAXES VERSUS DEFERRED TAXES

We believe there is a difference between accrued income taxes and deferred taxes, although we have seen some entities and resources describe them as one and the same. This topic has gray areas and consists of varying views. As discussed in Chapter 9, deferred taxes are created due to timing differences in accounting for GAAP purposes versus tax purposes. We described differing depreciation methods as one possible way to create a deferred tax liability. However, we have found accrued income taxes to be the actual amount of taxes owed in a given period but not yet paid. So whereas deferred taxes are projected based on some accounting timing differences, accrued income taxes can simply be projected as a percentage of the taxes due, and as such we will consider them operating.

We have now identified the following line items from the balance sheet to be used in our operating working capital schedule.

- Trade receivables.
- Other receivables.
- Total inventories.
- Prepaid expenses.
- Other current assets.
- Trade payables.
- Other payables.
- Accrued marketing.
- Other accrued liabilities.
- Accrued income taxes.

Relating Operating Working Capital Line Items to the Balance Sheet and Cash Flow Statement

You may notice that the 10 line items we have identified may not be defined as such in the cash flow statement. This is a common complication that arises when trying to link the operating working capital between the balance sheet and the cash flow statement. In other words, the operating working capital line items defined in the balance sheet may not be defined in the same exact way in the cash flow statement. It is our job as analysts to best reallocate the line items to match the operating working capital balance sheet line items to the cash flow statement without misrepresenting the original reported numbers. If we refer back to the cash flow statement in Figure 6.1, Heinz clearly labels a section within the cash flow from operating activities section as "Changes in current assets and liabilities, excluding effects of acquisitions and divestitures." This is actually helpful for us. Some companies do not define this section so narrowly, or they define it as something like "Changes in assets and liabilities" as opposed to "Changes in *current* assets and liabilities." If Heinz had labeled that section without the word *current*, we would have to caution that some of the line items within that section may not be current, and therefore may not truly be working capital items. However, because Heinz clearly lists this section as current, we can assume these should be related to operating working capital.

The items identified in this section of the cash flow statement are:

- Receivables.
- Inventories.

- Prepaid expenses and other current assets.
- Accounts payable.
- Accrued liabilities.
- Income taxes.

You may notice that there are only six items defined within this section, but we have defined 10 items as operating working capital in the balance sheet. This is a common problem that arises when trying to relate the operating working capital line items between the cash flow statement and the balance sheet. We need to find a way either to consolidate balance sheet line items or to add more cash flow line items to match everything up. See Figure 10.1, which lists the balance sheet items we have defined and the cash flow statement items defined in the "Changes in current assets and liabilities, excluding effects of acquisitions and divestitures" section.

Reading from the top down, we can clearly make some comparisons. "Trade receivables" and "Other receivables" we can relate to the "Receivables" in the cash flow statement. "Total inventories" is clearly related to "Inventories." The next two balance sheet line items, "Prepaid expenses" and "Other current assets," can be related to the "Prepaid expenses and other current assets" line item in the cash flow statement. We can group all "Payables" together, so "Trade payables" and "Other payables" can be combined and related to "Accounts payables" in the cash flow statement. Since "Accrued marketing" is an accrued liability, we can combine this with "Other accrued liabilities" and relate this to the "Accrued liabilities" in

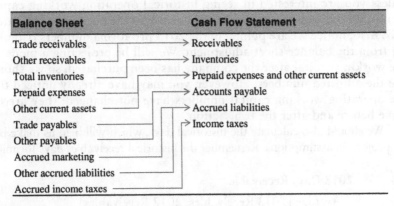

FIGURE 10.1 Operating Working Capital Comparison

the cash flow statement. Finally, "Accrued income taxes" will be related to "Income taxes" in the cash flow statement.

Note that we do not know, and will probably never know for sure, if this is the right way to match up these line items. It is a best guess, and there could be other configurations. Also, going back to the historical years and trying to back into the numbers as a means to try to figure out how to match up the line items rarely works out. As balance sheet line items are often written up or written down, and as reporting adjustments are made, don't expect to match the historical cash flow statement and balance sheet numbers. This is unfortunately an unsatisfying component to such financial reporting. The goal is to be sure, however, that our projections match up, and this is the first step.

We can now proceed to the operating working capital schedule in the model and rework the schedule so that we have the six line items from Figure 10.1.

Receivables

As we had done with the net property, plant, and equipment in the depreciation schedule, it is recommended to actually pull these numbers from the balance sheet adjustments into the operating working capital schedule. We need to keep in mind consolidating the balance sheet items where noted previously. So in the operating working capital schedule for "Receivables, net," we can pull in the sum of the "Trade receivables" and "Other receivables" from the Heinz balance sheet. So in Cell I230 we will have "=H113+H114." Notice we do not have historical balance sheet information prior to the 3Q data, and it's not 100 percent necessary here unless you are interested in seeing historical operating working capital trends. We will not go into that level of detail for the purposes of this analysis. Also, notice we are pulling in the 2013 pro forma numbers (Column H) from the balance sheet adjustment. We will be projecting a model of the working capital after the company has been purchased, so we should use the adjusted numbers. However, you may have already noticed that the operating working capital numbers have not changed; they are the same before and after the transaction.

We should also calculate the historical days, which will help us make better projection assumptions. Remember the historical receivables days formula:

$$2013 \text{ Days Receivable}$$
$$= \frac{\text{Average}\left(2013 \text{ Receivables}, 2012 \text{ Receivables}\right)}{2013 \text{ Revenue}} \times 360$$

TABLE 10.1 Heinz Historical Operating Working Capital Receivables

Operating Working Capital (OWC) Schedule (in US$ millions except per share amounts)						
			Estimates			
On January 27	2013PF	2014E	2015E	2016E	2017E	2018E
Current assets						
Receivables	$1,098.8					
Days receivable	*33.8*					
Inventories						
Inventory turnover days						
Prepaid expenses and other current assets						
Days prepaid						
Total current assets						
Current liabilities						
Accounts payable						
Days payable						
Accrued liabilities						
Days payable						
Income taxes						
Days payable						
Total current liabilities						
Total operating working capital						
Change in total operating working capital						

However, we have only one year of balance sheet information, so we will eliminate the "average" component to this formula. We will also use last twelve months (LTM) revenue in place of 2013 revenue, as that is the time frame closely related to the 2013 pro forma data.

$$2013 \text{ Days Receivable} = \frac{2013 \text{ Receivables}}{\text{LTM Revenue}} \times 360$$

In operating working capital Cell I231, we can do the following:

2013 Days Receivable (Cell I231)

Excel Keystrokes	Description
Type "="	Enters into "formula" mode
Select Cell I230	Receivables

(continued)

Type "/"	Divides
Select Cell I6	LTM revenue
Type "*360"	Multiplies times 360
Hit Enter	End
Formula result	=I230/I6*360

This should give us 33.8 days. This is pretty standard. As a customer is typically expected to pay anywhere from 30 to 90 days (depending on the business), 33.8 days of receivables outstanding is at the low end of that range. A high level of accounts receivable days could imply there is a large portion of receivables that have not been collected—a potential concern. Again, this is a great example of how building these models can help test the soundness of a business.

Note: Do not copy this formula beyond 2013, as we will be providing our own assumption drivers for projections in 2014. This formula is solely for the purposes of calculating historical metrics. See Table 10.1.

Inventories

The same process can continue for the remaining operating working capital line items. We need to take care in understanding which income statement line item the operating working capital item is referring to. In some cases, this is obvious. For example, accounts receivable is always related to revenue, and inventory is related to cost of goods sold (COGS).

We can link "Inventories" in Row 232 directly in from the "Total inventories" in the balance sheet adjustments. So, I232 will read "=H115."

We can now calculate the inventory days (also known as turnover). The standard formula is:

$$2013 \text{ Inventory Days}$$
$$= \frac{\text{Average} \left(2013 \text{ Inventories}, 2012 \text{ Inventories}\right)}{2013 \text{ COGS}} \times 360$$

Adjusting because we have only the 2013 balance sheet and LTM income statement data gives us:

$$2013 \text{ Inventory Days} = \frac{2013 \text{ Inventories}}{\text{LTM COGS}} \times 360$$

So, in operating working capital Cell I233, we can do the following:

2013 Inventory Days (Cell I233)

Excel Keystrokes	Description
Type "="	Enters into "formula" mode
Select Cell I232	Inventories
Type "/"	Divides
Select Cell I8	LTM COGS
Type "*360"	Multiplies times 360
Hit Enter	End
Formula result	=I232/I8*360

This should give us 72.3 days. See Table 10.2.

Now let's move on to prepaid expenses.

Prepaid Expenses and Other Current Assets

The same process can be repeated for the next line item. "Prepaid expenses and other current assets" will be a combination of the "Prepaid expenses" and "Other current assets," so I234 will be "=H116+H117."

In this case it is not clear which income statement line item relates to prepaid expenses. We need to consider what income statement expense the company is actually prepaying. If it is expenses to the manufacturer, for example, then we can relate prepaid expenses to COGS. However, if it is rent payments, then we should be relating prepaid expenses to selling, general, and administrative (SG&A) expenses. Unfortunately, in this case, a search for "prepaid expenses" gives us is no further information in the Heinz annual report or the Heinz quarterly report. We will, then, make the educated guess that this is related to SG&A, as (1) we only have two choices in this case, COGS or SG&A, and (2) prepaid expenses have more often been related to SG&A than to COGS. Note that we are mainly concerned about trends here, and so it is safe to say that as both the SG&A and COGS costs are growing at the same rate of revenue, whichever one we relate prepaid expenses to, we will get a trend growing at the rate of revenue.

The traditional formula for the historical days prepaid is:

2013 Days Prepaid

$$= \frac{\text{Average (2013 Prepaid Expenses, 2012 Prepaid Expenses)}}{\text{2013 SG\&A}} \times 360$$

But adjusting out the average component gives us:

$$2013 \text{ Days Prepaid} = \frac{2013 \text{ Prepaid Expenses}}{\text{LTM SG} \& \text{A}} \times 360$$

So, in working capital Cell I235, we can do the following:

2013 Days Prepaid (Cell I235)

Excel Keystrokes	Description
Type "="	Enters into "formula" mode
Select Cell I234	Prepaid expenses
Type "/"	Divides
Select Cell I13	LTM SG&A
Type "*360"	Multiplies times 360
Hit Enter	End
Formula result	=I234/I13*360

This should give us 36.5 days.

We can now total the three current asset line items into Row 236, taking care not to include the "days" metric into the total, so Cell I236 should read, "=I230+I232+I234." We can copy this formula to the right, and we should have the same values as in Table 10.2.

TABLE 10.2 Heinz Historical Operating Working Capital Current Assets

Operating Working Capital (OWC) Schedule (in US$ millions except per share amounts)						
		Estimates				
On January 27	2013PF	2014E	2015E	2016E	2017E	2018E
Current assets						
Receivables	$1,098.8					
Days receivable	*33.8*					
Inventories	1,448.4					
Inventory turnover days	*72.3*					
Prepaid expenses and other						
current assets	261.1					
Days prepaid	*36.5*					
Total current assets	$2,808.2	$0.0	$0.0	$0.0	$0.0	$0.0

Accounts Payable

We can now repeat this procedure for the current liabilities line items, "Accounts payable," "Accrued liabilities," and "Accrued income taxes." We first link "Accounts payable" in as a sum of "Trade payables" and "Other payables" from the balance sheet adjustments. So in I238 we can type "=H130+H131" and hit Enter. Accounts payable is most commonly related to COGS, but it's always worth a bit of research to be sure. Unfortunately our research has not revealed any new information, so we will stay with the default assumption. We can calculate the historical days by the formula (adjusting out the average and for LTM):

$$2013 \text{ Days Payable} = \frac{2013 \text{ Accounts Payable}}{\text{LTM COGS}} \times 360$$

2013 Days Payable (Cell I239)

Excel Keystrokes	Description
Type "="	Enters into "formula" mode
Select Cell I238	Accounts payable
Type "/"	Divides
Select Cell I8	LTM COGS
Type "*360"	Multiplies times 360
Hit Enter	End
Formula result	=I238/I8*360

This gives us 64.3. See Table 10.3.
We can move on to "Accrued liabilities."

Accrued Liabilities

We considered "Accrued liabilities" as a combination of "Accrued marketing" and "Other accrued liabilities." So in Cell I240 we can have "=H132+H133." Accrued liabilities are commonly related to an operating expense. It is clear from simply the name "Accrued marketing" that this is related to an operating expense (marketing); however, "Other accrued liabilities" are a bit unclear. Further research does mention "Other accrued liabilities" in relation to one-off items, but it does not help us generalize what expense the majority of these other liabilities are based on. Since we only have one major operating expenses line item, SG&A, and given what we know about the accrued marketing, let's use SG&A.

We can calculate the historical days by the formula (adjusting for the average and LTM):

$$2013 \text{ Days Payable} = \frac{2013 \text{ Accrued Liabilities}}{\text{LTM SG \& A}} \times 360$$

2013 Days Payable (Cell I241)

Excel Keystrokes	Description
Type "="	Enters into "formula" mode
Select Cell I240	Accrued liabilities
Type "/"	Divides
Select Cell I13	LTM SG&A
Type "*360"	Multiplies times 360
Hit Enter	End
Formula result	=I240/I13*360

This gives us 131.9 days (see Table 10.3). This is a high number. An unusually high days number (typically >90) could indicate that there is a group of liabilities in this account that have been left outstanding for quite a long time. This most likely has to do with the "Other accrued liabilities"; either there are nonrecurring or one-time items buried in there, or these liabilities are simply not directly related to just the SG&A. Again, for projection purposes, we are mostly concerned about high-level trends. So we will not dig and adjust further.

Accrued Income Taxes

We are now left with "Accrued income taxes," which we link in from Row 134 on the balance sheet. So in Cell I243 we will have "=H134." Accrued income taxes are related to the income tax expense line item in the income statement. We can calculate the historical days by the formula (adjusting for average and LTM):

$$2013 \text{ Days Payable} = \frac{2013 \text{ Accrued Income Taxes}}{\text{LTM Income Tax Expense}} \times 360$$

2013 Days Payable (Cell I243)

Excel Keystrokes	Description
Type "="	Enters into "formula" mode
Select Cell I242	Accrued income taxes
Type "/"	Divides

Select Cell I35	LTM income tax expense
Type "*360"	Multiplies times 360
Hit Enter	End
Formula result	=I242/I35*360

This gives us 145.7 days. We can now total the three current liability line items into Row 244, taking care not to include the "days" metric into the total, so Cell I244 should read, "=I238+I240+I244." "Total operating working capital," the line directly underneath "Total current liabilities," is calculated by subtracting the Total Current Liabilities from Total Current Assets. So, in Cell I245 we can type "= 1236 – 1244." We can copy both Cells I244 and I245 to the right to get Table 10.3.

We can now start projecting the operating working capital schedule.

TABLE 10.3   Heinz Historical Operating Working Capital Schedule

Operating Working Capital (OWC) Schedule (in US$ millions except per share amounts)						
				Estimates		
On January 27	2013PF	2014E	2015E	2016E	2017E	2018E
Current assets						
Receivables	$1,098.8					
Days receivable	*33.8*					
Inventories	1,448.4					
Inventory turnover days	*72.3*					
Prepaid expenses and other current assets	261.1					
Days prepaid	*36.5*					
Total current assets	$2,808.2	$0.0	$0.0	$0.0	$0.0	$0.0
Current liabilities						
Accounts payable	1,287.8					
Days payable	*64.3*					
Accrued liabilities	944.0					
Days payable	*131.9*					
Income taxes	91.3					
Days payable	*145.7*					
Total current liabilities	$2,323.1	$0.0	$0.0	$0.0	$0.0	$0.0
Total operating working capital	$ 485.1	$0.0	$0.0	$0.0	$0.0	$0.0

PROJECTING OPERATING WORKING CAPITAL

In order to project operating working capital, we will use the days calculated for each line item as an indicator of next year's operating working capital performance. It is also recommended to pull in prior years' working capital numbers from previous financial reports for more color on historical days trends if you have time to dig up that information. On the other hand, this business will be most likely going through a lot of management changes, so the operating working capital may be managed differently; maybe more efficiently, or maybe less efficiently. We will stick to just the 2013 days for purposes of this analysis.

Receivables

We had calculated 33.8 days receivable. Thirty days is typical for receivables, but they could also be higher or lower. For good projections we want to know if the 33.8 days levels will continue, or if the company will start to perform above or below the historical levels. It is common to assume that last year's performance or an average of the past three historical years' performance will be an indicator of next year's performance. So, let's take the previous year's 33.8 days for our projections. Let's hard-code "33.8" into Cell J231 as our assumption for 2014, and copy this to the right. In order to use the projected days to drive estimated accounts receivable, we need to reverse engineer the standard days receivable formula:

$$2013 \text{ Days Receivable}$$
$$= \frac{\text{Average (2013 Receivables, 2012 Receivables)}}{2013 \text{ Revenue}} \times 360$$

But for 2014 the formula would read:

$$2014 \text{ Days Receivable}$$
$$= \frac{\text{Average (2014 Receivables, 2013 Receivables)}}{2014 \text{ Revenue}} \times 360$$

Now we have days receivable (our projected assumption), so we want to solve for 2014 receivables. We can divide both sides of the equation by 360, giving us:

$$\frac{2014 \text{ Days Receivable}}{360}$$
$$= \frac{\text{Average (2014 Receivables, 2013 Receivables)}}{2014 \text{ Revenue}}$$

And we can multiply both sides of the equation by "2014 Revenue," giving us:

$$\frac{2014 \text{ Days Receivable}}{360} \times 2014 \text{ Revenue}$$
$$= \text{Average (2014 Receivables, 2013 Receivables)}$$

So, in order to get 2014 receivables, the formula is:

$$\frac{2014 \text{ Days Receivable}}{360} \times 2014 \text{ Revenue}$$

Note that we could have taken the formula a step further and readjusted for the "Average (2014 Receivables, 2013 Receivables)" component. However, for standard projections, the days we choose as our driver should technically be a representation of average and standard indicators, so adjusting for the average can be considered overengineering the analysis. However, there are some advanced analyses (for example, backing into management's projections), where using the following formula is the only way to back into the exact metrics. So, for reference, we have furthered the analysis here.

First we convert the "average" formula into mathematical operations:

$$\text{Average (2014 Receivables, 2013 Receivables)}$$
$$= \frac{(2014 \text{ Receivables} + 2013 \text{ Receivables})}{2}$$

We can replace this version of the "average" formula into the equation:

$$\frac{2014 \text{ Days Receivable}}{360} \times 2014 \text{ Revenue}$$
$$= \frac{(2014 \text{ Receivables} + 2013 \text{ Receivables})}{2}$$

(continued)

We can multiply both sides of the equation by 2 to get:

$$\left\{ \frac{2014 \text{ Days Receivable}}{360} \times 2014 \text{ Revenue} \right\} \times 2$$

$$= (2014 \text{ Receivables} + 2013 \text{ Receivables})$$

And we can subtract the 2013 receivables from both sides of the equation:

2014 Receivables

$$= \left\{ \frac{2014 \text{ Day Receivable}}{360} \times 2014 \text{ Revenue} \right\} \times 2$$

$$- 2013 \text{ Receivables}$$

We will stick with the "2014 Days Receivable/360 * 2014 Revenue" formula to calculate the 2014 projections. And this should make sense. Remember that in the original basic formula, "Receivables/Revenue * 360," the "Receivables/Revenue" part of the formula gives us a percentage. This percentage answers, "What percentage of revenue booked is left outstanding?" Remember the first example in this chapter, where we had $25,000 of receivables after booking $100,000 in revenue, representing 25 percent of our revenue still outstanding. We then multiply the percentage by 360 to convert into an estimated number of days outstanding. So in the example 360 times 25 percent is 90 days. Now, in the reverse engineered formula, "2014 Days Receivable/360 * 2014 Revenue," the "2014 Days Receivable/360" part of the formula backs into that percentage outstanding, or 90/360, giving us 25 percent. We simply multiply that percentage by the projected revenue to get future estimated receivables.

2014 Receivables (Cell J230)

Excel Keystrokes	Description
Type "="	Begins the formula
Select Cell J231	2014 days receivable
Type "/360"	Divides by 360
Type "*"	Multiplies
Select Cell J6	2014 revenue
Hit Enter	End
Formula result	=J231/360*J6

We can copy this formula to the right through 2018 to complete our receivables projections shown in Table 10.4.

TABLE 10.4   Heinz Projected Operating Working Capital Receivables

Operating Working Capital (OWC) Schedule (in US$ millions except per share amounts)						
			Estimates			
On January 27	2013PF	2014E	2015E	2016E	2017E	2018E
Current assets						
Receivables	$1,098.8	$1,102.1	$1,106.5	$1,110.9	$1,115.4	$1,119.8
Days receivable	*33.8*	*33.8*	*33.8*	*33.8*	*33.8*	*33.8*

Inventories

We can repeat this process for each working capital line item. But remember that each item is related to different income statement line items, so for inventories we have:

$$2014 \text{ Inventories} = \frac{2014 \text{ Inventory Days}}{360} \times 2014 \text{ COGS}$$

So, in Cell J233, we can use the 72.3 days, hard-coding this as our future assumption, to project the inventories.

2014 Inventories (Cell J232)

Excel Keystrokes	Description
Type "="	Begins the formula
Select Cell J233	2014 inventory days
Type "/360"	Divides by 360
Type "*"	Multiplies
Select Cell J8	2014 COGS
Hit Enter	End
Formula result	=J233/360*J8

We can copy Cells J232 and J233 to the right.

Now we repeat for prepaid expenses and other current assets, relating them to the SG&A on the income statement.

Prepaid Expenses and Other Current Assets

$$2014 \text{ Prepaid Expenses} = \frac{2014 \text{ Days Prepaid}}{360} \times 2014 \text{ SG\&A}$$

So, in Cell J235, we can use the 36.5 days, hard-coding this as our future assumption, to project the prepaid expenses. Note here that cost savings have been estimated, which would reduce the SG&A and possibly the underlying prepaid expense balance. Let's make that similar adjustment by projecting the prepaid expenses off of the SG&A *less* the cost savings, or:

$$
\begin{aligned}
&2014 \text{ Prepaid Expenses} \\
&= \frac{2014 \text{ Days Prepaid}}{360} \times (2014 \text{ SG\&A} \\
&\quad - 2014 \text{ Cost Savings})
\end{aligned}
$$

2014 Prepaid Expenses (Cell J234)

Excel Keystrokes	Description
Type "="	Begins the formula
Select Cell J235	2014 prepaid expenses
Type "/360"	Divides by 360
Type "*"	Multiplies
Type "("	Begins addition formula
Select Cell J13	2014 SG&A
Type "+"	Adds
Select Cell J16	2014 cost savings (the value is negative so we add it to reduce)
Type ")"	Closes formula
Hit Enter	End
Formula result	=J235/360*(J13+J16)

It may have been easier to just calculate both the historical and future prepaid line items off of "Total operating expenses," but we don't believe that the line item "Fund management fee" would contribute to prepaid expenses; so we took only SG&A and cost savings into consideration.

We can copy Cells J234 and J235 to the right. (See Table 10.5.)

TABLE 10.5 Heinz Projected Operating Working Capital Current Assets

Operating Working Capital (OWC) Schedule (in US$ millions except per share amounts)

On January 27	2013PF	2014E	2015E	2016E	2017E	2018E
				Estimates		
Current assets						
Receivables	$1,098.8	$1,102.1	$1,106.5	$1,110.9	$1,115.4	$1,119.8
Days receivable	33.8	33.8	33.8	33.8	33.8	33.8
Inventories	1,448.4	1,452.2	1,458.0	1,463.8	1,469.7	1,475.6
Inventory turnover days	72.3	72.3	72.3	72.3	72.3	72.3
Prepaid expenses and other current assets	261.1	259.2	260.2	261.3	262.3	263.4
Days prepaid	36.5	36.5	36.5	36.5	36.5	36.5
Total current assets	$2,808.2	$2,813.5	$2,824.7	$2,836.0	$2,847.4	$2,858.8

Accounts Payable

We can now continue the process with the current liabilities, beginning with the accounts payable.

$$2014 \text{ Accounts Payable} = \frac{2014 \text{ Days Payable}}{360} \times 2014 \text{ COGS}$$

So, in Cell J239, we can use the 64.3 days, hard-coding this as our future assumption.

2014 Accounts Payable (Cell J238)

Excel Keystrokes	Description
Type "="	Begins the formula
Select Cell J239	2014 accounts payable
Type "/360"	Divides by 360
Type "*"	Multiplies
Select Cell J8	2014 COGS
Hit Enter	End
Formula result	=J239/360*J8

We can copy Cells J238 and J239 to the right.

Accrued Liabilities

For accrued liabilities, we hard-code "131.9" into Cell J241. Again, here cost savings have been estimated, which would reduce the SG&A and possibly the underlying accrued liability balance. Let's make that similar adjustment:

$$\begin{aligned}
2014 &\text{ Accrued Liabilities} \\
&= \frac{2014 \text{ Days Payable}}{360} \times (2014 \text{ SG\&A} \\
&\quad - 2014 \text{ Cost Savings})
\end{aligned}$$

2014 Accrued Liabilities (Cell J240)

Excel Keystrokes	Description
Type "="	Begins the formula
Select Cell J241	2014 accrued liabilities

Type "/360"	Divides by 360
Type "*"	Multiplies
Type "("	Begins addition formula
Select Cell J13	2014 SG&A
Type "+"	Adds
Select Cell J16	2014 cost savings (the value is negative so we add it to reduce)
Type ")"	Closes formula
Hit Enter	End
Formula result	=J241/360*(J13+J16)

We can copy Cells J240 and J241 to the right.

Accrued Income Taxes

For accrued income taxes, we hard-code "145.7" into J243 and use the following formula.

$$2014 \text{ Accrued Income Taxes}$$
$$= \frac{2014 \text{ Days Payable}}{360} \times 2014 \text{ Income Tax Expense}$$

2014 Income Taxes (Cell J242)

Excel Keystrokes	Description
Type "="	Begins the formula
Select Cell J243	2014 accrued income taxes
Type "/360"	Divides by 360
Type "*"	Multiplies
Select Cell J35	2014 income tax expense
Hit Enter	End
Formula result	=J243/360*J35

We can copy Cells J242 and J243 to the right. See Table 10.6.

TABLE 10.6 Heinz Projected Operating Working Capital Schedule

Operating Working Capital (OWC) Schedule (in US$ millions except per share amounts)

| On January 27 | 2013PF | Estimates | | | | |
		2014E	2015E	2016E	2017E	2018E
Current assets						
Receivables	$1,098.8	$1,102.1	$1,106.5	$1,110.9	$1,115.4	$1,119.8
Days receivable	*33.8*	*33.8*	*33.8*	*33.8*	*33.8*	*33.8*
Inventories	1,448.4	1,452.2	1,458.0	1,463.8	1,469.7	1,475.6
Inventory turnover days	*72.3*	*72.3*	*72.3*	*72.3*	*72.3*	*72.3*
Prepaid expenses and other current assets	261.1	259.2	260.2	261.3	262.3	263.4
Days prepaid	*36.5*	*36.5*	*36.5*	*36.5*	*36.5*	*36.5*
Total current assets	$2,808.2	$2,813.5	$2,824.7	$2,836.0	$2,847.4	$2,858.8
Current liabilities						
Accounts payable	1,287.8	1,291.5	1,296.7	1,301.8	1,307.1	1,312.3
Days payable	*64.3*	*64.3*	*64.3*	*64.3*	*64.3*	*64.3*
Accrued liabilities	944.0	936.7	940.5	944.2	948.0	951.8
Days payable	*131.9*	*131.9*	*131.9*	*131.9*	*131.9*	*131.9*
Income taxes	91.3	144.1	143.7	143.2	142.8	142.3
Days payable	*145.7*	*145.7*	*145.7*	*145.7*	*145.7*	*145.7*
Total current liabilities	$2,323.1	$2,372.3	$2,380.8	$2,389.3	$2,397.8	$2,406.4
Total operating working capital	$ 485.1	$ 441.1	$ 443.9	$ 446.7	$ 449.5	$ 452.4

OPERATING WORKING CAPITAL AND
THE CASH FLOW STATEMENT

It is important to explain the relationship between operating working capital line items and cash flow. Remember, one of the reasons for creating an operating working capital schedule is to serve as a bridge between balance sheet items and cash flow items. Now that we have our operating working capital projections, we can link each of these line items into the operating working capital section of the cash flow statement, Rows 69 to 74.

Let's first discuss this relationship between operating working capital and cash flow. If inventory increases from one year to the next, this results in a cash outflow. For example, if we had $0 in inventory in 2012, and in 2013 our inventory balance increases to $1,000, we may have purchased inventory. If inventory is purchased, money is spent, so the cash flow relating to the inventory change is –$1,000.

The same rules apply to all current assets within operating working capital (remember that cash is not included in operating working capital). If accounts receivable increases from year to year, this results in a cash outflow. But, what happens if a current assets account decreases from year to year? If we have $1,500 in accounts receivable in 2012, for example, and that balance has reduced to $0 by 2013, we must have collected on our accounts receivable. In other words, customers who owed us money for purchases they made on credit have paid us back. So, the receivables go down, and cash comes in. In this example, we have received cash of $1,500 from the reduction in accounts receivable. Similarly, if our inventory has reduced from, say, $2,000 in 2012 to $1,500 in 2013, we can assume we have sold that inventory and $500 in cash has been received.

Asset Balance Change	Cash Flow Effect
Current assets increase* (+)	Cash flow decreases (–)
Current assets decrease* (–)	Cash flow increases (+)
*Note: Current assets exclude cash when referring to operating working capital. If cash as an asset would increase, then cash on the cash flow statement would certainly increase accordingly.	

Current liabilities have the opposite effect on cash. Let's look at accrued liabilities, for example. If an accrued liability has increased from $1,000 in 2012 to $2,000 in 2013, this results in a positive cash flow. It's sort of hard to think through how an increase in a payable (an expense you have not yet paid) results in a positive cash flow line item, but remember that cash flow from operations represents noncash adjustments to the net income. So the payables increasing from $1,000 to $2,000 means we have more noncash expenses that we should be adding back to net income. This add-back is represented by a cash inflow, so an accounts payable account increasing from one year to the next results in a cash increase, or really, cash being added back to the net income. Conversely, if the accrued liability account decreases, we have paid down that liability; cash decreases. So if, for example, the accounts payable account was $7,500 in 2012 and is reduced to $0 in 2013, we have effectively paid off those expenses, resulting in a cash outflow of –$7,500. An increase in current liabilities reflects an increase in cash, and a decrease in current liabilities reflects a decrease in cash.

Liability Balance Change	Cash Flow Effect
Current liabilities increase (+)	Cash flow increases (+)
Current liabilities decrease (–)	Cash flow decreases (–)

The cash flow statement's operating working capital section refers to the cash impact based on the increase or decrease in each current asset and current liability from year to year. So we want to link the year-to-year changes of each operating working capital line item into the cash flow statement, taking care to properly adjust for the directional cash flows. Before we begin, let's look at the total operating working capital. Row 246 of the operating working capital schedule, entitled "Change in total operating working capital," represents the total change in operating working capital for each projected year. So in Cell J246, we can subtract the 2013 total operating working capital from the 2014 total operating working capital, or have J246 read "=J245-I245."

We can copy this formula to the right. This is showing that the operating working capital is decreasing in the first year, but then slightly increasing each year thereafter.

Since operating working capital is defined as current assets (not including cash) less current liabilities (not including debts), it can be considered a net asset. So, total operating working capital acts like an asset; if it is increasing, it represents a cash outflow, and if it is decreasing, it represents cash coming in. If Heinz's projected operating working capital is decreasing, we should see total cash from working capital as positive in the cash flow statement.

The match formula in Row 247 is another one of several checks we see throughout the model. It may read "N" right now, as we have not yet properly linked the operating working capital line items to the cash flow statement. Once done properly, the match should read "Y." The match checks to make sure the total operating working capital changes, Row 246, match the cash flow, Row 75. In the cash flow statement, we will subtract each individual line item making up working capital and total the changes. We are effectively calculating the same total operating working capital change in a different way. This helps ensure we have our changes flowing in the right direction.

Operating Working Capital	2011	2012
Accounts Receivable	20,000.0	25,000.0
Inventory	5,000.0	7,500.0
Prepaid Expenses	1,250.0	1,000.0
Accounts Payable	10,000.0	12,500.0
Accrued Expenses	12,500.0	15,000.0
Net Working Capital	**3,750.0**	**6,000.0**
Changes in Net Working Capital		**2,250.0**

Cash Flow	2012
Accounts Receivable	(5,000.0)
Inventory	(2,500.0)
Prepaid Expenses	250.0
Accounts Payable	2,500.0
Accrued Expenses	2,500.0
Total Working Capital	**(2,250.0)**

Changes in Receivables

Let's link each operating working capital line item into the cash flow statement beginning with the receivables. On the cash flow statement, Row 69, "Changes in receivables," represents "Receivables," so we clearly want to link this in from the "Receivables" row in the operating working capital schedule. However, on the cash flow statement we want to show the proper year-to-year change, representing an inflow or outflow depending on whether the item is an asset or a liability. We see that receivables in the operating working capital schedule have increased from 2013 to 2014. This should be represented as a cash outflow on the cash flow statement. So when we link the receivables from the operating working capital into the cash flow statement we should link the negative changes from 2013 to 2014, or Cash Flow Receivables = –(2014 Accounts Receivable – 2013 Accounts Receivable).

2014 Changes in Accounts Receivable (J69)

Excel Keystrokes	Description
Type "="	Begins the formula
Type "-("	Prepares to calculate the negative change
Select Cell J230	2014 receivables
Type "-"	Subtracts
Select Cell I230	2013 receivables
Type ")"	Closes the formula
Hit Enter	End
Formula result	=-(J230-I230)

We can copy this formula to the right through 2018. See Table 10.7.

Changes in Inventories

Every current asset within the operating working capital works the same way; that is, we want to pull the negative change into the cash flow statement because of the relationship between current assets in the operating working capital and their effect on cash. So, because inventory is also increasing year over year, we should expect to see a cash outflow in the "Inventories" line item of the cash flow statement.

2014 Changes in Inventories (Cell J70)

Excel Keystrokes	Description
Type "="	Begins the formula
Type "-("	Prepares to calculate the negative change
Select Cell J232	2014 inventories
Type "-"	Subtracts
Select Cell I232	2013 inventories
Type ")"	Closes the formula
Hit Enter	End
Formula result	=-(J232-I232)

We can copy this formula to the right through 2018. See Table 10.7.

Changes in Prepaid Expenses and Other Current Assets

Again, as prepaid expenses are current assets, we want to pull the negative change into the cash flow statement because of the relationship between current assets in the operating working capital and their effect on cash.

2014 Changes in Prepaid Expenses (Cash Flow Cell J71)

Excel Keystrokes	Description
Type "="	Begins the formula
Type "-("	Prepares to calculate the negative change
Select Cell J234	2014 prepaid expenses
Type "-"	Subtracts
Select Cell I234	2013 prepaid expenses
Type ")"	Closes the formula
Hit Enter	End
Formula result	=-(J234-I234)

We can copy this formula to the right through 2018. See Table 10.7.

Changes in Accounts Payable

For current liabilities, remember that an increase from year to year represents a cash inflow. So, we will simply subtract the next year from the prior year: 2014 Cash Flow Changes in Accounts Payable = 2014 Accounts Payable – 2013 Accounts Payable.

2014 Changes in Accounts Payable (J72)

Excel Keystrokes	Description
Type "="	Begins the formula
Select Cell J238	2014 accounts payable
Type "-"	Subtracts
Select Cell I238	2013 accounts payable
Hit Enter	End
Formula result	=J238-I238

This formula can be copied to the right through 2018. See Table 10.7.

Changes in Accrued Liabilities

We can repeat the process for accrued liabilities.

2014 Changes in Accrued Liabilities (Cash Flow Cell J73)

Excel Keystrokes	Description
Type "="	Begins the formula
Select Cell J240	2014 accrued liabilities
Type "-"	Subtracts
Select Cell I240	2013 accrued liabilities
Hit Enter	End
Formula result	=J240-I240

This formula can be copied to the right through 2018. See Table 10.7.

Changes in Accrued Income Taxes

We can repeat the process for accrued income taxes as well.

2014 Changes in Accrued Income Taxes (Cash Flow Cell J74)

Excel Keystrokes	Description
Type "="	Begins the formula
Select Cell J242	2014 accrued income taxes
Type "-"	Subtracts
Select Cell I242	2013 accrued income taxes
Hit Enter	End
Formula result	=J242-I242

This formula can be copied to the right through 2018. See Table 10.7.

TABLE 10.7 Heinz Projected Consolidated Statements of Cash Flows

Consolidated Statements of Cash Flows
(in US$ millions except per share amounts)

Period Ending	Estimates				
	2014E	2015E	2016E	2017E	2018E
Cash flows from operating activities					
Net income	$ 905.8	$ 903.0	$ 900.1	$ 897.2	$ 894.3
Depreciation	297.4	309.2	321.0	332.9	344.8
Amortization	30.0	30.0	30.0	30.0	30.0
Amortization of identifiable intangible assets	342.4	342.4	342.4	342.4	342.4
Deferred tax benefit/(provision)	(83.0)	(83.0)	(83.0)	(83.0)	(83.0)
Net losses on divestitures	0.0	0.0	0.0	0.0	0.0
Impairment on assets held for sale	0.0	0.0	0.0	0.0	0.0
Pension contributions	(80.0)	(80.0)	(80.0)	(80.0)	(80.0)
Asset write-downs from Fiscal 2012 productivity initiatives	0.0	0.0	0.0	0.0	0.0
Other items, net	10.2	10.2	10.2	10.2	10.2
Changes in operating working capital					
Changes in receivables	(3.3)	(4.4)	(4.4)	(4.4)	(4.5)
Changes in inventories	(3.8)	(5.8)	(5.8)	(5.9)	(5.9)
Changes in prepaid expenses and other current assets	1.8	(1.0)	(1.0)	(1.0)	(1.0)
Changes in accounts payable	3.7	5.2	5.2	5.2	5.2
Changes in accrued liabilities	(7.3)	3.7	3.8	3.8	3.8
Changes in accrued income taxes	52.9	(0.4)	(0.4)	(0.5)	(0.5)
Net changes in operating working capital	$ 44.0	$ (2.8)	$ (2.8)	$ (2.8)	$ (2.8)
Total cash provided by (used for) operating activities	$1,466.8	$1,429.0	$1,437.9	$1,446.9	$1,455.9

We notice that the match Row 247 in the operating working capital schedule should now read "Y." Again, this is a check to ensure we are linking each year-to-year operating working capital line item change into the cash flow statement. It is easy to confuse whether to include the direct year-over-year change or the "minus" year-over-year change when linking from the operating working capital into the cash flow statement. Having this check can help us avoid that potential issue and will ensure we have our cash flowing in the right direction.

We are now done with the operating working capital schedule and can continue on to projecting the balance sheet. Refer to Appendix 1 to ensure you are following the model building path.

CHAPTER 11

Balance Sheet Projections

Now that our cash flow is complete, we can proceed to the balance sheet, which begins in Row 158. Before actually projecting the 2014 balance sheet, we need to pull in the pro forma balance sheet numbers we had calculated in our balance sheet adjustments analysis. We can simply link those numbers into the pro forma Column I. However, remember that we had consolidated several balance sheet line items for the working capital section. Those working capital line items are effectively balance sheet line items too. We should also follow the same procedure here, consolidating where appropriate. It might be cleaner to go back to the balance sheet adjustments analysis and combine the line items there so they are consolidated everywhere, but for purposes of the book let's simply consolidate where needed in this balance sheet section.

To begin, we would like to link the cash balance in from the cash line in the Balance Sheet Adjustments section. So, I164 will read "=H112." The next line, "Receivables," is a consolidation of "Trade receivables" and "Other receivables" as per our discussions in Chapter 10, Working Capital. We should also consolidate here simply by adding both "Trade receivables" and "Other receivables" into Cell I165. Cell I165 will read "=H113+H114." We will repeat the same process until we have a representation of the pro forma balance sheet here to build our projections off of. Note that the "Totals" should continue to total top-down as one would in any year. See the following table and Table 11.1 as a guide.

Balance Sheet Item	Formula
Cash and cash equivalents (Cell I164)	=H112
Receivables (Cell I165)	=H113+H114 (sum of "Trade receivables" and "Other receivables")
Inventories (Cell I166)	=H115
Prepaid expenses and other current assets (I167)	=H116+H117 (sum of "Prepaid expenses" and "Other current assets")
Total current assets (Cell I168)	=SUM(I164:I167)

(continued)

Property, plant, and equipment, net (Cell I169)	=H119 (Hint: Since there is no more consolidation in this section, you can simply just copy Cell I169 down through Cell I173)
Goodwill (Cell I170)	=H120
Trademarks, net (Cell I171)	=H121
Other intangibles, net (Cell I172)	=H122
Other noncurrent assets (Cell I173)	=H123
Total assets (Cell I174)	=SUM(I168:I173)

When complete with the assets section, your total assets should match the total assets in the pro forma balance sheet adjustments section. See Table 11.1. We can continue with the liabilities:

Balance Sheet Item	Formula
Short-term debt (Cell I177)	=H127
Portion of long-term debt due within one year (Cell I178)	=H128
Revolving line of credit (Cell I179)	=H129
Accounts payable (Cell I180)	=H130+H131 (sum of "Trade payables" and "Other payables")
Accrued marketing and other accrued liabilities (Cell I181)	=H132+H133 (sum of "Accrued marketing" and "Other accrued liabilities")
Income taxes (Cell I182)	=H134
Total current liabilities (Cell I183)	=SUM(I177:I182)
Term facilities (Cell I184)	=H136 (Hint: Since there is no more consolidation in this section, you can simply just copy Cell I184 down through Cell I190)
The notes (Cell I185)	=H137
Long-term debt (Cell I186)	=H138
Deferred income taxes (Cell I187)	=H139
Nonpension postretirement benefits (Cell I88)	=H140
Other noncurrent liabilities (Cell I89)	=H141
Redeemable noncontrolling interest (Cell I90)	=H142
Total liabilities (Cell I91)	=SUM(I183:I190)

And we can now move on to the equity.

Balance Sheet Item	Formula
Capital stock (Cell I194)	=H146 (Hint: Since there is no more consolidation in this section, you can simply just copy Cell I194 down through Cell I199)
Common equity investment (Cell I195)	=H147
Preferred equity investment (Cell I196)	=H148
Retained earnings (Cell I197)	=H149
Treasury stock (Cell I198)	=H150
Accumulated other comprehensive loss (Cell I199)	=H151
Total stockholders' equity (Cell I200)	=SUM(I194:I199)
Noncontrolling interest (Cell I201)	=H153
Total equity (Cell I202)	=I200+I201
Total liabilities and equity (Cell I203)	=I202+I191

If this has all been input properly, the balance sheet match in Cell I205 should read "Y." See Table 11.1. Although it may have been slightly redundant to list out every single row in the preceding tables, doing so should be helpful in illustrating the ease of copying this column into the actual balance sheet we will now use for our projections.

TABLE 11.1   Pro Forma Balance Sheet

Consolidated Balance Sheets (in US$ millions except per share amounts)	
	Pro Forma
On January 27	2013PF
Assets	
Current assets:	
Cash and cash equivalents	$ 0.0
Receivables	1,098.8
Inventories	1,448.4
Prepaid expenses and other current assets	261.1
Total current assets	$ 2,808.2
Property, plant, and equipment, net	2,428.2
Goodwill	18,513.4
Trademarks, net	1,050.9
Other intangibles, net	5,519.3
Other noncurrent assets	1,053.6
Total assets	$31,373.5
	(continued)

TABLE 11.1 *(Continued)*

Consolidated Balance Sheets (in US$ millions except per share amounts)

On January 27	Pro Forma 2013PF
Liabilities	
Current liabilities:	
Short-term debt	0.0
Portion of long-term debt due within one year	0.0
Revolving line of credit	0.0
Accounts payable	1,287.8
Accrued marketing and other accrued liabilities	944.0
Income taxes	91.3
Total current liabilities	$ 2,323.1
Term facilities	10,500.0
The notes	2,100.0
Long-term debt	0.0
Deferred income taxes	776.7
Nonpension postretirement benefits	230.9
Other noncurrent liabilities	504.8
Redeemable noncontrolling interest	28.7
Total liabilities	$16,464.1
Total Equity	
Shareholders' equity	
Capital stock	0.0
Common equity investment	8,240.0
Preferred equity investment	8,000.0
Retained earnings	(1,381.1)
Treasury stock	0.0
Accumulated other comprehensive loss	0.0
Total shareholders' equity	$14,858.9
Noncontrolling interest	50.5
Total equity	$14,909.4
Total liabilities and equity	$31,373.5
Supplemental Data:	
Balance? (Y/N)	Y

CASH FLOW DRIVES BALANCE SHEET VERSUS BALANCE SHEET DRIVES CASH FLOW

There are two common methods used when modeling financial projections.

1. *The balance sheet drives the cash flow statement.* The cash flow statement is derived from subtracting year-over-year balance sheet changes.
2. *The cash flow statement drives the balance sheet.* The balance sheet is projected based on how cash is being sourced or spent.

Although both methods are utilized often, we strongly recommend the second method, using the cash flow to drive the balance sheet. It is a more logical approach and has been proven to be less prone to errors. Further, the first method of "back-solving" into a cash flow statement can lead to an incomplete picture of each individual cash flow. Let's take property, plant, and equipment (PP&E), for example. The net PP&E value increases by CAPEX spend and decreases by depreciation. So if PP&E on the balance sheet increases by $1,000, how do we know how much of that change is attributable to depreciation versus capital expenditures?

Cash Flow		Balance Sheet	2012	2013
Depreciation	?	→ Property, Plant, and Equipment	0.0	1,000.0
CAPEX	?			

One can possibly attribute that to CAPEX of $1,000.

Cash Flow		Balance Sheet	2012	2013
Depreciation	0.0	→ Property, Plant, and Equipment	0.0	1,000.0
CAPEX	(1,000.0)			

Or, CAPEX could be $1,500 and depreciation is $500, also resulting in the net $1,000 PP&E change.

Cash Flow		Balance Sheet	2012	2013
Depreciation	500.0	→ Property, Plant, and Equipment	0.0	1,000.0
CAPEX	(1,500.0)			

Further, the company could have purchased $2,000 in assets and written down $500 in assets. Several possibilities could account for this change in PP&E. But the cash flow statement clearly shows depreciation and CAPEX, so we can look to the cash flow statement. For this reason, if we use the cash flow statement to create the projected balance sheet, we may have a more complete picture of the business.

Note: We understand in this example that additional research on CAPEX and depreciation can reveal how the property, plant, and equipment number in the company financials is changing from year to year. However, this illustrates the possibility of other complex situations where important cash flows can be missed by back-calculating into the cash flow statement from the balance sheet.

We highly recommend following and adhering to the method we discuss in the next paragraph. One of the major challenges of a junior Wall Street analyst is keeping a balance sheet in balance. Remember, the formula "Assets – Liabilities = Shareholders' Equity" must always hold for a balance sheet to be in balance. The difficulty to balancing a balance sheet is having to make projections individually to each line item within the assets, liabilities, and shareholders' equity sections, and ensuring that the formula still holds. When a balance sheet doesn't balance, error checking to find out what's off can be a daunting task. This has been known to keep analysts up all night. However, with a clear and methodical approach to projecting a balance sheet, this task should no longer be so strenuous. Such all-nighters would be eliminated if one had a better conceptual understanding of the flows behind a balance sheet. With our methods, the maximum time it should take to error check an unbalanced balance sheet should be one hour, so we encourage you to read on.

The key to thinking about balance sheet projections is the cash flow statement. Cash flows affect assets, liabilities, and shareholders' equity items. If a company has spent cash, it might have purchased an asset, or maybe it paid back a loan. Conversely, if a company has received cash, maybe it has sold an asset or has raised funds. We look to the cash flow statement to help determine how our assets, liabilities, and shareholders' equity are being affected. If cash is spent, that must mean an asset is increasing (except cash), or a liability or shareholders' equity is decreasing; if cash is received, that must mean an asset is decreasing (except cash), or a liability or shareholders' equity is increasing. So, to project balance sheet line items, we look to each balance sheet line item and ask ourselves two questions:

1. Which cash flow statement item or items are affecting this balance sheet item?
2. In what direction should this cash flow statement item be driving the balance sheet item? Should it be increasing or decreasing?

Assets

Let's take the "cash" line item on the balance sheet as an example. If 2013 cash was $1,000 and we want to project 2014 cash, we look to the two questions.

Cash Flow	2014
?	?

Balance Sheet	2013	2014
Cash	1,000.0	?

The cash flow item "Total change in cash and cash equivalents" affects the balance sheet cash. Also, a positive value of cash should naturally increase the total balance of cash on the balance sheet. If the total change in cash and cash equivalents was $500, then the 2014 cash in the balance sheet should be $1,500.

Cash Flow	2014
Total Change in Cash	500.0

Balance Sheet	2013	2014
Cash	1,000.0	1,500.0

For 2014 cash on the balance sheet, we would take the 2013 cash from the balance sheet and add the 2014 change in cash and cash equivalents from the cash flow statement, or:

2014 Balance Sheet Cash = 2013 Balance Sheet Cash + 2014 Total Change in Cash and Cash Equivalents

In the same way, we can project the 2014 cash for Heinz in the model.

2014 Cash (Balance Sheet Cell J164)

Excel Keystrokes	Description
Type "="	Begins the formula
Select Cell I164	Cash
Type "+"	Adds
Select Cell J103	2014 total change in cash and cash equivalents
Hit Enter	End
Formula result	=I164+J103

This should give us $814.7. We can copy this formula to the right through 2018. See Table 11.2.

Receivables

Let's first take a typical receivables example and assume the 2013 receivables balance sheet balance was $1,000.

Cash Flow	2014
?	?

Balance Sheet	2013	2014
Receivables	1,000.0	?

To answer the first question, it's the 2014 "Changes in receivables" line item in the operating working capital section of the cash flow statement that drives the balance sheet receivables. Now remember the relationship between receivables on the cash flow statement and on the balance sheet as discussed in the operating working capital section of this book. If the cash change is positive, then we have collected on our receivables, or receivables should be reduced. So, for example, if the 2014 "Changes in receivables" is $250, then we have collected $250 in receivables, and the 2014 receivables balance should be reduced by $250 to $750.

Cash Flow	2014
Changes in Receivables	250.0

Balance Sheet	2013	2014
Receivables	1,000.0	750.0

or:

2014 Balance Sheet Receivables = 2013 Balance Sheet Receivables – 2014 Cash Flow Changes in Receivables

Notice here that the formula structure is similar to the formula for cash, but we are using a "–" instead of a "+" between the two terms.

So in the same way, we can project the 2014 receivables for Heinz in the model.

2014 Receivables (Balance Sheet Cell J165)

Excel Keystrokes	Description
Type "="	Begins the formula
Select Cell I165	Receivables
Type "-"	Subtracts
Select Cell J69	2014 changes in receivables
Hit Enter	End
Formula result	=I165-J69

This gives us $1,102.1. We can copy this formula to the right through 2018. See Table 11.4.

Inventories

In the same way we can look at inventories. Let's say 2013 inventories are $1,500.

Cash Flow	2014
?	?

Balance Sheet	2013	2014
Inventories	1,500.0	?

To answer the first of the two questions, the cash flow item relating to inventories is "Changes in inventories" in the working capital section of the cash flow statement. Let's say the "Changes in inventories" number in 2014 is –$250. A negative change in working capital would imply that we had purchased some more inventory, so the inventories balance should increase from $1,500 to $1,750.

TABLE 11.2 Heinz Projected Balance Sheet Cash

Consolidated Balance Sheets (in US$ millions except per share amounts)

On January 27	Pro Forma 2013PF	2014E	2015E	2016E	2017E	2018E
				Estimates		
Assets						
Current assets:						
Cash and cash equivalents	$ 0.0	$814.7	$1,589.6	$2,371.7	$3,160.8	$3,957.0
Receivables	1,098.8					
Inventories	1,448.4					
Prepaid expenses and other current assets	261.1					
Total current assets	$2,808.2					

Cash Flow	2014		Balance Sheet	2013	2014
Changes in Inventories	(250.0)	→	Inventories	1,500.0	1,750.0

2014 Balance Sheet Inventories = 2013 Balance Sheet Inventories –
2014 Cash Flow Changes in Inventories

Notice that the formula structure is similar to the accounts receivable formula structure. Also, note the "-" being used.

2014 Inventories (Cell J166)

Excel Keystrokes	Description
Type "="	Begins the formula
Select Cell I166	Inventories
Type "-"	Subtracts
Select Cell J70	2014 changes in inventories
Hit Enter	End
Formula result	=I166-J70

This gives us $1,452.2. We can copy this formula to the right through 2018. See Table 11.4.

It is important to note that, based on the preceding, the formula structure for projecting an asset on a balance sheet will *always* be (except for cash):

2014 Balance Sheet Line Item = 2013 Balance Sheet Line Item – 2014
Related Cash Flow Statement Line Item

The one exception, cash, will be:

2014 Balance Sheet Line Item = 2013 Balance Sheet Line Item + 2014
Related Cash Flow Statement Line Item

And this should make logical sense because next year's balance sheet item is last year's balance increased or decreased by the related cash impact. For assets, cash flow cash has the opposite effect, increasing the asset if cash is negative, or decreasing the asset if cash is positive, hence the need for the "-". The exception is the balance sheet cash asset, where positive cash increases the cash balance, and negative cash decreases the cash balance, hence the "+". This pattern in formula structure is part of the key to a well-built model. Although there are other ways to project some of these line items, we encourage you to keep this consistent structure throughout the model. The more straightforward and consistent your model is, the better it is to read, the higher the chances are that the model will be error free, and the simpler the model will be to error check if there do happen to be mistakes. These formulas should also make conceptual sense, as it is the better understanding of such concepts that can help an analyst think through where errors in models can possibly be.

We can continue this process throughout the assets section of the income statement, matching the following balance sheet items to the related cash flow statement items as per Table 11.3.

We can then copy each of these line items to the right through 2018. We can also copy the "Total current assets" Cell I168 and "Total assets" Cell I174 (which we had calculated when linking in the pro forma values) to the right. We have now completed the assets section of the balance sheet. See Table 11.4.

TABLE 11.3 Balance Sheet Asset Projections

Balance Sheet Item	Cash Flow Statement Item	Formula
Prepaid expenses and other current assets (Cell J167)	Changes in prepaid expenses and other current assets (Cell J71)	=I167-J71
Property, plant and equipment, net (Cell J169)	Depreciation (Cell J59), CAPEX (Cell J78), Proceeds from disposals of property and equipment (Cell J80), Acquisitions, net of cash acquired (Cell J81), Proceeds from divestitures (Cell J82) Note: As shown here, there may be more than one cash flow item that can relate to the balance sheet line item. Also, acquisitions, disposals, and divestitures could have some effects on other balance sheet items such as goodwill. But we will keep the assumptions simple for now and assume the majority of the balance sheet effects will be in the PP&E. As long as they are somehow captured in the balance sheet, this should not greatly affect our overall analysis.	=I169-J59-J78-J80-J81-J82
Goodwill (Cell J170)	0 Again, we could have assumed a portion of acquisitions, disposals, and divestitures could be related to goodwill, but we had made the simplifying assumption that they affect our property, plant, and equipment. Nothing else affects goodwill here.	=I170

(continued)

TABLE 11.3 (*Continued*)

Balance Sheet Item	Cash Flow Statement Item	Formula
Trademarks, net (Cell J171)	Amortization (Cell J60) Note: Amortization had affected both "Trademarks" and "Other intangible assets." However, we did not feel it necessary to split this line item up between the two. Rather, we could have combined the "Trademarks" and "Other intangible assets" balance sheet line items to simplify the balance. We have, however, kept the line items as is. Again, as long as they are captured somehow in the assets section of the balance sheet, we are okay.	=I171-J60
Other intangibles, net (Cell J172)	Amortization of identifiable intangible assets (Cell J161) Note: As per our balance sheet adjustments discussion (Chapter 8), we had assumed all new intangible assets created as a result of the purchase will be grouped into "Other intangibles," so the resulting amortization will be affected here.	=I172-J161
Other noncurrent assets (Cell J173)	Other items, net (J67), Sale of short-term investments (J83), Change in restricted cash (J84), Other items, net (J85) Note: As there is little indication of what is contained in "Other noncurrent assets," we've used this as a sort of catchall. Any line item that could be related to assets that doesn't have any other obvious place in the assets section we will link in here. "Other items, net" (there are two) of course we link into this line item. "Change in restricted cash" we thought would more likely go into a current assets line item, but, because we found no relevant item that it would directly link into, we placed it here.	=I173-J67-J83-J84-J85

TABLE 11.4 Heinz Projected Total Assets

Consolidated Balance Sheets (in US$ millions except per share amounts)

On January 27	Pro Forma 2013PF	Estimates 2014E	2015E	2016E	2017E	2018E
Assets						
Current assets:						
Cash and cash equivalents	$ 0.0	$ 814.7	$ 1,589.6	$ 2,371.7	$ 3,160.8	$ 3,957.0
Receivables	1,098.8	1,102.1	1,106.5	1,110.9	1,115.4	1,119.8
Inventories	1,448.4	1,452.2	1,458.0	1,463.8	1,469.7	1,475.6
Prepaid expenses and other current assets	261.1	259.2	260.2	261.3	262.3	263.4
Total current assets	$ 2,808.2	$ 3,628.2	$ 4,414.4	$ 5,207.7	$ 6,008.1	$ 6,815.7
Property, plant, and equipment, net	2,428.2	2,600.3	2,762.5	2,914.8	3,057.1	3,189.3
Goodwill	18,513.4	18,513.4	18,513.4	18,513.4	18,513.4	18,513.4
Trademarks, net	1,050.9	1,020.9	990.9	960.9	930.9	900.9
Other intangibles, net	5,519.3	5,176.9	4,834.5	4,492.1	4,149.6	3,807.2
Other noncurrent assets	1,053.6	1,094.8	1,135.9	1,177.1	1,218.3	1,259.4
Total assets	$31,373.5	$32,034.4	$32,651.6	$33,265.9	$33,877.3	$34,485.9

Liabilities

Let's look at the first line of the current liabilities section of the balance sheet, short-term debt. If a company is going to borrow money, say $500, the cash would increase and the liability also would increase, both by $500.

Cash Flow	2014
Short-Term Debt Issuances/(Retirements)	500.0

Balance Sheet	2013	2014
Short-Term Debt	0.0	500.0

Or, if the company, for example, has $1,000 in short-term debt and would like to pay back $500 of this liability, there would be a cash outflow and the liability would decrease.

Cash Flow	2014
Short-Term Debt Issuances/(Retirements)	(500.0)

Balance Sheet	2013	2014
Short-Term Debt	1,000.0	500.0

So, we will add any cash changes due to short-term debts to the short-term debt balance on the balance sheet.

2014 Balance Sheet Short-Term Debts = 2013 Balance Sheet Short-Term
Debts + 2014 Cash Flow Changes in Short-Term Debts

Remember, however, that we assumed that the company's debts have actually been paid down as a result of the transaction, so the original debt balances are zero. Regardless, we still have a line item in the cash flow statement entitled "Net payments on commercial paper and short-term debt." Although this is also zero, and technically these debts no longer exist in the future, to be complete and for illustration, let's still link up the short-term debts as if they exist (although you are welcome to just delete them).

We can project the 2014 short-term debt.

2014 Short-Term Debt (Cell J177)

Excel Keystrokes	Description
Type "="	Begins the formula
Select Cell I177	Short-term debt
Type "+"	Adds
Select Cell J94	2014 net payments on commercial paper and short-term debt
Hit Enter	End
Formula result	=I177+J94

Notice the next line, "Portion of long-term debt due within one year." This is of course the part of the long-term debt that should be paid back this year. You may notice there is no cash flow line item that is directly related to the pay-down of just the portion of long-term debt due within one year. Typically, in order to best handle this, either we would create a line item in the cash flow statement, driven from the debt schedule, or we would simply combine the current portion of long-term debts with the long-term debts. The book entitled *Financial Modeling and Valuation* steps through one way to handle this common situation. However, as we are modeling the purchase of Heinz, and therefore assuming the company's debts will be eliminated, it is not necessary to make such adjustments. We can either delete this row or continue to make the line item 0. We will do the latter so as not to further disturb the structure of the model for illustration. We will have J178 read "=I178."

Revolving Line of Credit

Now the revolving line of credit (the revolver), on the other hand, although it is 0, is a new debt issued as a result of the transaction. The press release had stated that $1.5 billion of a revolver will be issued but not yet drawn. So the value is currently 0, but we want to be sure that this is ready and properly linked through in case the company decides to draw funds from it. So we will link the revolver in using the "Revolver borrowings (repayments)" row in the cash flow statement. The flows are exactly the same as the other short-term debt flows. Notice we have not yet projected the cash flow revolver borrowings (repayments). These changes will ultimately come from the debt schedule and link into the cash flow statement. Even though we have not yet projected those items in the cash flow statement, we should still continue to link up the formulas in the balance sheet.

2014 Revolver (Cell J179)

Excel Keystrokes	Description
Type "="	Begins the formula
Select Cell I179	Revolver
Type "+"	Adds
Select Cell J88	2014 revolver borrowings (repayments)
Hit Enter	End
Formula result	=I179+J88

Accounts Payable

Let's assume the 2013 accounts payable balance sheet balance was $1,000.

Cash Flow	2014		Balance Sheet	2013	2014
?	?	→	Accounts Payable	1,000.0	?

To answer the first question of the two discussed earlier, it's the 2014 changes in the accounts payable line item in the working capital section of the cash flow statement that drives this item. Now remember the relationship between accounts payable on the cash flow statement and on the balance sheet as discussed in the working capital chapter of this book. If the cash change is positive, then we have increased our accounts payable. So, for example, if the 2014 accounts payable item is $500, then we have increased our payables by $500.

Cash Flow	2014
Changes in Accounts Payable	500.0

Balance Sheet	2013	2014
Accounts Payable	1,000.0	1,500.0

or:

2014 Balance Sheet Accounts Payable = 2013 Balance Sheet Accounts Payable + 2014 Cash Flow Changes in Accounts Payable

Notice here that the formula structure is similar to the formula for the assets but we are using a "+" instead of a "−"; this is due to the direct relationship between liabilities and cash (i.e., cash increasing results in liabilities increasing, and cash decreasing results in liabilities decreasing).

So in the same way, we can project the 2014 accounts payable for Heinz in the model.

2014 Accounts Payable (Cell J180)

Excel Keystrokes	Description
Type "="	Begins the formula
Select Cell I180	Accounts payable
Type "+"	Adds
Select Cell J72	2014 changes in accounts payable
Hit Enter	End
Formula result	=I180+J72

This gives us $1,291.5, and we can copy this formula to the right.

We can continue this process throughout the liabilities section of the balance sheet, matching the following balance sheet items to the related cash flow statement items as per Table 11.5.

We can then copy Cells J177 through J190 to the right through 2018. We can copy the total current liabilities, Cell I183, and the total liabilities, Cell I191, which we had calculated when linking in the pro forma balance sheet items to the right. We have now completed the current liabilities side of the balance sheet. See Table 11.6.

TABLE 11.5 Heinz Balance Sheet Liabilities Projections

Balance Sheet Item	Cash Flow Statement Item	Formula
Accrued marketing and other accrued liabilities (Cell J181)	Changes in accrued liabilities (Cell J73)	=I181+J73
Accrued income taxes (Cell J182)	Changes in accrued income taxes (Cell J74)	=I182+J74
Term facilities (Cell J184)	Term facilities borrowings (repayments) (Cell J89) Note: As with the revolver, we have not yet projected these line items, but we should continue to link this up anyway.	=I184+J89
The notes (Cell J185)	The notes borrowings (repayments) (Cell J90) Note: As with the revolver, we have not yet projected these line items, but we should continue to link this up anyway.	=I185+J90
Long-term debt (Cell J186)	Proceeds (payments) of long-term debt (Cell J93) Note: The long-term debt has been eliminated as a result of the purchase, so we could have alternatively just deleted this row.	=I186+J93
Deferred income taxes (Cell J187)	Deferred income taxes (Cell J62)	=I187+J62
Nonpension postretirement benefits (Cell J188)	0 Note: we could not find any line item that clearly contributed directly to nonpension postretirement benefits.	=I188
Other noncurrent liabilities (Cell J189)	Pension contributions (Cell J65) Note: Again, "other" line items can serve as catchalls. We had utilized most unknown items in the "Other assets" section. Having some of those items linked here instead would not have made any dramatic changes to the model.	=I189+J65
Redeemable noncontrolling interest (Cell J190)	0 There is no line item in the cash flow statement that is an obvious link into this line item.	=I190

TABLE 11.6 Heinz Projected Liabilities

Consolidated Balance Sheets (in US$ millions except per share amounts)

On January 27	Pro Forma 2013PF	Estimates				
		2014E	2015E	2016E	2017E	2018E
Liabilities						
Current liabilities:						
Short-term debt	$ 0.0	$ 0.0	$ 0.0	$ 0.0	$ 0.0	$ 0.0
Portion of long-term debt due within one year	0.0	0.0	0.0	0.0	0.0	0.0
Revolving line of credit	0.0	0.0	0.0	0.0	0.0	0.0
Accounts payable	1,287.8	1,291.5	1,296.7	1,301.8	1,307.1	1,312.3
Accrued marketing and other accrued liabilities	944.0	936.7	940.5	944.2	948.0	951.8
Income taxes	91.3	144.1	143.7	143.2	142.8	142.3
Total current liabilities	**$ 2,323.1**	**$ 2,372.3**	**$ 2,380.8**	**$ 2,389.3**	**$ 2,397.8**	**$ 2,406.4**
Term facilities	10,500.0	10,500.0	10,500.0	10,500.0	10,500.0	10,500.0
The notes	2,100.0	2,100.0	2,100.0	2,100.0	2,100.0	2,100.0
Long-term debt	0.0	0.0	0.0	0.0	0.0	0.0
Deferred income taxes	776.7	693.7	610.7	527.7	444.7	361.7
Nonpension postretirement benefits	230.9	230.9	230.9	230.9	230.9	230.9
Other noncurrent liabilities	504.8	424.8	344.8	264.8	184.8	104.8
Redeemable noncontrolling interest	28.7	28.7	28.7	28.7	28.7	28.7
Total liabilities	**$16,464.1**	**$16,350.4**	**$16,195.8**	**$16,041.3**	**$15,886.9**	**$15,732.4**

Shareholders' equity line items act the same way as liability line items. If cash is generated, that could mean equity was raised. Or, if cash is spent, a company could have purchased shares in a share buyback. So the general formula for a shareholders' equity balance sheet line item is:

2014 Shareholders' Equity Line Item = 2013 Shareholders' Equity Line Item + 2014 Related Cash Flow Statement Line Item.

That is, we always use a "+" between the two terms; so we can proceed using the same method as previously (see Table 11.7).

Then we are done! Copy each of the line items from Cell J194 through Cell J199 and Cell J201 to the right through 2018. We can also copy to the right the total shareholders' equity (Cell I200), the total equity (Cell I202), and the total liabilities and equity (Cell I203), which we had calculated when inputting the historical values. See Table 11.8.

After completing this process, we should have a balancing balance sheet. You may notice a second match line at the bottom of the balance sheet in Row 205. This match checks to be sure the balance sheet is in balance:

Assets = Liabilities + Shareholders' Equity

If the model does not balance, then we need to take the appropriate steps to identify where the problem could be. This is the daunting task we were referring to earlier. However, with our methodology, there are several

TABLE 11.7 Heinz Balance Sheet Shareholders' Equity Projections

Balance Sheet Item	Cash Flow Statement Item	Formula
Capital stock (Cell J194)	Exercise of stock options (Cell J97) Note: Again here, shareholders have been bought out so there will be no more public capital stock and no stock options. Technically we could have deleted these rows.	=I194+J97
Common equity investment (Cell J195)	Common equity (Cell J91) If any additional common equity is to be infused into the business in the future beyond the initial investment, it will be hard-coded in the cash flow statement row 91.	=I195+J91

(continued)

TABLE 11.7 (*Continued*)

Balance Sheet Item	Cash Flow Statement Item	Formula
Preferred equity investment (Cell J196)	Preferred equity (Cell J92) If any additional preferred equity is to be infused into the business in the future beyond the initial investment, it will be hard-coded in cash flow statement Cell J92.	=I196+J92
Retained earnings (Cell J197)	Net Income (Cell J58) and Dividends (Cell J95) Note: Retained earnings is always driven by net income after dividends (and possibly noncontrolling interests if there does not already exist a separate line item for it; Heinz separates noncontrolling interests in Row 201).	=I197+J58+J95
Treasury stock (Cell J198)	Purchases of treasury stock (Cell J96)	=I198+J96
Accumulated other comprehensive income (Cell J199)	Net losses on divestitures (Cell J63), Impairment on assets held for sale (Cell J64), Asset write-downs from Fiscal 2012 productivity initiatives (Cell J66), Acquisitions of subsidiary shares from noncontrolling interests (J98), Earn-out settlement (Cell J99), Other items, net (Cell J100), Effect of exchange rate on cash and cash equivalents (Cell J102) Remember, other unrealized gains and losses due to divestitures, closing operations, impairments, sales, and foreign currency adjustments are included in other comprehensive income. As a best guess, we included "other items, net" from the financing activities in here as well. Page 37 in the Heinz annual report explains a few line items that make up other comprehensive income.	=I199+ J63+J64+J66+J98+ J99+J100+J102
Noncontrolling interest (Cell J201)	0.	=I201

TABLE 11.8 Heinz Projected Balance Sheet

Consolidated Balance Sheets (in US$ millions except per share amounts)

On January 27	Pro Forma 2013PF	2014E	2015E	Estimates 2016E	2017E	2018E
Assets						
Current assets:						
Cash and cash equivalents	$ 0.0	$ 814.7	$ 1,589.6	$ 2,371.7	$ 3,160.8	$ 3,957.0
Receivables	1,098.8	1,102.1	1,106.5	1,110.9	1,115.4	1,119.8
Inventories	1,448.4	1,452.2	1,458.0	1,463.8	1,469.7	1,475.6
Prepaid expenses and other current assets	261.1	259.2	260.2	261.3	262.3	263.4
Total current assets	$ 2,808.2	$ 3,628.2	$ 4,414.4	$ 5,207.7	$ 6,008.1	$ 6,815.7
Property, plant, and equipment, net	2,428.2	2,600.3	2,762.5	2,914.8	3,057.1	3,189.3
Goodwill	18,513.4	18,513.4	18,513.4	18,513.4	18,513.4	18,513.4
Trademarks, net	1,050.9	1,020.9	990.9	960.9	930.9	900.9
Other intangibles, net	5,519.3	5,176.9	4,834.5	4,492.1	4,149.6	3,807.2
Other noncurrent assets	1,053.6	1,094.8	1,135.9	1,177.1	1,218.3	1,259.4
Total assets	$ 31,373.5	$32,034.4	$32,651.6	$33,265.9	$33,877.3	$34,485.9
Liabilities						
Current liabilities:						
Short-term debt	0.0	0.0	0.0	0.0	0.0	0.0
Portion of long-term debt due within one year	0.0	0.0	0.0	0.0	0.0	0.0
Revolving line of credit	0.0	0.0	0.0	0.0	0.0	0.0
Accounts payable	1,287.8	1,291.5	1,296.7	1,301.8	1,307.1	1,312.3
Accrued marketing and other accrued liabilities	944.0	936.7	940.5	944.2	948.0	951.8
Income taxes	91.3	144.1	143.7	143.2	142.8	142.3
Total current liabilities	$ 2,323.1	$2,372.3	$2,380.8	$2,389.3	$2,397.8	$2,406.4
Term facilities	10,500.0	10,500.0	10,500.0	10,500.0	10,500.0	10,500.0

(*continued*)

TABLE 11.8 (Continued)

Consolidated Balance Sheets (in US$ millions except per share amounts)

On January 27	Pro Forma	Estimates				
	2013PF	2014E	2015E	2016E	2017E	2018E
The notes	2,100.0	2,100.0	2,100.0	2,100.0	2,100.0	2,100.0
Long-term debt	0.0	0.0	0.0	0.0	0.0	0.0
Deferred income taxes	776.7	693.7	610.7	527.7	444.7	361.7
Nonpension postretirement benefits	230.9	230.9	230.9	230.9	230.9	230.9
Other noncurrent liabilities	424.8	424.8	344.8	264.8	184.8	104.8
Redeemable noncontrolling interest	28.7	28.7	28.7	28.7	28.7	28.7
Total liabilities	$16,464.1	$16,350.4	$16,195.8	$16,041.3	$15,886.9	$15,732.4
Total Equity						
Shareholder's Equity						
Capital stock	0.0	0.0	0.0	0.0	0.0	0.0
Common equity investment	8,240.0	8,240.0	8,240.0	8,240.0	8,240.0	8,240.0
Preferred equity investment	8,000.0	8,000.0	8,000.0	8,000.0	8,000.0	8,000.0
Retained earnings	(1,381.1)	(475.3)	427.7	1,327.7	2,224.9	3,119.2
Treasury stock	0.0	0.0	0.0	0.0	0.0	0.0
Accumulated other comprehensive loss	0.0	(131.2)	(262.5)	(393.7)	(525.0)	(656.2)
Total shareholder's equity	$14,858.9	$15,633.5	$16,405.2	$17,174.0	$17,939.9	$18,703.0
Noncontrolling interest	50.5	50.5	50.5	50.5	50.5	50.5
Total equity	$14,909.4	$15,684.0	$16,455.7	$17,224.5	$17,990.5	$18,753.5
Total liabilities & equity	$31,373.5	$32,034.4	$32,651.6	$33,265.9	$33,877.3	$34,485.9
Supplemental Data:						
Balance? (Y/N)	Y	Y	Y	Y	Y	Y

simple steps to find a balance sheet error without the need to pull an all-nighter.

BALANCING AN UNBALANCED BALANCE SHEET

With the proper understanding that balance sheet line items increase or decrease based on how cash is sourced or spent, it is easy to understand that an unbalanced balance sheet occurs when there is a mismatch between the cash flow statement and the balance sheet. More specifically, there are four major reasons why a balance sheet may not be in balance:

1. There is a line item in the cash flow statement that has not been linked to the balance sheet. This happens quite often, especially when cash flow statements have a lot of nonstandard line items. It is often the case that such nonstandard items are accidentally left out and forgotten about.
2. There is a line item in the cash flow statement that has accidentally been used more than once in the balance sheet. Again, this happens often in cash flow statements that have a lot of nonstandard line items. Remember: A balance sheet stays in balance when each cash flow statement item drives one of the assets, liabilities, or shareholders' equity line items—but only one. If you link one cash flow statement item in two places, the model will be out of balance.
3. A line item in the cash flow statement is linking to the correct balance sheet item, but it is moving the balance sheet item in the wrong direction, or the line item is pulling from the wrong year. This is where having a common structure of formulas as described earlier can be of great help. As you notice in the projected balance sheet we have built together, every formula has the structure:

   = Balance Sheet Item 2013 "+/–" Cash Flow Item 2014

   So we know that every formula should have an "I" in the first term, representing the 2013 (pro forma) balance sheet, and a "J" in the second term (and subsequent terms if applicable), representing the 2014 cash flow statement. We also know that every asset except cash should have a "-" between the first and second terms, and every liability and shareholders' equity line item should have a "+" between the first and second terms. Knowing all of this, we can easily scan each balance sheet formula to ensure the structure is correct. If that first term is not pointing to Column "I" and if that second term is not pointing to column "J," then one of those items is pulling from the wrong year. We also know that if there is a "-" where there should be a "+" or vice versa, then the projected balance sheet line item is moving in the wrong direction.

4. The totals are not calculating properly in the cash flow statement or balance sheet. It is possible that a balance sheet is out of balance simply because the total assets, for example, are not adding up properly or, more commonly, the total change in cash and cash equivalents does not properly include all line items in the total.

Here is an example of a simple balanced balance sheet. Each cash flow statement line item is properly driving the appropriate 2014 balance sheet line item, and the balance sheet is in balance.

Cash Flow	2014		Balance Sheet	2013	2014
Net Income	1,000.0		Cash	1,000.0	2,150.0
Changes in Receivables	(100.0)		Receivables	500.0	600.0
Changes in Inventories	250.0		Inventories	250.0	0.0
Total Changes in Cash	1,150.0		Liabilities	0.0	0.0
			Retained Earnings (Net Income)	1,750.0	2,750.0
			Balance?	Y	Y

If there happens to be a cash flow line item that was not included in the balance sheet, then we have detected a problem of type 1, as identified previously. We had left a cash flow line item out and need to link it to the balance sheet. In the following example, we had forgotten to link inventories into the balance sheet. This creates a total of $3,000 ($2,150 + $600 + $250) in assets, which, less $0 in liabilities, no longer matches the shareholders' equity of $2,750. If we had linked in the inventories properly, the balance sheet would balance.

Cash Flow	2014		Balance Sheet	2013	2014
Net Income	1,000.0		Cash	1,000.0	2,150.0
Changes in Receivables	(100.0)		Receivables	500.0	600.0
Changes in Inventories	250.0		Inventories	250.0	250.0
Total Changes in Cash	1,150.0		Liabilities	0.0	0.0
			Retained Earnings (Net Income)	1,750.0	2,750.0
			Balance?	Y	N

If a cash flow statement line item was linked into the balance sheet more than one time, then we have detected a problem of type 2. We have used the same cash flow line item in the balance sheet two times, but we can use a cash flow statement line item only once. In the following example, we accidentally linked inventories into two separate places in the balance sheet. So there is $250 less assets (inventories cash inflow reduces our asset balance) than we should have in the balance sheet, as we have double-counted the changes in inventories. This creates a total of $2,500 ($2,150 + $350) in assets, less $0 liabilities, versus $2,750 in shareholders' equity.

Cash Flow	2014
Net Income	1,000.0
Changes in Receivables	(100.0)
Changes in Inventories	250.0
Total Changes in Cash	**1,150.0**

Balance Sheet	2013	2014
Cash	1,000.0	2,150.0
Receivables	500.0	350.0
Inventories	250.0	0.0
Liabilities	0.0	0.0
Retained Earnings (Net Income)	1,750.0	2,750.0
Balance?	Y	N

If we have added the cash flow statement into the balance sheet when we should have subtracted, or vice versa, we have detected a problem of type 3. In the following example the inventories line item is linked into the balance sheet but has increased the asset from $250 to $500, when it should have decreased the asset from $250 to $0. A type 3 problem can also occur if the balance sheet item is linking from the wrong cash flow statement column; it is linking in from the wrong year.

Cash Flow	2014
Net Income	1,000.0
Changes in Receivables	(100.0)
Changes in Inventories	250.0
Total Changes in Cash	**1,150.0**

Balance Sheet	2013	2014
Cash	1,000.0	2,150.0
Receivables	500.0	600.0
Inventories	250.0	500.0
Liabilities	0.0	0.0
Retained Earnings (Net Income)	1,750.0	2,750.0
Balance?	Y	N

If there is a problem with a total item, either in the cash flow statement or in the balance sheet, this is a problem of type 4. In the following example, each cash flow item is properly linked to the balance sheet. However, the "Total Changes in Cash" is totaling wrong; it should be $1,150, not $900. This creates a mismatch because we have linked a total of $1,150 in individual cash flow items into balance sheet line items, but are showing only $900 in total changes in cash affecting our cash balance.

Cash Flow	2014
Net Income	1,000.0
Changes in Receivables	(100.0)
Changes in Inventories	250.0
Total Changes in Cash	**900.0**

Balance Sheet	2013	2014
Cash	1,000.0	1,900.0
Receivables	500.0	600.0
Inventories	250.0	0.0
Liabilities	0.0	0.0
Retained Earnings (Net Income)	1,750.0	2,750.0
Balance?	Y	N

There is a foolproof method for detecting where and why a balance sheet is out of balance. Even if the model you are working with is not structured as our model is, this method can still detect the error. We have proven this method time and time again with the most complex of models on Wall Street. We assure you, if you can get a handle on this process, balancing an unbalanced balance sheet will no longer be a daunting task.

New York School of Finance Balance Sheet Balancing Method

We strongly recommend printing out the cash flow statement and the balance sheet and performing this method on paper. Going through this method on paper with a pencil and calculator is the surest way to find the balance sheet errors the first time through. But, proofing the balance sheet in Excel can work as well. Whether using paper or Excel, the first step is to create a differences column on the balance sheet. The differences column will subtract the first year the model is not balancing from the previous balancing year. So, if 2013 is balancing but 2014 is not, the differences column will subtract 2013 from 2014 for each line item. It doesn't really matter which way you are subtracting, because we will just be matching the values here. In the example in Table 11.9, we have a column listing the differences for each balance sheet line item (the numbers in this example do not reflect Heinz).

These differences are essentially cash flows. So, we now need to match each of these differences to the cash flow statement. So for each balance sheet line item we ask ourselves two **balance sheet balancing** questions:

1. Does this difference number match the appropriate cash flows?
2. Is this balance sheet line item moving in the right direction?

Let's take receivables, for example. The difference in receivables is $146.5 (see Table 11.9). So for question 1, this difference should match the "Changes in accounts receivable" line item from the cash flow statement (see Table 11.10).

It does; the 2014 "Changes in accounts receivable" number is $146.5. For the second question, we notice that the "Changes in accounts receivable" number on the cash flow statement is positive, so that should be decreasing the asset on the balance sheet. Going back to the balance sheet, we notice the receivables are in fact decreasing from $5,937.0 in 2013 to $5,790.5 in 2014, so the receivables check out. It is crucial that we cross off the "Changes in accounts receivable" line item on the cash flow statement to indicate that we have already used this line item. Remember, one of the more common errors is accidentally including a cash flow line item in the balance sheet more than once or leaving it out altogether. Marking each cash flow line item as we go through this process helps make sure we are using every cash flow line item, but only one time. We can continue this process by moving to the next line item in the balance sheet, answering the two questions, and crossing off the cash flow line items accordingly. We should do this for every balance sheet line item, including cash; by the time we get down to the end of the balance sheet, we should have crossed off every line item in the cash flow statement, but only one time each.

TABLE 11.9 Balance Sheet Differences Example

Consolidated Balance Sheets (in US$ millions)

		Actuals			Estimates	
On January 31	2011A	2012A	2013A		2014E	Differences
Assets						
Current assets:						
Cash and cash equivalents		$ 7,395.0	$ 6,550.0		$ 8,691.8	$ 2,141.8
Receivables, net		5,089.0	5,937.0		5,790.5	(146.5)
Inventories		36,437.0	40,714.0		40,862.4	148.4
Prepaid expenses and other		2,960.0	1,685.0		2,458.9	773.9
Other current assets (discontinued operations)		131.0	89.0		89.0	0.0
Total current assets		$ 52,012.0	$ 54,975.0		$ 57,892.6	5,621.3
Property, plant, and equipment, net		107,878.0	112,324.0		117,945.3	
Goodwill		16,763.0	20,651.0		20,651.0	0.0
Other assets and deferred charges		4,129.0	5,456.0		5,576.0	120.0
Total assets		$180,782.0	$193,406.0		$202,064.9	

TABLE 11.10 Cash Flow from Operating Activities Example

Consolidated Statements of Cash Flows (in US$ millions)

Period Ending January 31	Actuals			Estimates
	2011A	2012A	2013A	2014E
Cash flows from operating activities				
Net income	$14,883.0	$16,993.0	$16,387.0	$18,685.2
Loss (income) from discontinued operations to net cash	79.0	(1,034.0)	67.0	0.0
Depreciation and amortization	7,157.0	7,641.0	8,130.0	8,591.7
Deferred income taxes	(504.0)	651.0	1,050.0	715.9
Other operating activities	318.0	1,087.0	398.0	318.0
Changes in operating working capital				
Changes in accounts receivable	(297.0)	(733.0)	(796.0)	146.5
Changes in inventories	2,213.0	(3,205.0)	(3,727.0)	(148.4)
Changes in prepaid expenses and other	0.0	0.0	0.0	(773.9)
Changes in accounts payable	1,052.0	2,676.0	2,687.0	701.2
Changes in accrued liabilities	1,348.0	(433.0)	59.0	1,425.7
Changes in accrued income taxes	0.0	0.0	0.0	(399.6)
Net changes in operating working capital	$ 4,316.0	$(1,695.0)	$(1,777.0)	$ 951.5
Total cash flows from operating activities	$26,249.0	$23,643.0	$24,255.0	$29,262.3

If the process is completed and there are cash flow line items not crossed off, then you know the problem is type 1 and you need to link that cash flow item into the balance sheet. If you find an item crossed off but used twice, then the problem is type 2, and you need to choose only one balance sheet item to link the cash flow item to. If the value in the differences column does not match the cash flow statement, then this is a problem of type 3. A type 3 problem also exists if the balance sheet item is moving the wrong way—that is, increasing when the cash flow item indicates it should be decreasing, or vice versa. There is a possibility that, after going through this method, everything checks out but the balance sheet still does not balance. If that is the case, then this is a problem of type 4: There must be a totaling error in either the cash flow statement or the balance sheet.

We encourage you to take the time to think through the relationship between the cash flow statement and the balance sheet. The method we have presented should make conceptual sense. With a complete understanding of the relationship between the cash flow statement and the balance sheet, it should be clear that outside of the four potential balance sheet problems mentioned, there is no other way a balance sheet can be out of balance.

With our completed balance sheet, we can now move on to the next schedule: the debt schedule. Refer to Appendix 1 to ensure you are following the model building path.

CHAPTER 12

Debt Schedule and Circular References

The debt schedule is designed to track every major type of debt a company has, and the associated interest and payment schedules for each. It also helps track the cash available that could be used to pay down those debts and any interest income that could be generated from cash or cash equivalents available. Simply put, a debt schedule helps us better track the debt and interest. There is also a very important "circular reference" that is created once the debt schedule is complete and properly linked through the rest of the model. This circular reference is crucial in helping us determine various debt situations, such as the absolute maximum amount of debt a company can raise while making sure there is still enough cash to meet the interest payments.

It is important to note that the debt schedule should be the very last statement to build due to this circular reference. Make sure you have a properly balancing balance sheet before beginning the debt schedule. If you do not have a balancing balance sheet, moving on to the debt schedule will only complicate things further.

DEBT SCHEDULE STRUCTURE

In the model, Rows 252 through 256 will help us track the amount of cash we have available to pay down the debt. This can be used if we want our

NOTE

Once the circular reference is created, you may receive an Excel error message. Refer to the "Circular References" section of this chapter on how to resolve circular reference errors.

model to pay down debts automatically as soon as we have the cash available to do so.

The following sections are grouped by type of debt. Here we will calculate each balance of debt from year to year, track the potential debt pay-downs or issuances, and calculate the interest. As this is a leveraged buyout (LBO), we are concerned only with the new debts that will be held in the business after the transaction. According to the latest transaction terms, and as represented in our uses, 3G Capital and Berkshire Hathaway will raise a revolving line of credit, term facilities, and notes. So our debt schedule will be designed to handle these three types of debts. Remember that part of the benefit of an LBO model is to be able to project the paying down of such debts by the cash generated in the business.

At the bottom of the debt schedule we will total all issuances and payments as "Total issuances/(retirements)" and all interests as "Total interest expense." We will then calculate cash at the end of the year and interest income associated with that cash, if any exists.

Notice there is a final match that will make sure the cash at the end of the year we are calculating here matches the cash on the balance sheet.

MODELING THE DEBT SCHEDULE

The very first step to modeling the debt schedule is to pull in the last reported balances of each cash and debt. We can begin with pulling the cash from Heinz's 2013PF balance sheet into the 2013PF "Cash at the end of the year" on the debt schedule. So Cell I280 on the debt schedule should be "=I164." Do not copy this formula across; we will re-calculate 2014E Cash later. We can now start looking at the debt balances. We have:

- Revolving line of credit.
- Term facilities.
- The notes.

We will create a separate debt section for each of these debts. There will be three sections, each labeled to match the debts listed. For each debt, we need to pull in the ending debt balances. Cell I261, "Revolving line of credit (end of year)" will be "=I179." We can continue on as per Table 12.1.

Revolving Line of Credit ("Revolver")

Once we have the ending balances linked in, we can build out each debt balance starting with the revolving line of credit. The 2014 revolving line of credit

TABLE 12.1 Debt Schedule Last Reported Balances

Debt Schedule Item	Balance Sheet Item	Formula
Revolving line of credit (Cell I261)	Revolving line of credit (end of year) (Cell I179)	=I179
Term facilities (Cell I268)	Term facilities (end of year) (Cell I184)	=I184
The notes (Cell I275)	The notes (end of year) (Cell I185)	=I185

(beginning of year) is the beginning balance of debt for that year. We assume this is the same value as the ending balance of debt from the year before. In other words, we assume that the balance of debt as of 1/1/2014 is the exact same as the balance of debt from 12/31/2013, for example. Or in Heinz's case, as the year-end is now 1/27/2013, we assume the beginning balance of debt as of 1/28/2013 (which is the beginning of Heinz's 2014 adjusted year-end) is the same as at 1/27/2013 (the end of Heinz's 2013 LTM year-end). So we will have:

$$2014 \text{ Revolving Line of Credit (Beginning of Year)} = 2013$$
$$\text{Revolving Line of Credit (End of Year)}$$

or in Cell J258, we will have "=I261," and we can copy this to the right through 2018.

Mandatory and Nonmandatory Issuances/(Retirements)

An issuance represents a debt raised and a retirement represents a debt paid down. In modeling we separate issuances and retirements into two categories, mandatory and nonmandatory. Mandatory issuances or retirements are those that have been planned or scheduled. For example, a yearly principal payment would be considered a mandatory payment, as the principal must be paid down as per the debt contract. A nonmandatory issuance or retirement is a payment or issuance made that is beyond the contractual requirements of the debt. In other words, let's say we happen to have a cash surplus at the end of one particular year. And, although it is not necessary, and assuming we are allowed to, we have decided to pay down some more debt beyond what has been required to be paid down so we can save on interest payments. This is nonmandatory. Nonmandatory payments are often used in revolving lines of credit, where one would pay down debt if there is a cash surplus. In modeling, as the mandatory payments are planned, we typically hard-code them in based on the debt contract terms. And, typically, non-mandatory payments are based on a formula created that compares the cash available to our outstanding debt balance. If we have excess cash available, we will automatically pay down our debt. In modeling it is important to separate our mandatory issuances and retirements from our nonmandatory ones, so we can have a place for our scheduled payments, and also be able to create this automatic formula and not have one disturb the other.

For now, we can keep them both as "0," and we will create these formulas once the debt schedule is complete. Let's hard-code J259 and J260 as "0," and we can copy to the right through 2018.

In order to calculate the revolving line of credit at the end of the year, we simply start with the debt at the beginning of the year and add our issuances and retirements. If we want to raise $1 million in debt, for example, we would hard-code "$1MM" into mandatory issuances, and our debt at the end of the year would be the beginning debt plus the $1 million. Conversely, if we wanted to pay down debt, we would hard-code "-$1MM" into mandatory issuances, and our debt at the end of the year would be the beginning debt minus the $1 million (or really, plus the negative $1 million).

2014 Revolving Line of Credit (End of Year) = 2014 Revolving Line of Credit (Beginning of Year) + Mandatory Issuances/(Retirements) + Nonmandatory Issuances (Retirements)

or Cell J261 would be "=SUM(J258:J260)."

We can copy this formula to the right and move on to the interest expense calculation. See Table 12.2.

For interest expense, it is better to take an average balance of debts of the beginning of the year and the end of the year. This is important if we do not know exactly when during the year potential issuances or retirements occur. For example, let's say we have $1 million of short-term debt outstanding and we are planning a mandatory retirement of $1 million in 2014. So, the ending balance of debt will be $0. Since we have paid down debt sometime during 2014, technically the interest on that debt will be incurred only during the time the debt has been outstanding. So if we had paid that $1 million down on the very first day of the year, we should technically not incur any interest (or very little interest) for the year. In contrast, if we had not paid down that debt until the very last day of the year, we should have incurred a full year of interest. Of course, if we know exactly when the debt is paid down, we can adjust accordingly; but assuming we do not have that information readily available, we take an average as a simplifying assumption.

Therefore, 2104 interest expense on the revolver is:

Average [2014 Revolving Line of Credit (Beginning of Year), 2013 Revolving Line of Credit (End of Year)] × 2014 Interest Rate

2014 Revolving Line of Credit Interest Expense (Cell J262)

Excel Keystrokes	Description
Type "="	Enters into "formula" mode
Type "average("	Creates the "Average" formula
Select Cell J258	2014 revolving line of credit (beginning of year)
Type ","	Separates the two values we want to average
Select Cell J261	2014 revolving line of credit (end of year)
Type "*"	Multiplies
Select Cell J263	2014 interest rate
Hit Enter	End
Formula result	=AVERAGE(J258,J261)*J263

We need to do some research to determine what Heinz's revolving line of credit interest rate actually is. In an 8-K filed on March 13, 2013, we found the following note regarding interest expense for all debts raised in the transaction:

Interest
At the Company's election, the interest rate per annum applicable to the loans under the Senior Secured Credit Facilities will be based on a fluctuating rate of interest determined by reference to (i)with respect to the New USD Term Loan B-1 Facility, New USD Term Loan B-2 Facility and New Revolving Credit Facility, either (a)a base rate determined by reference to the highest of (1)the prime rate of JPMorgan Chase Bank, N.A., (2)the federal funds effective rate plus 0.5 percent and (3)the Eurodollar rate applicable for an interest period of one month plus 1.00 percent, plus an applicable margin to be set forth in the definitive documentation for the Senior Secured Credit Facilities or (b)a rate determined by reference to LIBOR, adjusted for statutory reserve requirements, plus an applicable margin to be set forth in the definitive documentation for the Senior Secured Credit Facilities and (ii)with respect to the EUR New Term Loan B-1 Facility, EUR New Term Loan B-2 Facility, GBP New Term Loan B-1 Facility and GBP New Term Loan B-2 Facility, a rate determined by reference to LIBOR, adjusted for statutory reserve requirements, plus an applicable margin to be set forth in the definitive documentation for the Senior Secured Credit Facilities. Borrowings under each of the USD New Term Loan B-1 Facility, USD Term Loan B-2 Facility, EUR New Term Loan B-1 Facility, EUR New Term Loan B-2 Facility, GBP New Term Loan

B-1 Facility and GBP New Term Loan B-2 Facility will be subject to a LIBOR floor of 1.00 percent. The applicable margin for loans under the New Revolving Credit Facility will be adjusted after the completion of the Company's first full fiscal quarter after the closing of the Transactions based upon the Company's first lien leverage ratio.

(Heinz 8-K, March 13, 2013, www.sec.gov/Archives/edgar/
data/46640/000095010313001737/dp36939_ex9901.htm)

This is basically saying that the interest rate has yet to be decided and will most likely be variable. A few news sources have indicated the bonds will have a rate of somewhere between 4.25 percent and 5.25 percent, although again this will probably change. For now, let's put 5 percent in, and we can change this once more information is revealed. We also realize the seniority of the debts will affect the interest rate. We hope that, as the deal approaches a close, we can find better information on the interest rates for each debt. Also, since the revolver is not drawn, this will not affect our analysis at this time. So let's hard-code "5.0%" in Cell J263 for now. We can copy cells J262 and J263 to the right through 2018. See Table 12.2.

Term Facilities

We can now move on to the next debt, the term facilities. In order to build this out, we need to repeat the exact same process as we performed with the revolving line of credit.

The 2014 term facilities (beginning of year) is the same value as the ending balance of debt from the year before. So,

2014 Term Facilities (Beginning of Year) = 2013 Term Facilities (End of Year)

or in Cell J265, we will have "=I268," and we can copy this to the right.

We can make the mandatory and nonmandatory issuances "0" for now and we can calculate the term facilities (end of year), which will be:

2014 Term Facilities (End of Year) = 2014 Term Facilities
(Beginning of Year) + Mandatory Issuances/(Retirements) +
Nonmandatory Issuances (Retirements)

or Cell J268 would be "=SUM(J265:J267)."

We can then calculate interest expense as we had done with the revolver:

Average [2014 Term Facilities (Beginning of Year), 2014 Term Facilities (End of Year)] × 2014 Interest Rate

2014 Term Facilities Interest Expense (Cell J269)

Excel Keystrokes	Description
Type "="	Enters into "formula" mode
Type "average("	Creates the "Average" formula
Select Cell J265	2014 term facilities (beginning of year)
Type ","	Separates the two values we want to average
Select Cell J268	2014 term facilities (end of year)
Type "*"	Multiplies
Select Cell J270	2014 interest rate
Hit Enter	End
Formula result	=AVERAGE(J265,J268)*J270

Let's also hard-code the 5.0 percent into Cell J270. Again, at this point in time, we have little indication as to what the interest rates may be. We can easily adjust the interest rate as a variable once the model is complete. We can copy both Cells J269 and J270 to the right. See Table 12.2.

The Notes

We can now move on to the next debt, the notes. In order to build this out, we need to repeat the exact same process as what we have been doing.

The 2014 notes (beginning of year) is the same value as the ending balance of debt from the year before. So,

2014 Notes (Beginning of Year) = 2013 Notes (End of Year)

or in Cell J272, we will have "=I275," and we can copy this to the right.

We can make the mandatory and nonmandatory issuances "0" for now, and we can calculate the notes (end of year), which will be:

2014 Notes (End of Year) = 2014 Notes (Beginning of Year) + Mandatory Issuances/(Retirements) + Nonmandatory Issuances (Retirements)

or Cell J275 would be "=SUM(J272:J274)."

We can then calculate interest expense as we had done with the revolver:

Average [2014 Notes (Beginning of Year), 2014 Notes (End of Year)] × 2014 Interest Rate

2014 Notes Interest Expense (Cell J276)

Excel Keystrokes	Description
Type "="	Enters into "formula" mode.
Type "average("	Creates the "Average" formula
Select Cell J272	2014 notes (beginning of year)
Type ","	Separates the two values we want to average
Select Cell J275	2014 notes (end of year)
Type "*"	Multiplies
Select Cell J277	2014 interest rate
Hit Enter	End
Formula result	=AVERAGE(J272,J275)*J277

Again, until Heinz produces more clarity on the terms of the notes, let's use a core assumption. Given that the notes are subordinate to the term loans, they are a higher-risk security and so would most likely have a higher rate. Although with such a large landmark deal anything is possible, let's conservatively assume a 7.5 percent interest rate, hard-coding it into Cell J277. Again, we can always easily tweak this once the model is complete. We can copy both Cells J276 and J277 to the right. See Table 12.2.

Total Issuances/(Retirements)

We can now move on to the "Total issuances/(retirements)" in Row 278. As stated, this is a sum of all of the mandatory and nonmandatory issuances and retirements from the debts described previously. So, Cell J278 is "=J259+J260+J266+J267+J273+J274." The value will be 0 for now. We can copy this to the right.

Total Interest Expense

Row 279, "Total interest expense," is the sum of the above interests. So, Cell J279 is "=J276+J269+J262." We can copy this to the right.

Cash Available to Pay Down Debt

We can now consider the cash. Note the ending balance of cash that we had pulled into Cell I280. As we had done with the debts, this will link into the

TABLE 12.2   Projected Debts

Debt Schedule (in US$ millions except per share amounts)

| | | | Estimates | | | |
On January 27	2013PF	2014E	2015E	2016E	2017E	2018E
Cash available to pay down debt						
Cash at beginning of year						
Cash flow before debt-paydown						
Minimum cash cushion						
Total cash available to pay down debt						
Revolving line of credit						
Revolving line of credit (beginning of year)		$ 0.0	0.0	$ 0.0	0.0	$ 0.0
Mandatory issuances/(retirements)		0.0	0.0	0.0	0.0	0.0
Nonmandatory issuances/(retirements)		0.0	0.0	0.0	0.0	0.0
Revolving line of credit (end of year)	$ 0.0	$ 0.0	$ 0.0	$ 0.0	$ 0.0	$ 0.0
Revolving line of credit interest expense		0.0	0.0	0.0	0.0	0.0
Revolving line of credit interest rate		*5.00%*	*5.00%*	*5.00%*	*5.00%*	*5.00%*
Term facilities						
Term facilities (beginning of year)		10,500.0	10,500.0	10,500.0	10,500.0	10,500.0
Mandatory issuances/(retirements)		0.0	0.0	0.0	0.0	0.0
Nonmandatory issuances/(retirements)		0.0	0.0	0.0	0.0	0.0
Term facilities (end of year)	$10,500.0	$10,500.0	$10,500.0	$10,500.0	$10,500.0	$10,500.0
Term facilities interest expense		525.0	525.0	525.0	525.0	525.0

(continued)

TABLE 12.2 (Continued)

Debt Schedule (in US$ millions except per share amounts)

On January 27	2013PF	2014E	2015E	2016E	2017E	2018E
				Estimates		
Term facilities interest rate		*5.00%*	*5.00%*	*5.00%*	*5.00%*	*5.00%*
The notes						
The notes (beginning of year)		2,100.0	2,100.0	2,100.0	2,100.0	2,100.0
Mandatory issuances/(retirements)		0.0	0.0	0.0	0.0	0.0
Nonmandatory issuances/(retirements)		0.0	0.0	0.0	0.0	0.0
The notes (end of year)	$2,100.0	$2,100.0	$2,100.0	$2,100.0	$2,100.0	$2,100.0
The notes interest expense		157.5	157.5	157.5	157.5	157.5
The notes interest rate		*7.50%*	*7.50%*	*7.50%*	*7.50%*	*7.50%*
Total issuances/(retirements)						
Total interest expense						
Cash at the end of the year	$ 0.0					
Interest income						
Interest rate						
Match? (Y/N)		N	N	N	N	N

318

cash at the beginning of the year, Cell J253. So, Cell J253 will read "=I280." We can copy this to the right.

Cash flow before debt pay-down is a measure of all cash generated or paid, excluding cash issued or paid from debts. It is important for us to get a proper measure of cash excluding debts because in the debt schedule we want to determine how much cash we can use to pay down debts. At the bottom of the cash flow statement in Row 105 there is the line item "Cash flow before debt pay-down." In order to calculate this, we need to sum up everything in the cash flow statement that is not related to debts. We *exclude*:

- Revolver borrowings (repayments).
- Term facilities borrowings (repayments).
- The notes borrowings (repayments).
- Proceeds (payments) of long-term debt.
- Net payments on commercial paper and short-term debt.

And the formula will be "=J76+J86+J91+J92+J95+J96+J97+J98+J99+J100+J102," which is calculated in Cell J105 of the cash flow statement.

We are concerned only with the projected years, so we begin with 2014 and we can copy to the right through 2018. Take care to include the "Effect of exchange rate on cash," which is easy to leave out accidentally. Note that some believe we can simply take the total change in cash and cash equivalents and subtract the above debts. Although that is mathematically correct, doing so in the model would create a second circular reference. It is better to sum as we have done and exclude them from the formula altogether. Note the totals for now match the "Change in cash and cash equivalents". This will change once we start paying down debts. See Table 12.3.

TABLE 12.3 Projected Cash Flow before Debt Pay-Down

Consolidated Statements of Cash Flows (in US$ millions except per share amounts)					
		Estimates			
Period Ending	2014E	2015E	2016E	2017E	2018E
Total change in cash and cash equivalents	$814.7	$775.0	$782.0	$789.1	$796.2
Supplemental Data:					
Cash flow before debt pay-down	814.7	775.0	782.0	789.1	796.2

We can now link this into Row 254 of the debt schedule. Cell J254 in the debt schedule is "=J105," and we can copy this to the right through 2018.

"Minimum cash cushion" is the minimum cash balance a company maintains at the end of the year. There could be several reasons why a company would want to maintain a minimum cash balance. First, it is a safety cushion in order to avoid a potential cash shortfall. Second, lenders often require a company to maintain a minimum balance in order to ensure principal and interest payments are made. Projecting the minimum cash balance can vary from company to company. The minimum cash balance might be calculated as a percentage of sales, operating capital, or total cash, or it can be the collateral stated in the company's debt contracts that a company must maintain. It is not the most significant of projections, but we do recommend researching how the company has come up with its minimum cash balance for clues. Given that this is a leveraged buyout, which means we would want to free up as much cash as possible to pay down debt, let's be simple and conservative, estimating $100 million as a minimum cash cushion. We can enter "-100" into Cell J255 of the debt schedule. We enter the value as a negative number because we want to remove the minimum cash balance from the cash we can use to pay down debts. The total cash available to pay down debt is a sum of the cash at the beginning of the year and the cash flow before debt pay-down, less the minimum cushion, or in Cell J256 we will type "=SUM(J253:J255)." We can copy cells J253 through J256 to the right through 2018.

The total cash available to pay down debt is the amount of cash that is arguably free to be utilized. Should a company decide to manage its business in such a way, it can conceivably utilize all those funds to pay down debts in order to save on interest payments. However, it is important to note that not all debts can be paid at will without penalty. See Table 12.4.

We can now calculate "Cash at the end of the year" at the bottom of the debt schedule in Row 280. We calculate cash at the end of the year by starting with "Cash at beginning of year" and then adding to it "Cash flow before debt pay-down" and "Total issuances/(retirements)." This confuses many, but think about the fact that we want to capture a complete measure of cash from the first of the period to the end of the period, including capturing cash payments or issuances from debt pay-downs. We want to begin with "Cash at beginning of year" as we have done with any continuous balance, such as the debts. We then want to add all of the cash generated during the year. The "Cash flow before debt pay-down" is the closest measure of that on this particular sheet. So we have all cash except for cash raised or paid from debts. This is located in "Total issuances/(retirements)". It is often thought that we need to subtract interest here, but once linked in properly, interest will already be included in this

TABLE 12.4 Projected Total Cash Available to Pay Down Debt

Debt Schedule (in US$ millions except per share amounts)						
				Estimates		
On January 27	2013PF	2014E	2015E	2016E	2017E	2018E
Cash available to pay down debt						
Cash at beginning of year		$ 0.0	$ 0.0	$ 0.0	$ 0.0	$ 0.0
Cash flow before debt pay-down		814.7	775.0	782.0	789.1	796.2
Minimum cash cushion		(100.0)	(100.0)	(100.0)	(100.0)	(100.0)
Total cash available to pay down debt		$ 714.7	$ 675.0	$ 682.0	$ 689.1	$ 696.2

calculation. We will discuss this next. The formula for "Cash at the end of the year" is:

Cash at Beginning of Year + Cash Flow before Debt Pay-Down + Total Issuances/(Retirements)

or in Cell J280: "=J253+J254+J278," and we can copy this to the right.

Now that we have a value of cash at the end of the year, we can calculate interest income. Interest income is commonly the income received from cash held in savings accounts, certificates of deposit, and other investments. The interest income based on cash and cash equivalents is calculated in Row 281. As done with interest expense, we can take the average balance of the cash at the beginning of the year and the cash at the end of the year and multiply by some interest rate. So, interest income is:

Average (Cash at the Beginning of the Year, Cash at the End of the Year) × Interest Rate

2014 Interest Income (Cell J281)

Excel Keystrokes	Description
Type "="	Enters into "formula" mode
Type "average("	Creates the "Average" formula
Select Cell J253	2014 cash at beginning of year
Type ","	Separates the two values we want to average
Select Cell J280	2014 cash at end of year
Type "*"	Multiplies
Select Cell J282	2014 interest rate
Hit Enter	End
Formula result	=AVERAGE(J253,J280)*J282

It is not so easy to determine a proper interest income rate without solid detail on the cash investments. We also are not yet sure how cash under the new Heinz entity will be managed but we can assume there will be minimal cash outstanding as most will be utilized to grow the business and pay down debts to maximize profit. So a low interest rate of ~1 percent is a safe and conservative assumption. So let's hardcode 1% into Cell J282. We can copy J281 and J282 to the right through 2018.

Additional research can also to be done to see if a company has other investments beyond just the cash and cash equivalents that are generating interest within the interest income account.

We can now link the interest expense and interest income into the income statement. Rows 30 and 31 on the income statement have yet to be properly linked. So the interest expense in Cell J30 of the income statement will be "=J279," and we can copy this to the right. Similarly, we can link the interest income in from the debt schedule. Cell J31 in the income statement will be "=J281," and we can copy this to the right. Notice that levels of interest expense in 2014 have significantly increased and the levels of interest income have decreased in 2014 from the previous years. This makes sense as we have raised a significant amount of debt to fund the acquisition, and have minimized the outstanding cash in the business.

We finally have a complete representation of the income statement (see Table 12.5).

We have one final set of links left before the model is complete. We still need to link the debt payments and issuances into the financing activities of the cash flow statement from the debt schedule. Each debt in the debt schedule contains rows reflecting any issuances or payments made. These should be reflected in the financing activities of the cash flow statement. For example, Row 88 in the cash flow statement contains issuances and payments of the revolving line of credit. This should be linked in from the issuances/(retirements) line items in the revolving line of credit section of the debt schedule, both the mandatory and nonmandatory. Cell J88 in the cash flow statement should be "=J259+J260." We can copy this to the right through 2018.

Similarly, the next line on the cash flow statement, term facilities borrowings (repayments), should be linked in from the issuances/(retirements) line items in the term facilities section of the debt schedule, both the mandatory and nonmandatory. Cell J89 should be "=J266+J267." We can copy this formula to the right and continue with the last empty row referring to the notes, Cell J90: "=J273+J274"; and we can copy this to the right.

Now that the debt schedule is fully linked, we can make sure our final match checks out. Row 283 in the debt schedule checks to make sure the cash at the end of the year matches the cash at the top of the balance sheet. This match is important because we are effectively calculating cash two different ways in the model. The balance sheet cash is calculated from the prior-year balance sheet cash balance plus changes in cash from the cash flow statement. However, the cash at the end of the year on the debt schedule is calculated from the cash balance at the beginning of the year at the top of the debt schedule, and then adding in cash flow before debt pay-down and issuances and retirements. The point of this is to ensure we have the debt issuances/(retirements), interest expense, and interest income wired in correctly. See Table 12.6.

TABLE 12.5 Heinz Projected Income Statement with Interest

Consolidated Income Statements (in US$ millions except per share amounts)

Period Ending	Actuals			Last Twelve Months (LTM)			Estimates				
	2010A	2011A	2012A	9-Mo. 2012	9-Mo. 2013	LTM	2014E	2015E	2016E	2017E	2018E
Revenue	10,495.0	10,706.6	11,649.1	8,495.9	8,538.3	11,691.5	11,738.3	11,785.2	11,832.3	11,879.7	11,927.2
Y/Y revenue growth (%)		2.0%	8.8%			0.4%	0.4%	0.4%	0.4%	0.4%	0.4%
Cost of goods sold	6,397.8	6,455.4	7,306.8	5,260.2	5,160.4	7,207.0	7,230.8	7,259.7	7,288.7	7,317.9	7,347.2
COGS as a % of revenue	61.0%	60.3%	62.7%	61.9%	60.4%	61.6%	61.6%	61.6%	61.6%	61.6%	61.6%
Gross profit	4,097.1	4,251.2	4,342.3	3,235.7	3,377.9	4,484.5	4,507.5	4,525.5	4,543.6	4,561.8	4,580.0
Gross profit margin (%)	39.0%	39.7%	37.3%	38.1%	39.6%	38.4%	38.4%	38.4%	38.4%	38.4%	38.4%
Operating expenses											
Selling, general and administrative	2,235.1	2,304.4	2,548.4	1,814.2	1,841.5	2,575.6	2,582.4	2,592.7	2,603.1	2,613.5	2,624.0
SG&A as a % of revenue	21.3%	21.5%	21.9%	21.4%	21.6%	22.0%	22.0%	22.0%	22.0%	22.0%	22.0%
Fund Management Fee	0.0	0.0	0.0	0.0	0.0	0.0	0.0	0.0	0.0	0.0	0.0
Cost savings	0.0	0.0	0.0	0.0	0.0	0.0	(25.8)	(25.9)	(26.0)	(26.1)	(26.2)
Cost savings as a % of SG&A							1.0%	1.0%	1.0%	1.0%	1.0%
Total operating expenses	2,235.1	2,304.4	2,548.4	1,814.2	1,841.5	2,575.6	2,556.6	2,566.8	2,577.1	2,587.4	2,597.7
Other income	0.0	0.0	0.0	0.0	0.0	0.0	0.0	0.0	0.0	0.0	0.0
Equity in earnings of unconsolidated affiliates	0.0	0.0	0.0	0.0	0.0	0.0	0.0	0.0	0.0	0.0	0.0
EBITDA	1,862.1	1,946.9	1,794.0	1,421.5	1,536.4	1,908.9	1,950.9	1,958.7	1,966.5	1,974.4	1,982.3

EBITDA margin (%)	17.7%	18.2%	15.4%	16.7%	18.0%	16.3%	16.6%	16.6%	16.6%	16.6%	16.6%
Depreciation	254.5	255.2	295.7	217.6	221.5	299.6	297.4	309.2	321.0	332.9	344.8
Amortization	48.3	43.4	47.1	34.0	34.9	48.0	30.0	30.0	30.0	30.0	30.0
Amortization of identifiable intangible assets	0.0	0.0	0.0	0.0	0.0	0.0	342.4	342.4	342.4	342.4	342.4
Total Depreciation and amortization	302.8	298.7	342.8	251.6	256.4	347.6	669.8	681.6	693.4	705.3	717.2
EBIT	1,559.2	1,648.2	1,451.2	1,169.9	1,280.0	1,561.3	1,281.1	1,277.1	1,273.1	1,269.1	1,265.1
EBIT margin (%)	14.9%	15.4%	12.5%	13.8%	15.0%	13.4%	10.9%	10.8%	10.8%	10.7%	10.6%
Interest											
Interest expense	295.7	275.4	294.1	218.1	213.1	289.1	682.5	682.5	682.5	682.5	682.5
Interest income	45.1	22.6	34.6	25.6	22.3	31.3	1.2	3.9	6.8	9.8	12.9
Net interest expense	250.6	252.8	259.5	192.5	190.8	257.8	681.3	678.6	675.7	672.7	669.6
EBT	1,308.7	1,395.4	1,191.7	977.4	1,089.2	1,303.5	599.8	598.5	597.4	596.4	595.4
EBT margin (%)	12.5%	13.0%	10.2%	11.5%	12.8%	11.1%	5.1%	5.1%	5.0%	5.0%	5.0%
Income tax expense	363.6	373.9	245.2	192.6	172.8	225.5	166.7	166.4	166.1	165.8	165.5
All-in effective tax rate (%)	27.8%	26.8%	20.6%	19.7%	15.9%	17.3%	27.8%	27.8%	27.8%	27.8%	27.8%
Net income (Adjusted)	945.1	1,021.5	946.4	784.9	916.4	1,078.0	433.1	432.1	431.3	430.6	429.9
Non-recurring events											
Other expense, net	13.1	15.5	6.5	2.6	15.2	19.1	19.1	19.1	19.1	19.1	19.1
Loss from discountued operations, net of tax	49.6	0.0	0.0	19.9	72.1	52.2	0.0	0.0	0.0	0.0	0.0

(continued)

TABLE 12.5 (*Continued*)

Consolidated Income Statements (in US$ millions except per share amounts)

Period Ending	Actuals			Last Twelve Months (LTM)			Estimates				
	2010A	2011A	2012A	9-Mo. 2012	9-Mo. 2013	LTM	2014E	2015E	2016E	2017E	2018E
Effect of accounting changes	0.0	0.0	0.0	0.0	0.0	0.0	0.0	0.0	0.0	0.0	0.0
Extraordinary items, net of tax	0.0	0.0	0.0	0.0	0.0	0.0	0.0	0.0	0.0	0.0	0.0
Total non-recurring events	62.7	15.5	6.5	22.5	87.3	71.3	19.1	19.1	19.1	19.1	19.1
Net income (after non-recurring events)	882.3	1,005.9	939.9	762.3	829.1	1,006.7	414.0	413.0	412.2	411.5	410.8
Net income attributable to non-controlling interests	17.5	16.4	16.7	14.5	12.1	14.3	0.0	0.0	0.0	0.0	0.0
Net income (as reported)	864.9	989.5	923.2	747.8	817.0	992.4	414.0	413.0	412.2	411.5	410.8
Earnings per share (EPS)											
Basic	2.737	3.091	2.879	2.331	2.549	3.096					
Diluted	2.719	3.063	2.855	2.311	2.529	3.072					
Average common shares outstanding											
Basic	315.9	320.1	320.7	320.9	320.5	320.5					
Diluted	318.1	323.0	323.3	323.5	323.0	323.0					

TABLE 12.6 Projected Debt Schedule

Debt Schedule (in US$ millions except per share amounts)

On January 27	2013PF	2014E	2015E	2016E	2017E	2018E
				Estimates		
Cash available to pay down debt						
Cash at beginning of year		0.0	246.1	531.5	825.9	1,129.7
Cash flow before debt paydown		246.1	285.3	294.5	303.7	313.1
Minimum cash cushion		(100.0)	(100.0)	(100.0)	(100.0)	(100.0)
Total cash available to pay down debt		**146.1**	**431.5**	**725.9**	**1,029.7**	**1,342.7**
Revolving line of credit						
Revolving line of credit (beginning of year)		0.0	0.0	0.0	0.0	0.0
Mandatory issuances / (retirements)		0.0	0.0	0.0	0.0	0.0
Non-mandatory issuances / (retirements)	1.0	0.0	0.0	0.0	0.0	0.0
Revolving line of credit (end of year)	**0.0**	**0.0**	**0.0**	**0.0**	**0.0**	**0.0**
Revolving line of credit interest expense		0.0	0.0	0.0	0.0	0.0
Revolving line of credit interest rate		*5.00%*	*5.00%*	*5.00%*	*5.00%*	*5.00%*
Term facilities						
Term facilities (beginning of year)		10,500.0	10,500.0	10,500.0	10,500.0	10,500.0
Mandatory issuances / (retirements)		0.0	0.0	0.0	0.0	0.0
Non-mandatory issuances / (retirements)		0.0	0.0	0.0	0.0	0.0
Term facilities (end of year)	**10,500.0**	**10,500.0**	**10,500.0**	**10,500.0**	**10,500.0**	**10,500.0**
Term facilities interest expense		525.0	525.0	525.0	525.0	525.0
Term facilities interest rate		*5.00%*	*5.00%*	*5.00%*	*5.00%*	*5.00%*
The notes						
The notes (beginning of year)		2,100.0	2,100.0	2,100.0	2,100.0	2,100.0

(continued)

TABLE 12.6 (Continued)

Debt Schedule (in US$ millions except per share amounts)

| | 2013PF | | Estimates | | | | |
		2014E	2015E	2016E	2017E	2018E
On January 27						
Mandatory issuances / (retirements)		0.0	0.0	0.0	0.0	0.0
Non-mandatory issuances / (retirements)		0.0	0.0	0.0	0.0	0.0
The notes (end of year)	2,100.0	2,100.0	2,100.0	2,100.0	2,100.0	2,100.0
The notes interest expense		157.5	157.5	157.5	157.5	157.5
The notes interest rate		*7.50%*	*7.50%*	*7.50%*	*7.50%*	*7.50%*
Total issuances / (retirements)		0.0	0.0	0.0	0.0	0.0
Total interest expense		682.5	682.5	682.5	682.5	682.5
Cash at the end of the year	0.0	246.1	531.5	825.9	1,129.7	1,442.7
Interest income		1.2	3.9	6.8	9.8	12.9
Interest rate		*1.00%*	*1.00%*	*1.00%*	*1.00%*	*1.00%*
Match? (Y/N)		Y	Y	Y	Y	Y

CIRCULAR REFERENCES

In a fully linked model, there is one major, important circular reference flowing through the statements. This circular reference is related to the debt and interest. Specifically, if debt is raised in the debt schedule, cash at the end of the year will increase and therefore interest income will increase. As interest income links to the income statement, net income is increased. That net income increase flows to the top of the cash flow statement and increases cash and, more important, "cash flow before debt pay-down" at the bottom of the cash flow statement. This "cash flow before debt pay-down" links to the debt schedule and increases the cash available to pay down debt, and therefore increases the cash at the end of the year, which increases the interest income, and so on.

See the following example of raising $1,000 in debt. For purposes of explaining the circular reference, let's just focus on what happens to interest income.

NOTE

When this circular reference is created, an error message may pop up in Excel. Excel automatically assumes circular references in a model are errors. We need to adjust a setting in Excel to explain that we want the circular reference in the model. When doing so, we need to tell Excel how many of these circular iterations we want it to go through before stopping, as, theoretically, this loop can go on forever.

- *Excel 2010.* If you are using Excel 2010, you can find the Excel settings by selecting "File" in the menu bar, then "Options" at the bottom.
- *Excel 2007.* In Excel 2007, you can find the Excel settings by selecting the circular Microsoft Office icon at the top left of the Excel program, and you will find the "Excel Settings" button at the bottom.

Once the settings box pops open, select "Formulas," which should reveal a "Calculation options" section. Within this section there should be a selection box titled "Enable iterative calculations." Checking this box tells Excel to allow circular references. Once this box is checked, we can tell Excel how many iterations we want Excel to cycle through; 100 iterations are enough.

Debt Schedule	
Cash at beginning of year	$ 0.0
Cash flow before debt pay-down	0.0
Minimum cash	0.0
Long-term debt	
Beginning of year	0.0
Issuances	1,000.0
Interest (@ 10%)*	100.0
End of year	1,000.0
Cash at the end of the year	1,000.0
Interest income (@ 1%)*	10.0

*Note that we are trying to illustrate only the interest income flow, so let's ignore the interest expense for now. In order to keep this simple, we did not take the average of the beginning and end of the year.

Income Statement	
Interest Income	10.0
Taxes (@ 40%)	(4.0)
Net Income	**6.0**

Cash Flow	
Net Income	6.0
Long-Term Debt Issuance	1,000.0
Total Changes in Cash	**1,006.0**
Cash Flow before Debt Pay-Down	**6.0**

The interest income flows into the income statement and increases net income (after tax) by $6. Net income flows into the cash flow statement. With the $1,000 debt issuance, cash increases by $1,006. However, cash flow before debt pay-down excludes the cash from debt issuance, so it increases by only $6. Back to the debt schedule:

Debt Schedule	
Cash at beginning of year	$ 0.0
Cash flow before debt pay-down	6.0
Minimum cash	0.0
Long-term debt	
Beginning of year	0.0
Issuances	1,000.0
Interest (@ 10%)*	100.0
End of year	1,000.0
Cash at the end of the year	1,006.0
Interest income (@ 1%)*	10.1

Because the cash flow before debt pay-down has increased by an additional $6, the interest income has increased by $0.1 (really $0.06, rounded up to $0.1), and will flow back through the income statement and continue the cycle.

Let's take another example illustrating the circular reference, but this time with the interest expense on the debt.

If debt is paid down in the debt schedule, interest expense will decrease. As interest expense links to the income statement, a reduction in interest expense increases net income. That net income increase flows to the top of the cash flow statement, and increases cash and, more important, "Cash flow before debt pay-down" at the bottom of the cash flow statement. This cash flow before debt pay-down links to the debt schedule and increases the cash available to pay down debt. So, based on the interest savings from paying down debt, we now have a little more cash we can use to pay down more debt. If we do so, interest expense will be reduced further, which will reduce net income further, and the cycle will repeat.

See the following example of paying down $1,000 in debt. For purposes of explaining the circular reference, let's just focus on what happens to interest expense. We will also have to assume we had $1,000 of cash at the beginning of the year in order to pay down that $1,000 of debt:

Debt Schedule	
Cash beginning of year	$1,000.0
Cash flow before debt pay-down	0.0
Minimum cash	0.0
Long-term debt	
Beginning of year	1,000.0
Issuances	(1,000.0)
Interest (@ 10%)*	(100.0)
End of year	0.0
Cash at the end of the year	0.0
Interest income (@ 1%)*	0.0

*We are illustrating the idea that interest expense has reduced by $100. In order to keep this simple, we did not take the average of the beginning and end of the year. We are also assuming no interest income to illustrate just the interest expense movements.

Income Statement	
Interest Expense*	(100.0)
Taxes (@ 40%)	40.0
Net Income	**60.0**

Cash Flow	
Net Income	60.0
Long-Term Debt Issuance	(1,000.0)
Total Changes in Cash	**(940.0)**
Cash Flow before Debt Pay-Down	**60.0**

So, the reduction in interest expense flows into the income statement and increases net income (after tax) by $60. Net income flows into the cash flow statement. With the $1,000 debt retirement, cash decreases by $940. However, cash flow before debt pay-down excludes the cash from debt issuance, so it increases by $60. Now back to the debt schedule.

Debt Schedule	
Cash beginning of year	$1,000.0
Cash flow before debt pay-down	60.0
Minimum cash	0.0
Long-term debt	
Beginning of year	1,000.0
Issuances	(1,000.0)
Interest (@ 10%)*	(100.0)
End of year	0.0
Cash at the end of the year	60.0
Interest Income (@ 1%)*	0.0

*Again, we are illustrating the idea that interest expense has reduced by $100. In order to keep this simple, we did not take the average of the beginning and end of the year. We are also assuming no interest income to illustrate just the interest expense movements.

We now have $60 more we could use to pay down more debt. We can choose to pay down more debt if we have more debt, and reduce interest expense further, which will flow back into the income statement and repeat the cycle.

Technically, since the issuing and paying down of debt is hard-coded in the model, this particular loop is not an endless one. In other words, we have to manually adjust the pay-down after each iteration. But we will later look at automatic pay-down formulas, which will cause an endless loop. Having the Excel iteration settings set to a number such as 100 will limit the iterations.

Circular Reference #Value! Errors

It can often happen at this point in the model that the whole model becomes ridden with #Value! or other errors. This is because of the circular reference and happens when a formula is accidentally mistyped in a cell that is connected to the circular loop. If a particular formula is mistyped in such a way that Excel thinks it is a string as opposed to a number, an error message is produced because Excel cannot make the calculation. If such an error message is produced in the circular reference loop, that error message is caught in the loop and every cell in its path is affected.

You can try this (don't worry—we have a quick fix) by forcing a cell within the loop to be a string. We can type "test," for example, in one of the debt issuances cells, let's say J259. The model should now be filled with #Value! error messages. If you don't see the error messages right away, try hitting the F9 key, which is a shortcut to recalculate the Excel model cells (see Table 12.7).

To repair this, we first need to identify where the error is and change it back to an integer. So let's change "test" back to "0." Although this fixes the original mistake, the errors still exist because that #Value! message is caught in a loop. To repair this, we need to break the loop, allow Excel to recalculate normally, and relink the loop. An easy way to do this is to look to the interest expense and interest income on the income statement, Rows 30 and 31 (see Table 12.8).

We can easily highlight and delete these two rows, starting in Cell D30, selecting the first row by holding down Shift, tapping the space bar once, and then selecting the other row by holding down Shift and tapping the down arrow key. We can now hit the Delete button to erase the links. Excel should recalculate normally, and you should see those #Value! errors disappear. If those #Value! errors still exist then you have a different problem with the model other than a circular reference issue. At this point, we can put those links back in simply by undoing the deletion or typing "Ctrl" + "Z." Now everything should be back to normal (see Table 12.9).

TABLE 12.7 Debt Schedule #Value! Error

Debt Schedule (in US$ millions except per share amounts)

On January 27	2013PF	Estimates				
		2014E	2015E	2016E	2017E	2018E
Cash available to pay down debt						
Cash at beginning of year		0.0	#VALUE!	#VALUE!	#VALUE!	#VALUE!
Cash flow before debt pay-down		#VALUE!	#VALUE!	#VALUE!	#VALUE!	#VALUE!
Minimum cash cushion		(100.0)	(100.0)	(100.0)	(100.0)	(100.0)
Total cash available to pay down debt		#VALUE!	#VALUE!	#VALUE!	#VALUE!	#VALUE!
Revolving line of credit						
Revolving line of credit (beginning of year)		0.0	0.0	0.0	0.0	0.0
Mandatory issuances/(retirements)		test	0.0	0.0	0.0	0.0
Nonmandatory issuances/(retirements)		0.0	0.0	0.0	0.0	0.0
Revolving line of credit (end of year)	0.0	0.0	0.0	0.0	0.0	0.0
Revolving line of credit interest expense		0.0	0.0	0.0	0.0	0.0
Revolving line of credit interest rate		*5.00%*	*5.00%*	*5.00%*	*5.00%*	*5.00%*

TABLE 12.8 Income Statement #Value! Error

Consolidated Income Statements (in US$ millions except per share amounts)

Period Ending	Actuals			Last 12 Months (LTM)			Estimates				
	2010A	2011A	2012A	9-Mo. 2012	9-Mo. 2013	LTM	2014E	2015E	2016E	2017E	2018E
EBIT	$1,559.2	$1,648.2	$1,451.2	$1,169.9	$1,280.0	$1,561.3	$1,281.1	$1,277.1	$1,273.1	$1,269.1	$1,265.1
EBIT margin (%)	14.9%	15.4%	12.5%	13.8%	15.0%	13.4%	10.9%	10.8%	10.8%	10.7%	10.6%
Interest											
Interest expense	295.7	275.4	294.1	218.1	213.1	289.1	682.5	682.5	682.5	682.5	682.5
Interest income	45.1	22.6	34.6	25.6	22.3	31.3	#VALUE!	#VALUE!	#VALUE!	#VALUE!	#VALUE!
Net interest expense	$ 250.6	$ 252.8	$ 259.5	$ 192.5	$ 190.8	$ 257.8	#VALUE!	#VALUE!	#VALUE!	#VALUE!	#VALUE!
EBT	1,308.7	1,395.4	1,191.7	977.4	1,089.2	1,303.5	#VALUE!	#VALUE!	#VALUE!	#VALUE!	#VALUE!
EBT margin (%)	12.5%	13.0%	10.2%	11.5%	12.8%	11.1%	#VALUE!	#VALUE!	#VALUE!	#VALUE!	#VALUE!
Income tax expense	363.6	373.9	245.2	192.6	172.8	225.5	#VALUE!	#VALUE!	#VALUE!	#VALUE!	#VALUE!
All-in effective tax rate (%)	27.8%	26.8%	20.6%	19.7%	15.9%	17.3%	27.8%	27.8%	27.8%	27.8%	27.8%
Net income (adjusted)	$ 945.1	$1,021.5	$ 946.4	$ 784.9	$ 916.4	$1,078.0	#VALUE!	#VALUE!	#VALUE!	#VALUE!	#VALUE!

TABLE 12.9 Fixed Income Statement

Consolidated Income Statements (in US$ millions except per share amounts)

Period Ending	Actuals			Last 12 Months (LTM)			Estimates				
	2010A	2011A	2012A	9Mo. 2012	9Mo. 2013	LTM	2014E	2015E	2016E	2017E	2018E
EBIT	1,559.2	1,648.2	1,451.2	1,169.9	1,280.0	1,561.3	1,281.1	1,277.1	1,273.1	1,269.1	1,265.1
EBIT margin (%)	14.9%	15.4%	12.5%	13.8%	15.0%	13.4%	10.9%	10.8%	10.8%	10.7%	10.6%
Interest											
Interest expense	295.7	275.4	294.1	218.1	213.1	289.1	682.5	682.5	682.5	682.5	682.5
Interest income	45.1	22.6	34.6	25.6	22.3	31.3	1.2	3.9	6.8	9.8	12.9
Net interest expense	250.6	252.8	259.5	192.5	190.8	257.8	681.3	678.6	675.7	672.7	669.6
EBT	1,308.7	1,395.4	1,191.7	977.4	1,089.2	1,303.5	599.8	598.5	597.4	596.4	595.4
EBT margin (%)	12.5%	13.0%	10.2%	11.5%	12.8%	11.1%	5.1%	5.1%	5.0%	5.0%	5.0%
Income tax expense	363.6	373.9	245.2	192.6	172.8	225.5	166.7	166.4	166.1	165.8	165.5
All-in effective tax rate (%)	27.8%	26.8%	20.6%	19.7%	15.9%	17.3%	27.8%	27.8%	27.8%	27.8%	27.8%
Net income (Adjusted)	945.1	1,021.5	946.4	784.9	916.4	1,078.0	433.1	432.1	431.3	430.6	429.9

AUTOMATIC DEBT PAY-DOWNS

Earlier we discussed that the reason for a "Nonmandatory issuances/(retirement)" line item is to pay down debt automatically if there happens to be excess cash, or to raise debt if there is some cash need. Not all businesses choose to or are allowed to pay down debt at will, but let's walk through how to enter such a formula into the model. First, it is important to explain the particular conditions we want such a formula to handle. We want to set up a series of logical conditions that essentially compares a debt balance with cash available to pay down debt. If we have more cash than debt, then we can pay down all of the debt; if we have less cash than debt, then we can pay down only as much cash as we have; if our cash balance is negative, then we need to raise more debt to fulfill the cash need. Let's list these in a more formal set of logical conditions:

1. If cash available is negative, then we need to raise cash.
2. If cash available is positive, then:
   a. If cash available is greater than debt, then we can pay down the debt.
   b. If cash available is less than the debt, then we can pay down only as much cash as we have.

We can then rewrite these conditions as "If … then" statements. Taking condition 1, for example: if the cash is negative, we clearly have a cash need and we need to raise cash to fulfill that cash need. So the condition would be:

1. If Cash < 0, then return -Cash.

So the "-Cash" at the end of the formula literally means to have the output be the negative value of the cash. In other words, if we have –$500 in cash, then we need to issue $500 to fill that cash need. So the formula would read "- - $500" (yes, a double negative) or $500.

2a. If Cash > 0, then, if Cash Available > Debt, then return -Debt.

Or if cash is positive and if we have more cash than debt, then we can pay down the entire debt. A debt pay-down is represented by "-Debt," the negative balance of debt.

2b. If Cash > 0, then, if Cash Available < Debt, then return -Cash.

Or if cash is positive but if we have less cash then debt, then we can pay down only as much cash as we have. This is represented by the negative cash balance.

Notice that conditions 2a and 2b can be satisfied in another way: by taking the minimum balance of cash and debt. Let's take an example for 2a and say cash is $1,000 and debt is $500. In this case, cash is positive and is also greater than debt, so we can certainly pay down all of the debt. So the output will be –$500, or "-Debt." Let's now take an example for 2b and say cash is $1,000 and debt is $2,500. In this case, cash is positive but is less than debt, so we can pay down only as much cash as we have, –$1,000, or "-Cash." In either case we are taking the minimum of the two, cash or debt. And notice in both cases the output is the negative of the value. So the formula "-Min (Cash, Debt)" will satisfy both of the conditions. But what about condition 1, where cash is negative? In this case, "-Min (Cash, Debt)" also satisfies this case. We know that debt can never be negative, and so if this is the case where the cash is negative, the negative value (cash) will always be smaller than the positive value (debt). If cash is negative, the formula "-Min (Cash, Debt)" will always give us "-Cash," the desired result.

It is important to understand the details of the formula and how it works so one can adjust the formula to handle different tasks. For example, adding an additional "min" function to the formula can cap how much debt can be raised.

We can use this for the revolving line of credit. If there is a cash need at some point, we would like to be able to raise debt funding the need. However, the revolver has a cap of $1,500, which means we cannot raise more than that amount. So if the cash need is –$2,500, we can raise only the $1,500, which is the minimum of the two. Or, if the cash need is –$500, then we want to raise only $500, not $1,500, again the minimum of the two. So, we will just add another "minimum" formula around the formula designed earlier.

The formula will look like:

$$=\text{MIN}(-(\text{MIN}(\text{Cash, Debt})),1500)$$

A debt pay-down will always be negative and therefore will always be less than any positive number (or in this case 1,500). But if the output happens to be a positive number (a debt to be raised as a result of a cash need) greater than $1,500, that outer "min" function will prevent it from going beyond the 1,500.

We can enter this formula into the model for the revolving line of credit. In Cell J260 of the debt schedule we can enter "=MIN(–MIN(J258,J256), 1500)."

We can copy this to the right. Now we can test the functionality of this formula: We can force the cash balance to be very negative, resulting in the need to raise debt, by temporarily changing the value in Cell J255 to be "-1000." If you do this, you will notice that the revolver begins to raise debt to fund the cash shortfall. Let's test the formula further by changing Cell J255 to be "-2000." Here, the cash shortfall exceeds the $1,500 maximum debt allowed to be raised. We can see that the revolver does not raise more than the $1,500. If you have properly copied this formula to the right, you can also see that the formula automatically pays the debt back down in the next year because it has the cash to do so. The formula works. Keep this value at "-2000" for now so we can discuss how to turn these formulas on and off with a switch.

BASIC SWITCHES

It is also helpful to put in a simple switch to be able to turn on or off the use of this "min" formula. We can do this by simply multiplying the formula by a "1" or "0." Multiplying any formula by "0" will always produce "0," so the formula will be turned off; multiplying any formula by "1" will not change the output of the formula, so it will be turned on. So, for example, we can type a "1" in Cell I260. We can also append the formula in J260 to add "*$I$260," making sure to add dollar signs around the reference to I260, so that we can copy the formula to the right without affecting the reference to I260. The formula in J260 should read "=MIN(-MIN(J258,J256),1500)*$I$260." Now, if we type "0" into Cell I260, the formula will read "0" and be turned off. If we type "1" into Cell I260, the formula will read "1" and be turned on. Let's keep the formula switched on, and we can make the value in Cell J255 be "–100" again.

FINALIZING THE MODEL

Now that the core model is complete, it is important to step back and take a high-level look at the output. We had already taken a high-level look at operations growth in relation to other Wall Street analysts. Since this company is being bought out, management will change and the business projections will become more uncertain. As a result, we feel it is always important to test model boundaries around our first-cut assumptions by running several variations of variables and testing how the overall returns are affected. We will learn how to calculate the overall returns in the next chapter.

Aside from operations, we need to go back and take a second look at the projected balance sheet. We should not show negative assets or liabilities balances unless there is good reason to do so. Typically, an asset or a liability should not be negative. The balance sheet looks okay from this perspective.

We want to consider the debt pay-downs and conduct research to determine if they are being handled according to how the company will actually intend them to be handled. Unfortunately, further research does not include detail on the amortization of the term loans and the notes. Often the term loans will amortize over a specific period—for example, over the expected life of the transaction. If such an amortization exists, we would need to plug in mandatory retirements as principal payments each year. It is hoped that in the near future more relevant detail on the debts will be publicly released. We will see in the next section, the Heinz cash flow doesn't even seem strong enough to support any major amortization or debt paydown each year, which is slightly unusual for a leveraged buyout. As we have previously discussed, part of the leveraged buyout strategy is to have debt paydown convert to equity thus adding value to the return. Despite the less than stellar cash flow we will still assume the company proceeds upon exit will go to paydown debt. So let's keep the principal payments zero on all debts, and in the next chapter will illustrate the paydown of all debts upon exit. We will also analyze more complicated debt structures in Part III.

We are done and can move on to estimating the expected return of the investment. We have the complete three major statements in the next pages for reference (see Tables 12.10, 12.11, and 12.12).

TABLE 12.10 Heinz Consolidated Income Statements

Consolidated Income Statements (in US$ millions except per share amounts)

| | Actuals | | | Last 12 Months (LTM) | | | | Estimates | | | | | |
Period Ending	2010A	2011A	2012A	9Mo. 2012	9Mo. 2013	LTM	2014E	2015E	2016E	2017E	2018E
Revenue	10,495.0	10,706.6	11,649.1	8,495.9	8,538.3	11,691.5	11,738.3	11,785.2	11,832.3	11,879.7	11,927.2
Y/Y revenue growth (%)		2.0%	8.8%			0.4%	0.4%	0.4%	0.4%	0.4%	0.4%
Cost of goods sold	6,397.8	6,455.4	7,306.8	5,260.2	5,160.4	7,207.0	7,230.8	7,259.7	7,288.7	7,317.9	7,347.2
COGS as a % of revenue	61.0%	60.3%	62.7%	61.9%	60.4%	61.6%	61.6%	61.6%	61.6%	61.6%	61.6%
Gross profit	4,097.1	4,251.2	4,342.3	3,235.7	3,377.9	4,484.5	4,507.5	4,525.5	4,543.6	4,561.8	4,580.0
Gross profit margin (%)	39.0%	39.7%	37.3%	38.1%	39.6%	38.4%	38.4%	38.4%	38.4%	38.4%	38.4%
Operating expenses											
Selling, general and administrative	2,235.1	2,304.4	2,548.4	1,814.2	1,841.5	2,575.6	2,582.4	2,592.7	2,603.1	2,613.5	2,624.0
SG&A as a % of revenue	21.3%	21.5%	21.9%	21.4%	21.6%	22.0%	22.0%	22.0%	22.0%	22.0%	22.0%
Fund management fee	0.0	0.0	0.0	0.0	0.0	0.0	0.0	0.0	0.0	0.0	0.0
Cost savings	0.0	0.0	0.0	0.0	0.0	0.0	(25.8)	(25.9)	(26.0)	(26.1)	(26.2)
Cost savings as a % of SG&A							1.0%	1.0%	1.0%	1.0%	1.0%
Total operating expenses	2,235.1	2,304.4	2,548.4	1,814.2	1,841.5	2,575.6	2,556.6	2,566.8	2,577.1	2,587.4	2,597.7
Other income											
Equity in earnings of unconsolidated affiliates	0.0	0.0	0.0	0.0	0.0	0.0	0.0	0.0	0.0	0.0	0.0
EBITDA	1,862.1	1,946.9	1,794.0	1,421.5	1,536.4	1,908.9	1,950.9	1,958.7	1,966.5	1,974.4	1,982.3
EBITDA margin (%)	17.7%	18.2%	15.4%	16.7%	18.0%	16.3%	16.6%	16.6%	16.6%	16.6%	16.6%

(continued)

TABLE 12.10 (Continued)

Consolidated Income Statements (in US$ millions except per share amounts)

Period Ending	Actuals			Last 12 Months (LTM)			Estimates				
	2010A	2011A	2012A	9Mo. 2012	9Mo. 2013	LTM	2014E	2015E	2016E	2017E	2018E
Depreciation	254.5	255.2	295.7	217.6	221.5	299.6	297.4	309.2	321.0	332.9	344.8
Amortization	48.3	43.4	47.1	34.0	34.9	48.0	30.0	30.0	30.0	30.0	30.0
Amortization of identifiable intangible assets	0.0	0.0	0.0	0.0	0.0	0.0	342.4	342.4	342.4	342.4	342.4
Total depreciation and amortization	302.8	298.7	342.8	251.6	256.4	347.6	669.8	681.6	693.4	705.3	717.2
EBIT	1,559.2	1,648.2	1,451.2	1,169.9	1,280.0	1,561.3	1,281.1	1,277.1	1,273.1	1,269.1	1,265.1
EBIT margin (%)	14.9%	15.4%	12.5%	13.8%	15.0%	13.4%	10.9%	10.8%	10.8%	10.7%	10.6%
Interest											
Interest expense	295.7	275.4	294.1	218.1	213.1	289.1	682.5	682.5	682.5	682.5	682.5
Interest income	45.1	22.6	34.6	25.6	22.3	31.3	1.2	3.9	6.8	9.8	12.9
Net interest expense	250.6	252.8	259.5	192.5	190.8	257.8	681.3	678.6	675.7	672.7	669.6
EBT	1,308.7	1,395.4	1,191.7	977.4	1,089.2	1,303.5	599.8	598.5	597.4	596.4	595.4
EBT margin (%)	12.5%	13.0%	10.2%	11.5%	12.8%	11.1%	5.1%	5.1%	5.0%	5.0%	5.0%
Income tax expense	363.6	373.9	245.2	192.6	172.8	225.5	166.7	166.4	166.1	165.8	165.5
All-in effective tax rate (%)	27.8%	26.8%	20.6%	19.7%	15.9%	17.3%	27.8%	27.8%	27.8%	27.8%	27.8%
Net income (Adjusted)	945.1	1,021.5	946.4	784.9	916.4	1,078.0	433.1	432.1	431.3	430.6	429.9

Non-recurring events										
Other expense, net	13.1	15.5	6.5	2.6	15.2	19.1	19.1	19.1	19.1	19.1	19.1
Loss from discontinued operations, net of tax	49.6	0.0	0.0	19.9	72.1	52.2	0.0	0.0	0.0	0.0	0.0
Effect of accounting changes	0.0	0.0	0.0	0.0	0.0	0.0	0.0	0.0	0.0	0.0	0.0
Extraordinary items, net of tax	0.0	0.0	0.0	0.0	0.0	0.0	0.0	0.0	0.0	0.0	0.0
Total non-recurring events	62.7	15.5	6.5	22.5	87.3	71.3	19.1	19.1	19.1	19.1	19.1
Net income (after non-recurring events)	882.3	1,005.9	939.9	762.3	829.1	1,006.7	414.0	413.0	412.2	411.5	410.8
Net income attributable to non-controlling interests	17.5	16.4	16.7	14.5	12.1	14.3	0.0	0.0	0.0	0.0	0.0
Net income (as reported)	864.9	989.5	923.2	747.8	817.0	992.4	414.0	413.0	412.2	411.5	410.8
Earnings per share (EPS)											
Basic	2.737	3.091	2.879	2.331	2.549	3.096					
Diluted	2.719	3.063	2.855	2.311	2.529	3.072					
Average common shares outstanding											
Basic	315.9	320.1	320.7	320.9	320.5	320.5					
Diluted	318.1	323.0	323.3	323.5	323.0	323.0					

TABLE 12.11 Heinz Consolidated Statement of Cash Flows

Consolidated Statements of Cash Flows (in US$ millions except per share amounts)

	Actuals			Last Twelve Months (LTM)			Estimates				
Period Ending	2010A	2011A	2012A	9Mo. 2012	9Mo. 2013	LTM	2014E	2015E	2016E	2017E	2018E
Cash flows from operating activities											
Net income	882.3	1,005.9	939.9	762.3	829.1	1,006.7	414.0	413.0	412.2	411.5	410.8
Depreciation	254.5	255.2	295.7	217.6	221.5	299.6	297.4	309.2	321.0	332.9	344.8
Amortization	48.3	43.4	47.1	34.0	34.9	48.0	30.0	30.0	30.0	30.0	30.0
Amortization of identifiable intangible assets	0.0	0.0	0.0	0.0	0.0	0.0					
Deferred tax (benefit) / provision	220.5	153.7	(94.8)	(71.5)	(59.7)	(83.0)	342.4	342.4	342.4	342.4	342.4
Net losses on divestitures	44.9	0.0	0.0	0.0	19.8	19.8	(83.0)	(83.0)	(83.0)	(83.0)	(83.0)
Impairment of assets held for sale	0.0	0.0	0.0	0.0	36.0	36.0	0.0	0.0	0.0	0.0	0.0
Pension contributions	(539.9)	(22.4)	(23.5)	(15.5)	(53.3)	(61.2)	(80.0)	(80.0)	(80.0)	(80.0)	(80.0)
Asset write-downs from fiscal 2012 productivity initiatives	0.0	0.0	58.7	0.0	0.0	58.7	0.0	0.0	0.0	0.0	0.0
Other items, net	90.9	98.2	75.4	87.9	22.7	10.2	10.2	10.2	10.2	10.2	10.2
Changes in operating working capital											

Changes in receivables	121.4	(91.1)	171.8	46.1	(148.1)	(22.4)	(3.3)	(4.4)	(4.4)	(4.4)	(4.5)
Changes in inventories	48.5	(80.8)	60.9	(126.6)	(158.5)	29.1	(3.8)	(5.8)	(5.8)	(5.9)	(5.9)
Changes in prepaid expenses and other current assets	2.1	(1.7)	(11.6)	(13.7)	5.7	7.8	1.8	(1.0)	(1.0)	(1.0)	(1.0)
Changes in accounts payable	(2.8)	233.3	(72.4)	(182.3)	(42.9)	67.1	3.7	5.2	5.2	5.2	5.2
Changes in accrued liabilities	96.5	(60.9)	(20.0)	(77.0)	(5.4)	51.6	(7.3)	3.7	3.8	3.8	3.8
Changes in accrued income taxes	(5.1)	50.7	65.8	82.3	(24.9)	(41.4)	(23.8)	(0.1)	(0.1)	(0.1)	(0.1)
Net changes in operating working capital	260.6	49.5	194.6	(271.2)	(374.0)	91.8	(32.7)	(2.5)	(2.5)	(2.5)	(2.5)
Total cash provided by (used for) operating activities	1,262.2	1,583.6	743.5	1,493.1	676.9	1,426.5	898.3	939.3	950.3	961.5	972.7
Cash flows from investing activities											
Capital expenditures (CAPEX)	(277.6)	(335.6)	(418.7)	(274.5)	(259.2)	(403.4)	(469.5)	(471.4)	(473.3)	(475.2)	(477.1)
CAPEX % of revenue						4.0%	4.0%	4.0%	4.0%	4.0%	4.0%
Proceeds from disposale of property, plant & equipment	96.5	13.2	9.8	6.9	17.3	20.2	0.0	0.0	0.0	0.0	0.0

(continued)

TABLE 12.11 (*Continued*)

Consolidated Statements of Cash Flows (in US$ millions except per share amounts)

Period Ending	Actuals			Last Twelve Months (LTM)					Estimates			
	2010A	2011A	2012A	9Mo. 2012	9Mo. 2013	LTM	2014E	2015E	2016E	2017E	2018E
Acquisitions net of cash acquired	(11.4)	(618.3)	(3.3)	0.7	16.8	12.9	0.0	0.0	0.0	0.0	0.0
Proceeds from divestitures	18.6	1.9	3.8	(3.3)	0.0	7.1	0.0	0.0	0.0	0.0	0.0
Sale of short-term investments	0.0	0.0	56.8	48.0	0.0	8.8	0.0	0.0	0.0	0.0	0.0
Change in restricted cash	192.7	(5.0)	(39.1)	(39.1)	4.0	4.0	(39.1)	(39.1)	(39.1)	(39.1)	(39.1)
Other items, net	(5.4)	(5.8)	(11.4)	(9.4)	(10.3)	(12.3)	(12.3)	(12.3)	(12.3)	(12.3)	(12.3)
Total cash provided by (used for) investing activities	13.4	(949.6)	(402.0)	(270.6)	(231.4)	(362.7)	(520.9)	(522.7)	(524.6)	(526.5)	(528.4)
Cash flows from financing activities											
Revolver borrowings (repayments)	0.0	0.0	0.0	0.0	0.0	0.0	0.0	0.0	0.0	0.0	0.0
Term facilities borrowings (repayments)	0.0	0.0	0.0	0.0	0.0	0.0	0.0	0.0	0.0	0.0	0.0
The notes borrowings (repayments)	0.0	0.0	0.0	0.0	0.0	0.0	0.0	0.0	0.0	0.0	0.0
Common Equity	0.0	0.0	0.0	0.0	0.0	0.0	0.0	0.0	0.0	0.0	0.0
Preferred Equity	0.0	0.0	0.0	0.0	0.0	0.0	0.0	0.0	0.0	0.0	0.0

Proceeds (payments) of long-term debt	(183.3)	184.1	471.5	479.4	(14.6)	(22.5)	0.0	0.0	0.0	0.0	0.0
Net payments on commercial paper and short-term debt	(427.2)	(193.2)	(42.5)	(56.9)	31.1	45.5	0.0	0.0	0.0	0.0	0.0
Dividends (including preferred dividends)	(533.6)	(579.6)	(619.1)	(464.9)	(499.7)	(653.9)	0.0	0.0	0.0	0.0	0.0
Purchase of treasury stock	0.0	(70.0)	(201.9)	74.5	96.1	(180.3)	0.0	0.0	0.0	0.0	0.0
Exercise of stock options	67.4	154.8	82.7	(201.9)	(139.1)	145.5	0.0	0.0	0.0	0.0	0.0
Acquisitions of subsidiary shares from non-controlling interests	(62.1)	(6.3)	(54.8)	(54.8)	(80.1)	(80.1)	0.0	0.0	0.0	0.0	0.0
Earn-out settlement	0.0	0.0	0.0	0.0	(44.5)	(44.5)	0.0	0.0	0.0	0.0	0.0
Other items, net	(9.1)	27.8	1.3	5.5	1.6	(2.6)	(9.1)	(9.1)	(9.1)	(9.1)	(9.1)
Total cash provided by (used for) financing activities	(1,147.9)	(482.5)	(362.8)	(219.2)	(649.3)	(792.9)	(9.1)	(9.1)	(9.1)	(9.1)	(9.1)
Effect of exchange rate on cash and cash equivalents	(17.6)	89.6	(122.1)	(129.1)	(26.0)	(19.1)	(122.1)	(122.1)	(122.1)	(122.1)	(122.1)
Total change in cash and cash equivalents	110.1	241.1	606.1	124.6	(229.8)	251.8	246.1	285.3	294.5	303.7	313.1
Supplemental Data:											
Cash flow before debt paydown							246.1	285.3	294.5	303.7	313.1

TABLE 12.12 Heinz Consolidated Balance Sheets

Consolidated Balance Sheets (in US$ millions except per share amounts)

On January 27	2013PF	2014E	2015E	2016E	2017E	2018E
				Estimates		
Assets						
Current assets:						
Cash and cash equivalents	0.0	246.1	531.5	825.9	1,129.7	1,442.7
Receivables	1,098.8	1,102.1	1,106.5	1,110.9	1,115.4	1,119.8
Inventories	1,448.4	1,452.2	1,458.0	1,463.8	1,469.7	1,475.6
Prepaid expenses and other current assets	261.1	259.2	260.2	261.3	262.3	263.4
Total current assets	**2,808.2**	**3,059.6**	**3,356.2**	**3,662.0**	**3,977.0**	**4,301.5**
Property, plant and equipment, net	2,428.2	2,600.3	2,762.5	2,914.8	3,057.1	3,189.3
Goodwill	18,513.4	18,513.4	18,513.4	18,513.4	18,513.4	18,513.4
Trademarks, net	1,050.9	1,020.9	990.9	960.9	930.9	900.9
Other intangibles, net	5,519.3	5,176.9	4,834.5	4,492.1	4,149.6	3,807.2
Other noncurrent assets	1,053.6	1,094.8	1,135.9	1,177.1	1,218.3	1,259.4
Total assets	**31,373.5**	**31,465.8**	**31,593.4**	**31,720.2**	**31,846.2**	**31,971.7**
Liabilities						
Current liabilities:						
Short-term debt	0.0	0.0	0.0	0.0	0.0	0.0
Portion of long term debt due within one year	0.0	0.0	0.0	0.0	0.0	0.0
Revolving line of credit	0.0	0.0	0.0	0.0	0.0	0.0
Accounts payable	1,287.8	1,291.5	1,296.7	1,301.8	1,307.1	1,312.3
Accrued marketing and other accrued liabilities	944.0	936.7	940.5	944.2	948.0	951.8
Income taxes	91.3	67.5	67.3	67.2	67.1	67.0
Total current liabilities	**2,323.1**	**2,295.7**	**2,304.5**	**2,313.3**	**2,322.1**	**2,331.1**

Term facilities	10,500.0	10,500.0	10,500.0	10,500.0	10,500.0	10,500.0
The notes	2,100.0	2,100.0	2,100.0	2,100.0	2,100.0	2,100.0
Long term debt	0.0	0.0	0.0	0.0	0.0	0.0
Deferred income taxes	776.7	693.7	610.7	527.7	444.7	361.7
Nonpension postretirement benefits	230.9	230.9	230.9	230.9	230.9	230.9
Other noncurrent liabilities	504.8	424.8	344.8	264.8	184.8	104.8
Redeemable noncontrolling interest	28.7	28.7	28.7	28.7	28.7	28.7
Total liabilities	16,464.1	16,273.7	16,119.5	15,965.3	15,811.2	15,657.1
Total equity						
Shareholder's Equity						
Capital stock	0.0	0.0	0.0	0.0	0.0	0.0
Common equity investment	8,240.0	8,240.0	8,240.0	8,240.0	8,240.0	8,240.0
Preferred equity investment	8,000.0	8,000.0	8,000.0	8,000.0	8,000.0	8,000.0
Retained earnings	(1,381.1)	(967.2)	(554.2)	(142.0)	269.5	680.3
Treasury stock	0.0	0.0	0.0	0.0	0.0	0.0
Accumulated other comprehensive loss	0.0	(131.2)	(262.5)	(393.7)	(525.0)	(656.2)
Total shareholder's equity	14,858.9	15,141.6	15,423.3	15,704.3	15,984.5	16,264.1
Noncontrolling interest	50.5	50.5	50.5	50.5	50.5	50.5
Total equity	14,909.4	15,192.1	15,473.9	15,754.8	16,035.1	16,314.6
Total liabilities & equity	31,373.5	31,465.8	31,593.4	31,720.2	31,846.2	31,971.7
Supplemental Data:						
Balance? (Y/N)	Y	Y	Y	Y	Y	Y

CHAPTER 13

Leveraged Buyout Returns

Now that the model is complete, we are ready to begin estimating the expected return of the investment in the entity to 3G Capital and Berkshire Hathaway. As discussed in the beginning of the book, the returns assume there will be some sort of exit event in the business. Although we have built a five-year model of the business, we are not certain of any intent to actually exit the business after five years. However, calculating returns under the assumption that there will be an exit does give an indication of value. So even if 3G Capital or Berkshire Hathaway does not have any intent to sell the business after five years, they should be performing a similar what-if analysis to at least determine the value of their investment.

EXIT VALUE

As mentioned in Chapter 3, the exit is most likely based on an earnings before interest and taxes (EBIT) or earnings before interest, taxes, depreciation, and amortization (EBITDA) multiple. We can find appropriate exit multiples by looking at comparable companies or historical transactions. However, it is common to take a more conservative approach looking at the purchase multiples of the business. Whatever multiple was paid for the business can be used as the exit multiple. If we paid 5x EBITDA for a business today, we would hope to sell it for at least 5x EBITDA five years from now. Although the multiple is the same, we hope we have successfully grown EBITDA in five years so that the exit value will be higher. We further hope that we can in fact sell the business for a higher multiple and thus achieve an even greater return, but we do not want to count on this happening. This is, of course, a conservative method only if the purchase did not take place at a time when the company was extremely overvalued. We assume any rational investor would not perform such an overvalued buyout, so based on that rationale, this would be a conservative method. As a precaution, it is helpful to cross-reference the purchase multiple with comparable companies and precedent transactions. We would recommend rereading the high-level walk-through of a leveraged buyout (LBO) analysis found in Chapter 3 to better prepare yourself for understanding how this full-scale model that we build will be utilized to estimate returns.

We can now calculate our purchase multiples to be conservatively used as exit multiples. Let's move to the Assumptions tab. Here we notice the "Purchase Multiples" box beginning in Cell B11. We can calculate the enterprise value of the business by adding the purchase price to the net debt; the total consideration paid. The enterprise value (EV) based on a purchase multiple is calculated from the purchase price, not the market capitalization. So, in Cell C12, we can have "=J6+J7"

This should give us $27,458.9, which can be used to calculate EBIT and EBITDA multiples. Purchase multiples should be calculated around estimated time of purchase, which we have simplified to be January 2013. We calculate these multiples based on operating metrics at that time (our last twelve months [LTM] metrics). So for the "Implied EV/LTM EBITDA," or Cell C13, we will divide the enterprise value by the LTM EBITDA. Cell C13 will read "=C12/Financials!I21." We can do the same in Cell C13, but we use the LTM EBIT as the denominator, so Cell C13 will read "=C12/Financials!I27." This should give us 14.4x and 17.6x for the EBITDA multiple and the EBIT multiple, respectively. See Table 13.1.

We will use the 14.4x EBITDA multiple as our exit. We can link this calculated value into the Returns tab. Or we can select the Returns tab, and locate and highlight Cell F6. Here we can type "=" and then toggle over to the Assumptions tab, select the implied EV/LTM EBITDA multiple, and hit Enter. If done correctly, Cell F6 in the "returns" table should read "=Assumptions!C13."

The rest of the Returns tab lays out how we will structure the exit and subsequent payouts to the debt holders and equity holders. In short, we will calculate the exit, add in any cash left over in the business, and then subtract all remaining debts and obligations, including preferred security holders. This is the remaining value left to common shareholders.

TABLE 13.1   Purchase Multiples

Purchase Multiples	
Enterprise value	27,458.9
Implied EV/LTM EBITDA	14.4
Implied EV/LTM EBIT	17.6

In this chapter will we calculate only the return to 3G Capital. This is a simpler process than calculating the return to Berkshire Hathaway, as 3G has only a common equity investment. In the advanced Part Three section of this book, we will learn how to model in preferred securities with dividend payments. Only then can we calculate the returns to Berkshire Hathaway.

The main focus of Part Two is to ensure that you have a solid understanding of a full-scale LBO model without one-off added complexities such as preferred securities and dividends. I decided to layer this book in increasingly advanced parts; otherwise it would become too convoluted. I strongly recommend reviewing Part Two to make sure you fully understand the mechanics of a full-scale LBO before attempting to tackle the more advanced Part Three. Additionally, review the chapter-end questions and build the homework LBO located on the book's website at www.wiley.com/go/pignatarolbo.

Now that we have the exit multiple, we can go ahead and calculate the estimated exit value. The exit value is the estimated sale value assuming we would actually sell the business in year 5. So we will multiply this exit multiple by the 2018 (EBITDA + Management Fee). Notice the "+ Management Fee"; this is a tiny nuance often adjusted in leveraged buyouts. We are not sure if the buyers would in fact charge themselves an additional management fee, but if they would, that management fee would clearly not exist if the business was sold. In other words, if 3G, for example, charged itself $1 million per year while owning the business, once 3G sells its stake in the company, it would clearly not charge itself that fee anymore. So we would sell the business at a multiple of EBITDA adding back that management fee.

So let's calculate this value in Cell K7 in the Returns tab.

2018 Exit Value (Cell K7)

Excel Keystrokes	Description
Type "="	Enters into "formula" mode
Type "("	Groups EBITDA + Management Fee
Select Financials tab Cell N21	2018 EBITDA
Type "+"	Adds
Select Financials tab Cell N15	2018 management fee
Type ")"	Closes grouping of EBITDA + Management Fee
Type "*"	Multiplies
Select Returns tab Cell F6	EBITDA multiple
Hit Enter	End
Formula result	=(Financials!N21+Financials!N15)*F6

This should give us an estimated exit value of $28,515.1 million. Notice right away that this is not very much higher that the purchase value. This could cause a problem: not much growth to support adequate returns. However, note we are using very conservative Revenue and EBITDA growth assumptions. We will tweak this later. Further, this value does not yet represent the return to 3G. Once the company is sold, the lenders and the preferred security holders need to be paid. Only then can we determine how much money 3G will actually receive. So let's calculate on.

We need to adjust this exit value for the following items:

- Cash.
- Revolving line of credit.
- Term facilities.
- The notes.
- Preferred equity.

Rows 8 to 13 in the Returns tab lay out the adjustments to get to the equity to common shareholders. (Note: We will properly calculate preferred dividends in Part Three.) We can simply pull these items in from the company balance sheet in 2018. For example, the cash value in Cell K8 we can pull in from the 2018 cash on the balance sheet (Financials tab Cell N164). Cell K8 will read "=Financials!N164." We will continue to pull in the relevant items as per Table 13.2.

As noted, we have not yet modeled out the preferred dividends. According to the preliminary proxy document, Berkshire will be receiving a 9 percent annual dividend on its preferred securities. We will model this out to properly handle the flows through the income statement, cash flow statement, and balance sheet. For now, we made a quick estimate for what the total dividend payout will be:

$$\text{Preferred Securities} \times \text{Dividend Rate (\%)} \times \text{Years}$$

TABLE 13.2 Formulas for Equity to Common Shareholders

Formula Cell (in Returns Tab)	Formula
K8	=Financials!N164
K9	=Financials!N179
K10	=Financials!N184
K11	=Financials!N185
K12	=Financials!N196
K13	"=9%*K12*5"

or $8,000 × 9% × 5, which gives us $3,600. Again, we will more properly model this out in Part Three, but this shortcut will be enough for now to give us a return estimate for 3G.

We can now calculate the total equity to common shareholders by taking the exit value, adding the cash, and subtracting the debts, preferreds, and dividends. Cell K14 will read: "=K7+K8-K9-K10-K11-K12-K13" (note that we are adding the cash and subtracting the rest). See Table 13.3.

RETURNS TO 3G CAPITAL

Now we can proceed with calculating the returns to 3G. We will use the "IRR" Excel formula, which calculates returns of values listed across a row. In order to properly calculate the return, we need the entry value (the original 3G investment) pulled in as a negative value; the negative value indicates money invested. This value comes from the sources of cash. In Cell F15 in the Returns tab we can link in the 3G investment by typing "-Assumptions!F14" (note the negative).

Next we need to represent the equity returned to 3G. As far as we know, based on public information, 3G's equity investment will represent

TABLE 13.3 Equity to Common Shareholders

Investment Returns (in US$ millions except per share amounts)						
			Estimates			
Period Ending	LTM	2014E	2015E	2016E	2017E	2018E
Exit Multiple	14.4x					
Enterprise value [(EBITDA + Management Fee) × EBITDA multiple]						$28,515.1
Plus cash						1,442.7
Less revolving line of credit						0.0
Less term facilities						10,500.0
Less the notes						2,100.0
Less preferred equity						8,000.0
Less preferred dividends						3,600.0
Equity to common shareholders						$5,757.8

70 percent of the business. This may change slightly, however, if an equity component attached to other securities such as the preferred securities (which we assumed will be 0 percent up to this point) would hold some value and dilute the 70 percent stake down. Again, the 70 percent is represented in the sources, so as we gain more knowledge of the transaction we can simply make the adjustment there. We will multiply 70 percent to the Equity to Common in Cell K15. Or, K15 will read: "=K14*Assumptions!H14." Notice we put the return value in Column K, the 2018 column. The IRR formula notes periods (years) by how many columns are between the entry and exit values. However, in order for the IRR formula to properly count the columns in between as periods, we need to put some value in those cells: "0." So we should hard-code "0" in Cells G15 through J15. See Table 13.4.

TABLE 13.4 3G Returns

Investment Returns (in US$ millions except per share amounts)							
	Actuals		**Estimates**				
Period Ending	**LTM**	**2014E**	**2015E**	**2016E**	**2017E**	**2018E**	
Exit Multiple	14.4x						
Enterprise value [(EBITDA + Management Fee) × EBITDA multiple]						28,515.1	
Plus cash						1,442.7	
Less revolving line of credit						0.0	
Less term facilities						10,500.0	
Less the notes						2,100.0	
Less preferred equity						8,000.0	
Less preferred dividends						3,600.0	
Equity to common						$5,757.8	
Return to 3G	(4,120.0)	0.0	0.0	0.0	0.0	4,030.5	
IRR	(0.4%)						
Return multiple	1.0x						

We can now calculate the IRR formula in Cell F16.

3G IRR (Cell F16)

Excel Keystrokes	Description
Type "="	Enters into "formula" mode
Type "IRR("	Begins IRR formula
Select Cell F15	Entry value
Type ":"	Indicates we will be selecting a range of cells
Select Cell K15	Exit value, and the end of the range
Type ")"	Closes IRR formula
Hit Enter	End
Formula result	=IRR(F15:K15)

This gives us a –0.4 percent return. Such a return does not look good for 3G. However, note that we have used some very conservative revenue and EBITDA growth assumptions. Before discussing this further, let's calculate the return multiple. The return multiple is another popular way to look at the return on an investment. The return multiple is simply the exit value divided by the entry value. This basically shows how many times your investment is returned. For example, if your investment was $100, and you received a $1,000 return, that is a 10x return on investment (1,000/100). We can calculate this in Cell F17 simply by dividing the exit by negative the entry value. We need to negate the entry value because we had pulled it in as a negative. So Cell F17 will read "=K15/-F15." This should give you 1.0x return, also not very good. So far 3G is returning almost exactly what they put in 5 years later. See Table 13.4.

There are several potential factors contributing to such low returns, the greatest being the lack of EBITDA growth. Let's home in on the three ways a leveraged buyout creates value:

1. EBITDA improvements.
2. Multiple expansion.
3. Debt pay-down.

EBITDA Improvements

If you recall from Chapter 3, when discussing revenue growth, we kept in line with conservative Street estimates that suggested the growth will not be greater than ~1 percent. We would assume that both 3G and Berkshire believe they can further EBITDA growth beyond such low estimates.

Fairness Opinions

To get additional guidance on this, it is recommended to consult a fairness opinion. A fairness opinion is a professional evaluation by an investment bank or other third party as to whether the terms of a merger, acquisition, buyback, or spin-off are fair. This analysis on the business can be found in the preliminary proxy report. In the latest proxy report (at the time of writing this book) posted on March 4, 2013, there is a section beginning on page 59 entitled "Opinion of BofA Merrill Lynch." This is a fairness opinion. The first paragraph reads:

> *Heinz has retained BofA Merrill Lynch to act as Heinz's financial advisor in connection with the merger. BofA Merrill Lynch is an internationally recognized investment banking firm which is regularly engaged in the valuation of businesses and securities in connection with mergers and acquisitions, negotiated underwritings, secondary distributions of listed and unlisted securities, private placements and valuations for corporate and other purposes. Heinz selected BofA Merrill Lynch to act as Heinz's financial advisor in connection with the merger on the basis of BofA Merrill Lynch's experience in transactions similar to the merger, its reputation in the investment community and its familiarity with Heinz and its business.*

> **(Heinz Proxy Report, March 4, 2013, pages 59ff)**

And further, to clarify the fairness opinion definition, the next paragraph in the proxy reads:

> *On February 13, 2013, at a meeting of the Heinz Board held to evaluate the merger, BofA Merrill Lynch delivered to the Heinz Board an oral opinion, which was confirmed by delivery of a written opinion dated February 13, 2013, to the effect that, as of the date of the opinion and based on and subject to various assumptions and limitations described in its opinion, the merger consideration to be received by holders of Heinz common stock was fair, from a financial point of view, to such holders.*

This is one of several fairness opinions located in the report. Heinz had also retained Centerview, which detailed its fairness opinion in the report. There is also a fairness opinion done by Moelis.

There are a couple of interesting sections that are helpful in analyzing further the way we modeled our potential returns, one being the financial projections. There's a note on page 73 of the Proxy Report that reads:

> *Heinz does not generally publish detailed business plans and strategies or make external disclosures of its anticipated financial position or results of operations other than providing, from time to time, estimated ranges of certain expected financial results and operational metrics in its regular earnings press releases and other investor materials. In connection with the evaluation of a possible transaction, Heinz's management prepared a forecast for fiscal year 2013 (which forecast included seven months of actual results and is referred to as the "2013 Forecast") and two sets of projections for the following five fiscal years. The first set of projections (the "Projections Excluding M&A") assumed that Heinz would not make any acquisitions in emerging markets during the time period covered, and the second set of projections (the "Projections Including M&A") assumed that Heinz would continue to complete bolt-on acquisitions in emerging markets during the time period covered in line with recent practice. The 2013 Forecast, the Projections Excluding M&A and the Projections Including M&A are collectively referred to as the "Financial Forecasts." None of the Financial Forecasts were intended for public disclosure.*

This is stating that Heinz management has provided two sets of financial projections. One including M&A activity, and one excluding M&A activity. The difference is the projections including M&A activity assumes the new buyers will pursue a strategy of making further acquisitions to increase revenue growth. It is our choice whether to use the including M&A projections, which would be more aggressive, or to use the excluding, which would be more conservative. Let's use the more aggressive assumptions for now just to see how the new buyers are thinking about returns of the business. Note the differences between those two cases are not too significant. Ideally we would have a set of various scenarios toggling between different revenue assumptions, but in my opinion the most conservative is the case we have right now—keeping the street estimates. Also note if we are assuming additional M&A activity we really should be modeling such bolt on acquisitions. However, this is beyond the scope of this book and reserved for the next book "Mergers and Acquisitions: A practical guide to investment banking and private equity." Found on page 77 of the Proxy Report we have the following projections. (See Figure 13.1.)

Here we notice the revenue growth is slightly higher than what we have projected. It could be that the buyers are estimating the revenue growth to

Projection Including M&A

The following table summarizes the Projection Including M&A (including the 2013 Forecast) that were provided to the Heinz Board:

| | For Fiscal Year Ending April, | | | | | |
(Dollars in millions, except per share data)	2013E	2014P	2015P	2016P	2017P	2018P
Revenue	$11,675	$12,291	$12,975	$13,618	$14,461	$15,399
EBIT[1]	1,705	1,845	1,990	2,105	2,268	2,449
Fully diluted earnings per share	$ 3.58	$ 3.81	$ 3.89	$ 4.10	$ 4.44	$ 4.82

[1] Non-GAAP measure. For this purpose, EBIT represents net income before net interest expense, minority interest expense, and income tax.

FIGURE 13.1 Company Projections

be slightly higher than the ~1 percent. If we increase our revenue growth to 5.5 percent, it will come closer to the revenue numbers listed in the fairness opinion. Let's make that change and see if it increases the returns. We want to know how the buyers are thinking about driving value in the business. So, we can hard-code 5.5 percent in Cell J7 in the Financials tab and copy to the right. Note that lowering the percentage to 4.5 percent will match the revenue closer to the "Projections excluding M&A" values. Feel free to play around with different scenarios. Keeping the 5.5 percent revenue growth, we can now switch back to the Returns tab and see if this helps. We see our returns have increased to 19.7 percent. This is much better. Note that most private equity firms expect a ~20 to 25 percent hurdle. Now, EBITDA improvements do not have to come from revenue growth alone; they can also come from cost reduction. For example, the cost of goods sold (COGS) percentage of revenue had reduced from 62.7 percent in 2012 to 61.6 percent in the last twelve months (LTM) analysis. Let's assume there will be further cost reduction by changing our 2014E COGS percentage of revenue to 60 percent and copying to the right. Doing so would cause our overall return to leap to 26.2 percent. Reducing COGS therefore makes a huge impact to our returns. Neither 3G's nor Berkshire Hathaway's plan to achieve profitable returns has yet been clearly stated. But we can infer that the maximum revenue growth estimates must be achieved to scrape the low end of a 20%–25% expected return range. Or there must also be some cost-cutting initiatives in place for the company to achieve such expected returns.

There are two other areas where value can be created in a buyout. Let's look at them now.

MULTIPLE EXPANSION

Multiple expansion is the expectation that the implied value of the business will increase. This would result in an increase in the expected multiple one can sell the business for. If the company is exited in 2018 for a multiple higher than the 14.4x, then there will be significant additional profitability. We can easily test this in Cell F6 of the Returns tab. Right now it reads 14.4. Let's still use a version of the model with increased 5.5 percent growth and COGS reductions down to 60 percent of revenue. If the business is exited for 16x revenue as opposed to 14.4x, what would be the overall return? If we hard-code "16" into Cell F6 in the returns tab, we see the returns increase to 31.7 percent. This is much better; it is now even beyond the standard 20 to 25 percent hurdle.

How do we know if 3G and Berkshire will ever actually be able to exit the investment, and at what multiple? This may most likely remain a mystery until an exit actually happens. However, it is important to look at comparable company multiples and precedent transaction multiples. If such multiples are higher than the purchase price multiple of Heinz, for example, then the buyers have paid a low price for the business, and the likelihood that the multiple will increase closer to the range of other comparable companies is higher, which means the likelihood that 3G and Berkshire would be able to exit the business at a premium is higher.

On page 69 of the preliminary proxy report we find a comparable company analysis done by Moelis. See Figure 13.2.

This analysis indicates an LTM EV/EBITDA range of 9.3x to 13.0x. We can compare this to the 14.4x multiple paid for Heinz. However, the buyers have paid a 20 percent premium. Applying 20 percent to the comparable company range would give us 11.16x to 15.60x. It would be nice if, even at the 20 percent purchase premium, the multiple paid is in line with current market multiples, indicating the buyers paid for a company that was undervalued. This would increase the chances of a higher exit multiple. To get a better indication of other purchase price multiples, we can look at precedent transactions. On page 70 of the proxy report, Moelis has illustrated a precedent transactions analysis (see Figure 13.3).

Company	EV ($ in millions)	EV/EBITDA 2013E	P/E 2013E
Nestlé S.A.	$233,969	11.3x	17.6x
PepsiCo, Inc.	135,550	10.3x	16.5x
Unilever plc	123,112	10.5x	17.8x
Mondelēz International, Inc.	75,436	12.6x	17.6x
Group Danone S.A.	50,478	10.0x	16.0x
Kraft Foods Group, Inc.	37,387	11.1x	17.4x
General Mills, Inc.	37,561	10.4x	15.2x
Kellogg Company	29,064	10.8x	15.4x
The Hershey Company	19,605	12.5x	22.1x
ConAgra Foods, Inc.[1]	24,429	9.5x	12.8x
Campbell Soup Company	16,281	9.9x	14.6x
The J.M. Smucker Company	11,639	9.3x	16.2x
McCormick & Company, Inc.	9,614	13.0x	19.6x
Hormel Foods Corporation	$ 8,990	9.9x	18.0x

[1]Financial data were pro forma for the Ralcorp acquisition.

FIGURE 13.2   Comparable Company Analysis

We see that the LTM EV/EBITDA multiples range from 8.3x to 18.4x. The 14.4x we had calculated does fall within this range, but this is a very wide range of multiples. Again, it would have been better if the Heinz purchase multiple was lower, indicating that the company had been purchased at a discount, thus increasing the possibility of a higher exit multiple. It is also important to note that many of the transactions shown in the precedent transaction analysis were done in a different market environment—an inherent drawback of a precedent transactions analysis. It is also helpful to again cross-reference this analysis with the analyses in the Centerview and Bank of America fairness opinions. Further, it would be ideal to create your own comparable company and precedent transactions analysis. In conclusion, there is no major evidence supporting multiple expansion yet, so let's revert back to the 14.4x multiple. Make sure you have linked Cell F16 in the "Returns" tab back to cell C13 in the assumptions tab. It's not wrong to hard-code 14.4x instead, but if you do, some rounding differences may change your output from ours in the book.

Date Announced	Target	Acquirer	EV ($ in thousands)	EV/LTM EBITDA
Dec. 2012	Morningstar Foods, LLC	Saputo Inc.	$ 1,450	9.3x
Nov. 2012	Ralcorp Holdings, Inc.	ConAgra Foods, Inc.	6,775	12.1x
Feb. 2012	Pringles Business of Procter & Gamble Company	Kellogg Company	2,695	11.1x[1]
June. 2010	American Italian Pasta Co.	Ralcorp Holdings, Inc.	1,256	8.2x
Jan. 2010	North American Frozen Pizza Business of Kraft Food Global, Inc.	Nestlé S.A.	3,700	12.5x
Nov. 2009	Birds Eye Foods, Inc.	Pinnacle Foods Group, Inc.	1,371	9.5x
Sept. 2009	Cadbury Plc	Kraft Foods Inc.	21,395	13.3x
June 2008	The Folgers Coffee Company	The J.M. Smucker Company	3,398	8.8x
Apr. 2008	Wm. Wrigley Jr. Company	Mars, Incorporated	23,017	18.4x
Nov. 2007	Post Foods	Ralcorp Holdings, Inc.	2,642	11.3x[1]
July 2007	Global Biscuit Business of Groupe Danone S.A.	Kraft Foods Global, Inc.	7,174	13.6x[1]
Feb. 2007	Pinnacle Foods Group, Inc.	The Blackstone Group, L.P.	2,142	8.9x
Aug. 2006	European Frozen Foods Division of Unilever plc	Permira Advisors Ltd.	2,199	9.9x[1]
Aug. 2006	Chef America, Inc.	Nestlé S.A.	2,600	14.5x
Dec. 2002	Adams Confectionary Business of Pfizer Inc.	Cadbury Schweppes Plc	3,750	12.8x[1]
Oct. 2001	ThePillsbury Company	General Mills, Inc.	10,396	10.1x[2]
Dec. 2000	The Quaker Oats Company	PepsiCo, Inc.	14,010	15.6x
Oct. 2000	Keebler Foods Company	Kellogg Company	4,469	10.7x
June 2000	Nabisco Holdings Corp.	Philip Morris Companies Inc.	19,017	13.7x
June 2000	International Home Foods	ConAgra Foods, Inc.	2,909	8.5x
May 2000	Bestfoods	Unilever Plc	$23,503	15.4x

[1] Financial data were based on latest available fiscal year-end information, not latest quarter-end information.
[2] Financial data reflected revised deal terms pursuant to a second amended merger agreement.

FIGURE 13.3 Precedent Transactions Analysis

DEBT PAY-DOWN

The third and final way in which value is created in a buyout is by the cash being produced by the business over the years paying down debt. As debt is paid down, equity is created. The way we modeled the business, only about $200 million to $300 million of cash is generated each year. By increasing the revenue growth to 5.5 percent and reducing COGS percentage of revenue to 60 percent, that cash generation increases to between $450 million and $750 million each year. This is an improvement, but is not so significant as to make a dramatic impact on debt pay-down. We handle the paying down of debt at the end in the returns analysis when we subtract the net debt from the exit value. We can also model more periodic debt pay-downs in the debt schedule year over year to get additional savings on the reduction of interest. However, this will not make a dramatic difference to the overall IRR.

CONCLUSION

The company needs to significantly improve revenue growth to achieve their targets. Otherwise, significant cost-cutting initiatives must be in place to enhance returns. There is not enough cash to dramatically pay down debt, and we do not see evidence of huge multiple expansion. We also did not account for any fees or operating income, if any, that 3G may receive for managing the investment. This part of the buyers' plan had not been disclosed. Nor do we know what is in store for Heinz, and there could very well be some other angles that can take place to enhance the profitability of the company and turn the buyout into a lucrative investment.

Of course, the story for Berkshire Hathaway will be different. Berkshire has additional return potential based on the preferred securities. Part Three, Advanced LBOs, will give us an understanding of Berkshire Hathaway's returns. Before continuing on, we strongly recommend that you have a good handle on full-scale LBO modeling. You may want to reread this part and try to redo the model on your own, focusing only on the chapter-end solutions as a guide. Also do the homework leveraged buyout for additional practice. Modeling takes practice and must be exercised. Your understanding of the mechanics and concepts will be enhanced as you build and rebuild. Once you are more comfortable, then move on to Part Three.

See the file NYSF_Leveraged_Buyout_Model_Solution_Part_Two.xls for the solution of the model up to this point. In this solution, we have kept the management projected 5.5% revenue growth, but have changed the COGS % of Revenue back to the 61.6%. We also have a second model solution, "NYSF_Leveraged_Buyout_Model_Solution_Part_Three.xls," for Part Three.

Three

Advanced Leveraged Buyout Techniques

In this third part of the book, we focus on several advanced structures and further detail in the Heinz case. As this is a live case, the data are always changing. Newer proxy reports will be posted upon transaction close containing more explicit detail than what we have been given in the preliminary proxy. Additional adjustments to the levels of debt raised, the purchase price, or adjustments to line items on the balance sheet can change for example. Rest assured, however, the major concepts will not change, and these adjustments will not be crucial to understanding leveraged buyout mechanics.

To further your LBO skill set, Part Three steps through the second method of accelerating depreciation, and employs a switch to adjust between the two common methods of depreciation—straight-line and accelerated.

We will also model out preferred securities and dividends as adjustable whether they are paid out when incurred or deferred. This will help us assess the returns to Berkshire Hathaway.

Finally, we will discuss advanced debt structures, including paid-in-kind (PIK) securities, and we will learn how to handle the amortization of debt fees, which may be of benefit for those looking for more complex analyses.

Note, if you are matching numbers in your model with the book, we are using the original version of the model with 0.4 percent revenue growth, 61.7 percent cost of goods sold (COGS) as a percentage of revenue, and the 14.4x EV/EBITDA purchase multiple as the exit multiple (make sure that exit multiple is actually linked from the assumptions tab, not hard-coded).

Continue building out the current model, but we recommend saving it under a different name. Refer to the solution model in the advanced section, "NYSF_Leveraged_Buyout_Model_Solution_Part_Three.xls."

CHAPTER 14

Accelerated Depreciation

As mentioned in Chapter 9, the U.S. tax method for depreciating assets is the Modified Accelerated Cost Recovery System (MACRS). This is an accelerated method of depreciation. Because the straight-line method is more universal and better demonstrates the core uses of depreciating assets, we had originally built the Heinz model using the straight-line method. However, in such a buyout scenario as the one we are studying, where the company will be private, it will most likely no longer be required to produce generally accepted accounting principles (GAAP) financials. If a private Heinz only reports tax statements, then it may depreciate assets using the MACRS schedule. In such landmark deals, however, rules constantly change. So, as there is a bit of uncertainty, we will build both and incorporate a switch to toggle between the two possible methods. Once we know more detail about the transaction, we can toggle the switch accordingly. This will help us determine if the difference even makes a significant enough impact to the overall returns. If it does not, then we know this is not one of the primary assumptions that we need to focus on.

MACRS

The MACRS system is the current tax depreciation method in the United States.

> *Most business and investment property placed in service after 1986 is depreciated using MACRS.*
>
> (www.irs.gov)

This may be a good time to review Chapter 9, which gives a conceptual overview of the MACRS method. In this advanced section we will focus on the modeling and the toggle switch. Using the MACRS method of depreciation, we first need to input the percentages relating to the useful lives of both the net property, plant, and equipment (PP&E) and the capital expenditures

TABLE 14.1   MACRS Midquarter Convention Placed in Service in First Quarter

Year	Depreciation Rate for Recovery Period					
	3-year	5-year	7-year	10-year	15-year	20-year
1	58.33%	35.00%	25.00%	17.50%	8.75%	6.563%
2	27.78	26.00	21.43	16.50	9.13	7.000
3	12.35	15.60	15.31	13.20	8.21	6.482
4	1.54	11.01	10.93	10.56	7.39	5.996
5		11.01	8.75	8.45	6.65	5.546
6		1.38	8.74	6.76	5.99	5.130
7			8.75	6.55	5.90	4.746
8			1.09	6.55	5.91	4.459
9				6.56	5.90	4.459
10				6.55	5.91	4.459
11				0.82	5.90	4.459
12					5.91	4.460
13					5.90	4.459
14					5.91	4.460
15					5.90	4.459
16					0.74	4.460
17						4.459
18						4.460
19						4.459
20						4.460
21						0.565

(CAPEX). We will use the midquarter convention table where the asset is placed in service in the first quarter (Table 14.1).

We have estimated that the combined assets have a useful life of 8.5 years (see Chapter 9). There is no schedule for an asset with an 8.5-year useful life, so we will use the next closest above, the 10-year MACRS schedule. For the CAPEX, at a useful life of 40 years, we can use the maximum 20-year MACRS schedule.

We recommend adding the MACRS depreciation rates directly into the depreciation schedule section of the model, so let's first add 16 rows above Row 222.

As a reminder, we can easily add rows by first selecting any cell in Row 222. We can then highlight the entire row by holding down "Shift" and hitting the space bar. Let go of those keys, and hold down "Ctrl" and tap "Shift" + "+" 16 times (or you may not have to include "Shift" if you have a single "+" key, because "Shift" + "=" is the same as a "+"). Once you have 16 empty rows, let's label them as we have in Table 14.2. You can also see

TABLE 14.2 MACRS Template

Depreciation (in US$ millions except per share amounts)					
			Estimates		
Period Ending	2014E	2015E	2016E	2017E	2018E
Property, plant, and equipment beginning of year	$2,428.2				
Capital expenditures beginning of year	469.5	$471.4	$473.3	$475.2	$477.1
Straight-line depreciation					
Years (PP&E)	8.5				
Years (CAPEX)	40	40	40	40	40
Existing PP&E	285.7	285.7	285.7	285.7	285.7
2014 CAPEX	11.7	11.7	11.7	11.7	11.7
2015 CAPEX		11.8	11.8	11.8	11.8
2016 CAPEX			11.8	11.8	11.8
2017 CAPEX				11.9	11.9
2018 CAPEX					11.9
Total straight-line depreciation	$ 297.4	$ 309.2	$ 321.0	$ 332.9	$ 344.8
MACRS Depreciation Rates					
Existing PP&E					
2014 CAPEX					
2015 CAPEX					
2016 CAPEX					
2017 CAPEX					
2018 CAPEX					
MACRS Depreciation					
Existing PP&E					
2014 CAPEX					
2015 CAPEX					
2016 CAPEX					
2017 CAPEX					
2018 CAPEX					
Total MACRS depreciation					
Depreciation used					
Amortization	30.0	30.0	30.0	30.0	30.0
Amortization of identifiable intangible assets	342.4	342.4	342.4	342.4	342.4
Total depreciation and amortization	$669.8	$681.6	$693.4	$705.3	$717.2

the solution model on the website. We have effectively created two sections; one section, entitled "MACRS depreciation rates," will handle the MACRS percentages, and the other, "MACRS depreciation," will contain the calculated depreciation.

Now we can simply hard-code the MACRS depreciation rates for the PP&E into Row 223, and for the 2014 CAPEX into Row 224. Be sure you have formatted the percentages as per Table 14.3.

Now the 2015 CAPEX will not begin depreciating until 2015, so our first depreciation rate will be entered into Cell K225. We can continue entering depreciation rates for the remaining CAPEX projections (see Table 14.4).

We can now begin projecting the depreciation. We simply multiply the base asset value by the respective rate in each year. So we will multiply the PP&E value of $2,428.2 in Cell J210 by the 17.5 percent in Cell J223. So, Cell J230 will read "=J210*J223."

This will give us depreciation expense of $424.9. In the next year, we will multiply the same $2,428.2 PP&E value by the next year's 2015 MACRS rate. We want to reference the same J210 cell, but with the new Cell K223 rate. So the formula in Cell K230 will read "=J210*K223." You may notice it is wise to anchor the J210 reference in the previous formula. This way, you can simply copy the formula to the right; the reference to the PP&E (Cell J210) will stay fixed, but the reference to the MACRS rates will shift as we copy the formula to the right. You can add a "$" to the original formula in Cell J210 so the formula reads "=$J210*J223" instead of "=J210*J223" and copy this formula to the right (see Table 14.5).

Once we have this complete, we can calculate the depreciation for the 2014 CAPEX. Again, we want to start with, and anchor, the reference to the 2014 CAPEX in Cell J211, and we can multiply this by the depreciation percentage each year in Row 224. So, Cell J231 will read "=$J211*J224."

TABLE 14.3 MACRS Percentages through 2014 CAPEX

Depreciation					
		Estimates			
Period Ending	2014E	2015E	2016E	2017E	2018E
MACRS Depreciation Rates					
Existing PP&E	17.500%	16.500%	13.200%	10.560%	8.450%
2014 CAPEX	6.563%	7.000%	6.482%	5.996%	5.546%
2015 CAPEX					
2016 CAPEX					
2017 CAPEX					
2018 CAPEX					

TABLE 14.4 MACRS Percentages through 2018 CAPEX

Depreciation					
			Estimates		
Period Ending	2014E	2015E	2016E	2017E	2018E
MACRS Depreciation Rates					
Existing PP&E	17.500%	16.500%	13.200%	10.560%	8.450%
2014 CAPEX	6.563%	7.000%	6.482%	5.996%	5.546%
2015 CAPEX		6.563%	7.000%	6.482%	5.996%
2016 CAPEX			6.563%	7.000%	6.482%
2017 CAPEX				6.563%	7.000%
2018 CAPEX					6.563%

If we copy this to the right, again the numerator will stay fixed and the denominator will shift. The 2015 CAPEX depreciation will not begin depreciating until 2015, so we will begin entering formulas one column to the right, Column K. We can repeat this process with each projected CAPEX year, making sure to begin by shifting one column to the right for each projected year. Refer to the guide in Table 14.6 and the solution in Table 14.7.

For a more detailed step-through on building a MACRS depreciation schedule, refer to the book *Financial Modeling and Valuation: A Practical Guide to Investment Banking and Private Equity*.

We can now total the depreciation expense in each year summing Rows 230 through 235, so in Cell J236 we will have "=SUM(J230:J235)." We can copy this formula to the right. (See Table 14.7.)

TABLE 14.5 Projected MACRS Depreciation for PP&E

Depreciation (in US$ millions except per share amounts)					
			Estimates		
Period Ending	2014E	2015E	2016E	2017E	2018E
MACRS Depreciation					
Existing PP&E	$424.9	$400.6	$320.5	$256.4	$205.2
2014 CAPEX					
2015 CAPEX					
2016 CAPEX					
2017 CAPEX					
2018 CAPEX					

TABLE 14.6 Projected MACRS Depreciation through 2018 CAPEX

CAPEX Year	Formula Cell	Formula
2014	J231	=$J211*J224
2015	K232	=$K211*K225
2016	L233	=$L211*L226
2017	M234	=$M211*M227
2018	N235	=$N211*N228

ACCELERATED VERSUS STRAIGHT-LINE DEPRECIATION

Now that we have the MACRS depreciation, we need to decide whether we want this accelerated depreciation or the straight-line depreciation for our income statement, cash flow statement, and balance sheet financials. Currently, it's the straight-line depreciation that flows throughout the rest of the model. We can create a binary switch to toggle between the straight-line and accelerated depreciations. You might want to review the "Basic Switches" section in Chapter 12.

We will use Row 237, entitled "Depreciation used." We can set the switch up so that if the switch is set to "1," then the MACRS depreciation flows through into this "Depreciation used" row and on through the rest of the model. If the switch is set to "0," then the straight-line depreciation flows into this row. We would do this by setting a cell to act as a variable. Let's call it "Switch Value" for this example. We would then multiply the

TABLE 14.7 Total Projected MACRS Depreciation

Depreciation (in US$ millions except per share amounts)					
			Estimates		
Period Ending	2014E	2015E	2016E	2017E	2018E
MACRS Depreciation					
Existing PP&E	$424.9	$400.6	$320.5	$256.4	$205.2
2014 CAPEX	30.8	32.9	30.4	28.2	26.0
2015 CAPEX		30.9	33.0	30.6	28.3
2016 CAPEX			31.1	33.1	30.7
2017 CAPEX				31.2	33.3
2018 CAPEX					31.3
Total MACRS depreciation	$455.7	$464.5	$415.0	$379.4	$354.7

MACRS depreciation by "Switch Value" and the straight-line depreciation by "1 – Switch Value."

MACRS Depreciation × Switch + Straight-Line Depreciation × (1 – Switch)

So if the Switch Value = "1," then the MACRS depreciation would be multiplying by 1 (thus including it into the calculation) and the straight-line depreciation would be set to 0 (or 1 – "Switch Value" which is 1 - 1, thus excluding it from the calculation). Conversely, if the Switch Value = "0"), then the straight-line depreciation would be set to 1 (or 1 – "Switch Value" which is 1 - 0, thus including it in the calculation). MACRS depreciation would be multiplying by 0 (thus excluding it from the calculation).

So, we first need to create a box in which to place the switch. We can use Cell D237 and title it "MACRS? 1 = Y, 0 = N." This is where you can be a bit more creative with the title. You may also find it more appropriate to place these switches in some sort of control tab such as the Assumptions tab, but let's keep it here for now. Hard-code "1" into Cell D238 and make sure it's in blue type.

We can now create the formula in Cell J237:

Depreciation with Switch (Cell J237)

Excel Keystrokes	Description
Type "="	Enters into "formula" mode
Select D238	Switch
Hit F4	Anchors (adds "$") to Switch cell
Type "*"	Multiplies
Select J236	Total MACRS depreciation
Type "+"	Adds
Type "(1-"	Begins "(1-switch)"
Select D238	Switch
Hit F4	Anchors (adds "$") to Switch cell
Type ")"	Ends "(1-switch)"
Type "*"	Multiplies
Select J221	Total straight-line depreciation
Hit Enter	End
Formula result	=$D$238*J236+(1-$D$238)*J221

Notice we have anchored the reference to the switch with "$" so we can easily copy the now formula to the right. Now when the switch is set to "1," "Depreciation Used" is equal to the MACRS value of $455.7; set to "0,"

TABLE 14.8 Total Depreciation and Amortization

Depreciation (in US$ millions except per share amounts)

Period Ending	Estimates				
	2014E	2015E	2016E	2017E	2018E
Property, plant, and equipment beginning of year	$2,428.2				
Capital expenditures beginning of year	$ 469.5	$471.4	$473.3	$475.2	$477.1
Straight-line depreciation					
Years (PP&E)	8.5				
Years (CAPEX)	40	40	40	40	40
Existing PP&E	285.7	285.7	285.7	285.7	285.7
2014 CAPEX	11.7	11.7	11.7	11.7	11.7
2015 CAPEX		11.8	11.8	11.8	11.8
2016 CAPEX			11.8	11.8	11.8
2017 CAPEX				11.9	11.9
2018 CAPEX					11.9
Total straight-line depreciation	$ 297.4	$ 309.2	$ 321.0	$ 332.9	$ 344.8
MACRS Depreciation Rates					
Existing PP&E	17.500%	16.500%	13.200%	10.560%	8.450%
2014 CAPEX	6.563%	7.000%	6.482%	5.996%	5.546%
2015 CAPEX		6.563%	7.000%	6.482%	5.996%
2016 CAPEX			6.563%	7.000%	6.482%
2017 CAPEX				6.563%	7.000%
2018 CAPEX					6.563%

MACRS Depreciation					
Existing PP&E	424.9	400.6	320.5	256.4	205.2
2014 CAPEX	30.8	32.9	30.4	28.2	26.0
2015 CAPEX		30.9	33.0	30.6	28.3
2016 CAPEX			31.1	33.1	30.7
2017 CAPEX				31.2	33.3
2018 CAPEX					31.3
Total MACRS depreciation	$455.7	$464.5	$415.0	$379.4	$354.7
Depreciation used	$455.7	$464.5	$415.0	$379.4	$354.7
Amortization	30.0	30.0	30.0	30.0	30.0
Amortization of identifiable intangible assets	342.4	342.4	342.4	342.4	342.4
Total depreciation and amortization	$828.2	$836.9	$787.4	$751.9	$727.2

the "Depreciation Used" is equal to the straight-line value of $297.4. Also notice there is a difference in the depreciation values, as expected, but not such a major difference to drive a change in the overall returns. Notice by 2018 the difference between the straight-line and the MACRS depreciations lessens. This is because the MACRS depreciation schedule is accelerated; a greater portion of the depreciation occurs earlier and is reduced as time goes on, eventually approaching and later growing smaller than the straight-line rate.

We now need to append our "Total depreciation and amortization" formula to pull in from the "Depreciation Used" as opposed to the straight-line depreciation. So, Cell J240 will now read "=J237+J238+J239." We can copy this to the right. See Table 14.8.

Finally, we need to relink the "Depreciation used" into the income statement so that the depreciation we select based on the switch will flow into the rest of the model. Cell J23, which is now linked in from "Total straight-line depreciation," should now link in from "Depreciation used." So Cell J23 should now read "=J237." We can copy this to the right. Since the depreciation on the cash flow statement is pulling in from this depreciation on the income statement, this should properly flow into the cash flow statement, and further into the balance sheet. Now we can see how toggling the switch will flow through and affect the overall returns. Adjust the switch from "1" to "0" and observe how the IRR changes in each scenario. It looks like the effect is minimal, adjusting the return by only ~0.4 percent, shifting from −0.4 percent using straight-line depreciation to 0.0% percent using accelerated depreciation. This is not a huge difference.

There is a good lesson here. Although we have concluded there is not a material difference to our returns, the method of depreciation was a big question and concern for us in making sure we are properly representing the new entity. However, we have just proven it does not make much of a difference; we have eliminated a major variable. This top-down process of first building a core model and then running various analyses to limit major variables is key in using a well-built financial model as a tool for analysis. Beyond the modeling, this is an excellent process to determine which areas of the entity a buyer should focus on and be concerned about as a priority. Certainly the depreciation of fixed assets will be a topic of due diligence to the buyers. However, we have proven that revenue growth and implementing cost-cutting initiatives are still one of the biggest drivers of high returns and should be a priority.

If you are matching numbers with the tables in the book, let's keep the switch set to "0" for the next chapters.

CHAPTER 15

Preferred Securities, Dividends, and Returns to Berkshire Hathaway

Let's now discuss preferred securities and properly model out the preferred dividends so we can calculate returns to Berkshire Hathaway.

PREFERRED SECURITIES

Preferred securities (also known as "preferreds" or "preferred stock") are financing instruments that are senior to common stock but subordinate to bonds in terms of claim.

The following features are usually associated with preferred stock:

- *Preference in dividends.* Preferreds generally issue a dividend paid out before dividends to common stockholders.
- *Preference in assets.* In the event of liquidation, preferreds are senior to common stock but subordinate to bonds.
- *Convertibility to common stock.* Preferred securities may come with an equity component.
- *Callability at the option of the corporation.* Preferreds may come with the rights to call on the securities.
- *Nonvoting.* Quite often these securities do not have voting rights.

The precise details of the structure of preferred stock can differ from security to security. However, the best way to think of preferred stock is as a hybrid between debt and equity. The dividends associated with the security can be considered equivalent to the benefits of interest (debt), and the ability to convert the security to equity can give the upside potential of an equity security.

For the most part, preferred securities do not come with a tax advantage for corporations. Preferreds pay fixed dividends with after-tax dollars.

For the investor, based on current tax law, most dividends are taxed at the ordinary income tax rate. However, certain types of preferreds could qualify for qualified dividend income (QDI) until December 2013. Since 2003, certain dividends known as qualified dividends have been subject to the same tax rates as long-term capital gains, which are lower than rates for ordinary income. (The rates are 0%, 15%, 18.8%, and 23.8% for 2013, based on the investor's income.) However, these rules may change.

There are a few reasons why issuing preferred shares is a benefit for companies. For financing purposes, the securities are typically not recorded as debt on the company's books. This helps maintain the company's debt ratios and credit ratings. We will discuss credit ratios in the next chapter. Also, as preferred shares tend not to have voting rights, they will not dilute the company's common shares.

For Heinz, the exact terms of the preferred securities remain unclear aside from the expected 9 percent dividend. The most important unknown consideration for modeling purposes is whether the dividend will be periodically paid out or the dividends will accumulate in a payable account until transaction exit. For many leveraged buyouts, although dividends in preferred securities are incurred, in order not to strain the business cash flow, the incurred dividends are not paid until exit. However, Heinz may be a special case, and Berkshire Hathaway has informally hinted at interest in the dividend aspect of the investment, possibly indicating they are expecting an annual payout. But we are still unsure. So, for modeling purposes we should consider both possibilities and utilize a switch to toggle between the possibilities of dividends being paid out each year versus accumulating in a payable account. Let's see if the difference makes a significant effect to the overall returns. If it does not, it may not be worth belaboring over.

PREFERRED DIVIDENDS

Before modeling the preferreds out, let's discuss a simple example of a preferred security that is paying an annual dividend of $100 per share per year. We will step through the flow of how this affects the income statement, cash flow, and balance sheet. First, let's assume the dividend is paid out when it is incurred. The income and cash flows are shown in Table 15.1.

Preferred dividends are shown after net income. Notice the net income before the preferred dividends is the net income that continues to flow into the cash flow statement. Remember, the net income used for the cash flow statement is net income before dividends and minority interests are paid out;

TABLE 15.1   Preferred Dividends Income Statement and Cash Flow Impact

Income Statement		Cash Flow	
Net Income	$0.0	Net Income	$0.0
Preferred Dividends	(100.0)	Preferred Dividends	(100.0)
Net Income after Preferreds	**(100.0)**	**Total Changes in Cash**	**(100.0)**

it is the same for preferred dividends. This is because dividends are treated as a financing activity, and, as such, they are removed in the financing activities section of the cash flow statement: –$100 preferred dividends. Table 15.2 illustrates how these dividends flow into the balance sheet.

As shown in the table, the total change in cash of –$100 flows into the balance sheet cash balance. The preferred dividends affect retained earnings. Remember, retained earnings are linked to net income and dividends.

Now what if we would like to defer the actual preferred dividend payments so as to not immediately strain the cash flow of the business? Well, as shown in Table 15.3, the income statement remains unchanged. However, we need to add a payable line to the cash flow statement to indicate that the dividend, although incurred, is not yet paid. It may seem redundant to have two lines negating each other, but in order to properly have the cash flow statement drive the balance sheet, both lines should exist. Notice that cash does not change; the dividends were not actually paid out.

Table 15.4 shows how the cash flow affects the balance sheet. Here there is now no change to the cash balance. The retained earnings line, just like before, shows –$100; the dividends are incurred. But the liability account we created, "Preferred Dividends Payable," will accumulate until exit. The balance sheet balances.

Now we can model this impact into the Heinz case. Let's first model the standard dividend. We will then incorporate the "payable" with a switch. This way we can determine the Berkshire Hathaway returns and see if whether or not the dividends are paid out right away has an effect on the IRR. Notice the major difference between the two (see the cash flow statements in Tables 15.2 and 15.4) is in the inclusion of the "Preferred Dividends Payable" line. We will simply add a switch to that, multiplying by "1" or "0," turning the payable function on or off.

Note that there are always several ways to model such adjustments. This is our suggested and recommended method.

TABLE 15.2   Preferred Dividends Balance Sheet Impact

Cash Flow		Balance Sheet	
Net Income	$0.0	Cash	$(100.0)
Preferred Dividends	(100.0)	Retained Earnings (Net Income)	(100.0)
Total Changes in Cash	**(100.0)**		

TABLE 15.3 Preferred Dividends Payable Income Statement and Cash Flow Impact

Income Statement		Cash Flow	
Net Income	$0.0	Net Income	$0.0
Preferred Dividends	(100.0)	Preferred Dividends Payable	100.0
Net Income after Preferreds	(100.0)	Preferred Dividends	(100.0)
		Total Changes in Cash	0.0

We can begin in the income statement of the Financials tab. Although not entirely necessary for the model, let's add a row under "Net Income" to calculate and show the dividends. Remember, the preferred dividends are a result of the transaction, so this will be done only for the projected years.

There are several ways to do this, but let's just add two rows after the "Net income attributable to noncontrolling interests" row, Row 45. Once you have two empty rows, let's label the first row "Preferred dividend" and the second "Preferred dividend (%)." See Table 15.5.

This will, of course, be hard-coded "0" for the historical years. For 2014 through 2018, let's first hard-code the dividend rate, which is 9 percent. So we can hard-code "9%" into Cell J47. Make sure you adjust the formatting so the 9 percent appears as a percentage and in blue font.

Cell J46 will simply be the actual dividend amount, 9 percent, times the amount of preferred securities raised, which is found in the Assumptions tab in Cell F12. Cell J46 will read: "=J47*Assumptions!$F$12." We anchored the reference to the total preferred capital raised in the Assumptions tab so that we can easily copy these formulas to the right. Let's copy Cell J46 and J47 to the right through 2018. See Table 15.5.

Again, there were several possible ways we could have done this. We could have found a place in the Assumptions tab for the dividend rate, for example, as opposed to creating a separate line in the income statement. This is, of course, the art in modeling, and it's up to you to exercise a little creativity and to design the model as you would like. I had preferred to show the actual interest rates directly in the model as opposed to the Assumptions tab so you can see as you are looking at the income statement numbers what is driving them. There's no right or wrong method here.

Notice that the value $720 million per year is what Berkshire Hathaway is set to receive for its investment in the preferred securities. Not a bad source of income!

TABLE 15.4 Preferred Dividends Payable Balance Sheet Impact

Cash Flow		Balance Sheet	
Net Income	$0.0	Cash	$0.0
Preferred Dividends Payable	100.0	Preferred Dividends Payable	100.0
Preferred Dividends	(100.0)	Retained Earnings (Net Income)	(100.0)
Total Changes in Cash	0.0		

TABLE 15.5   Income Statement with Preferred Dividends

Consolidated Income Statements (in US$ millions except per share amounts)					
	Estimates				
Period Ending	2014E	2015E	2016E	2017E	2018E
Net income (Adjusted)	433.1	432.1	431.3	430.6	429.9
Non-recurring events					
Other expense, net	19.1	19.1	19.1	19.1	19.1
Loss from discountued operations, net of tax	0.0	0.0	0.0	0.0	0.0
Effect of accounting changes	0.0	0.0	0.0	0.0	0.0
Extraordinary items, net of tax	0.0	0.0	0.0	0.0	0.0
Total non-recurring events	19.1	19.1	19.1	19.1	19.1
Net income (after non-recurring events)	414.0	413.0	412.2	411.5	410.8
Net income attirbutable to non-controlling interests	0.0	0.0	0.0	0.0	0.0
Preferred dividend	720	720	720	720	720
Preferred dividend (%)	9.0%	9.0%	9.0%	9.0%	9.0%

Although it will not be used, we can calculate the net income in Row 48 to now also be after preferred dividends. So, Cell J48 will read "=J44-J45-J46." However, this line will not be used in the model. It is the net income before dividends that flows into the cash flow and balance sheet. Let's move on and make our next adjustments.

The next step is to adjust for preferred dividends in both the cash flow statement and the balance sheet. Refer to Table 15.3. Notice again that the net income pulling into the cash flow statement is before dividends. We need to add the dividends into the "Cash flows from financing activities." You may want to add a separate row for this, but let's just use Row 97, as it is not being used in the future projections. We can change the label from "Dividends" to "Dividends (including preferred dividends)." We can simply link this in from the dividends calculated on the income statement. We need to switch the signs here so that the dividends are represented as a negative. Cell J97 will be "=-J46." Copy this to the right and change the font to black as this is now a formula. See Table 15.6.

You may notice as you enter the formula that the revolving line of credit changes (make sure you have the automatic debt pay-down switch in Cell I278 turned on). The company at the current growth rate does not have adequate cash to support such dividends, so the revolving line of credit

TABLE 15.6 Cash Flow Statement with Preferred Dividends

Consolidated Statements of Cash Flows (in US$ millions except per share amounts)

Period Ending		Estimates			
	2014E	2015E	2016E	2017E	2018E
Cash flows from financing activities					
Revolver borrowings (repayments)	586.7	469.6	479.5	490.0	500.8
Term facilities borrowings (repayments)	0.0	0.0	0.0	0.0	0.0
The notes borrowings (repayments)	0.0	0.0	0.0	0.0	0.0
Common Equity	0.0	0.0	0.0	0.0	0.0
Preferred Equity	0.0	0.0	0.0	0.0	0.0
Proceeds (payments) of long-term debt	0.0	0.0	0.0	0.0	0.0
Net payments on commercial paper and short-term debt	0.0	0.0	0.0	0.0	0.0
Dividends (including preferred dividends)	(720.0)	(720.0)	(720.0)	(720.0)	(720.0)
Purchase of treasury stock	0.0	0.0	0.0	0.0	0.0
Exercise of stock options	0.0	0.0	0.0	0.0	0.0
Acquisitions of subsidiary shares from non-controlling interests	0.0	0.0	0.0	0.0	0.0
Earn-out settlement	0.0	0.0	0.0	0.0	0.0
Other items, net	(9.1)	(9.1)	(9.1)	(9.1)	(9.1)
Total cash provided by (used for) financing activities	(142.4)	(259.5)	(249.6)	(239.1)	(228.3)
Effect of exchange rate on cash and cash equivalents	(122.1)	(122.1)	(122.1)	(122.1)	(122.1)
Total change in cash and cash equivalents	100.0	0.0	(0.0)	(0.0)	(0.0)

kicks in to fund that cash need. Of course we have been very conservative with our growth estimates. Regardless, we will soon adjust the model so the dividends can be deferred, which will refrain from straining the cash in the business. However, this demonstrated well the functionality of the revolver; notice how the total cash change is 0 in the future. If the revolver had been switched off, the cash would have been negative, showing a cash deficit. The revolver has helped fund that cash need, keeping the cash flow change at "0." You may also notice that the balance of cash on the balance sheet will stay at $100, the minimum required that we established in the debt schedule.

We now need to make sure the dividends link into the retained earnings. We have linked the dividend row in Part Two of the book, so they should already be linked and the model should still balance.

We can now refer to Tables 15.3 and 15.4, illustrating the adjustments to defer payment of the dividends. We will need to add a row to the cash flow statement and create a balance sheet liability. Let's begin by adding a row above Row 97, the "Dividends" line, in the cash flow statement. Even though this is labeled as a payable, it is not considered working capital as (1) it is not short-term (payable in five years at exit) and (2) it is not operating (it is not a part of the net income used in the cash flow from operating activities). We can title this new row "Preferred dividends payable," and we can hard-code "0" in all the historical years. We also want to add a switch so we can turn the ability to defer dividends on and off. Here again you may prefer to have a separate tab for all of your switches, but I placed a box over to the right in Cell O96 and titled it "Preferred Dividend Deferred? 1=Yes; 0=No." Let's hard-code "1" in cell O97 and put it in blue type. See Table 15.7.

We can now link in the preferred dividends payable account. We can pull it either from the income statement or from the line directly underneath. Either way, we need to multiply this line by the switch so that if it's turned on ("1"), we will have a value, or if it's turned off ("0"), it will be zero. So Cell J97 will read "=-J98*$O$97" if you have decided to pull the values from the "Dividends" row. Notice the negative before "J98" and also notice we have anchored Cell O97 with dollar signs. You can copy this formula to the right, and make the formulas black.

You may notice that the revolving line of credit has not gone away. It should though if those dividends no longer need to be paid out. Since we have added a row, we need to amend the "Cash flow before debt paydown" formula to include this new row. So if you change the formula in Cell J108 to additionally add Cell J97, that should fix the problem. The revolver should go back to zero, and we should now have some cash flow again. Cell J108 should now read "=J78+J88+J93+J94+J98+J99+J100+J101+J102+J103+J105+J97." Copy Cell J107 to the right. See Table 15.8.

TABLE 15.7 Preferred Dividend Payable Switch

Consolidated Statements of Cash Flows (in US$ millions except per share amounts)

Period Ending		Estimates					Preferred Dividend Deferred?
	2014E	2015E	2016E	2017E	2018E		1=Yes; 0=No
Cash flows from financing activities							
Revolver borrowings (repayments)	586.7	469.6	479.5	490.0	500.8		
Term facilities borrowings (repayments)	0.0	0.0	0.0	0.0	0.0		
The notes borrowings (repayments)	0.0	0.0	0.0	0.0	0.0		
Common Equity	0.0	0.0	0.0	0.0	0.0		
Preferred Equity	0.0	0.0	0.0	0.0	0.0		
Proceeds (payments) of long-term debt	0.0	0.0	0.0	0.0	0.0		
Net payments on commercial paper and short-term debt	0.0	0.0	0.0	0.0	0.0		
Preferred dividends payable							1
Dividends (including preferred dividends)	(720.0)	(720.0)	(720.0)	(720.0)	(720.0)		
Purchase of treasury stock	0.0	0.0	0.0	0.0	0.0		
Exercise of stock options	0.0	0.0	0.0	0.0	0.0		
Acquisitions of subsidiary shares from non-controlling interests	0.0	0.0	0.0	0.0	0.0		
Earn-out settlement	0.0	0.0	0.0	0.0	0.0		
Other items, net	(9.1)	(9.1)	(9.1)	(9.1)	(9.1)		
Total cash provided by (used for) financing activities	(142.4)	(259.5)	(249.6)	(239.1)	(228.3)		
Effect of exchange rate on cash and cash equivalents	(122.1)	(122.1)	(122.1)	(122.1)	(122.1)		
Total change in cash and cash equivalents	100.0	0.0	0.0	0.0	0.0		

TABLE 15.8 Cash Flow with Preferred Dividends Payable

Consolidated Statements of Cash Flows (in US$ millions except per share amounts)

	Estimates				
Period Ending	2014E	2015E	2016E	2017E	2018E
Cash flows from financing activities					
Revolver borrowings (repayments)	0.0	0.0	0.0	0.0	0.0
Term facilities borrowings (repayments)	0.0	0.0	0.0	0.0	0.0
The notes borrowings (repayments)	0.0	0.0	0.0	0.0	0.0
Common Equity	0.0	0.0	0.0	0.0	0.0
Preferred Equity	0.0	0.0	0.0	0.0	0.0
Proceeds (payments) of long-term debt	0.0	0.0	0.0	0.0	0.0
Net payments on commercial paper and short-term debt	0.0	0.0	0.0	0.0	0.0
Preferred dividends payable	720.0	720.0	720.0	720.0	720.0
Dividends (including preferred dividends)	(720.0)	(720.0)	(720.0)	(720.0)	(720.0)
Purchase of treasury stock	0.0	0.0	0.0	0.0	0.0
Exercise of stock options	0.0	0.0	0.0	0.0	0.0
Acquisitions of subsidiary shares from non-controlling interests	0.0	0.0	0.0	0.0	0.0
Earn-out settlement	0.0	0.0	0.0	0.0	0.0
Other items, net	(9.1)	(9.1)	(9.1)	(9.1)	(9.1)
Total cash provided by (used for) financing activities	**(9.1)**	**(9.1)**	**(9.1)**	**(9.1)**	**(9.1)**
Effect of exchange rate on cash and cash equivalents	(122.1)	(122.1)	(122.1)	(122.1)	(122.1)
Total change in cash and cash equivalents	**246.1**	**285.3**	**294.5**	**303.7**	**313.1**

We now need to adjust the balance sheet. You may notice that the balance sheet no longer balances. (See Table 15.9.) This is because we have a line item in the cash flow statement that is not linking into the balance sheet—the preferred dividends payable. We should create a line item for this. Let's add a row above Row 192, "Other noncurrent liabilities," and label it "Preferred dividends payable." See Table 15.9.

We can hard-code "0" for the LTM year (Cell I192). Of course this was before the purchase, and no preferred dividends payable existed at that time. However, the next year we can use the standard balance sheet balancing formula for a liability, which is:

2014 Balance Sheet Payable = LTM Balance Sheet Payable + 2014 Cash Flow Payable

TABLE 15.9 Unbalanced Balance Sheet

Consolidated Balance Sheets (in US$ millions except per share amounts)

On January 27	Actuals	Pro-Forma	Estimates				
		2013PF	2014E	2015E	2016E	2017E	2018E
Liabilities							
Current liabilities:							
Short-term debt		0.0					0.0
Portion of long term debt due within one year		0.0	0.0				
Revolving line of credit		0.0	0.0				
Accounts payable		1,287.8	1,291.5	1,296.7	1,301.8	1,307.1	1,312.3
Accrued marketing and other accrued liabilities		944.0	936.7	940.5	944.2	948.0	951.8
Income taxes		91.3	67.5	67.3	67.2	67.1	67.0
Total current liabilities		2,323.1	2,295.7	2,304.5	2,313.3	2,322.1	2,331.1
Term facilities		10,500.0	10,500.0	10,500.0	10,500.0	10,500.0	10,500.0
The notes		2,100.0	2,100.0	2,100.0	2,100.0	2,100.0	2,100.0
Long term debt		0.0	0.0	0.0	0.0	0.0	0.0
Deferred income taxes		776.7	693.7	610.7	527.7	444.7	361.7
Non-pension postretirement benefits		230.9	230.9	230.9	230.9	230.9	230.9
Preferred dividends payable							
Other non-currents liabilities		504.8	424.8	344.8	264.8	184.8	104.8
Redeemable non-controlling interest		28.7	28.7	28.7	28.7	28.7	28.7
Total liabilities		16,464.1	16,273.7	16,119.5	15,965.3	15,811.2	15,657.1

Total Equity						
Shareholder's Equity						
Capital stock	0.0	0.0	0.0	0.0	0.0	0.0
Common equity investment	8,240.0	8,240.0	8,240.0	8,240.0	8,240.0	8,240.0
Preferred equity investment	8,000.0	8,000.0	8,000.0	8,000.0	8,000.0	8,000.0
Retained earnings	(1,381.1)	(1,687.2)	(1,994.2)	(2,302.0)	(2,610.5)	(2,919.7)
Treasury stock	0.0	0.0	0.0	0.0	0.0	0.0
Accumulated other comprehensive loss	0.0	(131.2)	(262.5)	(393.7)	(525.0)	(656.2)
Total shareholder's equity	14,858.9	14,421.6	13,983.3	13,544.3	13,104.5	12,664.1
Non-controlling interest	50.5	50.5	50.5	50.5	50.5	50.5
Total equity	14,909.4	14,472.1	14,033.9	13,594.8	13,155.1	12,714.6
Total liabilities & equity	31,373.5	30,745.8	30,153.4	29,560.2	28,966.2	28,371.7
Supplemental Data:						
Balance? (Y/N)	Y	N	N	N	N	N

So in Cell J192 we would have "=I192+J97." We can copy this to the right and you can now see the payables accumulating. The balance sheet should be back in balance. See Table 15.10.

Notice that the switch should work now. If the switch is set to "0," the cash flow statement preferred dividends payable should go to zero and the revolving line of credit will draw.

Let's keep the switch set to "1" for now and can calculate the returns to Berkshire Hathaway. We can then see if whether paying the preferreds out and drawing on the revolver or deferring the preferreds makes a difference to the overall returns.

RETURNS TO BERKSHIRE HATHAWAY

Now that we have properly modeled the preferred dividends, we can calculate the returns to Berkshire Hathaway. We can refer back to the Returns tab in the model. Here, if you remember, we had made a shortcut calculation for the "Preferred dividends" in Row 13. We can now replace this calculation with the preferred dividends payable in the balance sheet. So, if the switch is turned off, meaning the dividends have not been deferred until exit, this line should be zero. If the dividends are not paid at exit, they would have been paid periodically out of the cash flow. So, in Cell K13, let's link in Cell N192 from the balance sheet. Cell K13 should be "=Financials!N192." Notice the number is the same $3,600 from before.

We can now go to the Berkshire Hathaway returns section beginning in Row 18 of the "Returns" tab. As we had done with 3G, we first want to pull in the original investment Berkshire Hathaway made into the company. This will include both the common equity and the preferred, and it will be represented as a negative value. So, Cell F19 will be "=-(Assumptions!F12+Assumptions!F13)." Don't miss the negative sign here. See Table 15.11.

The next few rows refer to the returns, which will be modeled in Column K. The equity value in Row 20 refers to Berkshire's equity stake in the business. As far as we know, based on public information up to this point, Berkshire's equity investment will represent 30 percent of the business. We will first multiply the 30 percent by the equity to common in Cell K20. Or, K20 will read: "=K14*Assumptions!H13."

Cell K21, the preferred equity, represents the return of the preferred equity investment, so we can simply have K21 be "=K12." Or we could have taken this value from the sources in the Assumptions tab. Note that we are taking the conservative assumption that the original value of the preferred investment will be returned. Often, it is negotiated that the investor would receive some sort of premium on this return. This premium can be in the

TABLE 15.10 Balance Sheet Preferred Dividends Payable

Consolidated Balance Sheets (in US$ millions except per share amounts)

	Actuals			Estimates		
	Pro-Forma					
On January 27	2013PF	2014E	2015E	2016E	2017E	2018E
Liabilities						
Current liabilities:						
Short-term debt	0.0	0.0	0.0	0.0	0.0	0.0
Portion of long term debt due within one year	0.0	0.0	0.0	0.0	0.0	0.0
Revolving line of credit	0.0	0.0	0.0	0.0	0.0	0.0
Accounts payable	1,287.8	1,291.5	1,296.7	1,301.8	1,307.1	1,312.3
Accrued marketing and other accrued liabilities	944.0	936.7	940.5	944.2	948.0	951.8
Income taxes	91.3	67.5	67.3	67.2	67.1	67.0
Total current liabilities	**2,323.1**	**2,295.7**	**2,304.5**	**2,313.3**	**2,322.1**	**2,331.1**
Term facilities	10,500.0	10,500.0	10,500.0	10,500.0	10,500.0	10,500.0
The notes	2,100.0	2,100.0	2,100.0	2,100.0	2,100.0	2,100.0
Long term debt	0.0	0.0	0.0	0.0	0.0	0.0
Deferred income taxes	776.7	693.7	610.7	527.7	444.7	361.7
Non-pension postretirement benefits	230.9	230.9	230.9	230.9	230.9	230.9
Preferred dividends payable	0.0	720.0	1,440.0	2,160.0	2,880.0	3,600.0
Other non-currents liabilities	504.8	424.8	344.8	264.8	184.8	104.8
Redeemable non-controlling interest	28.7	28.7	28.7	28.7	28.7	28.7
Total liabilities	**16,464.1**	**16,993.7**	**17,559.5**	**18,125.3**	**18,691.2**	**19,257.1**

(continued)

TABLE 15.10 (*Continued*)

Consolidated Balance Sheets (in US$ millions except per share amounts)

On January 27	Actuals Pro-Forma 2013PF	2014E	2015E	Estimates 2016E	2017E	2018E
Total Equity						
Shareholder's Equity						
Capital stock	0.0	0.0	0.0	0.0	0.0	0.0
Common equity investment	8,240.0	8,240.0	8,240.0	8,240.0	8,240.0	8,240.0
Preferred equity investment	8,000.0	8,000.0	8,000.0	8,000.0	8,000.0	8,000.0
Retained earnings	(1,381.1)	(1,687.2)	(1,994.2)	(2,302.0)	(2,610.5)	(2,919.7)
Treasury stock	0.0	0.0	0.0	0.0	0.0	0.0
Accumulated other comprehensive loss	0.0	(131.2)	(262.5)	(393.7)	(525.0)	(656.2)
Total shareholder's equity	14,858.9	14,421.6	13,983.3	13,544.3	13,104.5	12,664.1
Non-controlling interest	50.5	50.5	50.5	50.5	50.5	50.5
Total equity	14,909.4	14,472.1	14,033.9	13,594.8	13,155.1	12,714.6
Total liabilities & equity	31,373.5	31,465.8	31,593.4	31,720.2	31,846.2	31,971.7
Supplemental Data:						
Balance? (Y/N)	Y	Y	Y	Y	Y	Y

form of a multiple (for example, 1.25x original investment) or some equity component. In this case it has been suggested in the preliminary proxy that there will be warrants attached to this security, and, of course, the 9 percent dividend.

Cell K22, the preferred dividends payable, can be taken from Row 13. So we can simply have K22 be "=K13." Or we could have taken this value directly from the balance sheet. Remember, this will turn to zero if we turn off the switch deferring dividend payments. If we do switch off deferred payments, we should calculate the return of the periodic payments coming in. We will do this in Row 23. So we need to pull in the actual value of the dividends only if the switch is turned off. There are a couple of ways to do this. If the switch is set to "0," meaning we want to show periodic dividends, then we should have the formula be:

$$\text{Dividends} \times (1 - \text{Switch})$$

If the switch is set to "0," the formula will return the value of the dividends, and if the switch is set to "1," the formula will return zero. In Cell G23 we will have "=-Financials!J98*(1-Financials!$O$97)." Note the negative sign after the equal sign, and we anchored the reference to the switch in Cell O97. We use the dividends, not the dividends payable line, because the dividends payable line becomes 0 when the switch is off. We can now copy G23 to the right through 2018. We can now add up all five rows and test the switch. Cell F24 should be "=SUM(F19:F23)." We can copy Cell F24 to the right through 2018. See Table 15.11.

TABLE 15.11   Returns to Berkshire Hathaway, Low Growth, Dividends Deferred

Investment Returns (in US$ millions except per share amounts)						
			Estimates			
Period Ending	LTM	2014E	2015E	2016E	2017E	2018E
Return to Berkshire Hathaway						
Equity investment	$(12,120.0)					
Equity value						$ 1,727.3
Preferred equity						8,000.0
Preferred dividends payable						3,600.0
Preferred dividends		0.0	0.0	0.0	0.0	0.0
Total return	$(12,120.0)	$0.0	$0.0	$0.0	$0.0	$13,327.3

Now if we change the preferred dividend deferred switch to "0," the payables should go away and be replaced by annual dividend payouts. See Table 15.12.

Let's determine what the actual IRR is based on these cases. Cell F26 should read, "=IRR(F24:K24)" and F27 should be "=SUM(G24:K24)/-F24." Note the "SUM(G24:K24)" portion of this formula. We want a total of all dividend payments as well. This gives us a 2.0 percent annual rate of return with the preferred dividend switch set to "0." If we switch the preferred dividend switch back to "1," the return lowers to 1.9 percent, so deferring the dividends does not make much difference at all (0.1%) to the overall returns. If you recall, back when calculating the expected returns for 3G, we ran a different case adjusting the growth to 5.5 percent annually and lowering COGS percentage of revenue to 60 percent. Let's make those adjustments now and see what difference that makes to the returns. See Table 15.13.

Using the expected growth rate as suggested in the fairness opinion, along with an exit multiple equal to the purchase multiple, the returns are 7.3 percent annually. Again, as discussed with 3G, these are not as high as one would expect. Remember, though, that this model is a tool meant to be adjusted. As the purchase approaches a close, maybe the terms will change, rendering higher returns. However, as discussed with 3G returns, in order to significantly increase returns (and remember, this is already with higher growth and some cost reductions), the company would need to grow revenue more aggressively or reduce costs more significantly. Or there might be some way to exit the investment at a higher multiple than the entry multiple. On

TABLE 15.12   Returns to Berkshire Hathaway, Low Growth, Dividends Paid Annually

Investment Returns (in US$ millions except per share amounts)						
				Estimates		
Period Ending	LTM	2014E	2015E	2016E	2017E	2018E
Return to Berkshire Hathaway						
Equity investment	$(12,120.0)					
Equity value						$1,646.5
Preferred equity						8,000.0
Preferred dividends payable						0.0
Preferred dividends		$720.0	$720.0	$720.0	$720.0	720.0
Total return	$(12,120.0)	$720.0	$720.0	$720.0	$720.0	$10,366.5

TABLE 15.13   Returns to Berkshire Hathaway, Moderate Growth, Dividends Deferred

Investment Returns (in US$ millions except per share amounts)							
			Estimates				
Period Ending	LTM	2014E	2015E	2016E	2017E	2018E
Return to Berkshire Hathaway							
Equity investment	$(12,120.0)						
Equity value						$ 5,645.6
Preferred equity						8,000.0
Preferred dividends payable						3,600.0
Preferred dividends		$0.0	$0.0	$0.0	$0.0	0.0
Total return	$(12,120.0)	$0.0	$0.0	$0.0	$0.0	$17,245.6
IRR	7.3%						
Return multiple	1.4x						

the other hand, if you believe this is a safe investment, receiving $720MM per year is not a bad source of income. Now that you know the estimated returns to each party, and the mechanics behind the returns, the intent and reasoning for making such investments given the inherent risks are open to subjective speculation.

This concludes analyzing the potential returns of the business investment. The next chapters are ancillary and go through nuances to LBO modeling that have been popular discussions and important to more recent buyouts.

CHAPTER 16

Debt Covenant Ratios, and Debt Fee Amortization

Debt covenant ratios are financial ratios detailing company thresholds needed to maintain certain levels of debt. Such ratios are typically determined by a lender and dictate the ability of a company to raise and maintain debt; important for determining how much of what type of debt one can raise in a leveraged buyout.

The most common types of financial ratios used in debt covenants are coverage ratios and leverage ratios. Depending on the company or lender, there can be a multitude of ratio combinations. Further the terms defining each ratio can be interpreted to have different meanings in different debt agreements. For example, total debt can mean all debts or just senior debt; total debt can include capital leases or exclude capital leases. Since the interpretations of these definitions differ from lender to lender or from company to company, it is always important to be very clear about the actual definition of the terms. A good analyst would always footnote his or her interpretation of the definitions. Because the definitions do vary, we will give general examples of a set of covenants here, but hold the understanding that this is just one view.

COVERAGE RATIOS

Coverage ratios help determine whether the cash or income produced by the business can meet the interest and other necessary payments to sustain the debt held in the business. There are several major types of coverage ratios.

- Debt service coverage.
- Interest coverage.
- Fixed charge coverage.

These terms are often used interchangeably, and companies have varying views on the definitions of such ratios; however, the numerator is most commonly some measure of income, and the denominator is some version of required payments to the lenders. Again, the purpose of such ratios is to determine the ability to meet such payments to the lenders.

Debt Service Coverage

One variation of the debt service coverage ratio is:

$$\text{Debt Service Coverage Ratio} = \frac{(\text{EBITDA} - \text{Taxes} - \text{Maintenance CAPEX})}{(\text{Principal Repayment} + \text{Interest Payments})}$$

If the debt coverage ratio is less than 1, the income generated from the business is not enough to cover the necessary payments. A property with a debt coverage ratio of more than 1 would mean the property does generate enough to cover such payments.

Typically, lenders expect a cushion, a ratio greater than 1, to ensure that there are more than enough funds available (for example, a ratio of 1.2 to 1.4 times EBITDA less taxes).

Other variations of the debt service coverage ratio could be a numerator based on net income or cash flow. We can also have simply EBITDA as the numerator. Further, the numerator may or may not include other fixed charges such as maintenance CAPEX, or the management fee paid to the buyer. This again depends on the company's or lender's interpretation.

Interest Coverage

The interest coverage ratio is similar in theory to the debt service coverage ratio; however, typically it measures the company's ability to pay down just the interest.

$$\text{Interest Coverage Ratio} = \frac{\text{EBITDA}}{\text{Interest Expense}}$$

Again, other variations of the interest coverage ratio could be a numerator based on net income, cash flow, or EBITDA less taxes.

Fixed Charge Coverage

The fixed charge coverage ratio is a measure of how well a firm covers their fixed costs. Fixed costs can most commonly include lease payments. Lease payments, like interest payments, must be met on an annual basis, so the fixed charge coverage ratio is important for firms that extensively lease equipment, for example.

One variation of a fixed charge coverage ratio is:

$$\frac{\text{Fixed Charge Coverage}}{\text{Ratio}} = \frac{\text{EBIT} + \text{Lease Payments}}{\text{Interest Expense} + \text{Lease Payments}}$$

So this formula attempts to explain the number of times a company can cover its fixed charges per year.

LEVERAGE RATIOS

Leverage ratios also help determine the ability to raise or maintain debt. The most common leverage ratios are Debt/Equity and Debt/EBITDA.

The Debt/Equity ratio helps indicate how much leverage the business has compared to the equity of the business. Another variation of the Debt/Equity ratio is Debt/Total Capital, where Total Capital is Debt plus Equity. Again, lenders would use such ratios to determine the advisability of lending to certain businesses.

The Debt/EBITDA ratio is another indicator of leverage. Such ratios not only help track and justify the lender's ability to lend a certain amount of debt, but are also helpful in trying to predict how much debt a company can possibly raise. For example, a lender may choose to lend only 3x a company's EBITDA. Let's take a company that has an EBITDA of $100,000 and is trying to borrow $1 million. This is a 10x Debt/EBITDA multiple, which is significantly higher than the lender's example requirement of 3x, so we know this loan would probably not be feasible.

Table 16.1 is an example of debt covenants for Heinz. We will not step through the calculations as they are simply divisions, but you can peer into the particular calculations by looking at the solutions file. If you are trying to match these numbers with the model you are working on, this output if from a version of the model with 5.5 percent revenue growth and 60 percent COGS as a percentage of revenue from 2014–2018.

TABLE 16.1 Heinz Debt Covenant Ratios

Consolidated Income Statements (in US$ millions except per share amounts)

Period Ending	Actuals		Estimates		
	2014A	2015A	2016A	2017A	2018A
Input Data					
EBITDA	2,247	2,371	2,501	2,639	2,784
Less taxes	(249)	(281)	(315)	(351)	(389)
Less: maintenance capex	(493)	(521)	(549)	(579)	(611)
Operating Cash Flow (OCF)	1,505	1,569	1,637	1,708	1,783
Debt service					
Total cash interest expense	683	683	683	683	683
Total principal repayments	0	0	0	0	0
Total Debt Service	683	683	683	683	683
Total Debt	12,600.0	12,600.0	12,600.0	12,600.0	12,600.0
Total Equity	14,686.4	14,546.8	14,495.4	14,537.4	14,678.3
Coverage Ratios					
EBITDA / Interest expense	3.3x	3.5x	3.7x	3.9x	4.1x
EBITDA / Total Debt Service	3.3x	3.5x	3.7x	3.9x	4.1x
OCF / Interest expense	2.2x	2.3x	2.4x	2.5x	2.6x
OCF / Total Debt Service	2.2x	2.3x	2.4x	2.5x	2.6x
Leverage Ratios					
Total Debt / EBITDA	5.6x	5.3x	5.0x	4.8x	4.5x
Total Debt / OCF	8.4x	8.0x	7.7x	7.4x	7.1x
Total Debt / Total Equity	0.9x	0.9x	0.9x	0.9x	0.9x
Total Debt / Total Capital	46.2%	46.4%	46.5%	46.4%	46.2%

We are also deferring preferred dividend payments and using straight line depreciation.

DEBT FEE CAPITALIZATION AND AMORTIZATION

Under certain conditions, the transaction fees related to the raising of debts can be capitalized and therefore amortized. Although a tiny nuance to the overall scope of a leveraged buyout (LBO) model, this topic has come up quite often and can lead to some tax savings. I'd like to illustrate how this works as a reference. Although we do not have details of the fees associated with the debts raised, they will typically be calculated as a percentage of the debts. For simplicity, let's assume that the fees related to both the term facilities and the notes will be 1 percent. So, 1 percent × ($10,500 + $2,100) = $126. It is this portion of the overall transaction fees that can be capitalized as an asset on the balance sheet and therefore amortized. To illustrate how this works, we will first create an asset in the balance sheet adjustments. We will then calculate an amortization that will affect the income statement and cash flow statement. Finally, we will reduce the asset in the projected years by the amount of debt amortization each year.

If you are matching numbers, we are using a version of the model with 5.5 percent revenue growth and COGS reduced to 60 percent.

In the model, we will first add a row in the long-term assets section of the balance sheet. We added an empty row above "Other noncurrent assets," Row 126, and labeled it "Capitalized debt fee." See Table 16.2.

We hard-coded the historical value as "0." We now need to illustrate the creation of the debt fee asset as a positive transaction adjustment. For simplicity, we linked in the formula of 1 percent times the initial debts raised, or Cell F126 equals "=1%*(Assumptions!F9+Assumptions!F10)." You may prefer to have a box in the Assumptions tab detailing the transaction fees. Again, the point here is to illustrate the flows. At this point you should have the tools to be creative with formatting and presentation. Now make sure the "Total" column H is properly calculating. So we have Cell H126 read "=E126+F126-G126." You can just copy this formula down from Cell H125 as well; it is the same structure.

At this point you may notice the pro forma balance sheet no longer balances. This is because we are double-counting the debt fees, having included them in the assets section and also in the shareholders' equity section. Remember, there is a key adjustment in the shareholders' equity section where we reduce shareholders' equity further by the total value of the transaction fees. However, since we are now capitalizing the transaction fees related to debt, we should not be including them as a shareholders' equity reduction. Rather,

TABLE 16.2 Capitalized Debt Fee

Consolidated Balance Sheet Adjustments (in US$ millions except per share amounts)

On January 27, 2013	Actuals LTM	Pro Forma Additions (+)	Pro Forma Subtractions (−)	Total
Assets				
Current assets				
Cash and cash equivalents	$1,100.7		$1,100.7	$0.0
Trade receivables, net	896.4			896.4
Other receivables, net	202.4			202.4
Total inventories	1,448.4			1,448.4
Prepaid expenses	173.0			173.0
Other current assets	88.0			88.0
Total current assets	$3,908.9			$2,808.2
Property, plant, and equipment, net	2,428.2	0.0		2,428.2
Goodwill	3,104.5	$15,408.8		18,513.4
Trademarks, net	1,050.9			1,050.9
Other intangibles, net	383.0	5,136.3		5,519.3
Capitalized debt fee	0.0	126.0		126.0
Other noncurrent assets	1,053.6			1,053.6
Total assets	$11,929.1			$31,499.5

as the capitalized debt fee is amortized, that amortization will reduce net income, which would then in turn reduce the shareholders' equity.

So, in Cell G153, the adjustments to the retained earnings, we have adjusted out the outstanding balance of retained earnings, plus we have removed the total fees, or as it currently stands: "=E153+Assumptions!J8."

We want to remove just the transaction fees related to everything except the debts. So, if you have a detailed transaction fee table, which is recommended, you would just replace the reference to the total transaction fees (Assumptions!J8) with all transaction fees excluding those relating to the debt fees we are capitalizing. However, since Heinz did not give us that detail (we only have assumed a total transaction fee of $1,381.1 million; there is no further breakout), we will adjust for the total fees less the debt fees by subtracting $126 from $1,381.1. We are, in summary, removing:

Retained Earnings + Total Fees – Debt Fees

We can adjust the formula in Cell G153 to remove the $126 of debt fees. It will now read "=E153+Assumptions!J8-F126." The pro forma balance sheet should now balance. See Table 16.3. I would like to note once more $1,381.1 in transaction fees seems extremely high. This was a result of the way we are back calculating into the fees with limited disclosure at this point. Please refer to the note in Chaper 4 for more detail.

Now that the debt fees have been capitalized as an asset, we need to amortize them, link them into the income statement, and adjust the amortization in the cash flow statement. For simplicity, let's assume the amortization rate for the capitalized debt fee is five years, the expected life of the transaction. Again, for presentation you may want to lay this out in a table in the Assumptions tab, but for this book let's agree that the fee is "126/5." So, we need to add a row in the depreciation schedule that will be linked into both the income and the cash flow statements. We cannot simply total this amortization into total depreciation and amortization, because we need to keep debt fee amortization separate in order to properly link to the balance sheet capitalized debt fee asset.

So we will add a row above the total depreciation and amortization, row 245, and label it "Capitalized debt fee amortization." For simplicity, we will link in the "126" we calculated in the balance sheet adjustments section and divide by 5. Cell J245 will read "=$F$126/5," making sure to anchor the reference to the balance sheet adjustment so we can copy this across.

Although this is not used in the rest of the model, you should amend the total depreciation and amortization formula to now include this new row. So J246 should now read "=J242+J243+J244+J245." We can copy Cell J246 to the right through 2018. See Table 16.4.

TABLE 16.3 Balance Sheet Adjustment with Capitalized Debt Fee

Consolidated Balance Sheet Adjustments (in US$ millions except per share amounts)

On January 27, 2013	Actuals LTM	Pro Forma Additions (+)	Pro Forma Subtractions (–)	Pro Forma Total
Assets				
Current assets:				
Cash and cash equivalents	$ 1,100.7		$ 1,100.7	$ 0.0
Trade receivables, net	896.4			896.4
Other receivables, net	202.4			202.4
Total inventories	1,448.4			1,448.4
Prepaid expenses	173.0			173.0
Other current assets	88.0			88.0
Total current assets	**$ 3,908.9**			**$ 2,808.2**
Property, plant, and equipment, net	2,428.2	0.0		2,428.2
Goodwill	3,104.5	$ 15,408.8		18,513.4
Trademarks, net	1,050.9			1,050.9
Other intangibles, net	383.0	5,136.3		5,519.3
Capitalized debt fee	0.0	126.0		126.0
Other noncurrent assets	1,053.6			1,053.6
Total assets	**$ 11,929.1**			**$ 31,499.5**
Liabilities				
Current liabilities:				
Short-term debt	14.7		14.7	0.0
Portion of long-term debt due within one year	1,038.5	0.0	1,038.5	0.0
Revolving line of credit	0.0			0.0
Trade payables	1,129.7			1,129.7
Other payables	158.1			158.1

Accrued marketing	320.1			320.1
Other accrued liabilities	624.0			624.0
Income taxes	91.3			91.3
Total current liabilities	**$ 3,376.3**			**$ 2,323.1**
Term facilities	0.0	10,500.0		10,500.0
The notes	0.0	2,100.0		2,100.0
Long-term debt	3,930.6		3,930.6	0.0
Deferred income taxes	776.7			776.7
Nonpension postretirement benefits	230.9			230.9
Other noncurrent liabilities	504.8			504.8
Redeemable noncontrolling interest	28.7			28.7
Total liabilities	**$ 8,848.0**			**$ 16,464.1**
Total Equity				
Shareholders' equity				
Capital stock	716.7		716.7	0.0
Common equity investment	0.0	8,240.0		8,240.0
Preferred equity investment	0.0	8,000.0		8,000.0
Retained earnings	7,877.4		9,132.6	(1,255.1)
Treasury stock	(4,675.8)		(4,675.8)	0.0
Accumulated other comprehensive loss	(887.7)		(887.7)	0.0
Total shareholders' equity	**$ 3,030.6**			**$ 14,984.9**
Noncontrolling interest	50.5			50.5
Total equity	**$ 3,081.1**			**$ 15,035.4**
Total liabilities and equity	**$ 11,929.1**			**$ 31,499.5**
Supplemental Data:				
Balance? (Y/N)	Y			Y

TABLE 16.4 Capitalized Debt Fee Amortization

Depreciation (in US$ millions except per share amounts)

Period Ending					Estimates			
		2014E	2015E	2016E	2017E	2018E
Depreciation used	MACRS? 1 = Y, 0 = N	$298.0	$311.0	$324.7	$339.2	$354.5
Amortization	1	30.0	30.0	30.0	30.0	30.0
Amortization of identifiable intangible assets		342.4	342.4	342.4	342.4	342.4
Capitalized debt fee amortization		25.2	25.2	25.2	25.2	25.2
Total depreciation and amortization		$695.6	$708.6	$722.4	$736.8	$752.1

We can now link the capitalized debt fee amortization into the income statement. Let's first create a row in the income statement below Row 25, "Amortization of identifiable intangible assets," and label it "Capitalized debt fee amortization." We can then hard-code "0" for the historical years and simply link in the projected values from the appropriate row in the depreciation schedule. So Cell J26 should be "=J246." We need to then adjust the total depreciation and amortization formula to now include this new row. Cell D27 should read "=D23+D24+D25+D26." We can copy Cells J26 and D27 to the right. See Table 16.5.

Next we have to ensure that the capitalized debt fee amortization properly flows into the cash flow statement. So let's add a row under "Amortization of identifiable intangible assets" (Row 64) and label it "Capitalized debt fee amortization." We can link each year in from the income statement, having Cell D65 be "=D26." We can then copy this to the right through 2018. See Table 16.6.

Finally, you may notice that the balance sheet does not balance. This is because there is now a line item in the cash flow statement that is not linked into the balance sheet. The capitalized debt fee amortization needs to reduce the capitalized debt fee asset we have created in the balance sheet adjustments. However, we first need to add a row in the long-term assets section of the balance sheet, as we had done in the balance sheet adjustments. We can add a row below Row 178, "Other intangibles, net," and label it "Capitalized debt fee." For the data in Column I, the pro forma number, we need to link this in from the pro forma balance sheet. We can simply copy formula I178 down one row or we can link formula I179 by having it read "=H128." See Table 16.7.

For the projected years, we can use the standard balance sheet balancing formula for an asset, which is:

2014 Balance Sheet Capitalized Debt Fee = LTM Balance Sheet Capitalized Debt Fee – 2014 Cash Flow Capitalized Debt Fee Amortization

So in Cell J179 we would have "=I179-J65." We can copy this to the right, and you can now see the debt fee amortizing eventually to 0. See Table 16.7. The balance sheet should be back in balance.

This concludes one simple way to model in the amortization of transaction fees related to debt. Of course the accounting rules governing the ability to capitalize such fees often change, so I always recommend double-checking the ability to amortize such items before doing so.

TABLE 16.5 Income Statement with Capitalized Debt Fee Amortization

Consolidated Income Statements (in US$ millions except per share amounts)

Period Ending	LTM	2014E	2015E	2016E	2017E	2018E
				Estimates		
EBITDA	$1,908.9	$2,247.3	$2,371.0	$2,501.4	$2,638.9	$2,784.1
EBITDA margin (%)	*16.3%*	*18.2%*	*18.2%*	*18.2%*	*18.2%*	*18.2%*
Depreciation	299.6	298.0	311.0	324.7	339.2	354.5
Amortization	48.0	30.0	30.0	30.0	30.0	30.0
Amortization of identifiable intangible assets	0.0	342.4	342.4	342.4	342.4	342.4
Capitalized debt fee amortization	0.0	25.2	25.2	25.2	25.2	25.2
Total depreciation and amortization	$ 347.6	$ 695.6	$ 708.6	$ 722.4	$ 736.8	$ 752.1
EBIT	1,561.3	1,551.7	1,662.3	1,779.0	1,902.1	2,031.9
EBIT margin (%)	*13.4%*	*12.6%*	*12.8%*	*13.0%*	*13.1%*	*13.3%*

TABLE 16.6 Cash Flow Statement with Capitalized Debt Fee Amortization

Consolidated Statements of Cash Flows (in US$ millions except per share amounts)

Period Ending	LTM	2014E	2015E	2016E	2017E	2018E
				Estimates		
Cash flows from operating activities						
Net income	1,006.7	610.1	693.5	781.8	875.2	974.2
Depreciation	299.6	298.0	311.0	324.7	339.2	354.5
Amortization	48.0	30.0	30.0	30.0	30.0	30.0
Amortization of identifiable intangible assets	0.0	342.4	342.4	342.4	342.4	342.4
Capitalized debt fee amortization	0.0	25.2	25.2	25.2	25.2	25.2
Deferred tax (beneft) / provision	(83.0)	(83.0)	(83.0)	(83.0)	(83.0)	(83.0)
Net losses on divestitures	19.8	0.0	0.0	0.0	0.0	0.0
Impairment of assets held for sale	36.0	0.0	0.0	0.0	0.0	0.0
Pension contributions	(61.2)	(80.0)	(80.0)	(80.0)	(80.0)	(80.0)
Asset write-downs from Fiscal 2012 productivity initiatives	58.7	0.0	0.0	0.0	0.0	0.0
Other items, net	10.2	10.2	10.2	10.2	10.2	10.2

TABLE 16.7 Balance Sheet Statement with Capitalized Debt Fee Amortization

Consolidated Balance Sheets (in US$ millions except per share amounts)

On January 27	2013PF	2014E	Estimates 2015E	2016E	2017E	2018E
Assets						
Current assets:						
Cash and cash equivalents	0.0	449.5	975.1	1,573.0	2,247.5	3,003.1
Receivables	1,098.8	1,158.1	1,221.8	1,289.0	1,359.9	1,434.7
Inventories	1,448.4	1,486.3	1,568.1	1,654.3	1,745.3	1,841.3
Prepaid expenses and other current assets	261.1	272.4	287.4	303.2	319.8	337.4
Total current assets	2,808.2	3,366.2	4,052.2	4,819.4	5,672.5	6,616.5
Property, plant and equipment, net	2,428.2	2,623.6	2,833.1	3,057.5	3,297.6	3,554.3
Goodwill	18,513.4	18,513.4	18,513.4	18,513.4	18,513.4	18,513.4
Trademarks, net	1,050.9	1,020.9	990.9	960.9	930.9	900.9
Other intangibles, net	5,519.3	5,176.9	4,834.5	4,492.1	4,149.6	3,807.2
Capitalized debt fee	126.0	100.8	75.6	50.4	25.2	0.0
Other non-currents assets	1,053.6	1,094.8	1,135.9	1,177.1	1,218.3	1,259.4
Total assets	31,499.5	31,896.5	32,435.6	33,070.6	33,807.4	34,651.6

CHAPTER 17

Paid-in-Kind Securities

Paid-in-kind (PIK) securities are securities in which interest payments are paid in additional securities instead of cash. At the end of the period the balance of debt increases in lieu of making interest payments in cash. Typically that increase in the balance also incurs additional interest; thus there is interest on interest. This is typically a more expensive type of security, but does less to strain the company's immediate cash flow. PIK interest securities have become quite popular in recent years, so I felt it important to touch upon, even if it's not core to the Heinz case.

Let's take an example to illustrate the flows of a paid-in-kind security. If we have an outstanding debt of $1,000 with 10 percent PIK interest, then at the end of the period, we incur a $100 PIK interest expense. If we assume a 40 percent tax rate, the net-of-tax amount, –$60, will flow into the cash flow statement. See Table 17.1.

Since the PIK interest expense is a noncash expense (it is actually not paid in cash), it is added back in the cash flow statement. Thus, the only effect to cash is the tax savings. Table 17.2 shows that the PIK interest accumulates as a liability on the balance sheet.

This balances because the cash adjustment of $40 less the $100 PIK liability equals the net income change of –$60.

Let's illustrate this in the model. The Heinz case does not contain a PIK interest security, but let's pretend the interest on the notes is PIK interest. I would recommend saving a version of your model in another name so as not to interfere with the core solution. We can assume for illustration that the 7.5 percent interest expense is PIK interest instead of cash interest. We will need to illustrate the fact that this interest will increase the overall debt balance, so we will add a new row under the interest to create a new

TABLE 17.1 Paid-in-Kind Interest Expense

Income Statement		Cash Flow	
Paid-in-Kind Interest	$(100.0)	Net Income	$(60.0)
Tax (40%)	40.0	Paid-in-Kind Interest Adjustment	100.0
Net Income	**(60.0)**	**Total Changes in Cash**	**40.0**

TABLE 17.2   Paid-in-Kind Interest Cash Flow and Balance Sheet Effects

Cash Flow		Balance Sheet	
Net Income	$(60.0)	Cash	$40.0
Paid-in-Kind Interest Adjustment	100.0	Paid-in-Kind Interest	100.0
Total Changes in Cash	**40.0**	Retained Earnings (Net Income)	(60.0)

end-of-year balance. Let's add a row below the notes interest rate, Row 302, and label it "The notes (after PIK)."

This row will be the debt end-of-year balance plus the interest expense. Remember, the structure of a PIK is such that the interest incurred is not paid in cash. Rather, the debt balance will increase indicating borrowing more debt to fund interest incurred. So in the new Cell J303 we will have "=J300+J301." We can copy this to the right. It is this new balance of debt that we want carried into the next year, so we need to change Cell K297 to be equal to the new Cell J303. We can then copy Cell K297 to the right. See Table 17.3.

Assuming that the PIK interest is tax-deductible, we need to be sure this links into the total interest expense; and it already does, as we had previously modeled notes interest to total into the total interest expense. However, as with the dividends payable, we need to add the PIK interest back into the cash flow statement and make sure a liability is incurred. See Table 17.1. We can add a row in the cash flows from operating activities. We add a row above the "Other items, net" Row 71 and label it "PIK interest." See Table 17.4. If you

TABLE 17.3   Notes with PIK Interest

Debt Schedule (in US$ millions except per share amounts)

				Estimates		
On January 27	2013PF	2014E	2015E	2016E	2017E	2018E
The notes						
The notes (beginning of year)		$2,100.0	$2,257.5	$2,426.8	$2,608.8	$2,804.5
Mandatory issuances/ (retirements)		0.0	0.0	0.0	0.0	0.0
Nonmandatory issuances/ (retirements)		0.0	0.0	0.0	0.0	0.0
The notes (end of year)	$2,100.0	$2,100.0	$2,257.5	$2,426.8	$2,608.8	$2,804.5
The notes interest expense		157.5	169.3	182.0	195.7	210.3
The notes interest rate		*7.50%*	*7.50%*	*7.50%*	*7.50%*	*7.50%*
The notes (after PIK)		$2,257.5	$2,426.8	$2,608.8	$2,804.5	$3,014.8

TABLE 17.4 Paid-in-Kind on the Cash Flow Statement

Consolidated Statements of Cash Flows (in US$ millions except per share amounts)

Period Ending	2014E	2015E	2016E	2017E	2018E
			Estimates		
Cash flows from operating activities					
Net income	610.7	686.7	767.0	851.8	941.4
Depreciation	298.0	311.0	324.7	339.2	354.5
Amortization	30.0	30.0	30.0	30.0	30.0
Amortization of identifiable intangible assets	342.4	342.4	342.4	342.4	342.4
Capitalized debt fee amortization	25.2	25.2	25.2	25.2	25.2
Deferred tax (benefit) / provision	(83.0)	(83.0)	(83.0)	(83.0)	(83.0)
Net losses on divestitures	0.0	0.0	0.0	0.0	0.0
Impairment of assets held for sale	0.0	0.0	0.0	0.0	0.0
Pension contributions	(80.0)	(80.0)	(80.0)	(80.0)	(80.0)
Asset write-downs from Fiscal 2012 productivity initiatives	0.0	0.0	0.0	0.0	0.0
PIK Interest	157.5	169.3	182.0	195.7	210.3
Other items, net	10.2	10.2	10.2	10.2	10.2
Changes in operating working capital					
Changes in receivables	(59.3)	(63.7)	(67.2)	(70.9)	(74.8)
Changes in inventories	(38.0)	(81.7)	(86.2)	(91.0)	(96.0)
Changes in prepaid expenses and other current assets	(11.3)	(15.0)	(15.8)	(16.7)	(17.6)
Changes in accounts payable	34.1	72.7	76.7	80.9	85.4
Changes in accrued liabilities	40.3	54.1	57.1	60.3	63.6
Changes in accrued income taxes	6.9	11.8	12.5	13.2	14.0
Net changes in operating working capital	(27.4)	(21.7)	(22.9)	(24.2)	(25.5)
Total cash provided by (used for) operating activities	1,283.6	1,390.0	1,495.6	1,607.3	1,725.5

are matching numbers with your model, we are running a version of the model using 5.5% revenue growth and 60% COGS as a percentage of revenue.

The PIK interest will link in from the interest in the debt schedule. We will hard-code "0" for the historical years. Cell J71 will read "=J302" and we can copy this to the right. We now need to double-check and make sure this new row is flowing into the total cash flow. See Table 17.4.

We now have to create a PIK liability in the balance sheet. Refer to Table 17.2. Notice that the balance sheet is now out of balance. Let's add a PIK row under the notes row, Row 193, and we can label it "PIK interest." We can hard-code "0" for the last twelve months (LTM) year. For the projected years we can use the standard balance sheet balancing formula for a liability, which is:

2014 Balance Sheet PIK Interest = LTM Balance Sheet
PIK Interest + 2014 Cash Flow PIK Interest

In Cell J194 we would have "=I194+J71." We can copy this to the right, and you can now see the PIK interest accumulating. The balance sheet should be back in balance. See Table 17.5.

Once the balance sheet balances, the PIK securities are complete. Note that one also needs to add the PIK securities to the Returns tab, as the accumulated interest would need to be paid down upon exit. So let's add a row in the Returns tab under the "Less the notes" Row 11 and label it "Less PIK interest." Cell K12 would then read "=Financials!N194." Finally, we need to amend the "Equity to common" formula to also subtract the PIK interest; the formula in Cell K15 should be changed to read "=+K7+K8-K9-K10-K11-K13-K14-K12." See Table 17.6.

The returns in Table 17.6 assume 5.5 percent growth and reduced cost of goods sold (COGS) percentage of revenue of 60 percent. We can see that this has a small effect on the overall returns, but the benefit of a PIK security freeing up cash still stands. The solution up to this point of the book can be found on the Wiley website under "Leveraged_Buyout_Model_Solution_Part_Three.xls."

For purposes of instruction in this book, the fundamental understanding of an ability to model through such one-off line items is an important and useful tool. We can go on and on creating similar one-off items and additional complexities to model. But for purposes of this introductory book, we have illustrated first-level complexities of LBO nuances. Leveraged buyouts can become significantly more complex, which will be illustrated in subsequent books. Although an uncommon situation, we felt Heinz was more relatable to all and a better case to utilize to illustrate the major movements of a leveraged buyout analysis. However, the minute details uncovered in private company buyouts, and the benefits realized and pitfalls encountered, are the next level. I hope you are looking forward to the next case as much as I am.

TABLE 17.5 Liabilities with PIK Interest

Consolidated Balance Sheets (in US$ millions except per share amounts)

| On January 27 | 2013PF | Estimates | | | | |
		2014E	2015E	2016E	2017E	2018E
Liabilities						
Current liabilities:						
Short-term debt	0.0	0.0	0.0	0.0	0.0	0.0
Portion of long term debt due within one year	0.0	0.0	0.0	0.0	0.0	0.0
Revolving line of credit	0.0	0.0	0.0	0.0	0.0	0.0
Accounts payable	1,287.8	1,321.8	1,394.6	1,471.3	1,552.2	1,637.5
Accrued marketing and other accrued liabilities	944.0	984.3	1,038.4	1,095.5	1,155.8	1,219.4
Income taxes	91.3	98.1	110.0	122.5	135.7	149.7
Total current liabilities	**2,323.1**	**2,404.3**	**2,543.0**	**2,689.3**	**2,843.7**	**3,006.6**
Term facilities	10,500.0	10,500.0	10,500.0	10,500.0	10,500.0	10,500.0
The notes	2,100.0	2,100.0	2,100.0	2,100.0	2,100.0	2,100.0
PIK Interest	0.0	157.5	326.8	508.8	704.5	914.8
Long term debt	0.0	0.0	0.0	0.0	0.0	0.0
Deferred income taxes	776.7	693.7	610.7	527.7	444.7	361.7
Non-pension postretirement benefits	230.9	230.9	230.9	230.9	230.9	230.9
Preferred dividends payable	0.0	720.0	1,440.0	2,160.0	2,880.0	3,600.0
Other non-currents liabilities	504.8	424.8	344.8	264.8	184.8	104.8
Redeemable non-controlling interest	28.7	28.7	28.7	28.7	28.7	28.7
Total liabilities	**16,464.1**	**17,259.8**	**18,124.8**	**19,010.2**	**19,917.2**	**20,847.4**

TABLE 17.6 Revised Equity Returns with PIK Security

Investment Returns (in US$ millions except per share amounts)

Period Ending	Actuals			Estimates			
	LTM	2014E	2015E	2016E	2017E	2018E	
Exit Multiple	14.4x						
Enterprise value [(EBITDA + management fee) ×							
EBITDA multiple)]						40,048.4	
plus cash						3,835.6	
less revolving line of credit						0.0	
less term facilities						10,500.0	
less the notes						2,100.0	
less PIK interest						914.8	
less preferred equity						8,000.0	
less preferred dividends						3,600.0	
Equity to common						**18,769.2**	
Return to 3G	(4,120.0)	0.0	0.0	0.0	0.0	13,138.5	
IRR	**26.1%**						
Return Multiple	**3.2x**						
Return to Berkshire Hathaway							
Equity investment	(12,120.0)						
Equity value						5,630.8	
Preferred equity						8,000.0	
Preferred dividends payable						3,600.0	
Preferred dividends		0.0	0.0	0.0	0.0	0.0	
Total return	(12,120.0)	0.0	0.0	0.0	0.0	17,230.8	
IRR	**7.3%**						
Return Multiple	**1.4x**						

Appendices

Model Quick Steps

For a full-scale leveraged buyout model, after completing core assumptions (purchase price, sources, and uses), the next steps should serve as a guide for modeling the rest of the model:

I. Income Statement
1. Input historical income statement data.
2. Project revenue.
3. Project all expenses.
   a. Leave "Depreciation" empty (to come from depreciation schedule, IV.1.a).
   b. Leave "Interest Expense" and "Interest Income" empty (to come from debt schedule, VII.8 and VII.9).
4. Build to Net Income.

II. Cash Flow
1. Input historical cash flow data.
2. Cash Flow from Operations projections.
   a. Pull in "Net Income before Distributions" from income statement.
   b. Leave "Depreciation" empty (to come from depreciation schedule, IV.1.b).
   c. Leave "Changes in Operating Working Capital" empty (to come from operating working capital schedule, V.1.a and V.2.a).
   d. Project "other" items.
3. Cash flow from investing.
   a. Project CAPEX.
   b. Project "other" items.
4. Cash flow from financing.
   a. Leave "Short-Term Borrowings (Repayments)" empty (to come from debt schedule, VII.10).
   b. Leave "Long-Term Borrowings (Repayments)" empty (to come from debt schedule, VII.11).
   c. Pull in "Dividends" from income statement.
   d. Project "other" items.
5. Sum Total Cash Flow.

III. Balance Sheet Adjustments
1. Input historical balance sheet data.
2. Perform balance sheet adjustments.

IV. Depreciation Schedule
1. Project depreciation.
   a. Depreciation links to income statement (I.3.a).
   b. Depreciation links to cash flow (II.2.b).

V. Operating Working Capital
1. Project each Current Assets line item.
   a. Each Change in Current Assets line item will link to cash flow (II.2.c).
2. Project each Current Liabilities line item.
   a. Each Change in Current Liabilities line item will link to cash flow (II.2.c).
3. Calculate Changes in Operating Working Capital.

VI. Balance Sheet Projections
1. Build future balance sheet balances using the cash flow statement movements.

VII. Debt Schedule
1. Pull in year-end debt and cash balances from balance sheet.
2. Calculate Cash Available to Pay Down Debt.
3. Build short-term debt balance.
   a. Calculate Interest Expense.
   b. Create mandatory and automatic issuances/(retirements).
4. Build long-term debt balance.
   a. Calculate Interest Expense.
   b. Create mandatory and automatic issuances/(retirements).
5. Calculate Total Interest Expense.
6. Calculate Total Mandatory and Automatic Issuances.
7. Calculate Cash at the End of the Year.
   a. Calculate Interest Income.
8. Link Total Interest Expense to income statement (I.3.b).
9. Link Total Interest Income to income statement (I.3.b).
10. Short-Term Mandatory and Automatic Issuances links to cash flow statement (II.4.a).
11. Long-Term Mandatory and Automatic Issuances links to cash flow statement (II.4.b).

Calculate returns and model is complete.

Financial Statement Flows

INCOME STATEMENT TO CASH FLOW

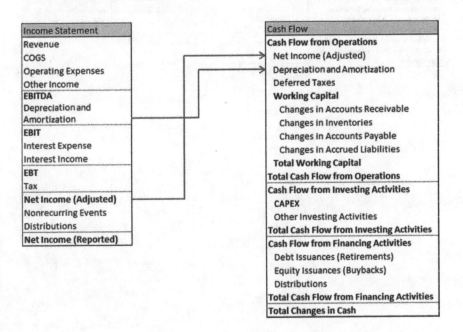

CASH FLOW TO BALANCE SHEET

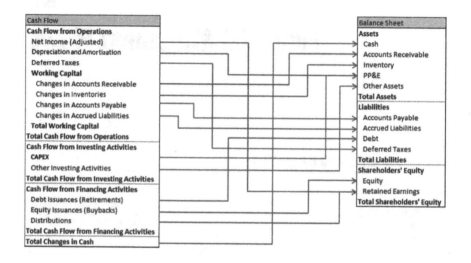

Excel Hot Keys

Description	Shortcut Key	Description	Shortcut Key
File Operations		**Cell Formatting**	
New file	Ctrl + N	Format cells	Ctrl + 1
Open file	Ctrl + O	Format as currency	Ctrl + Shift + 4
Save file	Ctrl + S	Format as date	Ctrl + Shift + 3
Close file	Ctrl + F4	Format as percentage	Ctrl + Shift + 5
Save as	F12	Format as number	Ctrl + Shift + 1
Exit Excel	Alt + F4	Bold	Ctrl + B
Print	Ctrl + P	Italicize	Ctrl + I
Cell Operations		Underline	Ctrl + U
Edit active cell	F2	Strikethrough	Ctrl + 5
Cancel cell editing	Escape key	Add cell borders	Ctrl + Shift + 7
Cut	Ctrl + X	Remove all borders	Ctrl + Shift + – (minus)
Copy	Ctrl + C	**Selecting Cells**	
Paste	Ctrl + V	Select entire worksheet	Ctrl + A
Copy right	Ctrl + R	Select group area	Ctrl + Shift + 8
Copy down	Ctrl + D	Select column	Ctrl + Space bar
Create cell comment	Shift + F2	Select row	Shift + Space bar
		Select manually	Hold Shift + Left, right, up, or down arrow key

Description	Shortcut Key	Description	Shortcut Key
Worksheet Navigation		**Other Operations**	
Up one screen	Page up	Find text	Ctrl + F
Down one screen	Page down	Replace text	Ctrl + H
Move to next worksheet	Ctrl + Page down	Undo last action	Ctrl + Z
Move to previous worksheet	Ctrl + Page up	Redo last action	Ctrl + Y
Go to first cell in worksheet area	Ctrl + Home	Create a chart	F11
Go to last cell in worksheet area	Ctrl + End	Spell check	F7
Go to formula source	Ctrl + {	Show all formulas	Ctrl + ~
Go to a cell	F5	Insert columns/ rows	Ctrl + Shift + + (plus sign)
		Insert a new worksheet	Shift + F11
		Move between open workbooks	Ctrl + F6
		Autosum	Alt + Equal sign

About the Companion Website

This book has a companion website, which can be found at www.wiley.com/go/pignatarolbo. The companion website contains models on H.J. Heinz Company. There you can build your own leveraged buyout model on Heinz step-by-step. The purpose of the model is for you to gain more practice and to further illustrate the application of skills learned in the book. Feel free to download and utilize these models; or try to create your own model and compare.

The website also contains chapter questions and answers and a second practice LBO model to help aid in your knowledge of the material presented in the book.

To access the site, go to www.wiley.com/go/pignatarolbo (password: buyouts)

About the Author

Paul Pignataro is an entrepreneur specializing in finance education. He has built and successfully run several start-ups in the education and technology industries. He also has over 13 years of experience in investment banking and private equity in business mergers and acquisitions (M&A), restructurings, asset divestitures, asset acquisitions, and debt and equity transactions in the oil, gas, power and utilities, Internet and technology, real estate, defense, travel, banking, and service industries.

Mr. Pignataro most recently founded New York School of Finance, which evolved from AnEx Training, a multi-million dollar finance education business, providing finance education to banks, firms, and universities throughout the world.

The New York School of Finance is a semester-long program, based in New York and geared toward helping business students from top tier and lower tier business schools prepare for jobs at the top firms on Wall Street.

At AnEx Training, Mr. Pignataro continues to participate on the training team, actively providing training at bulge bracket banks and for M&A teams at corporations, and has personally trained personnel at funds catering to high net worth individuals worth billions of dollars. AnEx continues to train at over 50 locations worldwide, and Mr. Pignataro travels extensively on a monthly basis training at sovereign funds and investment banks overseas.

Prior to his entrepreneurial endeavors, Mr. Pignataro worked at TH Lee Putnam Ventures, a $1 billion private equity firm affiliated with buyout giant Thomas H. Lee Partners. Before that, he was at Morgan Stanley, where he worked on various transactions in the technology, energy, transportation, and business services industries. Some of the transactions included the $33.3 billion merger of BP Amoco and ARCO, the $7.6 billion sale of American Water Works to RWE (a German water company), the sale of two subsidiaries of Citizens Communications (a $3.0 billion communications company), and the sale of a $100 million propane distribution subsidiary of a $3 billion electric utility.

Mr. Pignataro is the author of *Financial Modeling and Valuation: A Practical Guide to Investment Banking and Private Equity* (John Wiley & Sons, 2013). He graduated from New York University with a bachelor's degree in mathematics and a bachelor's degree in computer science.

Index